COMING TO MATURITY

How to Grow Up in God

by

Susan I. Smith, M.Ed., Th.D., Ph.D.

and

Rev. Stelman H. Smith, M.M., Th.M., Th.D.

 Unless otherwise identified, Scripture quotations are from The King James Version of the Bible.

Companion Press
P.O. Box 310
Shippensburg, PA 17257

"Good Stewards of the
Manifold Grace of God"

ISBN 1-56043-621-2

For Worldwide Distribution
Printed in the U.S.A.

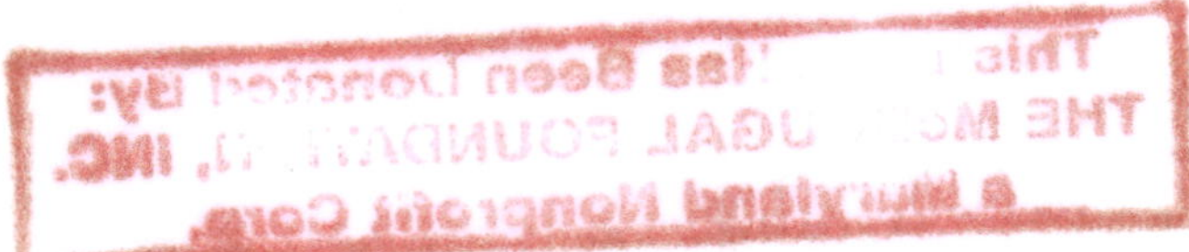

We gratefully acknowledge the commitment of
Zion's Hill Ministries
to the publishing of this book
and the invaluable assistance of
Ruth Hipkins
who is undoubtedly the world's greatest proofreader.

Lovingly dedicated to
Mom and Pop
Who stuck with us through all the years
while we were coming to maturity

CONTENTS

PART ONE
Exodus: Coming Out of Bondage

PART TWO
Joshua: Coming Into Inheritance

PART THREE
Ephesians: Coming Into Perfection

AUTHOR'S PREFACE

Learning From History

The nineteenth-century philosopher, Georg Hegel, perceptively and succinctly stated a most interesting principle:

> What experience and history teach is this, that people and governments never have learned anything from history or acted on principles deduced.

Sad commentary, isn't it! Then, the twentieth-century Spanish-born American philosopher, poet, and writer, George Santayana, told us the terrible price to be paid for this minor oversight when he wrote, "Those who do not learn from history, are condemned to repeat it."

In one form or another, the philosophers of almost every age have pondered this baffling question: Since man is the only animal gifted by God with the ability to contemplate and learn from the history of his species, what great heights might he have attained during his millennia on this earth if he had only done so? The answer can only be imagined. In a citizen of the world, this inability to learn from the history of both men and of nations may be pitiable; in a citizen of the heavenly kingdom, however, this little flaw could prove to be fatal.

God left man a magnificent Book containing, among other things, lots of history--the history of the earth upon which man lives, the history of the nations man inhabits, the history of man, himself, and the history of his dealings with his God. Obviously, God meant for man to read this history, to learn the lessons it teaches, and to act upon the principles which may be gathered from it so that he might never be condemned to repeat it and, quite possibly, be condemned for all eternity.

A Jewish Perspective on Biblical History

To be certain that they would not fail to learn the lessons of their own history, the Jews of ancient times had four methods of Biblical interpretation:

1. **Literal.** In the literal or historical interpretation of Scripture, each event recorded was seen as having literally happened, just as the Bible said. A literal stone brought down a literal giant; a literal whale swallowed a literal prophet, etc.
2. **Personal.** Once the Jewish reader understood the literal meaning of the Scriptures he read, he tried his best to apply those Scriptures to his own personal life.
3. **Spiritual.** In addition, the Jew believed that all Scripture had a spiritual or allegorical interpretation which must be understood. In this spiritual application, Jonah might become a type of the nation of Israel, swallowed for her disobedience to God by an allegorical whale called Babylon and disgorged to return to her land and to serve her Lord according to His commands.
4. **Prophetic.** The Jew also believed that every Scripture had prophetic, or futuristic, implications. For example, the story of Israel's restoration following her captivity might have previewed that day in 1948 when Israel was reborn as a nation.

The ancient Jews applied each of these methods to the interpretation of every Scripture, believing that only then could the full riches of God's Word be discovered. As has been observed, "Every passage of the Bible looks backward and forward and every way, like lights from the sun."[1]

Using these various interpretations of Scripture, the Jews were able to study the events of their history, learn the lessons of that history, and apply them to their own lives and to the life of their nation. This is evidenced by the fact that, after Israel was punished by God for their idolatry by seventy years of captivity in Babylon, Israel, as a nation, never again slipped into that same sin.

Learning to Mature

One of the distinguishing characteristics of the young and immature, as many a parent has noted, is their inability to use past experience to determine future consequences and thereby avoid the negative ones. "I just didn't think," they often say.

But, God, through His Son, Jesus, left a very specific command for His people in Matthew 5:48, *Be ye therefore perfect, even as your Father which is in heaven is perfect.*

The word twice translated perfect here is the Greek, *telios*, which means: "Having reached its end, finished, complete, perfect. It is used of persons, primarily of physical development, then, with ethical import, fully grown, mature."[2]

Clearly, it is the intent of the Lord that each of His children strive to attain this quality of spiritual maturity. But, how is the Christian to arrive at this God-ordained state of maturity? We can begin just as the ancient Jews began, by studying the history God recorded for us in His Word, learning its lessons, and applying them to our own lives. Using that history, we can examine the results of the actions of those who went before so that we might govern our own future conduct to avoid some of the unfortunate consequences so many of our predecessors suffered. As we study, we can grow spiritually and, finally, mature in Christ, just as He commanded.

A New Perspective Based on Old Methods

This study will explore two Old Testament books of history, Exodus and Joshua, and one New Testament book of applied principle, Ephesians. In particular, it will apply the ancient Jewish methods of Biblical interpretation--literal or historic, personal, and, in some cases, spiritual or allegorical--in a search for true spiritual growth leading to full Christian maturity. In Exodus, the child of God comes out of bondage; in Joshua, he conquers all God has for him; and, in Ephesians, he comes to perfection, a mature believer.

From this new perspective based upon age-old methods, it is hoped that the reader will learn from history and, having learned, will never be condemned to repeat it. Perhaps this was precisely what God had in mind when He gave His children a Bible containing so much history. No wonder God, through the apostle, Paul, in 2 Timothy 3:16 and 17, said,

> *All scripture is given by inspiration of God, and is profitable for doctrine, for reproof, for correction, for instruction in righteousness: That the man of God may be perfect (or mature), throughly furnished unto all good works.*

[1]Matthew Henry, *Matthew Henry's Commentary on the Whole Bible*, Volume 1, p. ix.

[2]W. E. Vine, *A Comprehensive Dictionary of the Original Greek Words With Their Precise Meanings for English Readers*, pp. 855 and 856.

PART ONE
EXODUS--COMING OUT OF BONDAGE

INTRODUCTION

A Look at One Man's Family

His large family had been starving in the world-wide famine. Twice, it had been necessary to send his grown sons to the far-away land of Egypt to purchase the food needed to keep his grandchildren alive. Then, he had discovered that his very favorite son, long thought dead, was alive, living in Egypt, of all places, and employed as Pharaoh's hand-picked supervisor over his food distribution program. As much as he loved his homeland, it seemed only logical to take the entire family to Egypt where he could be with his long-lost child and where his family's needs could easily be met.

So it was that the patriarch, Jacob, renamed Israel by Jehovah God, made the momentous decision to move the house of Israel to the land of Egypt, secure in God's promise that He would one day bring them home again, as Genesis 46:2 through 4 recounts:

And he said, I am God, the God of thy father: fear not to go down into Egypt; for I will there make of thee a great nation: I will go down with thee into Egypt; and I will also surely bring thee up again.

And, Jacob and his family were welcomed with open arms. Pharaoh even set aside the northeast section of the fertile Nile delta, Goshen, for their exclusive use. It seemed that life could not be better for Jacob and his descendants. With life so wonderful, would they ever want to go home to Canaan, the land God had always promised them?

But, by the time four hundred and thirty years had passed, life for the descendants of Jacob and his sons was not so wonderful at all. A new Pharaoh sat upon the throne of Egypt, a Pharaoh who saw the children of Israel as nothing more than slaves to be put to work on his various construction projects. Now, the Israelites longed to take advantage of the promise God had made to their ancestor, Jacob; now, they longed to return to the land from which he had come so long before.

But, how does an enslaved people obtain freedom? The Israelites began by crying out to the God of their father, Jacob, the God who had brought them to Egypt to save their lives, the very God who had made the promise in the first place, the promise to take them back home. And, their God heard their cries and set about to raise up His chosen deliverer, one who would gain their freedom and lead them on the long march home. But, they would have to do much growing up, much maturing on the way.

The Time Had Come

Yes, the time had come for God to move in behalf of His people. But, just exactly when was that time? For years, Bible scholars have argued the date of the Jewish exodus from Egypt. Some say it happened in the fifteenth century B.C., while others maintain that it occurred in the thirteenth century B.C. But, what does the Bible, itself, say? Does it contain any clues concerning the date of this pivotal point of all Judaism, the exodus? To answer these questions, we must begin many years later, in 1 Kings 6:1:

And it came to pass in the four hundred and eightieth year after the children of Israel were come out of the land of Egypt, in the fourth year of Solomon's reign over Israel...that he began to build the house of the LORD.

While Bible scholars may disagree about the date of the exodus, few dispute the date when Solomon began to build the beautiful Temple of Jehovah God in Jerusalem. Contemporary histories along with archaeological records prove to almost everyone's satisfaction that the Temple was begun in 966 B.C. In fact, this date is considered to be so certain, so clearly established in both history and archaeology, that everything else in the Old Testament can be accurately dated from it. So, if the exodus occurred four hundred and eighty years before Solomon began to build the Temple in 966 B.C., we need not be mathematicians to figure out that the Israelites left Egypt in 1446 B.C.

There is even more Scriptural evidence to support this conclusion. In order to conform to the Biblical account of the life of Moses, the same pharaoh had to have reigned for at least forty years. The only two pharaohs of Egypt which meet this requirement were Thutmose III, who reigned from 1504 until 1450 B.C., and Rameses II, who ruled from 1290 to 1224 B.C.

In fact, the only Biblical evidence used to support a thirteenth century date for the exodus is found in Exodus 1:11:

Therefore they did set over them taskmasters to afflict them with their burdens. And they built for Pharaoh treasure cities, Pithom and Raamses.

Since a treasure city called Raamses was constructed by Hebrew slave labor, many have concluded that their exodus came during the reign of Rameses II, which occurred during the thirteenth century B.C. But, a study of history shows that the geographical name, Raamses, which is spelled differently than Rameses, the name taken by two of Egypt's pharaohs, was composed of two Coptic words, *rem*, meaning, man, and *shos*, meaning, "shepherds."[1] The geographical name meant, "land of the shepherdmen,"[2] and was used to identify territory belonging to the pharaohs who were considered to be the shepherds of Egypt. It was a place name used well before the days of the pharaohs named Rameses. In fact, the pharaohs who chose the name, Rameses, may have done so because it identified them as the reigning shepherds of Egypt.

There is also much archaeological evidence to support the 1446 B.C. date for the exodus. For instance, the so-called "dream stela" of Thutmose IV, which is found on the sphinx, indicates that Thutmose was not the legal heir when he came to the throne in 1426 B.C. That may be because the true heir was one of the eldest sons who died in the tenth plague twenty years before. Archaeologists have also found that the last level of Hazor, which was destroyed by Barak and Deborah, contained Mycenaean IIIB pottery which was only produced in the late thirteenth century B.C. Since Barak and Deborah were well down the list of judges, the exodus had to have occurred at least a century and a half earlier. Finally, the Amarna Tablets, created in about 1400 B.C., mention a recent upheaval in Egypt caused by a people called the *Habiru*, a title many authorities believe to have been a corruption of the name, Hebrews. With so much evidence, it seems safe to conclude that the exodus did indeed occur in 1446 B.C. and that the Egyptian pharaoh before whom Moses stood was, in fact, Amenophis II, the successor to Thutmose III, whose daughter had reared the young Moses.

The Bible is even more specific about the exact date of this event. In Exodus 12:1 through 6, we are told that the first Passover lamb was to be chosen on the tenth day of the first month and sacrificed at sunset on the fourteenth day of the same month (comparable to our month of April). Since the Israelites left Egypt that very night (Exodus 12:31 and 42), we can conclude that the exodus took place on the fourteenth day of the first month of the Jewish calendar in the year 1446 B.C.

The Time Was Short

While it may seem that the events recorded in the Book of Exodus cover a lengthy period of time, such was not really the case. The last event recorded in the Book of Exodus was the erection of the tabernacle which Moses dated in Exodus 40:17:

> *And it came to pass in the first month in the second year, on the first day of the month, that the tabernacle was reared up.*

By Moses' own account, the tabernacle was erected in the second year of the journey (1445 B.C.), on the first day of the first month, just under one year after the exodus.

It was a brief time, less than twelve short months. Yet, there was much to do, many places to go, many wonders to see, many things to be accomplished. And, yes, there were many things to learn and much maturing to be completed along that rocky wilderness road. But, God would be with them, to guide them, to protect them, and to teach them. Under His omnipotent hand and with His help, it would all happen for them, just as He had planned.

Now, we start that long journey with them, learning with them, growing with them, maturing with them. The very same path God planned for their feet is the path He has designed for our feet, too. And, so, let us begin....

[1]Robert Jamieson, A. R. Fausset, and David Brown, *A Commentary Critical, Experimental, and Practical on the Old and New Testaments*, Volume I, p. 277.

[2]Ibid.

Chapter 1
BORN IN BONDAGE

Born With a Godly Heritage

In the very first sentence of the very first chapter of the Book of Exodus, as well as elsewhere in Scripture, the Jews are referred to as "the children of Israel." Just what did it mean to be a child of Israel? Let's go back to the Book of Genesis to find out.

The patriarch of the family had not always been called Israel. At his birth, in 2006 B.C., he had been named, Jacob (Genesis 25:26). This name meant, "a supplanter,"[1] and carried the sense of one who defrauds. And, in a time when the meaning of the name chosen for a child had great significance and often carried clues to the character of that child, no name could have been more appropriate. Jacob was an accomplished "con artist" from his earliest days. He conned his mother, Rebekah, into showing him favoritism from childhood (Genesis 25:27), conned his elder twin brother, Esau, out of the senior heir's birthright (Genesis 25:29 through 34), and finally conned his aged and almost blind father, Isaac, into bestowing upon him the blessing due the eldest son (Genesis 27:1 through 29).

Jacob's behavior finally caught up with him. Forced to flee the wrath of the brother he had so flagrantly defrauded, Jacob traveled to the home of his mother's brother, his uncle Laban. And, if ever there were a bigger con artist than Jacob, it was Laban. When Jacob contracted to marry his younger daughter, Rachel, Laban conned him into a marriage with his elder daughter, Leah, first (Genesis 29:18 through 26). When Jacob contracted to work for Laban in return for cattle, Laban changed his wages no less than ten times (Genesis 31:41), in an effort to con him out of the huge herds he was amassing. At last, Jacob decided it would be better to take his two wives, two concubines, eleven sons, and one daughter and return home, even if he did risk the revenge his brother had planned for him twenty years before. On the way, Jacob was blessed with a twelfth son, but, also on the way, Jacob, the con man, the supplanter, met the one Person he couldn't con; Jacob had a one-on-one confrontation with God, recorded in Genesis 32:24 through 28:

> *And Jacob was left alone; and there wrestled a man with him until the breaking of the day. And when he saw that he prevailed not against him, he touched the hollow of his thigh; and the hollow of Jacob's thigh was out of joint, as he wrestled with him. And he said, Let me go, for the day breaketh. And he said, I will not let thee go, except thou bless me. And he said unto him, <u>What is thy name?</u> And he said, <u>Jacob</u>. And he said, <u>Thy name shall be called no more Jacob, but Israel</u>: for as a prince hast thou power with God and with men, and hast prevailed.*

Notice that the first question God asked was Jacob's name. That seems to indicate that God didn't even know to whom He was speaking. But, in forcing Jacob to respond, to give his name, complete with all that it indicated about his character, God also forced Jacob to admit just what sort of a man he had always been, a supplanter, a defrauder of the worst sort. God had brought him face to face with the reality of his own sordid past. Often, admitting what one is, is the first step to change. In the next instant, God changed Jacob's name to Israel, which means, "a prince of God,"[2] or, "one who rules with God."[3] Since one must first be ruled <u>by</u> God before he can rule <u>with</u> God, Jacob, the supplanter, the con man, had just become a God-ruled man, instead. So, by the very definition of the words, the children of Israel were those whose father had had a life-changing experience with God, an experience that even caused him to walk differently (due to the dislocation of his thigh in Genesis 32:25 and 31), and was, as a result, ruled by Him. The children of Israel were those whose father was, in New Testament parlance, born again.

In addition, the children of Israel had clearly had religious training or they never would have known to cry out to God. They had even maintained their religious identity as children of Israel, also known as Hebrews, possibly from the Akkadian word, *Habiru*, which meant a people with no land and no citizenship. But, natural or religious heritage is never a guarantee of anything. Each previous generation had had to deal with God for themselves. The children would have to deal with God, personally, too.

These children of Israel illustrate an important truth: God doesn't have any grandchildren. Just because the father of their family had been a man who came to be ruled by God, didn't mean the children were; just because the father had learned to walk differently, didn't mean the children had; and just because the father had found spiritual freedom, didn't mean the children found it. Still, today, while parents may be God-ruled Christians, that doesn't mean the children are or that they are relieved of their responsibility to have a personal encounter with God. Each of us must meet God ourselves; each of us must have a life-changing experience with Him; each of us must learn to walk differently and to be ruled by Him.

Born Fruitful

Even though the children of Israel did not yet know the God of their father for themselves, there was a blessing inherent in the fact that they were the offspring of a man who did. This eternal principle of God is found in Deuteronomy 28:2 through 4:

> *And all these blessings shall come on thee, and overtake thee, if thou shalt hearken unto the voice of the LORD thy God. Blessed shalt thou be in the city, and blessed shalt thou be in the field. Blessed shall be the fruit of thy body.*

Jacob had become the God-ruled man, Israel. Because he had obeyed the Lord's voice, God's blessing just naturally overtook his children, even before they had met God for themselves. This blessing was first given by God, Himself, to Jacob in Genesis 46:3, *"And he said, I am God, the God of thy father: fear not to go down into Egypt; for I will make of thee there a great nation."* It's clear, from Exodus 1:7, that God had kept His promise, *"And the children of Israel were fruitful, and increased abundantly, and multiplied, and waxed exceeding mighty; and the land was filled with them."* Obviously, the blessing of God was on the children of Israel then, just as it is often upon the children of Christians today, even if those children are not yet Christians themselves. It happened then and it happens now for two very important reasons: First, God never forgets a promise and, second, God's promises never go out of date. But, even though the blessing of God rests upon the children of the righteous, this does not mean that those children aren't born in bondage.

Born Bound

These children of Israel, these children with such a godly heritage, these children who had been living in the promised blessing of God--these very same children, every single one of them, were born bound, born enslaved in a land in which they had no citizenship and that land was Egypt. The very definition of the name, Egypt, paints certain spiritual pictures. It can mean, "black,"[4] perhaps a reference to the darkness of the mud along the fertile Nile River, but indicative of spiritual darkness and sin, as well. It can also mean, "oppressors,"[5] an evidence of the nature of the people who dwelt there. Both definitions would clearly indicate a type of the world, a place of spiritual darkness and sin, a place where the offspring of the God-ruled man are ever oppressed.

And, the children of Israel were indeed oppressed in Egypt, oppressed in their bondage by the king of Egypt called Pharaoh, a title which may be translated, "the Sun."[6] Here, we see a type of Satan, himself, who was first called Lucifer, which means, "the light bearer, son of the morning, the bright star,"[7] all clear references to the sun. Pharaoh was unimpressed by the religious heritage of the children of Israel and had no acquaintance whatever with Joseph, the favored son of Jacob who had become governor of Egypt during the days of famine. Pharaoh was motivated by only one, overriding concern:

> *Come on, let us deal wisely with them; lest they multiply, and it come to pass, that, when there falleth out any war, they join also unto our enemies, and fight against us, and so get them up out of the land.*

This is exactly the same motivation, the same concern, evidenced by Satan, as he seeks to oppress. He cares nothing for humanity and is not even impressed by those who can boast a godly heritage. In that eternal state of war which exists between himself and Jehovah God, he cares only that man might come into a relationship with his Enemy (God) and fight against him. It's been that way from the very beginning.

When God first created man upon this earth, He made him in His own image, as Genesis 1:26 declares, *"And God said, Let us make man in our image, after our likeness: and let them have dominion."* Just as God was a Trinity, a tri-part Being, He made man a trinity, a tri-part being, too. God made man with a spirit, to commune with Him, a soul, to make decisions based on that communion, and a body, to carry out those decisions. And, God made this man to have dominion over everything in this world, including a certain sinful angel who was cast down to earth, Lucifer (Isaiah 14:12), otherwise known as Satan.

To prevent man from exercising this dominion over him, Satan conceived a brilliant strategy. God had already communed with man in his spirit and had set one limit upon man's conduct: man was not to eat of the tree of the knowledge of good and evil. But, Satan deceived man's companion, Woman, and caused her, and later tempted man, too, to make the decision in their souls to disobey the clear command of God (Genesis 3:1 through 6). Their bodies simply carried out the decision their souls had made, as their hands trembled to touch what their mouths longed to taste.

The consequence of their sin was cataclysmic, as a terrible punishment was meted out to them by God. He had told them that failure to obey His one command would result in death, and God is always true to His word. While their bodies lived on outside of the perfect garden God had made for them and their souls survived to continue to make decisions, their spirits, that precious part of their nature which communed with God, died. In that state, they no longer posed any threat to Satan; they were no longer able to fight against him and on the side of his Enemy, God. Because that first man, Adam, was the father of the human race, all human beings born since have inherited a dead spirit and each has committed sin and become enslaved by it as a result. As the father of the children of Israel led them into the land of bondage, so the father of the human race led all of his descendants into the slavery of sin.

In all the ages of history since, Satan has had only two objectives for mankind. First, he seeks to master, to prevent man from going over to his Enemy to obtain salvation, that born-again experience in which the spirit of man is reborn to commune with God once again (John 3:3 through 8). Second, he seeks to murder, to bring eternal death to the soul of man. He would prefer the second, but he will temporarily settle for the first secure in the knowledge that it will ultimately result in the second.

Born Under Taskmasters

It would seem that Pharaoh had the very same objectives in mind for the children of Israel. To achieve the first, mastery, Pharaoh placed over them taskmasters who had only two functions: First, they perpetuated the bondage under which the children of Israel suffered. Second, they orchestrated the building of Pharaoh's kingdom (Exodus 1:11 through 14), by constructing storage cities for his treasures. These taskmasters of ancient Egypt may be seen as typical of the demonic influences of sin which enslave unregenerate man, perpetuating his bondage and building up the kingdom of Satan in this world. As Paul so aptly put it in Romans 6:16:

> *Know ye not, that to whom ye yield yourselves servants to obey, his servants ye are to whom ye obey; whether of sin unto death, or of obedience unto righteousness.*

The effects of living in slavery, under the domination and control of the taskmasters were not pleasant. As described in Exodus 1:13 and 14, it was a life of affliction, bitterness, hardness, difficulty, and strict servitude. And, this life had only one end in sight--death. So it has ever been; so it will ever be. While there may be pleasure in sin for a season, the end is always pain and death.

Born to Die

But, even slavery was not enough for Pharaoh, as it is never enough for Satan. It was also Pharaoh's plan to bring about the destruction of the entire race of Hebrews. His diabolical plan began at birth. To accomplish his aim, he ordered the Jewish midwives to murder every male child born to a Jewish mother. Had his plan succeeded, there would have been no men to father future generations and Pharaoh would soon have been rid of the race he feared would one day rise up against him.

How often, in the course of history, has Satan thought to destroy the children of the righteous? How often has he longed to be rid of them, once and for all? But, by a miracle of the grace of God, those children have always prospered best when persecuted most and, somehow, God has always used such adversity to temper His people like steel, to strengthen their resolve, to set their priorities, to clarify their thinking, and to forge in them a determination like iron. It has always been such persecution which has gotten man's attention and turned him to his God. Was that the plan all along?

While God's plan is always destined to succeed, Pharaoh's plan was destined to fail. Two midwives who feared God more than they feared Pharaoh claimed that all Hebrew children were born before they reached the homes of their patients. For this, the women were richly rewarded by God (Exodus 1:21). God has always had such people in His employ. There have always been those who fear nothing so much as His frown of displeasure and will risk anything to earn His smile of favor.

Born to be Born Again

We, too, are children of the first father, Adam, sold in severe slavery to sin through the inheritance he passed on to us. (Gee, thanks, Dad!) In addition, many of us are children of Israel, children of a godly father (or mother), who may have trusted in our religious heritage to save us from Satan and his taskmasters. And, all of God's people are Hebrews, Habiru, with no real homeland on this earth, no citizenship in this world.

Because of this background, all of us were born in bondage, under the domination of Satan, enslaved to his sin, living in bitterness and affliction, and building his kingdom in the world. Satan has no other end in mind than our eventual and eternal death, and, until that day comes, he has no other concern than to keep us under his mastery, unable to deter us from coming to the side of his Enemy, to prevent us from finding salvation. The plan begins at birth and it continues until the day of death. But, the first step to spiritual life and spiritual maturity is taken when we realize our lost and hopeless state, admit our sinful nature, and begin to cry out to God for the help that only He can bring. With that first cry, He begins to move in our behalf; He begins the chain of events which will bring the Saviour to us and us to the Saviour; He begins the marvelous work of our salvation.

We sometimes wonder why. Why did God permit us to be born in bondage to sin and to Satan? Why did God permit life to be so difficult? Why did God permit us to come so close to being lost forever? The answer rings down through the corridors of time: It was all a part of God's eternal plan. It was the suffering of slavery which He designed to show us the futility of our situation; it was the discontent of captivity which He conceived to bring us to our senses; it was the bitterness of bondage which He used to turn us to Him. Praise God, it worked! We reached out to God, we cried out for His mercy, we took those first tentative steps to escape pharaoh and his diabolical taskmasters, to flee to the side of the Saviour. Thus did God set our feet upon that long road to spiritual maturity.

[1]George Barr, *Who's Who in the Bible*, p. 83.

[2]Ibid., p. 80.

[3]Herbert Lockyer, *All the Men of the Bible*, p. 161.

[4]Finis Jennings Dake, *Dake's Annotated Reference Bible*, p. 65.

[5]William Smith, *Dr. William Smith's Dictionary of the Bible*, Volume 1, p. 668.

[6]Ibid., Volume III, p. 2461.

[7]Ibid., Volume II, p. 1689.

Chapter 2
BORN TO DELIVER

The Birth of the Deliverer

Moses, the future lawgiver and deliverer of Israel, was born at Heliopolis, Egypt, just south of the delta of the Nile River,[1] in about 1526 B.C. He was born at a time when the Egyptian pharaoh, likely Thutmose III as previously noted, had ordered the deaths of all male Hebrew babies. The Jewish historian, Josephus, records that this order may have been the result of a prophecy given to Thutmose which predicted the birth of a Hebrew boy who would become the deliverer of his people and the destroyer of Egypt.[2] But, Josephus also says that the father of Moses, Amram, had received similar information in the form of a dream,[3] and he was determined to keep the child alive in spite of Pharaoh's order. The labor of Moses' mother, Jochebed, must have been so mild and the delivery so easy that Jochebed was able to do without the services of the midwives who usually attended the Hebrew women, thus enabling her and her newborn son to evade detection. Still, the beautiful baby boy had been born into the same human condition as his fellow countrymen and, in the normal course of events, would have suffered the same death sentence pronounced upon them. As he grew, his cries became stronger and louder. Within three months, his heartbroken parents knew that they would be unable to hide him much longer (Exodus 2:2).

The Salvation of the Saviour

To save her son, Jochebed constructed a small boat which she called an ark (Exodus 2:3), probably in the hope that it would provide the same salvation for her son that the ark of Noah's day had provided for his righteous family. This ark was made of bulrushes (Exodus 2:3), a strong reed which grew along the banks of the Nile River, and was waterproofed with a coating of pitch or bitumen, a tar-like substance which sometimes bubbles forth from underground petroleum reserves. (It is interesting to note that the discoverer of oil in the Middle East thought to search in that area based upon this very Scripture, certain that the pitch described there would be the precursor to great quantities of petroleum. He believed the Bible and he was richly rewarded.)

When the time came, Jochebed put her precious son inside the ark she had made and placed it in an arm of the Nile River near Zoan or Avaris.[4] The location had evidently been chosen with great care. It lay on the eastern boundary of the land of Goshen, the Jewish quarter of Egypt. It was also near one of the residences of Egyptian royalty. As such, the river bank had been beautified by flags (Exodus 2:3) and the river itself had been cleared of the crocodiles which infested every other part of the Nile, to permit the royal family to swim and bathe safely. But, although this section of the Nile may have been safer, it was also an area where the child was more likely to be discovered. His mother could only imagine the horrors which awaited him if he were.

It was as the daughter of Pharaoh, identified by Josephus as Thermuthis, was bathing in the river that she heard the infant's cries, found the tiny ark, and rescued the baby inside (Exodus 2:5). Although she knew immediately that she had found a Hebrew baby (Exodus 2:6) who was under her father's death sentence, she was captivated by the child and determined to raise him as her own. She named him Moses, meaning "to draw out," because she had drawn him from the waters of the Nile (Exodus 2:10).

Miriam, the elder sister of Moses, had been watching from a location nearby, observing everything which had transpired, determined to know the fate of her baby brother. When she saw that Thermuthis was planning to keep the baby she had found, Miriam thought quickly, approached Thermuthis, and offered her mother's services as wetnurse to the infant (Exodus 2:7). Tradition holds that, when the child refused the milk of the Egyptian wetnurses, Jochebed was immediately summoned and handsomely paid to care for the very child she thought she had lost forever.

The Education of the Educator

It was through this chain of events that Moses came to receive his first education at his mother's own breast, despite the death sentence pronounced upon him by Pharaoh. This brief period before he was weaned, which, according to Egyptian custom, lasted only three to five years, would prove to be the most formative of his life and would forge the unbreakable link which would forever tie him to his people, the Hebrews.

What could a mother teach that would have such a lasting impact on a three to five year-old child? One can only guess. She doubtless told him of his heritage as a Jew, as a member of the tribe of Levi, as a descendant of the colorful and revered patriarchs, Abraham, Isaac, and Jacob. These stories of family history would have been enough to inflame the imagination of any child. She probably also told her son of the suffering of his countrymen under the hand of their Egyptian taskmasters. Having those seeds thus planted in his young mind, it would have been easy for them to take root and grow after he was returned to Thermuthis and began to see with his own eyes the truth of all his mother had told him. It's also reasonable to assume that Jochebed told the young Moses of all of the promises Jehovah God had made to his people, promises of a return to the land in which they had once wandered, promises that that land would one day be their own. Later, as he observed the bitter bondage and sorrowful suffering of his own people, Moses heart must have gone out to them. Finally, it must be assumed that all of Jochebed's lessons for her son were taught in an atmosphere of love and nurture. The remembrance of that love, of the feelings of warmth and security it stirred in the young child's heart, must have stayed with Moses all of his life and tied him irrevocably to the woman who had lavished this love upon him and to the people she represented.

Most believe that the years of infancy are the most formative in any child's life. It is thought that it is during these years that the basic personality is formed, that the deepest drives are initiated, and that the most purposeful lines of thought are conceived. These are the roots which will grow and blossom and bear fruit throughout the remainder of one's life. There could be no more perfect anecdotal evidence to support this theory than the life of Moses. There is no historical evidence that, once Moses was weaned and returned to the care of Thermuthis, he ever saw his natural mother again. Yet, those few short years in her nurture and admonition would govern the remainder of his life.

The education of Moses would continue under the direction of Thermuthis. In ancient Egypt, formal education began as soon as weaning was completed. According to the testimony of Stephen, as recorded in Acts 7:22, Moses was indeed well educated, *"And Moses was learned in all the wisdom of the Egyptians, and was mighty in words and in deeds."*

There was no nation in the ancient world which attached more value to education than Egypt. In fact, it was in the royal schools of Egypt that the heirs to the thrones of the

Syro-Palestinian territories dominated by Egypt were educated. As a result, Moses would have been privileged to attend school with royal princes from as far away as the great Euphrates River.

According to Jewish tradition, Moses was educated at the school of the Temple of the Sun in Heliopolis, the same city just south of the Nile delta in which he had been born. His education began early, as soon as he was weaned, because hieroglyphics, the Egyptian system of picture writing, was quite complicated and required many years to master. In addition, Moses would have been taught such complex mathematical concepts as duodecimal and decimal scales of notation, geometry, and trigonometry. In the sciences, he would have learned astronomy, chemistry, medicine, dentistry, and metallurgy. He would also have learned all of the literature of the Greek, Chaldee, Assyrian, and Egyptian masters. In his philosophy classes, Moses would have learned the complicated religious beliefs of the Egyptians, the philosophies and religions of other nations, and the systems of law of Egypt and other nations, as well. It is proof of the divine inspiration of the books subsequently written by Moses that none of these philosophies, religions, or legal systems crept into them. Music was another subject which was considered to be of great importance in the royal Egyptian schools. Moses would have been trained in this art, too. Another art to be mastered was the art of composition. The writing of letters, prose, and poetry were all stressed. The young Moses would also have completed these courses.

All in all, God arranged for Moses to be formally educated in all of the skills and sciences he would need to accomplish the task for which he was destined. Yet, God also somehow enabled him to reject all of those ideas and thoughts which were contrary to divine truth. It was, indeed, quite an educational feat. And, it was just the beginning of the maturing process God had in mind for the deliverer He had chosen.

The Leadership Training of the Leader

There is no record of the age at which the formal education of Moses was completed. There is, however, much tradition and history which gives a glimpse of his life as a prince between the time of his graduation and his flight from Egypt at the age of forty. Josephus holds that, following the completion of his studies, Moses entered the military service of Egypt, as further preparation for the heir apparent, the young prince who was to succeed Pharaoh.[5] In the military, Moses used the engineering skills he had been taught to invent boats and engines for building and instruments of war which used principles of hydraulics. He is credited with leading an invasion of Ethiopia during which he miraculously cast out the serpents he discovered there, founded the city of Hermopolis as a monument to his victory, and, finally returned to Egypt in total triumph.

While in the military service of Egypt, Moses would have continued to learn lessons which would prove to be of great value to him in the future. He would have learned all of the military strategies and secrets of the Egyptians, how to predict the actions of her generals and commanders, and the weaknesses and vulnerabilities of his future adversaries. All of these lessons would stand him in good stead.

Having completed this "post-graduate" course, God knew that there were still some lessons Moses needed to learn and He had prepared just the right "school" for him.

The Shepherd's Training of the Shepherd

At the age of forty, Moses decided to reject the fame and fortune which would have been his as heir and ultimately as pharaoh, and to cast his lot with his own people, the

Hebrew slaves he had learned about at his mother's breast. Hebrews 11:24 through 27 puts it this way:

> *By faith Moses, when he was come to years, refused to be called the son of Pharaoh's daughter; Choosing rather to suffer affliction with the people of God, than to enjoy the pleasures of sin for a season; Esteeming the reproach of Christ greater riches than the treasures of Egypt: for he had respect unto the recompense of the reward. By faith he forsook Egypt, not fearing the wrath of the king: for he endured, as seeing him who is invisible.*

As an act of rejection of his Egyptian upbringing and acceptance of his true heritage as a Hebrew, Moses killed an Egyptian who was mistreating one of his Hebrew brothers (Exodus 2:11 and 12). He thought he had acted in secret, but, by the next day, he realized that his deed had been witnessed and was known to the authorities (Exodus 2:14). As a result, Pharaoh made clear his intention to execute Moses and, according to tradition, several assassination plots were actually formulated against him. Tradition also holds that Moses was forewarned of these plots by Aaron, his elder brother. Moses fled for his life to the land of Midian (Exodus 2:15), the home of the descendants of Midian, a son of Abraham by his second wife, Keturah (Genesis 25:1 and 2). It lay on the east bank of the Jordan River and the Dead Sea and also encompassed the southern and eastern parts of the Sinai Peninsula. As he fled, Moses learned the geography and topography of the very places through which the Lord would one day take His people to their promised land. Thus was he educated for the command of that journey for which he had been chosen by God.

Once in the land of Midian, Moses met Reuel, or Jethro, a priest of the Midianites, and his seven daughters, one of whom, Zipporah, he subsequently married (Exodus 2:21). God blessed their union with two sons, Gershom and Eliezer (Exodus 18:2 and 3). Moses assumed the quiet, pastoral life of a shepherd to Reuel's flocks, gently leading them from pasture to pasture and oasis to oasis. During his forty years as a shepherd in Midian, Moses learned the important skill of shepherding, as Psalm 77:20 recalls, *"Thou leddest thy people like a flock by the hand of Moses."* He learned how to lead the weak, the young, the stubborn, and the strong, all at the same time, all along the same path. He learned how to survive in the wilderness and how to locate food and water even in the most primitive places. In short, he learned everything he would need to know to lead his people from slavery to their promised land. God had arranged his courses well to bring him to maturity.

Moses, a Type of Man

Through this brief glimpse of the early life of Moses, we can often see him as a type of man. This is especially obvious at those times in his life when his human frailty and vulnerability were evident and at those times when he failed in his human efforts. For example, we see him born a defenseless infant, unable to provide for his own salvation, much less the salvation of others. Later, we see him hidden in an ark, a Biblical type of the salvation and deliverance without which man is destined to die. And, when rescued by Pharaoh's daughter, we see him drawn out of the water, a type of water baptism which is illustrative of man's rebirth following salvation.

Nowhere is the humanity of Moses more in evidence than when, at the age of forty, he tried to save his people by his own human effort just as man, all too often, attempts some form of "do-it-yourself" salvation. He does his best to turn over a proverbial new leaf, effect a life change, or, in some other way, save himself. His salvation is indeed God's will, but this kind of effort is never done in God's time or in God's way. In Moses' attempt, we see the true nature of unregenerate man revealed. We see man's pride in his own ability, his temper, his hatred of his fellowman, his prejudice against those who are different from him, his lawlessness and rebellion to the point of murder, his violence as his answer to his problems, and his deception in thinking that any effort of this kind could succeed in securing his salvation. Such a plan, based as it is on human logic, human motivations, human characteristics, and human failings, is always destined to falter.

In Moses' effort at "do-it-yourself" deliverance, we see the four results such attempts always bring, the four F's of man's way. First, there was failure; second, Moses experienced frustration with his failure; then, Moses became fearful to try again; and, finally, Moses fled any further attempts to accomplish his goal. We see this pattern repeated often in the life of man. For example, a man may decide to quit a bad habit, a seemingly simple thing. He tries to turn over a new leaf and may explore plan after plan of his own devising to achieve his goal. But, he fails miserably and finds himself frustrated with his own failure. As a result, he is afraid to try again, fearful that he will only fail once more. Finally, he flees any future attempt to accomplish his goal. Using his methods, he has lost a battle which God's methods can easily win.

As we seek to see ourselves in the life of Moses, we can begin to learn from his example. We learn that we, too, are born into the human condition of sin and death, that we need an Ark we cannot build for ourselves in order to save us, and that we, too, must go through the water of baptism to illustrate our salvation. We learn than no amount of human effort, no matter how well-conceived or well-executed can ever succeed in changing our state of slavery in sin to salvation in God. We also learn that only in God, only according to His will, only by following His plan can we truly find the freedom we seek.

Moses, a Type of Christ

In the life of this same, very human man, Moses, we also see a type of the divine Man, Christ Jesus. This is particularly true when observing God's sovereignty in preparing, preserving, and presenting Moses to be the deliverer of His people and at those times when Moses was executing his divinely-appointed mission.

For example, we see that Moses was born to be the deliverer and lawgiver of his people, just as Jesus was. We find that the mothers of both children had no midwife to attend them at the birth of their babies. We see that both were born under the death sentence of the rulers of their nations and, in both cases, these death sentences were ordered for masses of male infants simply because of prophecies which had reached the rulers' ears concerning the future destiny of a single male child. But, both babies were spared through dreams given to their fathers. Both were hidden and saved from death in Egypt where both received their first education from their mothers. We also see that both were born into the same human condition faced by all other members of their race.

A careful study of history shows that both Moses and Jesus were educated in the best schools available in the times in which they lived. Luke 4:16 describes an occasion when Jesus read from the Torah in the synagogue at Nazareth, making it obvious that He had, at some point, been taught to read, probably in that very synagogue school. Since the Sanhedrin, the ruling body of Judaism in Jesus' day, had ruled that formal education in a synagogue school was a mandatory requirement for all boys who wished to be welcomed into Temple worship, and since Jesus was, according to Luke 2:41, 42, and 46, thus received into the life of the Temple at the age of twelve, it is clear that He had been so educated. In addition, Jesus was called Rabbi more often than any other single title recorded in the

New Testament, proving that He had gone on to higher education in one of the rabbinical schools of the time.

We also find that both Moses and Jesus once lived in great splendor, in kingly palaces. But, both laid aside status, position, and kingship to suffer. Both identified themselves with their own people, the Jews, and both identified with the bondage which held their people helpless. Then, both became the shepherds of their own.

Both Moses and Jesus suffered great hardships. Both spent time in the wilderness before they could be revealed. Both were rejected by the very people they had come to deliver. Both were often lonely, slandered, and misunderstood.

As the end came, both Moses and Jesus died on a mount appointed by God. Then, both were resurrected to return to this earth for a time.

As we observe Moses as a type of Christ, there are also some important lessons for us to learn on the way to maturity. Foremost among them is the truth of what God can accomplish with one life lived in His will, governed by His guidance, and dedicated to His direction.

[1]William Smith, *Smith's Dictionary of the Bible*, Volume III, p. 2017.

[2]Flavius Josephus, *The Complete Works of Josephus*, Antiquities of the Jews, Book 2, Chapter 9, Verse 2.

[3]Josephus, Antiquities of the Jews, Book 2, Chapter 9, Verse 3.

[4]Alfred Edersheim, *Old Testament Bible History*, The Book of Exodus, p. 36.

[5]Ibid., Antiquities of the Jews, Book 2, Chapter 10, Verse 1.

Chapter 3
GOD'S PLAN FOR SALVATION

Man's Decision

Moses had chosen to reject the fame and fortune of the life fate had bestowed upon him, along with his pleasures and privileges as a prince of Egypt. Instead, he had decided to cast his lot with the people of God. Yet, when he arrived in Midian at the age of forty in 1486 B.C., this is the testimony we read of him in Exodus 2:19, "And they said, *"An Egyptian delivered us out of the hand of the shepherds."* Although Moses had left behind the world he had known, that world had not left him. He looked more like an Egyptian, more like the world, than he looked like a child of God. That's why he was still being identified as an Egyptian.

In the ancient world, it was easy to recognize a citizen of Egypt. While the inhabitants of Midian wore the long flowing robes and head coverings of nomads, the Egyptians wore decorated loin cloths and sphinx-like headdresses. While the Midianites allowed their hair and beards to grow freely, the Egyptians shaved their heads and beards completely. This case of mistaken identity probably occurred because Moses had not yet had time to change his clothes or allow his hair and beard to grow. He still looked like an Egyptian. It was a condition only time and growth would change.

Whenever a citizen of this sinful world chooses to reject his imperfect past and walk into the unknown future with God, he may discover that others just don't recognize the difference instantly. Even when an inner change has indeed taken place, an outer change may not yet be apparent. Like Moses, the confusion may simply be the result of such inconsequential things as clothes and hair, and, like Moses, these outer markers may only be brought into harmony with the inner state through a process of growth occurring over a period of time. The very same Bible that assures us that God looks at the inner man and is never puzzled by man's true state, also tells us that others see only the outer man and are often mistaken in their assessment of him (1 Samuel 16:7).

Have patience, child of God; in time, God, Himself, will produce in you the growth which will result in a total transformation which will be obvious to all.

God's Knowledge

Forty years passed. God and time had done their work. The impetuous Egyptian murderer had become the patient, settled shepherd--the very man God could use to accomplish the very task the old Moses had so terribly bungled. Time had also changed the political situation in Egypt and the spiritual situation of God's people who were suffering in slavery there, as we read in Exodus 2:23 through 25:

> *And it came to pass in the process of time, that the king of Egypt died: and the children of Israel sighed by reason of the bondage, and they cried, and their cry came up unto God by reason of the bondage. And God heard their groaning, and God remembered his covenant with Abraham, with Isaac, and with Jacob. And God looked upon the children of Israel, and God had respect unto them.*

The words used here are strong and revealing ones. Sighed is the Hebrew, *anah*, which refers to the public displays of grief and mourning, associated with the frenzied weeping and wailing of Middle Eastern funerals. For the Jews, it seems life in Egypt had become one, long, continuous funeral, one, long, continuous period of mourning their state. Cry, is the Hebrew, *shaw'a*, which means, a cry for help. It is used to describe cries of anguish associated with oppression, the cries of those who are close to the breaking point.

God knew exactly how close to the breaking point His people were. Respect, is from the Hebrew root, *yada*, meaning, knowledge or recognition, and is used of God's knowledge of man and his circumstances. God had complete knowledge of all that His people were suffering, He knew that they had reached the breaking point, and He knew that they were finally ready to reach out to Him and to receive His help. God always knows the situation of His people. He realizes when they have reached the point of despair. It is then that His people cry out to Him for the help that only He can give; it is then that He can begin to keep His promises to them; it is then that He can finally move in their behalf.

God's first move in behalf of His people in Egypt, however, would come in the far-away land of Midian.

God's Call

As the eighty year-old Moses led his flock of sheep to the top of Mount Horeb, a desert promontory in the wilderness of Sinai where a rich oasis of fruit trees and pastures awaited Bedouin shepherds,[1] did he wonder if he would spend the rest of his life in pastoral pursuits? Did he ponder the fate of the people he had once tried to save? One can only imagine. But, his days of obscurity and anonymity were about to come to a screeching halt.

It was probably not unusual to see some bit of the scrub brush of Horeb burst into flame from spontaneous combustion in the desert heat. But, the burning bush Moses saw that day, was not being consumed by the flames which enveloped it. Any well-educated shepherd who viewed this scene would know in an instant that this phenomenon defied the laws of nature. It couldn't be happening, but somehow it was.

Now, it's a fact that, when any little bush is willing to be on fire for God, people will come to watch it burn. It's also a fact that God is a recognized Expert in the use of visual aids to teach important lessons. God certainly got Moses' attention with this one! The lesson God illustrated was significant. That little bush was exactly like the Israelites; they, too, were undergoing fiery trials, but they were not consumed.

At this point, Moses had a choice to make. He could continue in the comfortable and secure pastoral life he had lived for the past forty years and ignore anything, including a burning bush, which did not directly impact on himself and his sheep. Or he could move into the insecure unknown, a move closer to the fire, closer to the source, closer to the miracle-working power of God. The child of God is sometimes called upon to make that same kind of choice. Little does he realize that the decision made in that moment may determine the course of the rest of his life.

It was only when Moses made the decision to move in the direction of God, that God spoke to him, as we read in Exodus 3:4 and 5:

> *And <u>when the LORD saw that he turned aside to see, God called unto him</u> out of the midst of the bush, and said, Moses, Moses. And he said, Here am I. And he said, Draw not nigh hither: put off thy shoes from off thy feet, for the place whereon thou standest is holy ground.*

Moses had clearly moved a great deal further than a few feet across the desert sands. He had moved into a new relationship with the God who knew him by name, and moved into a new revelation of the God who was so holy that He could not be approached in the same shoes which had walked through the filth of the world below. This kind of a relationship can be so intense as to be terrifying and so profound as to be paralyzing (Exodus 3:6).

God identified Himself to Moses as the God of his ancestors, Abraham, Isaac, and Jacob (Exodus 3:6), the very God who had made certain promises that they had lived and died believing would one day be kept. And, He identified Himself as the God who has full knowledge of the condition of His people. He had seen (Exodus 3:7), seen the torment in which His people suffered, heard (Exodus 3:7), heard their heart-wrenching cries for help, and acted (Exodus 3:8), acted to deliver them from the bondage out of which they could not deliver themselves and take them into His promises. But, God also revealed Himself as the God who chooses to move in the human realm using human instruments when God gave Moses the following command in Exodus 3:10: *"I will send thee unto Pharaoh, that thou mayest bring forth my people the children of Israel out of Egypt."*

God wants to deliver people, to set them free of sin. But, it was not His design to descend in a chariot of fire to do the work Himself and it is not His aim to send angels to witness to the lost. He wants to use believers to accomplish this task, not in their strength or according to their will, but clothed in His strength and obedient to His will.

Man's Response

A real one-on-one, face-to-face encounter with the omnipotent God of this universe will always produce true humility in man as he recognizes God's greatness compared to his own insignificance. Moses was no exception. His initial reaction to God's call was a modest, *"Who am I, that I should go"* (Exodus 3:11). Was this the same Moses who, just forty years earlier, had impetuously volunteered his services as the heroic defender and deliverer of his enslaved countrymen? Indeed it was. But, this Moses had grown greatly during the course of those forty years. The older, more settled, more mature man realized his own insufficiency and accepted his own inadequacies.

Still, even true meekness cannot be an excuse for inactivity in response to God's call. God promised to be with Moses in the endeavor (Exodus 3:12), and one man and one God are always a majority. If God promises to be in it, it promises to succeed.

God's Identity

Once the question, "Who am I" was settled, Moses asked another question, "Who are you?" (Exodus 3:13). Indeed, when one experiences what he believes to be the call and leading of the Lord, he has a right, even a responsibility, to be certain it is truly God who is speaking. Deception is possible and it is often difficult, especially for the new Christian, to discern the voice he hears. Those to whom he is sent will also want to know about the God who is doing the sending, too.

In response to Moses' question, God's answer in Exodus 3:14 echoes through the ages, *"And God said unto Moses, I AM THAT I AM: and he said, Thus shalt thou say unto the children of Israel, I AM hath sent me unto you."* Here, God introduced Himself to Moses as "*Eheyeh Asher Eheyeh*," in the original, "*Jehovah Elohey*," "I AM THAT I AM." This title combined the concept of Jehovah, the self-existent and eternal One, with the idea of unchangeableness of character. It was by the name, Jehovah, that God instituted and signed His unalterable covenants with man. By instructing that this name be given to the children of Israel, God was reminding them that it had been He who had made the covenants with their forefathers in the first place, He who still remembered them, and He who would fulfill them. In addition, this name of God may also be translated, "I am because I am," an indication of the unconditional, independent, and eternal existence of God. By this name, I AM THAT I AM, God signified that He intended to be whatever His people needed. Did they need a Deliverer? God said, "I am that Deliverer." Did they need a Guide across the wilderness? God said, "I am that Guide." Did they need a Supplier to meet their needs? God said, "I am that Supplier."

Using this name to sign Moses' marching orders, God instructed him in precisely the way to proceed (Exodus 3:15 through 17). He also proved that He knew exactly what would occur and had already planned to deal with it (Exodus 3:18 through 20). In addition, God promised that His children would be able to spoil the enemy which had held them in bondage for so long (Exodus 3:21 and 22). God also avowed that this was His name, His identity to His people, and would be forever (Exodus 3:15).

Some things never change. It's interesting to note that, in the Gospel of John, Jesus often identified Himself in this same way. For example, He said, *"I am the bread of life"* (John 6:35), *"I am the light of the world"* (John 8:12 and 9:5), "I am the good shepherd" (John 10:11), *"I am the resurrection and the life"* (John 11:25), *"I am the way, the truth and the life"* (John 14:6), *"I am the true vine"* (John 15:l and 5). And, in John 8:58, he said, *"Before Abraham was, I am."* That same I AM, still is and ever shall be.

Man's Humanity

But, Moses raised objections to answering the call of God, objections only too common to human beings who realize the enormity of the task He has placed in their hands. First, Moses was concerned that his countrymen, most of whom probably didn't even remember him or knew him only as a fleeing felon, wouldn't believe that God had sent him to set them free (Exodus 4:1). It was a valid concern. It is the same concern expressed by many who are sent to witness to the saving power of God.

In response, God gave Moses two signs to prove the authenticity of his claims. First, He enabled Moses to throw down his shepherd's staff, causing it to become a serpent. Then, to illustrate the authority He had given Moses over the serpents of sin and slavery and the serpent which was the emblem of royal power in Egypt, God empowered Moses to retrieve the serpent, whereupon it reverted to its previous form, causing no harm to God's servant (Exodus 4:4 and 5). The second sign involved the use of leprosy, the disease most dreaded in the ancient world. At God's instruction, Moses was able to place his hand inside his robe and withdraw it full of leprosy. Then, to illustrate the power of God over illness, Moses was able to replace his same hand in his same robe and remove it as clean as before (Exodus 4:6 and 7).

The subjugation of the serpent and the destruction of disease are just two signs that should still follow those who believe in God, as Mark 16:17 and 18 declares:

> *And these signs shall follow them that believe; In my name shall they cast out devils; they shall speak with new tongues; They shall take up serpents; and if they drink any deadly thing, it shall not hurt them; they shall lay hands on the sick, and they shall recover.*

In fact, the very words translated "miracle" in both the Old and New Testaments mean, a sign or a token. Both indicate a sign used to authenticate the minister and point the spectator to God.

God had overcome the first objection of Moses. He promised that such miraculous signs as the ability to turn water to blood, would convince even the most obdurate observer (Exodus 4:9).

The second objection Moses raised had to do with his powers of eloquence. Moses admitted that he was slow in both speech and tongue (Exodus 4:10). Did he have an actual impediment in his speech, such as a lisp or a stutter, as some suppose? Had he simply forgotten so much of the Egyptian language and syntax over the past forty years that he feared he would not be able to communicate God's message effectively? Or, did he feel that he simply did not possess the gift to put words together well? Whatever the situation in which Moses found himself, God had the answer. His promise to Moses is recorded in Exodus 4:12, *"Now therefore go, and I will be with thy mouth, and teach thee what thou shalt say."* God must have been as good as His word. In Acts 7:22, Stephen gave this account of Moses' powers of speech, *"And Moses was learned in all the wisdom of the Egyptians, and was mighty in words and deeds."*

Still, God knew Moses; He knew the reluctance of his heart. Although He was angered by the lack of faith Moses evidenced, God acquiesced to his human frailty and arranged for Aaron, his elder brother, to accompany him to Pharaoh's court (Exodus 4:14 through 16). It would not be long, however, before Moses would assume full duties as spokesman, just as God had originally ordained. The child of God soon learns that the will of God cannot be resisted and that the message of God is a fire in the bones which cannot long be contained.

God had overcome all of Moses' objections. So, Moses bid his father-in-law a fond farewell, took his wife and sons, and left to go back to Egypt. Fully prepared by God for all that lay ahead of him (Exodus 4:21 through 23), Moses had made the decision to obey the command and commission of his Lord.

The Deliverer Must First Be Delivered

As they traveled the long road home, a seemingly inexplicable event occurred. God accosted Moses and his family along the way and attempted to kill the very servant He had just dispatched (Exodus 4:24). How could such a thing happen? Why might such a thing happen? The answer to those questions is given in 1 Peter 4:17:

> *For the time is come that judgment must begin at the house of God: and if it first begin at us, what shall the end be of them that obey not the gospel of God?*

Moses had doubtless heard the stories of his ancestors and of God's command to Abraham (Genesis 17:9 through 14) to circumcise every male child born to his family. This would explain why Moses had circumcised one son, probably the elder, but, for whatever reason, possibly the objection of his wife who may have been horrified by the first circumcision, he had failed to obey God's command to circumcise his other son.

One cannot disobey the clear command of God on the one hand and hope to carry out His commission on the other. In such cases, the judgment of God will fall upon the child of God, just as it almost fell upon Moses. Only the quick, if clearly resentful, compliance of Zipporah in performing the circumcision herself saved her husband's life.

Just as the Saviour of the world had to be without sin in order to carry out His divinely-appointed mission, so the deliverer of the Hebrew slaves had to be free of offense to God before he could execute God's plan for his life. So, the true servant of God must be pure in his Lord's sight before he can be used. Secret sin and rebellion must be confessed, repented of, and forgiven; incomplete obedience must be corrected and total compliance achieved. Nothing less is acceptable; nothing else will do; nothing more is expected. It took near-tragedy for Moses and his family to learn this lesson; may those who follow after take note and learn in a less frightening fashion.

The Vision Shared

With the judgment of God avoided, Moses continued traveling toward Egypt while God spoke to his brother, Aaron, and instructed him go into the wilderness. The two men met on Mount Horeb, the very mount of God where Moses had first heard God's call, and enjoyed a private reunion there (Exodus 4:27). Moses shared all that God had told him and, together, the two traveled on to Egypt to proclaim freedom to God's people (Exodus 4:29 through 30). The people believed, rejoiced in the good news they had so long awaited, and worshipped the God who had sent them a deliverer.

But, freedom was not yet a reality. As so often happens, there was to be a time of waiting and warring before revelation became realization. Things were going to get far worse before they got any better. But, then, that's another story for another chapter....

A Dynasty of Deliverers

Every child of God is called to be a Moses, in one way or another. All are called to bring the good news of deliverance from the bondage of sin. And, most, if they are truly honest, react, to one extent or another, just as Moses did. We all wonder if we are really hearing from God; we all fear the disbelief of those to whom we are sent; we all question our qualifications to complete the assigned task. But, the same God who calmed Moses' fears will calm ours; the same God who empowered him will empower us; the same God who assigned a co-laborer to share the duty will call others to our corner of the vineyard. It is, after all, His work and He never initiated an action He did not plan to complete; it is, after all, His battle and He never declared a war He was not determined to win.

As the child of God matures, he learns the amazing art of moving and resting at the very same time. He learns to move without question at God's clear command and, at the same time, to rest in God's strong arms without concern. He also learns that nothing can be accomplished in his own strength or in his own way. The battle can only be won as he goes forth in total obedience to God's will and proceeds in complete compliance to God's plan. He finds, too, that he can have no success so long as secret sin lies in his camp. It is only after he has crucified his own flesh that he is able to present the grandeur of the Cross to others.

[1]Alfred Edersheim, *Old Testament Bible History*, The Book of Exodus, p. 45.

Chapter 4
SALVATION: GOD VS. SATAN

The Battle Begins

God's time had arrived. He had heard the anguished cries of His people, commissioned His chosen deliverer, and sent him to bring the good news of coming freedom. With him, God sent an aide, an assistant, a spokesman, Moses' elder brother, Aaron. Just who was this second in command in the battle against bondage?

Aaron was three years older than Moses, although he was younger than their older sister, Miriam. He must have been born prior to the death decree issued by Thutmose III against all male Hebrew babies for we read of no ark of bulrushes or mother's plan to save his life. While Aaron was noted throughout Scripture for his eloquence, the ideas he expressed were usually those of his brother. Scripture also takes note of his "warts," such as his inability to resist peer pressure. This was the flaw which resulted in his complicity in the golden calf affair. But, Aaron was also a spiritual man, a praying man, the man chosen by God to initiate a priesthood which would serve Israel for more than a millennium and a half. As it was said in Israel:[1]

From the tribes of Israel came the warriors.
From the tribe of Levi came the workers.
From the family of Aaron came the worshippers.

This, then, was the man who stood at the deliverer's side, the man who formed half of one of the most effective ministry teams in all of recorded history. Together, they would bring freedom to hundreds of thousands who were born in bitter bondage.

In Exodus 4:29 through 31, we read that Moses and Aaron went first to the elders of Israel, the heads of the various families, and, later, to the people, with the message of salvation for which they had been crying out for so long. The people accepted this message gratefully, worshipfully. It was just the message they had been waiting to hear.

From there, Exodus 5:1 says that Moses and Aaron took their message to none other than Pharaoh, himself, Amenophis II, the successor to Thutmose III who had been upon the throne of Egypt for only four years. That message, *"Thus saith the LORD God of Israel, Let my people go."* Now, that's a message which would strike terror into the hearts of most. Unfortunately, Pharaoh had an entirely different reaction to the audacious Jews who stood before him and the message they brought, as we read in Exodus 5:2:

And Pharaoh said, Who is the LORD, that I should obey his voice to let Israel go? I know not the LORD, neither will I let Israel go.

Just reading those words is enough to send chills down the spine of any child of God. Pharaoh had just challenged the God of this universe to a battle he could not possibly hope to win. Oh, he would come to know who the "LORD" was, but it would be too late when he did. And, he would let God's people go, just as God had demanded, but it would cost the life of his son and lots of other Egyptian sons before it happened.

But, Pharaoh, who, for the purposes of our study, stands as a type of Satan, was, as a result of the message delivered by Aaron and Moses, alerted to the potential danger of losing his hard-working slaves. Of course, Satan does not give up his slaves without a struggle. Even a young Christian can attest to this fact. Once alerted to the danger, Satan will act; he will take action, just as Pharaoh did.

As Exodus 5:4 through 18 details, Pharaoh moved immediately to consolidate his hold upon his slaves, to make them wish they had never heard of Moses or the deliverance he proposed, to cause them to long for the "good old days" of bondage. He instructed his taskmasters to stop supplying the Hebrews with the straw they had been receiving, the straw they needed, the straw which was mixed with the mud or clay to solidify it and hold it together. (It is fascinating to note that archaeological expeditions in Egypt have found buildings constructed of brick in which the lower levels contain bricks composed of mud and straw, the middle levels are built with bricks containing straw and stubble, and the highest levels are constructed of bricks made of mud or clay alone.[2] These finds conform to the Biblical account exactly.) In the future, the slaves would be required to gather the stubble of the ground, a backbreaking task at best, wherever they could find it. As if that were not enough, they would be required to manufacture exactly the same number of bricks as before. That should keep their minds off of their God and making sacrifices to Him! As bad as life in bondage had been, it had just become worse. In much the same way, at the first sign of faith, Satan begins to scheme to keep the sinner enslaved. Craftily using his taskmasters, those things which hold in bondage, those things with build his kingdom, Satan seeks to perpetuate, even to increase that bondage and to encourage the sinner to believe that there is no hope of freedom. And, all too often, the sinner's situation seems to get much worse before it gets any better.

The reaction of the children of Israel to this turn of events was only too human. Instead of blaming Pharaoh or his taskmasters, the true agents of their enslavement, they blamed the preachers who had dedicated their lives to obtaining their release from slavery (Exodus 5:19 through 21). The prayer of Moses, recorded in Exodus 5:22 and 23, illustrates the heartfelt pain and the discouraging doubts this caused him. But, the battle had just begun. It was no time to get angry at the preachers; it was about time to get incensed at Satan, the slavemaster. It was time for God to have the last word.

The Battle is God's

In response to the prayer of Moses, God spoke. In Exodus 6:1 through 8, He issued His covenant of deliverance to His people, the eight "I wills" of God Almighty:

1. I will bring you out with a strong hand - Exodus 6:1.
2. I will lift your burden - Exodus 6:6.
3. I will set you free - Exodus 6:6.
4. I will redeem you - Exodus 6:6.
5. I will take you as My own - Exodus 6:7.
6. I will be your God - Exodus 6:7.
7. I will bring you into My promises - Exodus 6:8.
8. I will give you everything I promised - Exodus 6:8.

The God who wrote the covenant signed it with His own name when, in Exodus 6:8, He said, *"I am the LORD."* That name, that signature, is most important. See what God, Himself, said of it in Exodus 6:3:

> *I appeared unto Abraham, unto Isaac, and unto Jacob, by the name of God Almighty, but by my name JEHOVAH was I not known to them.*

God declared that Abraham, Isaac, and Jacob knew Him as God Almighty, in the Hebrew, *El Shadda*i, the all-sufficient and bountiful God who meets every need. It could even be translated, "the breasted One,"[3] the God who, like a nursing mother, nourishes and satisfies His children. Indeed, God did meet every need of the early patriarchs.

Here, as in Exodus 3:14, however, God chose to reveal Himself to Moses, by His most solemn and reverenced name, Jehovah, a name which appears approximately seven thousand times in the Old Testament. It was originally a tetragrammaton, a four-letter name, and was spelled *YHVH* or *YHWH*. The exact pronunciation of it has been lost to history because, for centuries, devout Jews considered it too sacred to be spoken aloud. In fact, even today, Jews avoid speaking or writing it as much as possible. It was during the Middle Ages when the Masoretic Jewish scribes of the time combined the consonants of the tetragrammaton with the vowels of the divine name, Adonai, to form the title, Jehovah, which literally means, "the eternal One."[4] It also reveals God as the self-existent One. The idea conveyed is not just continuous existence, but existence in motion rather than at rest. This motion is not that of change, for God is immutable; it is, rather, the motion of action. God is continually moving to reveal Himself to His people as He acts in their behalf.

Jehovah is also the name of God in covenant relationship; it is the name by which God "signs" His contracts with man, the name by which He obligates Himself to move in man's behalf. In the covenant of deliverance, God promised the children of Israel redemption out of Egypt and the fulfillment of all of the promises He had made to their forefathers. To seal this redemptive covenant, He used His name, Jehovah, to conclude the contract. In the English, it is translated, *"LORD,"* and appears, as Jehovah always does in the King James Version of the Bible, in all capital letters. It was this name by which God revealed Himself to Moses and, through him, to all of the children of Israel, because He was undertaking a contractual obligation, making a personal covenant, to do all that He had promised them. He swore by His own self-existence, because there is, in the entire universe, nothing greater by which to swear.

It must be noted that the early patriarchs, Abraham, Isaac, and Jacob, had heard the name, Jehovah, and God had indeed made covenants with them. They had not, however, had God revealed to them as the covenant-keeping God because the time of the execution of those covenants had not come during their lifetimes. But, the day of the fulfillment of the ancient covenants had now come. Moses and the generation of Jews he led would meet Jehovah God, the covenant-making, covenant-keeping God.

Indeed, whenever the name, Jehovah, is spoken, whenever the name, *"LORD"* (in all caps), appears in Scripture, God is revealing Himself as the eternal, self-existent One who is ever moving to show Himself to His people, the promise-making, promise-performing, covenant-keeping God who will never fail in a single point. No wonder this was the name God used to "sign" His deliverance covenant in Exodus 6:8.

Moses delivered these precious promises to the children of Israel but, as Exodus 6:9 reveals, they refused to listen. Just as God was about to move in their behalf, their discouragement caused them to rebuff Him. But, their rejection did not deter God at all. He simply proceeded to outline His battle plan, a classic in spiritual warfare.

First, Moses was instructed to speak to Pharaoh (Exodus 6:29). He was commanded to tell Pharaoh everything God had said. Standing before the malignant power of Pharaoh, speaking the word of the God he did not even acknowledge, was a frightening prospect for Moses, as we see in Exodus 6:30. But, the command of God was clear. Whether Satan cares to acknowledge it or not, the words of the Lord have a great effect against him. Whether he cares to admit it or not, he has to listen to those words God has spoken. And, whether he cares to assent or not, he is bound by the exercise of the promises of God done in faith by the believer.

The second step of the battle plan was accomplished by God, Himself. In Exodus 7:1, He gave Moses this strategically important information: *"See, I have made thee a god to Pharaoh: and Aaron thy brother shall be thy prophet."* God would see to it that Pharaoh was totally intimidated by Moses and Aaron. In his superstition and deception, he would see them as gods. In the same way, when Satan looks at the believer who has taken a stand of faith for his freedom from bondage, he does not see the believer. Instead, God arranges for him to see Christ in the believer. It is in that authority, and only in that authority, that man becomes a match for the enemy.

Next, God planned to further harden Pharaoh's already stony heart (Exodus 7:3 and 13). Why? Why not simply cause Pharaoh to concede defeat from the outset and allow the children of Israel to go free without the destruction of Egypt which was to follow? The answer is two-fold. First, God had already resolved to ravage Egypt for reasons which we shall see shortly. Second, since Pharaoh stands as a type of Satan, God showed that there is nothing nice about Satan. It is his fallen nature to be hard-hearted, especially against the people of God. There is not one ounce of compassion, kindness, or fairness in him. It is impossible to reason with him and he will never give up or give in easily. He will fight in any and every way he can, usually unfairly, to defeat the child of God, and the only way his power can be broken is by the superior power of almighty God.

Finally, God's battle plan called for the use of signs and wonders (Exodus 7:3 through 5), as His might was pitted against Pharaoh's. In this regard, Aaron threw down his rod, just as God had taught Moses to do, and it became a serpent wriggling before Pharaoh's throne (Exodus 7:10). Then, Pharaoh's magicians, identified in 2 Timothy 3:8 as Jannes and Jambres, did the very same thing (Exodus 7:11). Still, the God Moses served was proven superior, as the serpent formed by Aaron's rod feasted upon the serpents of the sorcerers (Exodus 7:12).

This encounter between Moses and Pharaoh's magicians serves to illustrate the very real power of Satan which can sometimes be quite frightening. But, notice two things about the power of the enemy. First, his action was not original; it was merely a counterfeit of what God had already done. Satan is a show-off, but he hasn't had one original idea in centuries. Second, it's obvious how quickly and easily the superior power of God was able to annihilate every manifestation of the enemy. Praise God!

The Battle Rages

The battle continued, and so did the signs and wonders of God. Ten terrible plagues were brought against Egypt, plagues conceived by God to carry out His plan, plagues designed by God to execute the design He detailed in Exodus 12:12, *"...and against all the gods of Egypt I will execute judgment: I am the LORD."* God did, indeed, strike a blow against every major god and goddess of the polytheistic Egyptian religion with its emphasis on death and the world beyond the grave. Yet, as the plagues devastated Egypt, the children of God were safe and secure in Goshen, providentially protected from the onslaught. Here are the ten plagues and some of the Egyptian gods defeated by them:

1. **The Nile River turned to blood** (Exodus 7:20). This plague struck a direct blow against Hapimou, the god of the Nile, upon which the Egyptians depended for their very lives. This plague remained for seven days and, although Pharaoh's magicians were able to duplicate it, they were never able to defeat it or undo its damage.

2. **Frogs** (Exodus 8:6). Ptha, the frog-headed god, and Heka, the frog goddess, were probably the targets of this plague. In addition, Geb or Leb, the earth god, was shown to be unable to prevent the frogs from covering his territory.
3. **Lice** (Exodus 8:17). Since lice are parasites, living on the blood of hosts, this plague struck Khopri, the scarab beetle, a sun god believed to be the self-creator.
4. **Flies** (Exodus 8:24). The plague of flies damaged the reputations of Shu, the wind god, since flies flew on the wind; Horus, the god of the rising sun, since flies come only in the daytime; and Itum, the god of the setting sun, since flies usually left at dusk.
5. **Cattle-killing murrain** (Exodus 9:6). This plague struck Apis, also known as Seraphis, the bull-god of death, and Amon, the ram-god known as "the king of the gods."
6. **Boils** (Exodus 9:10). Since boils destroyed the flesh of the sufferers, this plague was directed against Anubis, the jackal-headed god of the dead, which the Egyptians believed controlled the decaying of the flesh and preserved their mummified dead.
7. **Hail and fire** (Exodus 9:24). This plague showed Nut, the goddess of the sky, Iris, the water deity, and Osiris, the god of fire, to be powerless.
8. **Locusts** (Exodus 10:13). Thermouthis, the goddess of crops, Nepri, the corn god, Shu, the god of the air, and Sebek, the insect god, were all defeated by this plague.
9. **Darkness** (Exodus 10:22). This plague was directed against the two most revered of the Egyptian deities, Ra, also called Atun Re, the hawk-headed sun god and supreme deity of Egyptian religion, and Sekhmet, the female Ra and goddess of power.
10. **Death of the firstborn son** (Exodus 12:29). This final blow was struck against Osiris, the god of fire and of the underworld, a perfect type of Satan, himself.

One can almost hear the pitiful wails of the Egyptian citizens, as they cried out to their gods, just as the children of Israel had cried out to Jehovah for so long. But, those gods in which they had trusted, the gods to whom they had sacrificed everything, were powerless before the King of kings and Lord of lords.

God will always find a way to deal with man's idols, a way designed to prove those idols powerless, a way conceived to bring man to the only true God, Jehovah. What anguish man could avoid by willingly laying aside his idols to serve the living Lord! What pain he could prevent if only he would reach out to the God of this universe!

There were other reasons why God initiated these ten terrible plagues against Egypt. Here are some of them:

1. The plagues provided positive public proof that the God of Moses was indeed God (Exodus 9:16). It was proof that Pharaoh and his magicians could not conceal, proof apparent to the citizens of Egypt, proof that none could deny (Exodus 8:19).
2. The plagues were the punishment of God against the Egyptians for their cruel mistreatment of His people. In all ages of history, God has taken very personally the abuse of His children and He has dealt with it very personally, too. Pharaoh did not miss this message (Exodus 10:16).
3. The plagues stood as an obvious warning to any nation which would dare to stand against the people of God. This lesson was not lost on other nations, as Joshua 2:8 through 11 makes clear.

Still, the demand of God remained the same, total and unconditional freedom for His people. Still, the response of Pharaoh remained the same, arrogant refusal. Like Satan, Pharaoh resisted all attempts to obtain the freedom of God's people, even when it meant confronting the superior power of their God, even when it meant sure and certain defeat.

Of course, Pharaoh had his own strategy. Four times, he feigned contrition, pleading for relief and promising release if it were granted (Exodus 8:8; 8:28; 9:28; and 10:17). And, four times, he reneged on his commitment. As soon as the plagues were lifted, he reverted to his previous hard-hearted stance. In the same way, Satan offers relief to the child of God seeking freedom if that child will only end the plague of prayer directed against him and his bondages. But, like Pharaoh's, Satan's promises cannot be trusted and will vanish as the pressure does.

Pharaoh also offered to compromise with his Hebrew slaves on four occasions. Those compromises may have seemed reasonable, but acceptance would have resulted in the ultimate defeat of the children of Israel and their continued bondage. The compromises and their modern parallels are explored below:

1. **Conduct your sacrifices in the land** (Exodus 8:25). This is the offer of nominal Christianity, the offer to maintain nominal identity as a Christian while remaining a part of the world. This compromise perpetuates bondage and is unacceptable to God according to 2 Timothy 3:5.
2. **Don't go very far** (Exodus 8:28). This kind of compromise speaks of incomplete commitment. Unless one's ties to the past are forever severed, backsliding will occur, according to 2 Corinthians 6:17.
3. **Let the men go** (Exodus 10:7). This compromise affords no opportunity for salvation for families; neither does it make any provision for the babes in Christ. All are abandoned to the enemy's devices and, if left to remain so, will ultimately go back into bondage, as we see in 1 Kings 19:20.
4. **Let your flocks and your herds remain** (Exodus 10:24). Had this compromise been accepted, there would have been no lamb for the sacrifice. Without the shedding of blood there can be no remission (Hebrews 9:22). Therefore, this kind of compromise results in a bloodless religion which can never provide salvation. In addition, failure to commit one's material possessions to God always results in materialism. Eventually, the heart will seek to return to its treasure (Luke 12:34).

Whenever Satan is losing a battle, he will attempt to offer a compromise. "Get saved someday," he will say. "Just don't do it now." Since no one knows how many days he has, delay can result in death.

"Go ahead, be a Christian," he taunts. "Just don't be a fanatic." But, God requires complete commitment.

"You can get rid of your bad habits," he offers. "But, there's no need to change everything." But, how, then, can we be changed into the image of Christ?

"You can deal with your really nasty spiritual problems," he cajoles. "But, why go looking for trouble by bothering with the others?" But, God wants total freedom for every one of His children.

It's clear that there can be no compromise with the enemy. Compromise is simply a continuation of captivity. It is unacceptable to God and should be equally unacceptable to every one of His children.

Finally, when all else had failed, when Pharaoh could do nothing else, he threatened Moses with death in Exodus 10:28. Yes, Satan will sometimes rant and rave and threaten dire consequences. But, like Moses, the child of God need never fear. He need only be determined to see the last of Satan (Exodus 10:29); he need only stand still to see the salvation of his God. That salvation is never long in coming.

[1]Herbert Lockyer, *All the Men of the Bible*, p. 20.
[2]Michael Esses, *Jesus in Exodus*, p. 33.
[3]Herbert Lockyer, *All the Divine Names and Titles in the Bible*, p. 14.
[4]Chafer, Volume 1, p. 263.

Chapter 5
SALVATION PROVIDED

Salvation Foretold

The battle between Jehovah God and Pharaoh was about to come to a crashing conclusion. As the ninth plague drew to a close and before the final plague was poured out upon Egypt, God paused to have a conversation with Moses, as recorded in the eleventh chapter of Exodus. There, God predicted exactly what would happen when the tenth plague came. Pharaoh, whose heart had been so completely hardened, whose resolve had been so totally unrelenting, would undergo a cataclysmic change, a change only God could have foretold. When the final plague fell, not only would Pharaoh permit the people of God to leave, he would actually order them out (Exodus 11:1).

This is so like Satan. Alerted to the fact that he is about to lose one of his slaves, he will fight, unfairly, unjustly, and unremittingly. But, once the power of God has been proven superior to his, he will eject that slave from his kingdom and slink silently off into the sunset, only to surreptitiously stalk, waiting for an opportunity to recapture what he lost.

Next, God promised that the children of Israel would be permitted to spoil their former captors (Exodus 11:2 and 3), an important military concept in the ancient world. It was the act of spoiling which separated the victors from the vanquished, the conquerors from the conquered. To forever prove whose God had triumphed, it was necessary that His soldiers be permitted to spoil their enemies. In an ironic twist which only God could conceive, the Egyptians would not even have to be beaten into submission on a battlefield first. The Jews would need only to ask. The word translated, borrow, in Exodus 11:2 is the Hebrew, *sha'al*, which means, to ask, request, or demand, and indicates what a superior demands from an inferior. This word is not generally used of things that are borrowed and are to be returned. Imagine it! The Hebrew slaves were to become the superiors, demanding valuables, as though the Egyptians were inferiors defeated in battle. When the time came, the Egyptians would be only too happy to comply, just to bring relief to their troubled land. The Hebrew slaves, it seems, were to be well paid for their years of labor in the brick kilns of Egypt. The servant of God is often permitted to spoil the kingdom of his defeated foe, Satan, too. Each time the child of God is successful in converting a sinner to Christ, each time he succeeds in spiritual warfare, he has spoiled Satan's kingdom. And, Satan, whose power is and ever shall be inferior to God's, is unable to resist.

The true story is told of the young full-gospel church which had rented a meeting hall over a bank. As the Depression raged, the pastor and his people were often hard pressed to meet the monthly rental. One month, as eviction loomed on the horizon, the pastor arrived early one Sunday morning to open the building to his worshippers, only to be met by the unsaved and unsavory husband of one of his parishioners. The man, unshaven and unkempt from a Saturday night spent in sin, accosted the petrified pastor, extended his hand in an almost threatening gesture, and thrust a wad of crumpled currency into the pastor's palm. "Take it," the man ordered, angrily. "God won't let me get any sleep until I give this to you." The startled servant of God quickly counted the bills and found just enough to retire the church's outstanding debts. That morning, instead of the sermon on surviving adversity that he had been planning, God gave the pastor a new message titled, "If God Can't Meet Your Need Any Other Way, He'll Send the Devil To Do It."

Finally, God predicted the final fatal plague that would soon fall. At midnight on the appointed night, God, Himself, would strike down the firstborn in every home in Egypt (Exodus 11:4 and 5), from the heir in the royal palace, to Pharaoh's serfs and servants, even to the cattle which had somehow survived previous plagues. The honored firstborn of every family, whether rich or poor, high or low, would be struck dead, as the cries of kin cut through the cold night air. The valued champion breeding stock in every barn, provided a massive sacrifice to the God whose might had been proven superior to that of the helpless gods the Egyptians trusted to protect their livestock. The message was clear. There is no escape from the judgment of God on those who do not honor Him. Riches and resources, power and position, cannot rescue. All that avails then is obedience to God.

But, in the midst of it all, God had prepared a way of escape for His people. They would remain untouched and untroubled, safe and secure in the protection of their Lord. Here, we find a futuristic message, a prophetic interpretation. There will be another midnight hour when the judgment of God will fall upon the unjust of every class in every place. There will be no escape for any who do not know Christ. But, God has given a way of escape for His own. Under the blood of the Lamb, they need never fear coming under the judgment of the Lion. Instead, they shall go forth into His eternal freedom.

Consider the various perspectives on the coming event. To Pharaoh (Satan), it would be a plague (Exodus 11:1) in which the power of God would be proven to be superior and his slaves would be lost to him forever, as Paul said in Romans 9:17 and 18:

> *For the scripture saith unto Pharaoh, Even for this same purpose have I raised thee up, that I might shew my power in thee, and that my name might be declared throughout all the earth.*

To Pharaoh's people, this event represented a spoiling (Exodus 11:2 and 3) that would eternally confirm their defeat and dangerously deplete Egypt's prosperity. To the Egyptians, it would also mean the loss of offspring, of heirs, of hopes of immortality, a time of unremitting sorrow and sadness. The vengeance of God would be executed, not just against the dead, but against the living, as well.

To the firstborn, this night would mean death (Exodus 11:4 and 5), not because of anything they had done, but simply because of their relationship to their fathers. The first birth produces children of sin and always results in death. Only the second birth produces a child of God and results in eternal life, as Jesus told Nicodemus in John 3:3 and 16:

> *Jesus answered and said unto him, Verily, verily, I say unto thee, Except a man be born again, he cannot see the kingdom of God....For God so loved the world, that he gave his only begotten Son, that whosoever believeth in him should not perish, but have everlasting life.*

To Moses, the spokesman of God, this time of grief for others would bring greatness (Exodus 11:3), as the demonstration of the power of his God resulted in his own reputation being recognized among all who heard of it. Among the servants of sin, his stature would be increased because of the defeat they had suffered at his hands, and, among the children of God, his fame would be the stuff of legend forever.

To God's people, this event would mean the breaking of their bonds and the end to their enslavement. It would mean their total freedom, from the plagues as well as their captivity, just as Jesus frees the child of God from sin, as He declared in John 8:34 and 36:

Jesus answered them, Verily, verily, I say unto you, Whosoever committeth sin is the servant of sin....If the Son therefore shall make you free, ye shall be free indeed.

And, to God, this night would be one of glory (Exodus 11:9), as He was glorified against the gods and goddesses of Egypt, against an arrogant enemy, among His redeemed people, and in the record of history. God would establish for Himself a lasting reputation which would span the centuries, as 1 Samuel 4:8 records:

Woe unto us! who shall deliver us out of the hand of these mighty Gods? these are the Gods that smote the Egyptians with all the plagues in the wilderness.

This testimony was given by the pagan Philistines almost three hundred and fifty years after the event. Even later, the wonders wrought by God would be immortalized in the Psalms (Psalm 78:43 through 51; Psalm 135:8; and Psalm 136:10).

Salvation Instructed

As God's conversation with Moses continued, He gave these specific and detailed directions for the salvation of His people during the long night of death. Only complete obedience to each detail would result in their salvation and the destruction of their enemies.

First, God established a new calendar (Exodus 12:2) that would begin with the month of deliverance from Egypt, originally called *Abib* or "the month of ears" since it was at this time of year when the first ears of wheat would appear. Later, it became known as *Nisan* (Esther 3:7; Nehemiah 2:1) and is our month of April. Prior to this, it would seem that the Hebrew calendar had begun with the month of *Tisri*, which is roughly equivalent to October. It is still at this time of year that Jews around the world mark the beginning of the new civil year. The religious or ecclesiastical year, however, continues to commence in *Nisan* or April. This God-ordained change in the religious calendar of Israel forever links the concepts of redemption and regeneration and reminds us that we begin the first day of the rest of our lives at salvation. It is to that point that we look back; it is at that point that our new lives begin; it is from that point that we reckon our existence.

With this new calendar, specific days were set as a part of God's deliverance plan. On the tenth day of *Abib*, a spotless, perfect lamb was to be chosen for each household or group of small households (Exodus 12:3 through 5). The lamb was to be kept under observation for four days, until the fourteenth of *Abib*, so that its perfection might be validated (Exodus 12:6). Finally, as dusk descended on the fourteenth, traditionally at the ninth hour or three in the afternoon, the time of the evening sacrifice, the congregation of Israel was to sacrifice the lamb (Exodus 12:6). Since the Hebrew day began at sunset, the Jews would leave Egypt later that same day, the fourteenth of *Abib*.

In the year, 32 A. D., the year in which it is believed by many that our Lord laid down His life as the last Lamb, the tenth of *Nisan* (or *Abib*) fell upon a Sunday, that first Palm Sunday on which Jesus entered into Jerusalem and was chosen and hailed as King (John 12:1 and 12 through 16). For the next four days, Jesus remained among His people, undergoing their scrutiny. Finally, as the fourteenth began at sunset, equivalent to our Thursday evening, He was arrested and condemned to be killed. It was only an "accident" of history and politics that postponed the death of Jesus until later that day according to Jewish reckoning, but comparable to our Friday, the very day when Jews from all over the known world gathered in Jerusalem to celebrate the Passover and to sacrifice their spotless lambs at sunset (John 19:31). Since Israel was under the domination of the Roman Empire, it was necessary that the Jewish authorities obtain the consent of the Roman officials before executing a death sentence (John 10). This permission could not be obtained until the next morning. Thus it was that Jesus came to be crucified (the Roman, not the Jewish method of execution, but the method clearly prophesied in Deuteronomy 21:23 and fulfilled according to Galatians 3:13) on Friday, still the fourteenth of *Nisan*, 32 A. D., the day of the annual Passover observance, the very day on which the exodus had occurred centuries before, the day to which every Jew traced his freedom from bondage, the day to which every Christian now traces his freedom from sin. Thus it was that Jesus, our perfect Passover Lamb, came to die at exactly the ninth hour or three o'clock in the afternoon (Mark 15:33 through 37). Thus it was that the words of John the Baptist, recorded in John 1:29 were fulfilled: *"Behold the Lamb of God, which taketh away the sin of the world."*

Once the blood of the sacrificial lamb had been poured out, God instructed the Hebrews to place it upon the sideposts and the upper beam, known as the lintel, of their doors (Exodus 12:7). It was this application of blood, done in faith, that provided protection against the destruction to come and supplied salvation during that long night. It doesn't take much imagination to realize that, if blood is placed on the sideposts and across the lintel of a door, it would form a cross on either side of the door, signifying the cross of Christ. But, notice that no blood was to be placed upon the door itself. In John 10:7 and 9, Jesus, Himself, explained this:

> *Then said Jesus unto them again, Verily, verily, I say unto you, I am the door of the sheep....I am the door: by me if any man shall enter in, he shall be saved, and shall go in and out, and find pasture.*

As the perfect and spotless Sacrifice, Jesus, our Door, needed no application of blood. Consequently, as God planned the first Passover, He decreed the blood be placed upon the house itself. In the same way, the blood of Christ must be applied to the earthly house of His own, the earthen vessel in which the treasure is to be contained.

Following the application of the blood of the Passover lamb to the doorposts and lintels, the children of Israel were to feast upon that lamb, consuming it all and allowing nothing to be wasted (Exodus 12:8 through 10). Along with lamb, they were to serve bitter herbs and unleavened bread, not the most appetizing accompaniments. This menu was carefully planned by God since, only after the blood has been applied, can we begin to feast on the Lamb who provided it. Those bitter herbs, typifying the bitterness and tears of bondage, also typify the bitterness and tears, the sorrow and sadness which result from our own slavery to sin. The unleavened bread, made without the yeast which would ferment and grow, symbolized freedom from the leaven of unrighteousness, which grows in sinful man, as Paul explained in 1 Corinthians 5:6 through 8:

> *Your glorying is not good. Know ye not that a little leaven leaveneth the whole lump? Purge out therefore the old leaven, that ye may be a new lump, as ye are unleavened. For even Christ our passover is sacrificed for us: Therefore let us keep the feast, not with the old leaven, neither with the leaven of malice and wickedness: but with the unleavened bread of sincerity and truth.*

Even God's instruction that none of the meat of the lamb be saved until morning was important. It foreshadowed that day when Jesus was removed from the cross before the new day began at sunset because the Jews would not permit a body to remain upon the tree on Passover (John 19:31 through 42).

Those who ate the first Passover feast were to eat quickly and be dressed for a hasty departure (Exodus 12:11) for the order to depart would indeed come before that long night ended (Exodus 12:31). Here, we see the children of the Lord, continually feasting upon the Lamb of God, always ready for a sudden summons, His second coming.

If the children of Israel obeyed the instructions God had given them, precisely as God had given them, God promised in Exodus 12:12 and 13 that some specific and memorable events would occur as a result:

> *For I will pass through the land of Egypt this night, and will smite all the firstborn in the land of Egypt, both man and beast; and against all the gods of Egypt I will execute judgment: I am the LORD. And the blood shall be to you for a token upon the houses where ye are: and when I see the blood, I will pass over you, and the plague shall not be upon you to destroy you, when I smite the land of Egypt.*

The Hebrew words translated, pass, in these verses are not the same words and do not carry the same meaning. The difference between them carries an important message for the child of God. The first word, pass (pass through), is the Hebrew, *abar*, which means, "pass over, by, through, do away, take away, overflow."[1] The main idea conveyed is one of movement, as God moved against Egypt in His overflowing power. But, the second word translated, pass (pass over), is the Hebrew, *pasah*, from which the Hebrew name of the feast, *Pasach*, comes. It means, "to pass over, to protect."[2] The idea is of protectively overshadowing and defending. The use of these different terms indicates that God meant to hover protectively over those who were under the protection of the blood, at the very same time His judgment was moving against their enemies. Still, the Lord protects and defends His own, even as He judges sinners, and that day will come when, as the final terrible judgments of God fall upon a sinful earth, He will gather those who love Him under His vast and sheltering wings, protecting them from all harm.

Finally, God ordered that this pivotal event of all Jewish history be commemorated each year on the same day of the same month (Exodus 12:14) so that every generation would know and understand all that God had provided for His people in that first Passover (Exodus 12:26 and 27). To this day, throughout the world, wherever there are Jews, the Passover is kept just as God commanded. The Paschal supper, called the Seder, still features lamb, bitter herbs, and unleavened bread. To this day, wherever Christians gather to worship their Lord, they celebrate the Passover, too, as they observe the Last Supper of Christ and His disciples, which occurred on this day, in their service of Communion. On that night in the upper room, Jesus explained all of the symbolism of the Jewish Passover to His disciples, and to all of us, as Paul detailed in 1 Corinthians 11:23 through 26:

> *For I have received of the Lord that which also I delivered unto you, That the Lord Jesus the same night in which he was betrayed took bread: And when he had given thanks, he brake it, and said, Take, eat: this is my body, which is broken for you: this do in remembrance of me. After the same manner also he took the cup, when he had supped, saying, This cup is the new testament in my blood: this do ye, as oft as ye drink it, in remembrance of me. For as often as ye eat this bread, and drink this cup, ye do shew the Lord's death till he come.*

The Passover feast also speaks of life after salvation. Just as the Jewish wife painstakingly searches every cupboard to remove all yeast, the child of God, no longer enslaved to sin, must undertake a careful and continual search to find and remove all sin from his life. Only then, can he remain free of sin, free to serve his God.

This was, however, not the first time that blood had been shed to provide salvation for God's children. After Adam and Woman had sinned, Genesis 3:21 records that God,

Himself, shed the blood of innocent animals to obtain skins from which coats were made to cover their nakedness. This event was also commemorated, just as the Passover would be remembered, in Abel's sacrifice of an animal from his flock (Genesis 4:4). His brother, Cain, made the same mistake his parents once made (Genesis 3:7) in attempting to make his sacrifice and cover his sin with plants or produce from the field (Genesis 4:3).

Salvation Initiated

His conversation with God ended, Moses went immediately to the elders of Israel, and explained every detail of the salvation plan, just as God had outlined it to him (Exodus 12:21 through 27). In response, God's people acknowledged Him and proceeded to execute the plan precisely as God had commanded it be done, as Exodus 12:27 and 28 records:

> *And the people bowed the head and worshipped...and did as the LORD had commanded Moses and Aaron, so did they.*

The lambs were slain, the blood applied, the bitter herbs gathered, the unleavened bread prepared, and the feast begun. While none of it could have made much sense to the Israelites at the time, they complied with every detail. Their total obedience, carried out in complete faith, brought exactly the results God had promised. At midnight, the tenth and final plague fell. God moved against Egypt and every firstborn in the land of Egypt was slain, just as God had said. Even Pharaoh's own firstborn died that night (Exodus 12:29) in one, final demonstration that the power of the God of Moses was superior to his own and to that of his gods (Exodus 12:12).

In the middle of that ghastly night, Pharaoh sent for Moses and Aaron (Exodus 12:31). As they went to the palace of their enemy who had just lost his firstborn to their God, they must have wondered what might be his reaction to this terrible turn of events. They need not have worried. Pharaoh was defeated and he knew it. Just as God had promised, he capitulated, ordering the Israelites to leave his land and to take everything they owned with them, just as he had originally been commanded to do in Exodus 5:1. He had gained nothing from his stubbornness and obstinacy; on the contrary, he had lost much of what he most valued, including his own firstborn child.

As a sign of their total triumph and as vindication of the victory of their God, the Hebrews were able to spoil the Egyptians--and, the Egyptians permitted themselves to be spoiled voluntarily (Exodus 12:35 and 36), just as God had also promised.

In these events, we see that salvation may be obtained only through complete obedience to God's plan. Down through the years, men have wondered why God conceived a plan in which it was necessary for His own Son to die as the final Lamb as His blood was shed to provide for man's redemption, just as the Israelites, who had so little of worth, must have questioned the sacrifice of a valuable lamb. Some have even tried to devise a "better" way, a less grisly Gospel. But, in Genesis 9:4, God had said, *"But flesh with the life thereof, which is the blood thereof, shall ye not eat."* Again, in Deuteronomy 12:23, he reiterated this governing principle of redemption, "Only be sure that thou eat not the blood: for the blood is the life; and thou mayest not eat the life with the flesh."

God had spoken. Life must be given; the blood, in which the life resides, must be shed. The principle, as recorded in Hebrews 9:22, is this, *"And almost all things are by the law purged with blood; and without shedding of blood is no remission."*

Only by obeying the command of God to embrace the offering already made, only by accepting the atonement already accomplished, only by receiving the sacrifice already completed--only by the blood of Jesus Christ--may man be saved. There is no other way.

It is only according to this plan of God, that man's eternal enemy may be defeated and deliverance from his determined and deliberate enslavement may be obtained. Then, we may spoil his kingdom, proving forever the superior power of our God. Those who were once poor in sin, may rejoice in the riches of redemption.

Salvation, a Reality

The Hebrew slaves were free. That very night, they left Egypt by way of Rameses, one of the treasure cities their slave labor had built (Exodus 12:37). How glad they must have been to put it behind them! They traveled as far as Succoth, near the western bank of the Red Sea, a distance of approximately thirty miles. In the group which left Egypt that night were six hundred thousand adult men, not counting the women and children (Exodus 12:37). Since each probably had a wife and one or more children, the number of freed Hebrews has been estimated between 1,200,000 and six million, a great increase from the seventy which had come to Egypt just four hundred and thirty years before.

Also in the group was a "mixed multitude" (Exodus 12:38). These may have been Egyptians, anxious to leave the devastation of the plagues behind. They may also have been others enslaved by the Egyptians who saw their opportunity to leave and took it. Whatever their identity, it is clear they were not God's people. The children of God have always been followed by the "mixed multitude" of this world. They may attend church, hold church membership, even wear crosses, but they are not truly saved. Others, although slaves to their sins, may be related to those who have been set free. Such will follow for a while, but will not be there when it comes time to enter in.

In Exodus 12:41, we read of the careful timing of the beginning of the exodus of God's people from Egypt:

> *And it came to pass <u>at the end of the four hundred and thirty years, even the selfsame day</u> it came to pass, that all the hosts of the LORD went our from the land of Egypt.*

Four hundred and thirty years, <u>to the very day</u>, after Jacob and his family left their homeland to go to Egypt, God brought his descendants out, just as He had promised in Genesis 46:3 and 4. The Lord had planned quite an anniversary! To conclude the festivities, God reiterated and elaborated upon His commands concerning the annual Passover observance (Exodus 12:43 through 49). Every member of His congregation was expected to attend. In addition, any stranger who wished to eat of the Passover supper, was welcomed to do so, so long as he was willing to be circumcised, symbolic of his new relationship with God, and abide by the same Law (Exodus 12:49).

The message is clear. The believer, who has accepted the sacrifice of the Lamb's blood, is a part of the congregation of the Lord and may rejoice in his freedom, regularly remember his day of freedom, and feast upon the Lamb. But, the Passover was not the private property of the Jew, just as the Gospel does not belong to the Christian alone. It is to be shared with the stranger, the unregenerate. If, by a decision of his will, the sinner chooses to partake of the Passover Lamb, to embrace the circumcision of the heart (Romans 2:29), and to abide by the Law of God, he is invited to the table of feasting and welcomed into the family of faith. Centuries later, the Apostle Paul would find this principle most important, as we shall see.

Redeemed and Rejoicing

The entire twelfth chapter of Exodus gives us our first glimpse of God's plan of redemption. Once revealed, its principles are then explained in Leviticus 25:47 through 49:

And if a sojourner or stranger wax rich by thee, and thy brother that dwelleth by him wax poor, and sell himself unto the stranger or sojourner by thee, or to the stock of the stranger's family: After that he is sold he may be redeemed again; one of his brethren may redeem him: Either his uncle, or his uncle's son, may redeem him, or any that is nigh of kin unto him of his family may redeem him: or if he be able, he may redeem himself.

Often, in Old Testament times, the poor had to sell a possession, a house, a field, themselves, or even a child. God granted the right of redemption, the right to buy back, to the nearest relative who possessed the intent and the money or goods to do it. Or, if it became possible, one might redeem himself or his previous possession. According to the Law, a redeemer must possess these three specific qualifications:

1. He must be a member of the family.
2. He must be willing.
3. He must have the purchase price.

The whole house of Israel had been sold into bondage in Egypt and they could never hope to free themselves. But, their heavenly Father, arranged for their redemption. He willingly paid the purchase price and bought them back to Himself.

Adam also sold the human family into slavery to sin and we could not redeem ourselves. Our right to return to God's family could only be bought back for us by another member of our human family whose life was untouched by sin, unenslaved by it. We needed a Redeemer. There was only One who possessed the necessary qualifications to make the transaction--Jesus Christ. He came to earth in human form, for there was no other way He could become our Kinsman, a Member of the family of man. He lived a perfect, sinless life, remaining free of our bondage, so that He could be in a position to buy us back. Then, He freely and willingly offered the purchase price, His own life, His own blood, to redeem us, to buy us back into God's family, to set us free from sin. By sending Jesus to be our Kinsman-Redeemer, God made the first move to reconcile us to Himself, just as, so long ago, He made the first move to redeem His people, Israel.

The children of Israel were finally free, saved by the blood of the Lamb and rejoicing in their redemption. They are now representative of all of the newborn babes in Christ. As we follow their path of growth and maturity in relationship to their Redeemer, we shall learn the lessons of growth and maturity in relationship to our Redeemer. And, so, the journey begins....

[1]R. Laird Harris, Gleason L. Archer, Jr., and Bruce K. Waltke, *Theological Wordbook of the Old Testament*, p. 641.

[2]Ibid., p. 728.

Chapter 6
SANCTIFICATION ORDERED

Commands Given

After four hundred and thirty years, the children of Israel had been redeemed out of Egypt and traveled as far as Succoth, no more than about thirty miles. Yet, the sense of emancipation and excitement must have been palpable in the camp. It was probably like that feeling of freedom of the new convert to Christianity, the new babe in Christ. But, the Lord reserves the right to rule those He has redeemed. It is possible that on that very night, God approached His servant, Moses, to discuss that specific subject, as Exodus 13:2 records, *"Sanctify unto me all the firstborn....it is mine."*

Sanctify, is the Hebrew, *qadash* or *kaddesh*. It originally meant, to cut or separate, and came to mean, holiness, sanctification, or sacredness; in the verb form, it meant, to be holy or sanctified or to consecrate, sanctify, or dedicate.[1] These words used to define *qadash* are also the various words used to translate it throughout the Old Testament and carry essentially the same idea. In its strictest sense, the word, sanctify, does not indicate immediate perfection or instant purity, as some suppose. Rather, the term signifies that which is set apart or separated.

It would follow, logically, that the thing set apart must be separated from something and set apart to or for something else. Indeed, this is exactly the case. That which is sanctified is separated from the world and set apart to the Lord and for His use. It is a thing dedicated to Him and devoted to whatever purpose He may choose.

The concept of sanctification is codified in the Law and explained in even greater detail in Leviticus 20:7 and 8. There, the Lord, as *Jehovah M'Kaddesh*, a name that comes from the same Hebrew root word and presents God as Sanctifier, commanded:

> *Sanctify yourselves therefore, and be ye holy: for I am the LORD your God....I am the LORD which sanctify you.*

Here, we see two sides of sanctification, one accomplished by the Lord as Sanctifier and one His people must do for themselves. Following redemption, the Lord sanctifies or sets apart those He has freed. But, then, the Lord expects those He has separated to sanctify themselves, to separate themselves from the world, from sin, and for His exclusive use, just as He called upon His people to do in both Exodus 13:2 and Leviticus 20:7. The Lord accomplishes His part of the process in an instant; for His people, it is a process which requires a lifetime to complete.

Sanctification, or holiness, is also a clear command of God in the New Testament. There, in Romans 12:l, the Paul issued this clarion call to the Christian:

> *I beseech you therefore, brethren, by the mercies of God, that ye present your bodies a living sacrifice, holy, acceptable unto God.*

Again, the sanctification expected of the saint (which, by the way, means, one who is sanctified one) is linked to what is accomplished by God. If He did not do His part, it would be impossible for the believer to ever hope to do what God requires of him. So, the holy God who demands sanctification from His people is also the merciful God who makes it possible for them to obey.

Exodus 13:3 through 7 seems to be out of place. It's a reminder of God's redeeming power in bringing His people out of Egypt and a reiteration of the Feast of Unleavened Bread, situated between two commands of God, which appear in Exodus 13:2 and 11 through 16, to sanctify the firstborn. But, a closer examination reveals that it is not out of place at all. Instead, God established, in type, the principles of sanctification which He later established in Law in Leviticus 20:7 and 8. He had separated His people from Egypt (Exodus 13:3 and 4) and they were to respond by setting themselves apart from leaven, symbolizing sin, to keep the Feast of Unleavened Bread, just as God had said.

According to Exodus 13:8 through 10, all of this--sanctification of the firstborn, remembrance of the day of redemption, and keeping of the Passover--was to be done as a sign, a memorial, of everything God had done for His people and their obedience to Him as a result. To all who saw (Exodus 13:14), these things would be a constant reminder of all God had done. He had delivered; in return, He demanded, as He had earned the right to do, the dedication of the firstborn to Him.

Indeed, the living of a sanctified life in this world is still a sign to all who see it. It is a memorial of God's work of redemption and sanctification and the obedience to God which man returns. It is the Christian's walk of sanctification that holds up the mirror of God's holiness before a watching world and makes them look.

God also specified that it was to be the <u>redeemed</u> firstborn which were to be sanctified according to Exodus 13:12 and 13:

> *That <u>thou shalt set apart unto the LORD all that openeth the matrix...all the firstborn of man among thy children shalt thou redeem</u>.*

It is a law of this universe that the first birth, the natural birth, always ends in physical death. It is inevitable. But, it is the law of God that the natural born can be redeemed and, once redeemed, spiritual death has no more hold (1 Corinthians 15:54 through 57). He has been bought with the price of blood and is no longer his own. He is free, free to be set apart <u>by</u> God, free to set himself apart <u>for</u> God. Redemption or death, sanctification or servitude--the choice is man's to make.

There is another sense in which the child of God must set apart his firstborn. To the ancients, the firstborn was the favored child, the exalted offspring, the honored heir, the most valued. The family devoted the most attention, the best education, and the greatest portion of the inheritance to him. This typifies the time, the talents, the material possessions, etc., all that is valued, all that is held dear by man, all to which he devotes himself. These, too, are claimed by God as His by right and might; these, too, must be redeemed and set apart for God's use or they are worthless.

Guidance Given

Once the command to sanctify had been issued, God, in Exodus 13:17 and 18, gave His first guidance to the people He had just rescued from Egypt:

> *And it came to pass, when Pharaoh had let the people go, that <u>God led them</u> not through the way of the land of the Philistines, although that was near; for God said, Lest peradventure the people repent when they see war, and they return to Egypt. But <u>God led the people</u> about, through the way of the wilderness of the Red sea: and <u>the children of Israel went up harnessed</u> out of the land of Egypt.*

There were two possible routes from Egypt to Canaan. The shortest and most direct was the caravan road which began in Tanis, Egypt, and followed a path beside the

Mediterranean Sea to Palestine. It was well-traveled and would have brought the Hebrews to the border of the Promised Land in about four or five days. It was the short cut to Canaan. The second path was much longer and required much more time to traverse. It took the traveler on a rather circuitous route to the southeast, through the rocky and unforgiving wilderness of the Arabian Desert on the Sinai Peninsula.

Although logic would have chosen the first route--for convenience, time, and distance--God chose the second. The first path would have brought the Israelites into direct confrontation with the Philistines who dwelt along the Mediterranean Sea and controlled the coastal road from Egypt, and they were noted, in Scripture as well as history, for fighting skills on land and sea. This being the case, God moved to protect His people from an inevitable conflict which would only have served to discourage them.

Harnessed, in Exodus 3:18, is the Hebrew, *hamushim*, which means, full battle array. It indicates that the men of Israel were fully armed. Why, then, was God concerned about a possible confrontation with the Philistines, so concerned that He rejected a much shorter route? First, there was the matter of the Egyptians. God, in His foreknowledge, certainly knew that they would follow and attempt to recapture His people to enslave them again. The northern route would have placed the Israelites between the Egyptians, stung by their defeat at the hands of God, and the Philistines, violent defenders of their borders. While armed, God's people were not qualified, either by previous training or experience, for such an encounter. They would have been defeated, disheartened, and disenchanted, easy prey for the Egyptians and easily enslaved by them. But, the southern route would bring the Egyptians to the brink of the Red Sea, where God would be able to deal with them, permanently. Second, God had promised Moses that the people he was sent to save would worship in the very mountain, Mount Horeb, where Moses had first received his call (Exodus 3:12). God never forgets a prophecy and He faithfully fulfills every one. Finally, there was the matter of maturity. Had the Israelites entered immediately into Canaan, they would not yet have reached the level of unity and maturity required to take and hold it. Momentary euphoria would soon have given way to the melancholy of failure, in the extremes of emotion so common to the immature. So, the Lord took His people by a longer but safer route where He could begin to try them and test them, prepare them, and prove them, where He would lead them to complete spiritual maturity.

Those God redeems, He dedicates in sanctification. And, those He dedicates, He directs. The path He chooses may not be the shortest or even the easiest, but it will result in the ultimate best (Romans 8:28). On that path, God's children will encounter no more spiritual warfare than they are able to fight or be accosted by no greater spiritual enemies than they are able to defeat. Also on that path God will bring His people to full spiritual maturity, as stable spiritual adults, so they can confidently conquer, own, and occupy all that God has for them.

When God offers guidance along the road, it is faith which takes the step. Exodus 13:20 records the faith of two of God's heroes to insure understanding of this principle:

> *And Moses took the bones of Joseph with him: for he had straitly sworn the children of Israel, saying, God will surely visit you; and ye shall carry up my bones away hence with you.*

Three hundred and fifty years previously, before Joseph, who was Jacob or Israel's son and Pharaoh's governor, died, he made this request in Genesis 50:24 through 26:

> *And Joseph said unto his brethren, I die: and God will surely visit you, and bring you out of this land unto the land which he sware to Abraham, to Isaac,*

and to Jacob. And Joseph took an oath of the children of Israel, saying...ye shall carry up my bones from hence. So Joseph died, being an hundred and ten years old: and they embalmed him, and he was put in a coffin in Egypt.

Imagine the faith of Joseph! In a society which doted on death, glorified the grave, and exalted the tomb, Joseph refused to permit his own burial. He believed the promise God had made to his father in Genesis 46:4, believed it so much that he wanted to be a part of the event, even in death. As a clause in his will, he asked his surviving brothers to preserve and protect his remains until the day of departure came. He preferred the lowliest crypt in Canaan to the loftiest tomb Egypt had to offer. With the eye of faith, Joseph could see the Promised Land and that's where he wanted to be.

Imagine the faith of Joseph's brothers and their sons and their sons' sons! For generations, Joseph's remains had been preserved. For generations, there had been those who had believed the promise, too, who longed for that day, just as Joseph had. In over three hundred and fifty years, not one among the children of Israel violated Joseph's sacred trust, not one gave up the hope that their enslavement was not as endless as it seemed, not one entombed their famous forefather in Egypt.

Imagine the faith of Moses! Not knowing how long the journey might be or what he might encounter along the way, Moses assumed the obligation the Israelites had kept inviolate for centuries. He carried the coffin of Joseph into the unknown. He knew God's promise to the patriarchs and God's promise to him. He knew that God never breaks a promise. Moses believed God would enable him to bring Joseph home.

It is just such faith which finds a foothold on the journey God has planned, which sees the prize in the distance, which will travel any distance, bear any burden, fight any foe, and overcome any obstacle to reach the goal. It is the faith that spans generations, unites families, and defeats death. It is the faith of our fathers. It can be our faith, too.

The Holy Spirit Given

In John 14:17, Jesus taught His disciples some vitally important facts about the Holy Spirit:

Even the Spirit of truth; whom the world cannot receive, because it seeth him not, neither knoweth him; but ye know him; for he dwelleth with you, and shall be in you.

Here, we are introduced to two aspects of the ministry of the Holy Spirit among men. First, He dwells with man. If He didn't, it would be impossible for anyone to be converted since it is the Holy Spirit, who, according to John 16:8 through 11, convicts man of sin and convinces him of his need of a Saviour. Once man is born again, the Holy Spirit remains with him in His role as Paraclete, one who is called to be by one's side, one who walks beside another to help. Second, the Holy Spirit's moves into the believer and fills him to overflowing. This ministry is foreshadowed throughout the Old Testament, prophesied in the Book of Joel (Joel 2:28 and 29), and fulfilled in the Book of Acts (Acts 2:1 through 4). It is at this point that the Holy Spirit does exactly what Jesus said He would do. He moves inside the believer, takes up permanent residence, and begins to work through the believer to transform him into the image of Christ, to help him to reach out to touch the lives of others, and to make him perfect (mature).

Immediately after the children of Israel were redeemed and sanctified, we see the Holy Spirit coming to be with them, walking along the wilderness road beside them, overshadowing, protecting, and guiding them. We see Him in type in the fire and the cloud sent by God to lead His people by day and by night in Exodus 13:21 and 22:

> *And the LORD went before them by day in a pillar of a cloud, to lead them the way; and by night in a pillar of fire, to give them light; to go by day and night: He took not away the pillar of the cloud by day, nor the pillar of fire by night, from before the people.*

This cloud, the same *shekinah* glory of God which, in 1 Kings 8:10 and 11, filled the Temple so intensely that it was impossible for the priests to minister, stood above the children of Israel. It led them along the right path, gave them shelter from the heat of the desert day, and blocked the view of Pharaoh, the type of Satan, and his warriors. Since a cloud would be difficult to see at night, the Holy Spirit came then in the form of a pillar or a column of fire. The fire brought light and warmth against the chill of the wilderness night, gave them guidance, and presented a barrier to Pharaoh (Satan). Either the fire or the cloud was always visible to God's people along their journey. According to Exodus 13:22, He never once removed this holy Presence from them. In time, the Holy Spirit would come to dwell in their very midst, but they would never forget those precious days and nights when the comforting closeness of the Holy Spirit was with them, even in the midst of the hottest days and the darkest nights.

The Holy Spirit ever walks alongside the child of God. He comes to direct, to shelter, to warm, to light, and to protect every one of God's redeemed. And, just as He never left the children of Israel in the wilderness, He will never forsake the child of God in this world today. No matter how high the mountain, how deep the valley, how dry the desert, how hot the day, or how dark the night, He is there. No matter what the world brings against the believer, no matter what Satan has in store, the believer can always sense the abiding presence of the Spirit of God in the midst of it all.

And, so, the children of Israel wait in the wilderness. They are redeemed, they are sanctified, and they have the precious presence of the Holy Spirit beside them. But, the journey is long and the road is not easy. A horror they cannot now imagine is hasty on their heels. The path to maturity continues....

[1]R. Laird Harris, Gleason L. Archer, and Bruce K. Waltke, *Theological Wordbook of the Old Testament*, p. 786.

Chapter 7
RESCUED AND REJOICING

The Prophecy Given

The children of Israel had been emancipated and embarked on the long journey which was to take them to their promised land for only a matter of days. Freedom felt fabulous and, no doubt, the former captives were certain they could meet all challenges. They did not know it, but a terrifying trial was on its way at that very moment. But, no challenge to the believer ever takes God by surprise. He already knew what was about to occur and He was already on the scene, preparing to manage the coming menace, putting His plan for victory into effect. This final confrontation between God and Pharaoh is detailed in the fourteenth chapter of the Book of Exodus.

For the first few days of the journey, God had been taking the Israelites along a southeastern route which would have taken them into the desert and beyond the reach of the Egyptians. Suddenly, however, God led His people due south (Exodus 14:1 and 2), a course which would keep them within range of Egypt's armies, sitting duck decoys, shut in between their enemies, the mountains, and the sea, almost inviting attack. Still, they were not instructed to run or to make any attempt to fight by ordinary human means; they were simply told to make the turn and set up their camp, just as they had done before. They would have to trust God for their security, whatever happened.

Why would God deliberately place His people in such obvious jeopardy? Why would He put them in a position of such impending doom? Why would He permit them to walk into such imminent danger? He explained His strange strategy in Exodus 14:4:

> *And I will harden Pharaoh's heart, that he shall follow after them; and I will be honoured upon Pharaoh, and upon all his host; that the Egyptians may know that I am the LORD.*

Clearly, the change of course was a part of God's plan. Observed and reported by spies, this deviation in direction indicated to Pharaoh that his former slaves had become lost in the wilderness and were conveniently easy prey for pursuit and recapture. In addition, Pharaoh found himself with economic and political problems produced by his previous decision to expel his Hebrew hostages as Exodus 14:5 details. There were complaints on every hand. The very citizens who couldn't wait for the captives to depart so that the plagues would be lifted, the very Egyptians who had sped them on their way with spoils, now suddenly saw that they had no servants to do their most unpalatable work, build their prodigious public works projects, and tolerate their prolific insults and abuse. The citizens were up in arms and the Egyptian economy was at a standstill. Such predicaments could present a risk to the rule of Pharaoh who found himself forced to act. It was all a part of God's carefully conceived strategy and it was all going to work together for good to God's people (Romans 8:28).

The freedom of redemption feels wonderful. The burdens of bondage are gone and a new life has begun. Often, after this initial experience, there is, for the child of God a respite, a time of release, a time of rest. Some call it "a spiritual honeymoon." But, it's a basic fact of spiritual life that Satan does not give up his captives without a struggle. There may be a brief break in his activity, often just enough to lull one into a false sense of security. He may be depended upon, however, to pursue after his lost slave, to plan a strategy by which he may recover that slave, and to seek an opportunity to put that diabolical plan into effect. In short, eventually, he will be back.

In the euphoria of escape, the child of God may not be aware of the certainty of coming combat. But, God knows what is ahead. He permits Satan's devious designs to go forward, not so His newborn babes can be destroyed, but only so that He can bring Satan down to defeat. This battle, in which God engages Satan and the existence of the believer hangs in the balance, is known as spiritual warfare. The Christian has no choice concerning whether or not this conflict will come. Because Satan is Satan, it will happen. The only decision left to the believer is one of flight or fight. Flight, the instinctive human response to threat, brings only death, for spiritual warfare cannot be won using natural logic or carnal weapons. The decision to stand and fight, on the other hand, brings God into the situation and allows Him to execute a battle plan guaranteed to conclude with Satan's ignominious defeat and God's glorious victory.

The Prophecy Fulfilled

Pharaoh mobilized immediately. Taking command in his own chariot, he led his entire force against the rag-tag company of former captives camped in the wilderness (Exodus 14:6 and 7). Make no mistake about it, Pharaoh's force was considerable, almost more than the mind of man could imagine. According to the noted Jewish historian, Josephus, the Egyptian army contained six hundred chariots, fifty thousand horsemen, and two hundred thousand foot soldiers,[1] all to pursue after a disorderly assemblage of slaves. Clearly, when Satan sees an opportunity to move against the believer, he will mobilize everything he has for the fight. In the hardness of his heart, he will seek only to capture and to kill. Peter explained it well in 1 Peter 5:8, *"Be sober, be vigilant; because your adversary the devil, as a roaring lion, walketh about, seeking whom he may devour."*

There are two ways to view every attack of the enemy. Because of the new convert's lack of experience with the might and majesty of his God, he, like the Israelites in the wilderness, often sees only the problem (Exodus 14:10), and, at first glance, Satan's forces look impressive. But, this view fosters fear, not faith. The initial reaction is to surrender, to avert certain death by a voluntary return to servitude. Then, even bondage and burial begin to look better than the defense of freedom (Exodus 14:11 and 12). Rationality and reason are lost in the menace of the moment. But, the more mature servant of the Lord, typified by Moses, takes a confident view of the same crisis. In faith, he gets his gaze off the problem and lifts his eyes a little higher. He sees salvation, help on the horizon, a vista of victory, according to Exodus 14:13 and 14:

> *And Moses said unto the people, Fear ye not, stand still, and see the salvation of the LORD, which he will shew to you to day: for the Egyptians whom ye have seen to day, ye shall see them again no more for ever. The LORD shall fight for you and ye shall hold your peace.*

Rescue Promised

In response to Moses' confident declaration of faith, God spoke once more (Exodus 14:15 through 18). He chided the people for their cries and complaints. It was not anguish which was needed, but action, and God ordered it to begin immediately. He commanded His people to proceed forward, all the way to the shores of the Red Sea (Exodus 14:15). Then, He promised a divine deliverance that would make history.

The raging Red Sea, which seemed like a wall to the children of Israel, trapping them before their enemies, would soon become a road. God would divide the sea, creating a dry path right through the middle by which His people could escape their pursuers (Exodus 14:16). Only God could such a thing. And, as if that were not enough, the Lord planned to use that same sea to obliterate their enemies, once and for all. In this way, God would execute His final revenge on Pharaoh and his hordes (Exodus 14:17 and 18). God would have victory and vengeance in one smooth stroke.

This is precisely the way God moves in response to the active faith of His servants. He bares His mighty arm in a display of power none can deny. He will fight for His followers, if they will only stand their ground. He is still resolved to have His vengeance upon the enemies of His people; He is still determined to grant His children the victory.

Rescue Provided

At that moment, the pillar of cloud which had been before the children of Israel to guide their procession forward, suddenly moved to the rear of the company, stopping only when it stood directly between God's people and their enemies (Exodus 14:19 and 20). From that position, the very same cloud was able to provide light all through the night for the Israelites and, at the same time, plunge the armies of Egypt into total darkness. The mighty Egyptian army was paralyzed, unable to move all night. God delights in such displays of His strength. Satan and his forces of darkness are immobilized while the believer is forcefully freed from his grip.

During the night, the Israelites, under the direction of Moses, reached the brink of the Red Sea. As God had commanded, Moses lifted up his miraculous staff over the waters of the sea. What happened next is best related by the historian, Josephus:[2]

> When Moses had said this, he led them to the sea, while the Egyptians looked on, for they were within sight. Now these were so distressed by the toil of their pursuit that they thought proper to put off fighting till the next day. But when Moses was come to the sea-shore, he took his rod, and made supplication to God, and called upon him to be their helper and assistant; and said, 'Thou art not ignorant, O Lord, that it is beyond human strength and human contrivance to avoid the difficulties we are now under; but it must be thy work altogether to procure deliverance to this army, which has left Egypt at thy appointment. We despair of any other assistance or contrivance, and have recourse only to that hope we have in thee; and if there be any method that can promise us an escape by thy providence, we look up to thee for it. And let it come quickly, and manifest thy power to us; and do thou raise up this people unto good courage and hope of deliverance, who are deeply sunk into a disconsolate state of mind. We are in a helpless place, but still it is a place that thou possessest; still the sea is thine, the mountains also that enclose us are thine; so that these mountains will open themselves if thou commandest them, and the sea also, if thou commandest it, will become dry land. Nay, we might escape by a flight through the air, if thou shouldst determine we should have that way of salvation.' When Moses had thus addressed himself to God, he smote the sea with his rod, which parted asunder at the stroke, and receiving those waters into itself, left the ground dry, as a road and a place of flight for the Hebrews.

With that, God's miraculous rescue of His people proceeded, just as He had predicted. The laws of nature no longer applied in the face of the Lord of nature; the impossible was made possible under His omnipotent hand. Scripture reveals that God sent an unusually strong east wind which divided the water of the Red Sea, forcing it to stand like a bulwark on either side and providing the dry path God had already promised. His people strolled through the sea, just as though it were a paved road (Exodus 14:21 and 22). They didn't even get their feet wet!

Many hypotheses have been advanced to explain this event but wonders aren't meant to be explained and every one of these explanations is found wanting. It is enough to know that Jehovah God did it--miraculously, marvelously, and mysteriously. It is enough to recognize that the same God who fought for Israel, now fights for the family of faith.

The Enemy Overcome

Simply delivering the Israelites wasn't enough to satisfy God's requirements. There was the matter of vengeance which God had determined to exact upon the Egyptians, too. They were no longer after the servants of God; God was now after them.

As morning dawned, the Egyptians saw what had happened and tried to follow the Hebrews on the same path their God had made for their feet (Exodus 14:23). God allowed them to proceed just so far--just to the middle of the Red Sea--and no further. Then, God dealt with them, finally and forever (Exodus 14:24 through 28). He caused the wheels of their chariots to break, leaving them stranded in the seabed. Then, He had Moses wave the water back into its place. Pharaoh's best troops were drowned.

God is ever able to deal with the diabolical designs of the devil, as he seeks to pursue and recapture the redeemed. Satan may raise old habits, old temptations, old spiritual problems--all the old enemies--to pursue God's children and end their freedom. But, all will be to no avail against the faithful followers of God. He will devise a divine strategy, guaranteed to defeat Satan, to trouble him, slow his forward progress, and, finally, overwhelm his forces completely. The seeds of Satan's destruction are sown in the deliverance of God's people. And, it will be total destruction, until not one foe is left to hinder them. It was all accomplished by faith, as Hebrews 11:29 reveals, "*By faith they passed through the Red sea as by dry land: which the Egyptians assaying to do were drowned.*"

Results of the Rescue

In Exodus 14:30 and 31, we see the glorious results of the miraculous rescue of God's people:

> *Thus the LORD saved Israel that day out of the hand of the Egyptians; and Israel saw the Egyptians dead upon the sea shore. And Israel saw that great work which the LORD did upon the Egyptians: and the people feared the LORD, and believed the LORD, and his servant Moses.*

Three things had happened. First, to the amazement of the Hebrews, they saw the raw, exposed power of their God against the Egyptians. He was able to overcome any obstacle, able to defeat any foe. In addition, the people of God came to fear or respect Him more than they had ever feared their adversaries. Such a miraculous deliverance will always engender faith for future spiritual battles in the believer. Finally, the skeptics among the Israelites had come to believe in Moses, the leader God had chosen for them. At last, they were convinced.

This divine deliverance became another pivotal point of Jewish history. It was the subject of psalmists' writings (Psalm 78:13 and 14; Psalm 106:7 through 11 and Psalm 135:13

through 15) and the theme of a prophet's musings (Isaiah 63:12). And, its deeper symbolism was not lost on the early Church. In 1 Corinthians 10:1 and 2, Paul wrote:

> *Moreover, brethren, I would not that ye should be ignorant, how that all our fathers were under the cloud, and all passed through the sea; And were all baptized unto Moses in the cloud and in the sea.*

Paul viewed this Old Testament event as a type of New Testament water baptism. Note that it was only after Stephen's recital of this incident that the martyr referred to the Israelites as *"the church in the wilderness"* (Acts 7:38). Thus baptized, these believers became God's church fifteen hundred years before the first mention of the word.

There are times when every child of God shares the same feelings of fear and frustration which the Israelites must have had with the Red Sea before them and the Egyptians advancing behind them. There are times when every believer feels overcome, overwhelmed, and ambushed. But, somewhere in the darkest night, God is there, leading, guiding, and protecting. Nothing takes Him by surprise. It's all a part of His plan to test, try, and perfect (mature) His own as He defeats and destroys their enemies. God's people can trust His guidance, just as Moses did, knowing that God will never lead them where His presence can't go with them or His power can't protect them. Their profession of faith becomes the starting point for God's action in their behalf. They, too, can stand still and watch in wonder as the God of might and majesty parts their personal Red Seas and defeats their personal enemies. In the aftermath, the believer's fear of the foe is banished, only to be replaced by awe of his God. Doubt becomes belief and skepticism is transformed into trust. This is the inheritance of the child of God; this is the heritage of His Church.

Rejoicing in Rescue

Any great victory of God deserves the recognition and appreciation of His people. So, as soon as their feet had found the far bank of the river, Moses ordered a pause to sing a song of victory before the Lord who had given it. That song and the celebration it initiated is recorded in Exodus 15:1 through 21. God's people worshipped Him for who He is--their strength, their salvation, their God (Exodus 15:2 and 3). Then, they praised Him for what He had done--delivering them from their enemy and defeating his plan to recapture and re-enslave them (Exodus 15:4 through 10). Finally, Israel meditated on the marvelous nature of their God. There was, they realized, no God like Him. He, alone, was holy, worthy of praise, and capable of great wonders (Exodus 15:11); He, alone, had a strong, right arm which was able to sweep away His enemies (Exodus 15:12); He, alone, was the Redeemer (Exodus 15:13); He, alone, was, at one and the same time, the Source of fear to the world and the inheritance of His people (Exodus 15:14 through 17); He, alone, was eternal and everlasting (Exodus 15:18); He, alone, could destroy the destroyer (Exodus 15:19). The celebration of God's victory concluded with a victory dance led by Miriam and performed by all the women.

Here, Miriam, the elder sister of Moses who was so instrumental in his care as an infant, is called a prophetess, from the Hebrew word, *nab*a, which comes from a root which meant, to bubble up, and came to mean, an authorized spokesman who bubbles over with his message. It identifies one who sings or speaks by divine inspiration and is used, not necessarily of one who occupies the office of prophet but of one who exercises the gift of prophecy.

Miriam was the eldest child of Amram and Jochebed and the elder sister of both Aaron and Moses. Her name, the Hebrew form of the Greek, Mary, meant, bitterness or rebellion, and, unfortunately, this side of her nature would emerge later. Although Scripture records no marriage of Miriam, Josephus states that she was the wife of Hur, who was appointed by Moses to be an elder of Israel.[3] In this passage, however, Miriam's main motive was to glorify her God in spiritual song and dance. In the aftermath of victory, it was that song of praise and worship which proved that the children of Israel had finally lifted their gaze. In it, there was little of Pharaoh and even less of anything man had accomplished. They saw only God's provision of protection and preservation.

Such a season of praise, worship, and meditation is essential after spiritual victory. It is only in giving the glory back to God that the believer relinquishes his own hold on it and, it is only by so doing that he overcomes his own ego. This is often done in the form of a testimony, but it must be a testimony which does not exalt the enemy or man; it must, instead, reflect man's recognition of all that God has accomplished in his behalf.

It is the psalmist who best reveals the importance of this time of praise, worship, and meditation upon the greatness of God following His victories. In the Book of Psalms (or songs) of Israel, the pattern for perfect praise is prescribed. In Psalm 99:5, the believer is instructed to <u>worship</u> God; in Psalm 9:11, to <u>praise</u> God; in Psalm 77:12, to <u>meditate</u> upon God; in Psalm 68:4, to <u>celebrate</u> God; and, finally, in Psalm 9:1, he is to <u>testify</u> to God's victory. It is a complete and a comprehensive plan, a plan whose purpose is to glorify the God who gives the victory, but it is also fashioned to protect the follower of God from one of his greatest pitfalls, his own human pride. It is a plan every mature child of God will choose to follow, for his own spiritual safety.

[1]Flavius Josephus, *The Complete Works of Josephus*, The Antiquities of the Jews, Book II, Chapter XV, Verse 3.

[2]Ibid., The Antiquities of the Jews, Book II, Chapter XV, Verses 1 and 2.

[3]Herbert Lockyer, *All the Women of the Bible*, p. 111.

Chapter 8
LIVING ON GOD'S PROVISION

Water Provided

The wilderness journey had just begun. No more than one short week had elapsed since God had freed His people from Egypt and only a few short days (Exodus 15:22) since the Red Sea had opened before them and closed upon their enemies, initiating a day of praise and worship for God's great victory. You'd think that, on the basis of past experiences, alone, the children of Israel would never doubt or fear again.

But, the trouble with people is that they are human and, no matter how many difficulties God has safely carried them through, each new crisis brings those same old feelings of fear and doubt and frustration. The song of victory which is sung beside the sea is seldom heard in the desert. To compound the problem, children of God tend to think that a great spiritual victory heralds their arrival in some new realm of Christian living, one where Satan is a stranger, crises never come, and negative emotions never intrude. It always comes as quite a shock to discover that it is often after just such a spiritual mountaintop experience that one is plunged into the deepest valley he has ever known. After all, a valley is simply a small depression between two mountains. From that valley, the next mountain peak may be shrouded in fog and difficult to discern in the distance; nevertheless, it is there. The children of Israel had scaled a spiritual mountaintop, but the valley was drawing closer every day.

After leaving the eastern bank of the Red Sea, Moses led God's people into the wilderness of Shur. It was to be a time of testing and trying, just as Jesus, after His baptism at the Jordan, was led into the wilderness to be tried and tested (Luke 4:1). It's amazing how often this method to maturity seems to be the one God chooses! The wilderness of Shur is an immense area which includes nearly all of the western part of the Arabian Peninsula. Although it adjoins the Red Sea, it is a plain of pure white desert sand which seems to go on forever. Having gone three days' journey into this wilderness, a distance of perhaps thirty miles, the children of Israel discovered that they had no water, not a single, solitary drop and the desert can be deadly difficult without water. The Bible, itself, clarifies the symbolism of water in John 7:38 and 39:

> *He that believeth on me, as the scripture hath said, out of his belly shall flow rivers of living water. (But this spake he of the Spirit, which they that believe on him should receive: for the Holy Ghost was not yet given; because that Jesus was not yet glorified.)*

In Ephesians 5:26, Paul refers to, *"The washing of water by the word."* Clearly, water typifies the Holy Spirit and the Word of God which sanctifies, or sets apart, and cleanses those who drink. To be without this water would signify suffering the greatest thirst of all, that unquenchable spiritual thirst experienced by those who do not have the Spirit of God in their lives and who do not drink in the Word of God.

The Israelites had seen the power of God and had even witnessed His miracles. But, they were not yet partakers of the Spirit of God or drinking the Word of God. That made them thirsty people--both physically and spiritually. Then, the children of Israel decided to make what may have been an unscheduled detour to Marah (Exodus 15:23). There are three reasons to wonder about this particular stop. First, Exodus 15:22 states that it was Moses who brought the children of Israel to this place with no mention of the cloudy column or the fiery pillar. Second, when it was discovered that the water of Marah was unpalatable, it was Moses who incurred the wrath of his countrymen. They did not speak out against God. Third, just six miles away from Marah was the oasis of Elim with twelve wells and seventy palm trees (Exodus 15:27). This was the next place Israel camped and may have been the Lord's destination all along. No matter! Whether or not God had guided them to this location, He would use it to prove them (Exodus 15:25), to test their faith and obedience.

Marah was always noted for its bitter water. In fact, that is exactly how it had gotten its name, which means, bitter water, long before the children of Israel ever stopped there. At Marah, an underground spring fed a basin-shaped well about six feet in diameter that usually contained no more than two feet of water. That wasn't much to quench the thirst of perhaps millions. As if that were not enough, what water there was had always been bitter, brackish by reason of its mineral deposits, and quite unpleasant to drink.

God's people had searched for water (the Spirit and the Word) in a convenient place, much like many modern-day believers attend any easily available church, only to find false doctrine or incomplete gospel that leaves them bitter. Indeed, there are times when even the true Word of God will seem bitter, as John experienced in Revelation 10:8 through 10. It may be difficult to hear, particularly if it portends God's judgment, difficult to understand, especially for the novice, and difficult to obey for all. But, sometimes the bitter is necessary to prove the child of God. Soon, the Holy Spirit will always lead into sweetness of the truth, if only He is followed and obeyed.

As the first thirsty travelers tasted the waters of Marah and recoiled from its biting bitterness, God's people instantly forgot His past miracles because of their present miseries. They saw only the impossibility of their situation, not the possibilities in God, and began to murmur against Moses (Exodus 15:24). Murmur, is the Hebrew, *lun*. In its strictest sense, it means, to lodge, and refers to a stop, such as one might make for the night. But, it can also refer to a stop caused by obstinacy or a grudge.

After all Moses had done for the Israelites, after all his leadership had given them, it's difficult to understand why they formed an instant grudge against him at the first sign of trouble. But, such a reaction is just human nature. When man doesn't like the location to which he has been led, he blames the leadership; when he doesn't like the message, he faults the messenger. In the home, it's all the parents' fault; on the job, it's all the boss's fault; in society, it's all the government's fault; and, in the Church, it's all the pastor's fault. Blaming others is the tendency of all, especially the young and immature. Before God, however, the believer bears personal responsibility. In a crisis, it is his responsibility, not to blame others, but to seek God for the answer. Then, God will fulfill His responsibility to meet man's need according to Philippians 4:19, *"But my God shall supply all your need according to his riches in glory by Christ Jesus."*

The children of Israel had not yet learned this lesson of maturity, but Moses had. Immediately, he went to prayer (Exodus 15:25), as was his habit in such situations. In response to the mature prayer of the mature man of God, the Lord answered, as was His habit in such situations, directing Moses to a particular tree which, when cast into the water, made it sweet (Exodus 15:25). Now, according to Jewish tradition, this tree was bitter all by itself, just one further indication that the sweetness was not in the tree; it was in the humble obedience of the man who reached out to touch the tree.

This tree is typical of Christ, the Source of the sweet Water of Life (John 4:14). In Scripture (Zechariah 3:8), Jesus is called *"the Branch."* It is also typical of the cross of Christ, the tree which, when applied to even the most bitter life, can make it sweet.

This incident is, of course, symbolic of so much in the believer's life. No matter how critical the crisis or how dire the dilemma, when the mature child of God reaches out to embrace Christ and His cross, he will find sweetness and life. In addition, he will find the sweet promises of God to sustain him in every circumstance.

Healing Provided

At the same time God's prescription caused the waters to be healed, God, in Exodus 15:16, gave Moses a new promise of healing for His people:

And said, If thou wilt diligently hearken to the voice of the LORD thy God, and wilt do that which is right in his sight, and wilt give ear to his commandments, and will keep all his statutes, I will put none of these diseases upon thee, which I have brought upon the Egyptians: for I am the LORD that healeth thee.

Here, God revealed Himself to His people by another of His covenant names, *Jehovah Rophi*, which means, "the Lord our Healer" or "the Lord our Physician."[1] It was not a new name. God had first revealed Himself by this name to Abraham as he prayed for the healing of Abimelech and his wives (Genesis 20:17). The Hebrew word for healing, as used in this name, indicates mending, in the sense that a garment is mended, repair, in the way that a building might be repaired, and curing, in the sense that a disease may be cured. It is in all of these senses that the Lord, our Physician, heals His people. This mortal body which man wears as a garment is often in need of mending; this earthly building in which man dwells, is often in need of repair; the diseases to which man is vulnerable are often in need of cure. It is only *Jehovah Rophi*, who made the garment, constructed the building and can heal its diseases.

Although Abraham received the first revelation of this name of God, it was not until about six hundred years later that the full healing contract was given to Moses, here in Exodus 15:26, a contract which incorporates all of the legal elements. First, it is an agreement between two parties, in this case, God and His people. Second, it contained conditions, four of them, to be exact. God required that His people obey His voice, live right, listen to His commands, and keep His Law. As in most contracts, the clear implication was, if they would, He would. Third, the contract was signed with God's covenant name, Jehovah, the name by which He swears performance because there is nothing and no one greater in the universe by which He can swear, and *Rophi*, by which He swears to be the Healer of His people. Such a contract with the signature of the covenant-making, covenant-keeping Lord of this universe will be kept forever.

That contract is still in force today. When doctors have prescribed all of their medicine, performed all of their surgery, stitched and set and done all that they can do, the mature child of God realizes that it is *Jehovah Rophi*, and *Jehovah Rophi* alone, who can cause healing to happen. Sometimes, it happens instantly; sometimes it occurs gradually; but, it is only *Jehovah Rophi* who can make it happen at all.

Rest Provided

As chapter fifteen of Exodus comes to a close, the children of Israel have traveled to a new location, as Exodus 15:27 records:

And they came to Elim, where were twelve wells of water, and threescore and ten palm trees: and they encamped by the waters.

Just six miles away from Marah, God's people came to the very campsite their Lord had prepared for them, Elim, an oasis like a jewel in the desert in the wilderness of Sin. There, the Hebrews were welcomed by twelve wells, one for each of the tribes, and rested in the shade of seventy palm trees. Nine of these wells remain to this day and the seventy palm trees have multiplied to over two thousand. A flowing stream also traverses the oasis, bringing life and health to all who pause there in their journeys.

As water typifies the Holy Spirit and the Word of God, the oasis symbolizes that place of rest the believer finds in the comfort of the Holy Spirit and the guidance of God's Word, a place of relaxation, of refreshment, of respite from this dry world. This spiritual oasis is a place to be alone with God, delight in His presence, and enjoy the water of life freely. God's mature servants will seek it without detour and drink in all its benefits. Such pauses are found all too seldom and the journey continues all too soon.

Bread and Meat Provided

After only one month, the Israelites camped in the wilderness of Sin (Exodus 16:1), a wasteland which stretched along the eastern coast of the Red Sea between Elim and the Sinai desert. Whatever provisions they had brought were now exhausted and it was impossible for such a throng to survive on the few wild olives and scarce wild honey which was all that was available. They were hungry and there seemed no hope of provision. Quickly forgetting all that God had already done for them and failing to petition God for what was needed, the Israelites immediately lapsed into murmuring and complaining against Moses and Aaron (Exodus 16:2). Once more, their thoughts returned to Egypt. The recollection of bondage had faded; they now recalled only the sufficiency of food provided to them there. Since man's strongest instinct is survival, the children of Israel found enslavement in Egypt preferable to death in the desert.

The child of God does not live in the natural realm, alone; he also resides in a spiritual kingdom where the King has promised to provide for His own, both physically and spiritually. When provision seems impossible to the natural eye, the spiritual eye must see the sufficiency of the Saviour. All too often, however, man seeks to satisfy the appetites of the natural man, even if he has to live in bondage to sin to do it.

The Lord was sufficient to this situation. He would provide His people with food, but in a way which would help them mature in trust and obedience (Exodus 16:4). Each morning, God would rain down heavenly bread and each individual was to gather one day's supply (Exodus 16:4); on the morning before the Sabbath, each was to gather enough for two days, since God did not plan to make deliveries on His day of rest (Exodus 16:5). Only perfect obedience to these orders would prove one's faith in God since, to gather extra on a weekday implied that God might not provide on the next and, to fail to gather extra for the Sabbath implied that God had not meant what He said. In addition, God taught all to budget their supply and live within their means, both essential lessons for the maturing child of God. Moses and Aaron passed along God's promise of provision. Every morning, their Lord would give them bread to eat and, each evening, He would send meat for dinner.

But, there was more at stake here than mere provision; there was also an important principle (Exodus 16:6 through 8). Moses reminded the children of Israel that he and Aaron were their God-appointed leaders, but God, Himself, was their ultimate Authority; when they murmured and complained against Moses and Aaron, they were really murmuring and complaining against the One who had chosen them, as seen in the last line of Exodus 16:8, *"...your murmurings are not against us, but against the LORD."* When God's people begin to murmur against, complain about, or gossip about the leaders He appoints, He takes it personally, since He called them and placed them in their positions. No wonder David refused to slay King Saul, the very man who sought his life, saying in 1 Samuel 24:10, *"I will not put forth mine hand against my lord; for he is the LORD's anointed."* Later, David put this principle in writing, as recorded in 1 Chronicles 16:22, *"Saying, Touch not mine anointed, and do my prophets no harm."*

God personally affirmed the words of Moses and the principle he set forth. His spectacular *shekinah* glory personally appeared in the form of a cloud, confirming all that Moses had said and confirming his call to lead Israel (Exodus 16:10).

That evening, the first meat arrived in the form of quail which littered the camp. Many have tried to identify the type of birds God used to fulfill His promise. Suffice it to say that there are several kinds of birds whose migratory route might take them over the Sinai Peninsula, but none could be expected in such large numbers, at this time of year, so regularly, or at the exact moment God said. This was clearly a miracle of God's provision for His people just as David wrote in Psalm 78:27 through 29:

> *He rained flesh also upon them as dust, and feathered fowls like as the sand of the sea: And he let it fall in the midst of their camp....So they did eat, and were well filled: for he gave them their own desire.*

The next morning, the first heavenly bread fell as a tiny, white, sweet-tasting, dew-like substance which the people called manna, from the Hebrew, *man* or *manna*, since they didn't know what it was. It's been suggested that manna was actually the *mannu* of ancient Egyptian manuscripts. It seems that, in the summers of very rainy years, the tamarisk tree, which is native to the Arabian desert, exudes small, sticky, light-colored drops of sap when its branches are punctured by insects. This hardens into little white grains which are collected before sunrise and used for food. While this might explain the name the Hebrews gave to the food and conform in some ways to the description of manna (Exodus 16:31), it can't explain the mysterious arrival of that food for many reasons. First, the Hebrews milled their manna into flour for bread (Exodus 16:23 and Numbers 11:8), but mannu could not be ground. Second, manna arrived every morning all year, not just during the summer season. Third, manna was found continuously for forty years, not just during the years that were rainy. In addition, the Bible contains certain clues to the source of the manna which prove beyond doubt that it was the miraculous provision of God. For example, in Psalm 78:24 and 25, David wrote:

> *And had rained down manna upon them to eat, and had given them of the corn of heaven. Man did eat angel's food: he sent them meat to the full.*

Here, manna is identified as angel's food which was rained down from heaven. Then, in John 6:31, the Jews of Jesus' time describe the event this way:

> *Our fathers did eat manna in the desert; as it is written, He gave them bread from heaven to eat.*

Whatever manna was, the Israelites scrambled to get their daily supply of it and discovered that, no matter how much or how little one collected, each portion measured the exact amount God permitted. Those who had selfishly attempted to amass more had nothing left over and those who hadn't gathered enough lacked nothing (Exodus 16:17 and 18). Those who did not trust God enough to follow His instructions to the letter, those who saved some of their day's supply until the next morning were surprised to discover that it spoiled overnight, breeding worms, and emitting a terrible odor (Exodus 16:20). Saddest of all, they failed God's test of faith and obedience and were rewarded with nothing but garbage. These people must have been equally surprised to find that the extra manna collected for the Sabbath did not spoil (Exodus 16:21 through 26) because it had been gathered in faith and obedience to God and according to His orders. And, there were those who didn't believe God and were out early on the Sabbath morning seeking manna. They were surprised to find that there was none (Exodus 16:27). For failing God's test, they went hungry until the next day.

In Exodus 16:28, we find a curious question, posed by God, Himself, *"How long refuse ye to keep my commandments and my laws?"* This inquiry may seem strange because the Mosaic Law was not yet given. Man has, however, been under the law of God, since his earliest days. The first law of God was given to Adam and Woman in the Garden of Eden. It, too, was concerned with man's natural need for food and his spiritual need for discipline. It was recorded in Genesis 2:16 and 17:

> *And the LORD God commanded the man, saying, Of every tree of the garden thou mayest freely eat: But of the tree of the knowledge of good and evil, thou shalt not eat of it: for in the day that thou eatest thereof thou shalt surely die.*

Man broke that law (Genesis 3:6) with disastrous results for himself and all of his descendants, as detailed in 1 Corinthians 15:21 and 22:

> *For since by man came death, by man came also the resurrection of the dead. For as in Adam all die, even so in Christ shall all be made alive.*

Sadly, Adam did it deliberately, as Paul explained in 1 Timothy 2:14, *"And Adam was not deceived, but the woman being deceived was in the transgression."* It was then that God made the first animal sacrifice to get the hides from which man's first clothes were fashioned (Genesis 3:21). Similar sacrifices continued to be made by Adam's son, Abel (Genesis 4:4) and all of the patriarchs who came after.

God's rules and regulations concerning the gathering and eating of manna were the second laws relating to food. It is a law of the universe that, wherever man exists, God will set some standard in his natural realm by which man's spiritual faith and obedience may be tested and determined. Too often, like the children of Israel, man fails that test.

There is much that the maturing child of God may learn from the Israelites and their manna and meat. For example, manna, or bread, in Scripture is always typical of Jesus Christ, as He, Himself, explained in John 6:32, 33, and 35:

> *Then Jesus said unto them, Verily, verily, I say unto you, Moses gave you not that bread from heaven; but my Father giveth you the true bread from heaven. For the bread of God is he which cometh down from heaven, and giveth life unto the world....And Jesus said unto them, I am the bread of life: he that cometh unto me shall never hunger; and he that believeth on me shall never thirst.*

But, Jesus is also the Word of God. It is by this title that He is first introduced by John and presented as the Personification of truth, in John 1:1 and 14:

> *In the beginning was the Word, and the Word was with God, and the Word was God....And the Word was made flesh, and dwelt among us, (and we beheld his glory, the glory as of the only begotten of the Father,) full of grace and truth.*

And, Scripture presents meat as a type of deep, spiritual truth, the spiritual truth of the mature child of God. In 1 Corinthians 3:1 and 2, Paul wrote:

> *And I, brethren, could not speak unto you as unto spiritual, but as unto carnal, even as unto babes in Christ. I have fed you with milk, and not with meat: for hitherto ye were not able to bear it, neither yet now are ye able.*

It is as a type of the Word, the profound spiritual truth of God, that the manna and the quail speak to the maturing child of God and there are many lessons one may learn about spiritual truth from them. Notice, for example, that, although Moses led them through the wilderness, the children of Israel were expected to gather their own manna and quail. In the same way, while the pastor may lead his flock into the truth of God, he is never expected to eat it for them. Each must search out both the manna and the meat (Acts 17:10 and 11). Each must gather for himself all that he can of Christ.

It is also interesting that the manna came in the morning, while the meat came in the evening just as the more easily to be understood spiritual truths, come early in the Christian experience while the more difficult ones, the profound revelations and the deep mysteries, come with maturity, in the evening of the Christian life.

Manna, the type of Christ and His Word, was to be gathered according to specific rules, just as the believer must approach Christ according to the commands given by His Father. Here are a few of those rules and the lessons they teach the maturing believer:

1. Manna was gathered daily (Exodus 16:4), indicating that, to maintain a growing relationship with Christ, it is necessary to partake of Him daily.
2. Manna was gathered in exact portions, according to need (Exodus 16:16 through 18). Jesus is the exact Portion which meets the need of the believer.
3. Failure to gather according to the rules resulted in spoilage and loss (Exodus 16:16 and 17), just as failure to gather more of Christ each day will cause one's relationship with Him to decay and perhaps even be lost.
4. Each was to gather only what he could digest (Exodus 16:18), just as each believer must take care not to try to digest the spiritual truth of another; each must live in the level of spiritual truth God has specified for him.
5. Manna was to be gathered in the morning, <u>before</u> it would be needed (Exodus 16:21), just as the believer must invite Christ into every aspect of his life early in his Christian experience, <u>before</u> the crises of life arise.
6. The gathering of manna, a type of Christ and His Word, was not to be done on the Sabbath (Exodus 16:23). For the believer, the private search for Christ is to be done every day, while the Sabbath is a day to use what has been gathered before and to rest in its blessings, a time to share what has been gathered previously, so that the needs of all can be met.
7. Failure to gather according to the rules will, then as now, result in spiritual hunger (Exodus 16:26 and 27).

Through the manna and quail, God provided all of the food His people would need for all their years in the wilderness. They supplied every vitamin and protein necessary to sustain human life. In the same way, God has provided all of the spiritual nourishment the believer will ever need to safely make the journey from earth to glory.

To commemorate this provision, God ordered that one portion of the miraculous manna be preserved (Exodus 16:32) so that future generations might see for themselves the reality of what God had done for their forefathers. Once the Ark of the Covenant was built, the pot of manna was permanently placed inside of the Ark for safe-keeping. Interestingly enough, for all the centuries that the Ark and its precious cargo remained in the hands of the Israelites, this manna never spoiled. Perhaps this portion of manna remains unspoiled to this day in the Ark's present place of honor in Heaven (Revelation 11:19). Perhaps, one day, the saints will be permitted to view it for themselves.

This memorial is most reminiscent of Communion, whose emblems stand as tangible evidence of all that Jesus has done for His own. In this service, the believer recalls Christ's provision of salvation. This Communion ceremony will continue as a testimony to Christ's death until He returns (1 Corinthians 11:23 through 26).

The testimony of God's marvelous miracles in the life of the believer may also be memorialized, shared with the Body of Christ and future generations of Christians. These testimonies help to build the faith and feed the souls of those who will come after, to help them mature in trust in God's provision and obey His commands, to keep alive the ageless wonder of God's working in behalf of His own.

A River From a Rock Provided

The Israelites continued to follow their Lord's leading through the wilderness of Sin, stopping to make camp at Rephidim, an area of rocky cliffs and a fertile valley near Horeb. It seemed, at first sight, to promise abundance, but sight was deceiving. There was no abundance and there was no water (Exodus 17:1). Again, the children of Israel forgot past provision. Again, they began to murmur and complain against their God-given leader (Exodus 17:2), even violently threatening to stone him in an area where stones seemed to be the only thing in abundance (Exodus 17:4). Again, they looked back longingly to Egypt, the place of their captivity (Exodus 17:3). Again, Moses, the God-appointed mature servant of God, looked to His Lord, instead (Exodus 17:4). And, again, God had still another plan for providing for His people, one that could only be accomplished in accord with His commands, as given to Moses in Exodus 17:5 and 6:

> *And the LORD said unto Moses, Go on before the people, and take with thee of the elders of Israel; and thy rod, wherewith thou smotest the river, take in thine hand, and go. Behold, I will stand before thee there upon the rock in Horeb; and <u>thou shalt smite the rock, and there shall come water out of it</u>, that the people may drink. And Moses did so in the sight of the elders of Israel.*

These elders were not the seventy judges Moses chose to help administer justice in the congregation. They had not yet been appointed. These were the ruling princes of the twelve tribes of Israel who were to represent their families, to observe the miracle of provision God was about to perform, and to report it to their tribesmen, just as the head of the Christian family stands as God's representative in that home and the pastor serves as God's representative to his church. There was much for the elders to report to their kinsmen, too. When Moses struck the rock, a river of water flowed out which was sufficient to satisfy the needs of every member of a congregation perhaps two million strong. It must have been an occurrence which was told and retold, from the eldest to the youngest in the camp, from generation to generation. It is the subject of much Old Testament writing (Deuteronomy 32:13 through 18, 30 and 31, and 37; Job 24:8; Psalm 78:20 and 35; Psalm 92:15; Psalm 94:22; Psalm 101:41; Psalm 114:8; Isaiah 2:10; and Isaiah 48:21). It is a story of the water of life which continues to be told and retold wherever the name of Christ is reverenced since this rock and the water which poured forth from it are clearly identified and explained in 1 Corinthians 10:4:

> *And did all drink the same spiritual drink: for they drank of that spiritual Rock that followed them: and <u>that rock was Christ</u>.*

Jesus, Himself, in John 4:14, identified the water as typical of that which He will give to all who stand upon Him, the smitten Rock:

But whosoever drinketh of the water that I shall give him shall never thirst: but the water that I shall give him shall be in him a well of water springing up into everlasting life.

Since that long-ago day when our Rock was smitten in the judgment halls of Caiaphas and Pilate, since that day when water and blood flowed forth from Calvary, that Rock has followed the believer and poured forth the water of life freely for whosoever will drink. Out of that Rock, a river of life will continue to flow until that day when His children shall stand on the banks of His river of life in Heaven (Revelation 22:1).

In addition, the water speaks of the Holy Spirit, which also flows forth to the believer from the Rock, Christ. In John 7:37 through 39, we read:

In the last day, that great day of the feast, Jesus stood and cried, saying, If any man thirst, let him come unto me, and drink. He that believeth on me, as the scripture hath said, out of his belly shall flow rivers of living water. (But this spake he of the Spirit, which they that believe on him should receive: for the Holy Ghost was not yet given; because that Jesus was not yet glorified.)

Now, the Rock is glorified and has given the Holy Spirit to believers. Out of the life of Christ in them, the Holy Spirit flows in His gifts (1 Corinthians 12:8 through 10) to meet the needs of all. This is the miraculous abundance of Christ, the Rock.

All Provided

God is still in the business of providing all that His people need, so well, in fact, that few ever need to trust Him for every bite of food or every drop of water. The sad truth is, God has provided so consistently that, often, He is taken for granted. No testimony is preserved to be shared with others and no expression of gratitude is given.

But, all of us have needs from time to time, both temporal and spiritual, and we can learn much about faith in God and obedience to Him at such times. In need, do we forget God's past provision? Do we begin to murmur and complain against God's appointed servants? Do we try to rely upon our own human wisdom and effort to meet the need? Or do we simply take our needs to God, trust Him to meet them, and obey His commands in the process?

It is still God's good pleasure to provide for the needs of His own, but He still may use those needs to test their faith, their obedience, and their maturity. God, like the Marine Corps, is looking for a few good men to trust Him and to do it His way, a few good men into whom He may pour His water of life, a few good men and women out of whom the Holy Spirit can flow to a thirsty world.

[1]Herbert Lockyer, *All the Divine Names and Titles in the Bible*, p. 24.

Chapter 9
FIGHTING FAITH'S FOES

Attacked By Faith's Foes

The children of Israel remained at Rephidim, eating of the manna which fell each morning and drinking of the water from the rock, until they were attacked by the Amalekites (Exodus 17:8). Although this attack came shortly after a challenge to God's appointed leadership when it seemed no water was available, it also came on the heels of a great spiritual victory as water flowed from the rock. Again, we find that menacing spiritual attacks often follow immediately after monumental spiritual victories.

The attacking Amalekites were actually blood relatives of the Hebrews. They were descendants of Esau, the brother of Jacob (or Israel) the patriarch of the Israelites, through his grandson, Amalek (Genesis 36:12). Here, we see that the attack on faith may come from within one's own family or from other members of the human family. In addition, this attack typifies the constant state of war which exists between the two natures of the believer for the flesh always has and always will fight against the spirit (Galatians 5:17). And, all such attacks issue from a common source for they symbolize that greater warfare between good and evil, God and Satan, which will perpetually involve the believer in warfare, as Paul warned in Ephesians 6:12:

> *For we wrestle not against flesh and blood, but against principalities, against powers, against the rulers of the darkness of this world, against spiritual wickedness in high places.*

It must also be noted that the attack of the Amalekites was completely unprovoked, just as are all such attacks upon faith. It was motivated by their knowledge that God was working in behalf of His people and their fear of their own destruction at His hands, as reported by the Jewish historian Josephus:[1]

> The...Hebrews began...to be everywhere renowned, and rumours about them ran abroad. This made the inhabitants of those countries to be in no small fear. Accordingly they sent ambassadors to one another, and exhorted one another to defend themselves, and to endeavour to destroy these men. Those that induced the rest to do so...were called Amalekites, and were the most warlike of the nations that lived thereabout...whose kings exhorted one another...to go to this war against the Hebrews; telling them that an army of strangers...lay in wait to ruin them; which army they were...to crush...before they could gather strength, and...perhaps attack them first in a hostile manner...but...those who endeavour to crush a power in its first rise are wiser than those that endeavour to put a stop to its progress when it is become formidable....After they had sent such embassages to the neighbouring nations..., they resolved to attack the Hebrews in battle.

This is exactly the plan Satan employs as he assaults the children of faith: attack the slaves escaped from sin before they have the spiritual strength to attack the satanic strongholds first. It is a battle plan which has resulted in the destruction of far too many children of God who did not recognize their enemy, did not know how to withstand his attacks, and did not understand how to win the battle against him.

The Believer's Battle Strategy

The enemy may have attacked suddenly and without provocation; he may have had an extremely effective battle plan. But, the children of God had a specific spiritually-based strategy which is detailed in Exodus 17:9:

And Moses said unto Joshua, Choose us out men and go out, fight with Amalek: to morrow I will stand on the top of the hill with the rod of God in mine hand.

Notice that this battle plan involved three major strategies. First, the battle was to be fought by the men. Spiritual warfare is the province of the spiritually-mature, the men in the kingdom of God, not the new babe in Christ who is unprepared for this kind of intense spiritual warfare. Second, the battle required standing. When faced with a spiritual battle, the child of God must not fall or faint or flee; he must stand firm to gain the victory as Exodus 14:13 and Ephesians 6:13 and 14 reiterate. Third, the battle was conducted under the rod of Moses, symbolic of his personal authority and that of his miracle-working God. This is the only battle plan which can win spiritual warfare.

Following God's Leaders

God always has His designated leaders who are specially qualified, specially prepared, and specially empowered to win spiritual battles. The names of the chosen warriors in the battle against the Amalekites are listed in Exodus 17:10:

1. **Joshua** - Born in Egypt, his name was the Hebrew form of the Greek name Jesus which meant, "Jehovah is salvation."[2] When he wasn't leading the men of Israel in military campaigns under the direct authority of Moses, he was serving as Moses' personal servant or attendant. Later, following the death of Moses, he would become the new God-appointed leader of all Israel. By name and by profession, he stands as a type of Christ, leading God's people in spiritual warfare, personally serving the Commander-in-Chief.
2. **Moses** - His name meant, "drawn out of the water,"[3] referring to the method of his deliverance from death shortly after his birth. He was born to Jewish parents, reared in the royal palaces of Egypt, nurtured by Pharaoh's own daughter, and educated in the best schools of the day. He was trained in military matters and had served as a commander in the army of Egypt before he cast his lot with his people. He was well-qualified formulate the spiritual battle against Amalek. Here, he stands as a type of God, Himself, directing the strategy to defeat the enemy of His people.
3. **Aaron** - He was the elder brother of Moses whose name may have meant either, "teaching, singing, or messenger."[4] He was his brother's spokesman and later became the first of the Aaronic priests, whose order was named for him. By name and by occupation, he stands as a type of the Holy Spirit, teaching, speaking, singing, and ministering to the people of God.
4. **Hur** - This man, whose name meant, "white or white product,"[5] or "freeborn,"[6] assisted in the execution of the battle strategy in whatever way he could, in this case, just by supporting the efforts of his leader. Having proven himself, he would later be selected to serve with Aaron as one of the elders who governed Israel while Moses communed with God on Mt. Sinai (Exodus 24:14). He may also have been the husband of Miriam. By his name, as one made white, one freeborn in Christ, and by his assignment as a supporting elder, Hur stands as a type of the mature and righteous believer who supports God's program and serves as elder to the elect. Notice that each participant had a particular task to perform in the execution of the battle plan. Moses, as a type of Jehovah God, determined strategy; Joshua, as a type of Christ, executed it; Aaron, as a type of the Holy

Spirit, ministered; and Hur, as a type of the mature man of God, was led by his commander, supporting and serving him. Without any one of them, the outcome of the conflict may have been very different. As clearly illustrated here, successful spiritual warfare will always involve the participation of the entire Trinity with the mature believer, working in concert with each other.

The children of Israel may have been no match for the warlike Amalekites, just as the believer is, in himself, no match for Satan. But, fighting together under the direction of their leaders, the Hebrews overcame their enemies, just as the child of God, acting in concert with his Lord, may gain the victory over Satan.

Unity Brings Victory

Indeed, unity was the key to victory. The warriors, though mature men, could not carry the conflict alone. Whenever the hands of Moses grew heavy and dropped and the warriors could not discern the hand of their leader in the battle, they began to fail before their foes (Exodus 17:11). But, whenever Moses' hands were supported by Aaron and Hur and the hand of the commander was clearly visible, they were able to prevail (Exodus 17:11 and 12). Neither did the leaders, whatever their qualifications and spiritual power, fight the battle alone. Instead, they worked with God's people to win the war just as God fights with His attacked followers to help them achieve success in spiritual warfare. Together, the soldiers of the Lord with God, Himself, as their Commander, are an unbeatable combination. This is symbolized in the fact that Moses was seated upon a stone, typical, in Scripture of man, himself, as 1 Peter 2:5 declares:

> *Ye also, <u>as lively stones</u>, are built up a spiritual house, an holy priesthood, to offer up spiritual sacrifices, acceptable to God by Jesus Christ.*

So, fighting under the authority of God and His appointed leaders, battling according to His strategy, and performing in total unity, the children of God achieved victory in the spiritual warfare imposed upon them by an implacable enemy (Exodus 17:13).

Since Joshua, here, stands as a type of Christ, and the sword can be none other than the sword of His word (Ephesians 6:17 and Revelation 19:15), the ultimate victory of Christ over all of His enemies is clearly previewed here. And, through Christ, all believers are more than conquerors, too. With Jesus as General, with Jesus directing the fray, with Jesus wielding the sword, the child of God cannot be defeated.

The Victory Remembered

God always means for His victories in behalf of His people to be remembered. In this case, the victory was to be memorialized in three important ways, as follows:

1. **By Word.** God told Moses to write a full account of the battle in a book and to retell it often. Such accounts are typical of one's testimony of victory, detailing God's deliverance in spiritual battle, which instructs and encourages all who may enter into spiritual warfare. Moses' testimony became a part of the Book of books and testifies still to all who read it, just as the believer's testimony of victory is meant to be shared with all.
2. **By Worship.** In addition, Moses built an altar, where the God who gave success could be worshipped. Indeed, the Giver of victory in spiritual warfare is to be worshipped as Conqueror and King by His triumphant army.
3. **By Revelation.** Each new victory in God brings a new revelation of God. This battle was no exception. After it, Moses saw God as *Jehovah Nissi*, meaning, "the Lord our Banner."[7] In ancient times, banners identified fighting forces and, often, the mere sight of the banner of an army with a particularly good reputation would send its enemies scurrying

for cover. God meant to be the Banner of His people, identifying Himself to their potential enemies, announcing His own reputation for victory. Marching behind such a Banner, the children of God need never fear defeat.

Future Warfare Predicted

There was a specific reason God revealed Himself as *Jehovah Nissi*, the covenant-keeping God who promises to go before His people into battle as Exodus 17:16 reveals: *"For he said, Because the LORD hath sworn that the LORD will have war with Amalek from generation to generation."* God warned the Israelites that, just because they had won a single battle did not mean that warfare with this enemy was over forever. They would continue the conflict for centuries to come. As a matter of actual historical fact, Israel did not totally annihilate the Amalekites until four hundred and twenty years later, during the reign of King Saul (1 Samuel 15:2 through 35). This continual conflict symbolizes the constant contention between the child of God and Satan. This spiritual warfare has persisted for centuries and will end only when the Lord returns to defeat His foes forever. Until then, one may win each battle as he marches behind the banner of *Jehovah Nissi*, obeys His orders, and conquers according to His commands.

Victory in the Victor

Spiritual warfare is the perpetual lot of the Christian, but the believer can be victorious over all his enemies as Jesus made abundantly clear in John 16:33: "In the world ye shall have tribulation: but be of good cheer; I have overcome the world." While the mature child of God must recognize that he must take his appointed place on the battlefield, he must also remember that his Lord, the same *Jehovah Nissi* Moses met at Rephidim, will give him the victory. He must never forget that the foes of faith may seem overwhelming, but his Lord delights in overcoming them all.

[1]Flavius Josephus, *The Complete Works of Josephus*, Antiquities of the Jews, Book III, Chapter II, Verse 1.

[2]George Barr, *Who's Who in the Bible*, p. 101.

[3]Ibid., p. 122.

[4]Ibid., p. 1.

[5]Ibid., p. 74.

[6]John Ritchie, *From Egypt to Canaan*, p. 78.

[7]Herbert Lockyer, *All the Divine Names and Titles in the Bible*, p. 30.

Chapter 10
COMING INTO THE BODY

The Family Reunited

It is at this point that we learn for the first time that, for the many months Moses had been engaged in the most important events of his life, he had been alone. His wife, Zipporah, and his two sons, had not been there for him. It's possible that Zipporah had been so horrified by the emergency circumcision of her son under the most primitive conditions to prevent God's judgment from falling on her husband (Exodus 4:25 and 26), that she had been unable to go on and Moses had sent her and the boys back to her father's home. Or, perhaps Moses made this decision in order to protect his family from the stress of the confrontation to come. Maybe Zipporah, whose name means, "little bird or sparrow,"[1] an indication of her fragility, just could not continue. The tradition of the Jewish rabbis indicates Moses was acting on the advice of his elder brother, Aaron.[2] In any event, the decision was reached and Moses traveled on alone.

Notice that Moses, a type of Christ, did not force his wife, a type of the Church to continue at his pace, just as Jesus doesn't force the believer to progress faster or further than he can bear. If she were reluctant, she would only have become embittered; if she were fearful, she would only have panicked; if she were angry, she would only have become filled with rage. The Lord permits His children to travel the road to spiritual maturity at their own pace; Moses permitted his wife the same liberty.

Moses was not the only one ever to suffer such rejection and loneliness. Often, when one becomes a deeply committed Christian, family members, even other Christian family members or other members of the church, do not understand or accept the change. They may counsel moderation; they may mock and belittle; they may even withdraw. For a while, at least, the child of God must walk alone. This is no new phenomenon. Perhaps, it is even to be expected. In Galatians 5:11, Paul refers to it as *"the offense of the cross,"* while Peter, in 1 Peter 2:8, calls it *"the offense of Christ."* Whatever the title, it happens, it must be endured in faith, and, in time, it can be resolved. God is, after all, in the business of restoring relationships and reuniting families.

Enter Jethro, the father of Zipporah and the father-in-law of Moses, a man with many names, all significant. He is identified as the priest of Midian (Exodus 3:1), his ancestral name which meant, "strife or contention,"[3] from the name of Midian, the son of Abraham and Keturah, (Genesis 25:2) whom he married after the death of Sarah. So, Midian was of Hebrew stock and Jethro, as his descendant, was of Hebrew blood, too. In the land of Midian, the place where this son of Abraham and his offspring had settled, Jethro was priest to the many descendants of Abraham living there. Jethro was also known by his given name Reuel (Exodus 3:18) or Raguel (Numbers 10:29), which meant, "friend of God."[4] But, the name by which he is most often identified, Jethro, was not a name at all; it was an honorary title of respect, which meant, pre-eminence, excellence[5] or abundance.[6] The meanings of his names say much about this man. For example, while he had come from strife and contention (Midian), he had chosen to become a friend of God, a definite inner change. As a result, he had become pre-eminent in his position, excellent in his profession, and abundant in his prosperity.

In Exodus 18, Jethro symbolizes the Holy Spirit for two reasons. First, he's trusted by Moses, a type of Christ, with the safety and protection of his bride (Exodus 18:2), as the Holy Spirit is trusted with the care and comfort of the Bride of Christ in this world (John 16:7). Second, as soon as Jethro heard that the exodus had occurred, he escorted the bride to her husband (Exodus 18:1 through 6), as the Holy Spirit will accompany the Bride of Christ to the heavenly home of her Husband (Matthew 25:1 through 13).

So, Zipporah was brought to her waiting husband, just as the Church will flee to the waiting arms of Christ on the last day. With her came their two sons, the fruit of their relationship. The elder was Gershom, which means, "a stranger there,"[7] indicating Moses' natural feelings of alienation in Midian, the same feelings Jesus must have often felt as He dwelt on earth, the same feelings common to the child of God in this world. The younger was Eliezer, which meant, "God is my help,"[8] typifying Moses' total dependence on God in his new life, the same dependence Jesus placed in His Father, the same dependence which characterizes the life of the believer. And, a real relationship with the Lord will produce fruit, including those who are won to Christ by the believer's witness. But, it may also result in alienation from this sinful society and a deep dependence on God as the only Source of help for the believer in this world.

The Lord Exalted

Jethro is also seen as a type of the Holy Spirit after his arrival in the camp. He received the honor of Moses, became his confidant, and inspired his testimony of all God had accomplished (Exodus 18:7), just as the Holy Spirit motivates the believer to testify of all God has done for him (Acts 1:8). Notice, that testimony of Moses included all that God had done to Pharaoh, not all that Pharaoh had done to Israel. He mentioned the hardships God's people had endured, but only to illustrate the way in which the Lord had delivered them (Exodus 18:7), just as the Holy Spirit glorifies the Lord (John 16:14), not the enemy or the problems he causes. The Spirit-inspired testimony of the believer will always honor God, not Satan nor the difficulties he causes. Jethro, just as the Holy Spirit testifies of Christ (John 15:26), rejoiced in the Lord and in all He had done (Exodus 18:9) and exalted and blessed Him in Exodus 18:10 and 11:

> *Blessed be the LORD, who hath delivered you out of the hand of the Egyptians, and...the hand of Pharaoh....Now I know that the LORD is greater than all gods: for in the thing wherein they dealt proudly he was above them.*

Then, Jethro worshipped God (Exodus 18:12). Since he was a priest and the Levitic priesthood was not yet established, he was privileged to make offerings to God and was joined in the feasting which followed by Moses and the elders of Israel. Only the Holy Spirit can initiate such a time of feasting on the Lord and His truth among men, as He leads, teaches, feeds, and calls to remembrance all which has been learned (John 14:26).

Guidance Given

Finally, Jethro performed one other function that the Holy Spirit accomplishes in the Body--he gave godly guidance (Exodus 18:13 through 27; John 16:13) concerning the body, the congregation of Israel, which was lacking in one area. There was no order, nor organization, no authority structure. Just as Paul, under the inspiration of the Holy Spirit and in a discourse concerning Him, advised the young Corinthian church, order was necessary to a smoothly functioning body. In 1 Corinthians 14:40, Paul wrote, *"Let all things be done decently and in order."* In this organizational vacuum, Moses was working alone from dawn to dusk trying to answer every question, settle every dispute, and guide every decision in the camp (Exodus 18:15 and 16). Still, the work wasn't getting done for the task of pastoring a congregation of millions was impossible. There wasn't even any time left for family, a natural concern of Jethro since Moses' family consisted of his own daughter and grandsons. As Jethro observed, in Exodus 18:17 and 18:

> *The thing that thou doest is not good. Thou wilt surely wear away...for this thing is too heavy for thee; thou art not able to perform it thyself alone.*

For centuries, the Holy Spirit has issued the warning of Jethro to those who would try to carry out the work of God alone, those who guard their perceived power jealously, those who would endanger their health and neglect their families in the process. For centuries, the Holy Spirit has pointed to a way which is better for the servant of the Lord, for the body he leads, for his family, for all concerned. Just as Paul, under the anointing of the Holy Spirit, designed an organizational plan for the operation of the church at Corinth (1 Corinthians 14:23 through 40), so Jethro, standing as a type of that same Holy Spirit, suggested an organizational plan for Israel (Exodus 18:19 through 23), the church in the wilderness (Acts 7:38). That plan was as follows:

1. **Moses.** As the apostle and acknowledged prophet or spokesman of God (Acts 7:37 and 38), Moses was to lead the people (Exodus 18:19), teach them the laws, statutes, and ordinances of God, show them how to walk in holiness, and oversee them (Exodus 18:20). In addition, while authority may be delegated to others, responsibility cannot be; Moses was to be ultimately responsible for the judgments rendered by those under him in the chain of command (Exodus 18:22). Here, Moses stands, once again, as a type of Christ, the Apostle and Prophet given responsibility for all judgment (John 5:22).
2. **Aaron.** Though not mentioned here, he was second in command. He would be ordained priest (Exodus 28:1) and charged with the tasks of ministering to the Lord, conducting worship (Exodus 32:1), and making all of the sacrifices (Exodus 30:10), all foreshadowing Christ to God's people. He would also serve as pastor or shepherd of God's flock, and, as a type of the Holy Spirit (John 16:12 through 15), tend to their spiritual needs and feed them on the Word of God. He also stands as a forerunner of the pastor, to whom similar responsibility is given in Ephesians 4:11 and 12.
3. **The Elders.** These were carefully chosen men who feared God, loved the truth, and hated greed (Exodus 18:21). They were ordained by the apostle, Moses, and worked under his immediate supervision, recognizing his ultimate authority (Exodus 18:25 and 26). They presided over groups of ten, fifty, one hundred, or one thousand. These first elders were forerunners of the elders of the early church, whose qualifications and duties are detailed in 1 Timothy 3:1 through 7, and to the modern church elders, all of whom were to lead the Body of Christ under the ultimate responsibility of Christ. In Numbers 11:16 and 17, God confirmed the advice of Jethro, determined the exact number of elders to be chosen, and promised to anoint them for the service they were to perform:

> *And the LORD said unto Moses, Gather unto me seventy men of the elders of Israel, whom thou knowest to be the elders of the people, and officers over them; and bring them unto the tabernacle of the congregation, that they may stand there with thee. And I will come down and talk with thee there: and I will take of the spirit which is upon thee, and will put it upon them; and they shall bear the burden of the people with thee, that thou bear it not thyself alone.*

The selection of seventy elders foreshadowed the Sanhedrin, the seventy-man ruling body of Judaism of Jesus' time. The rule of the elders over specific numbers of citizens provided an appeal procedure so that all could be assured of a full hearing and a fair verdict, and so that the elders would have a chain of command through which they might obtain assistance with their cases. The appeal procedure worked this way:

1. **First Step.** Any citizen with a complaint or a question went first to his captain of ten, an elder who was charged with responsibility over the ten families under his control. If the citizen was satisfied with the reply he received, there was no need to proceed further. If, however, he were not satisfied, he had the right of appeal.
2. **Second Step.** The citizen's appeal went to the ruler of fifty, the elder who oversaw fifty families and their five captains. If the citizen was unhappy with the verdict of the appeal judge, he was permitted to take his case to an even higher court.
3. **Third Step.** Next, the citizen could go to the magistrate of one hundred, the designated leader of one hundred families, their ten captains and two rulers. If the citizen was still displeased with the verdict, he proceeded still higher.
4. **Fourth Step.** The citizen next went to the ruler of one thousand, the elder chosen to judge one thousand families, their one hundred captains, twenty rulers, and ten magistrates. A dissatisfied citizen had one further step in the appeal procedure.
5. **Fifth Step.** The last level in the appeal procedure, the "Supreme Court," was Moses. A citizen, or any of the rulers in the chain of command, could refer an unpopular decision or an especially difficult case to him (Exodus 18:26). His verdict was final.

Moses accepted the counsel of Jethro, a type of the guidance of the Holy Spirit, as given and approved by God. He established the exact organizational plan Jethro had suggested. Consequently, he found that the body functioned more smoothly (Exodus 18:26) and his own burden of leadership was lightened considerably (Exodus 18:26).

Often, one in leadership is reluctant to relinquish any aspect of his responsibility. He wonders if others will labor as diligently, care as deeply, or sacrifice as much for the work committed to his trust. When necessity or the leading of the Holy Spirit requires such a surrender of power, however, the leader usually discovers, to his own amazement, that, through the involvement of many hands, the work is given more attention, done with greater concern for detail, and completed more consistently. It is then he discovers that no man is indispensable and that the Body ministry, all believers working together to achieve the Lord's goals, just as the Holy Spirit through the Apostle Paul detailed in 1 Corinthians 12:12 through 27, is really best, after all.

The Realities of Ruling

Being selected to be a judge or an elder of God's own people seems to be a great honor--and it is. But, lest we think it is all power and position, we must consider the commensurate problems and difficulties which the elder might confront in the performance of his daily duties, as well as the stresses on him, on his family relationships and personal friendships, he might encounter as he strives to perform his duties with honesty and integrity.

CASE ONE: Joe Judah claims that Bob Benjamin stole one of his sheep and produces a witness. What verdict should the judge render? Suppose he knows that Joe Judah is wealthy enough to have paid his witness, wealthy enough to spare the sheep, even wealthy enough to destroy his position as judge? Suppose Bob Benjamin is poor and may have been tempted to steal a sheep to feed his family? Suppose Joe Judah is a good friend of the judge? Suppose Bob Benjamin is an even better friend? What will people think if the judge decides in favor of Joe Judah? What will they think if he decides in favor of Bob Benjamin?

CASE TWO: Al Asher's and Larry Levi's ox carts collided on the way to Rephidim. Al says Larry was driving recklessly, while Larry claims that Al was speeding. There were no witnesses to the collision. What should the judge decide? Suppose he knows that Al Asher has a reputation for tipping a few flagons of wine as he drives? Suppose he discovers that Larry Levi's oxen are young and do not yet work well in yoke? Suppose the judge's daughter is engaged to Al Asher's son? Suppose his wife and Larry Levi's wife belong to the same club? What will happen if the judge rules in favor of Al Asher? What will happen if he decides for Larry Levi?

Clearly, the task of serving as a judge in Israel involved a great deal more than met the eye. So, too, does the task of serving as elder in a modern congregation. It isn't always the honor it seems. Consider our third case.

CASE THREE: In a more modern body of Christ, an elder has been selected to judge spiritual gifts in accord with the instructions given by Paul in 1 Corinthians 14:29 and 30. The whole congregation knows that Betty Busybody and Nora Nosy are non-stop gossips. One Sunday, Betty gives a word of knowledge which contains a juicy tidbit about Nora. Not to be outdone, Nora lays a personal prophecy on Betty which reveals a suspect relationship between Betty and a certain deacon, Wally Womanizer. What should the elder do? Suppose he has good reason to believe that both women's revelations are true? Suppose Betty Busybody is the pastor's wife? Suppose Nora Nosy is his mother-in-law? What will people think if he rules against Betty Busybody? What will they think if he decides against Nora Nosy?

The Holy Spirit, now as then, appoints dedicated and devoted elders to govern His people and to relieve the burden of responsibility upon their leader. These elders should meet rigid qualifications and adhere to the strict standards of Scripture in their judgments. Still, theirs is not an easy task. While such an office carries a degree of prestige and power, it has inherent problems, too; while it deserves the honor and respect of the congregation, it should never be sought for that reason. All who are a part of the Body of Christ and governed by the elders of His church, should never envy the elder, but do all within their power to make his task as easy as possible. An elder must be a mature man of God who executes his responsibilities as best he can; the people he serves should maturely accept and follow his leadership, as well.

[1]Herbert Lockyer, *All the Women of the Bible*, p. 168.

[2]Robert Jamieson, A. R. Fausset, and David Brown, *A Commentary Critical, Experimental and Practical on the Old and New Testaments*, Volume 1, p. 347.

[3]Herbert Lockyer, *All the Men of the Bible*, p. 243.

[4]Ibid., p. 288.

[5]Ibid., p. 188.

[6]George Barr, *Who's Who in the Bible*, p. 94.

[7]Ibid., p. 126.

[8]Ibid., p. 101.

Chapter 11
GOD'S RULEBOOK WRITTEN

The People Sanctified

Every parent knows that children need certain things to grow and mature. These include the basics--food, shelter, clothing--and lots of love. Every child needs caring discipline, too, if he is to conform his behavior to reasonable standards. In addition to His other attributes, God is a good Parent. Once His children have come out of slavery to sin, been redeemed, and entered the congregation of God, He begins to discipline them. He does it for the same reason as human parents--for His children's own good. The Lord disciplines them so that they can avoid the pitfalls and penalties of sin, learn to conform their behavior to His eternal standards, grow up in Him, and come to full spiritual maturity.

Discipline involves rules and regulations. When a rule is broken, consequences result and punishment is imposed. A child learns that wrong behavior brings reprimand and right behavior brings reward. It's the process by which people achieve emotional maturity; it's also the process by which every child of God reaches spiritual maturity.

Ever since the Israelites had been redeemed out of captivity, God had cared for them as spiritual newborns, provided for their every need, ignored their tantrums, and carried them all the way. But, God knew His maturing children had to come under His parental discipline. God issued a call for discipline on the first day of the third month (Exodus 19:1), after the Israelites left Rephidim and camped in Sinai (Exodus 19:2), and He issued it to Moses, who had gone into the mountains to meet Him. It was based on the previous experience of His people, on all that He had done to the Egyptians and for Israel (Exodus 19:4). It was also based upon future expectations and contained an awesome offer. But, while God's love for His people is unconditional, like the love of all good parents for their children, many of God's special blessings and covenants are conditional. God's offer and its conditions are in Exodus 19:5 and 6:

> *Now therefore, if ye will obey my voice indeed, and keep my covenant, then ye shall be a peculiar treasure unto me above all people....And ye shall be unto me a kingdom of priests, and an holy nation.*

These same promises are, according to Revelation 1:5 and 6, still available to the obedient child of God:

> *And from Jesus Christ, who is the faithful witness, and the first-begotten of the dead, and the prince of the kings of the earth. Unto him that loved us, and washed us from our sins in his own blood, And hath made us kings and priests unto God and his Father; to him be glory and dominion for ever and ever.*

One can still be a precious treasure that Jesus Christ is willing to purchase with His own blood and become one of His kings and priests. To do it, one must still accept the Lord's discipline and live according to His rules as a mature child of God.

Finally, God's promise was based upon the people's consent (Exodus 19:7 through 9). God did not then and does not now force obedience from His children. He knows outward obedience must be based upon inner conviction, a desire to comply. He knows that, while external conformity might be coerced, inward motivation never can be. So, while God is the Creator and Sovereign of this universe and, as such, has every right to demand

and command compliance, He prefers, instead, that His children obey Him by choice, because they love Him and trust that His laws governing their behavior are best for them.

When Moses relayed the message of God, the children of Israel had an important choice to make--the path of obedience or the road to rebellion. Their answer is recorded in Exodus 19:8, *"And all the people answered together, and said, All that the LORD hath spoken we will do."* Certainly, the children of Israel could not yet comprehend the loftiness of God's Law, the magnitude of their own moral weaknesses, or the severity of God's judgment. But, it is just as certain that their answer came from honest hearts which really wanted to please God. Their acceptance established a legal contract, a covenant, an agreed upon constitution for the kingdom of God.

Each reborn child of God confronts such a moment of decision when faced with the blessings and benefits of serving God and the rules and regulations which condition them. Each must decide to obey God's laws unconditionally or travel the path of carnal Christianity, ungoverned and ungovernable, reaping the terrible tares he sows, incurring the consequences of his actions, enduring God's rebuke rather than enjoying His rewards.

Those who opt to obey God, must set themselves apart from sin (Romans 6) and to God (Psalm 4:3). So, to prepare His people for His personal approach to give them His Law, God ordered a three-day period of cleansing and sanctification (Exodus 19:10 through 25). It takes time to come up to God's standard of holiness and there are no short cuts. During this season of sanctification, strict standards were set. All were to cleanse their clothes (Exodus 19:10), typical of setting apart everything touching both body and soul, just as Zechariah viewed the ceremonial cleansing of Joshua, the high priest, and his clothing (Zechariah 3:1 through 7). Then, before God approached, the Israelites were to place protective boundaries around Mount Sinai so that no one would come too close. No one was to walk within, touch, stray too near (Exodus 19:12 and 13), or even look longingly across those boundaries (Exodus 19:21) just to satisfy their own curiosity. Death would be the result of disobedience. They were even to abstain from sexual activity (Exodus 19:15), a temporary time of celibacy (1 Corinthians 7:5) to end when the sanctification concluded. Destruction awaited those who disregarded any of these directives (Exodus 19:12 and 13).

God has set clear boundaries for His children in His Law. Those who are wise won't seek to violate them or walk near enough to touch sin; they won't see how close they can come to sin's fire without getting burned; they won't even look longingly at sin or those who commit it. They will set themselves completely apart from sin, obeying God's commands, observing the boundaries He has established, separating themselves from their flesh and all of its sinful desires, realizing that those who do not are destroyed. While sanctification sometimes seems synonymous with self-denial, it has its benefits. The Israelites would see God more clearly (Exodus 19:11), witness His wonderful power (Exodus 19:16), and hear His gentle voice (Exodus 19:9). Today's child of God gains the same blessings from sanctification. He, too, will see God more clearly in every aspect of his life, see the power of God against sin, and be more attuned to the still, small voice of God, guiding him along the path to perfection. But, separation must be maintained or destruction will result (Exodus 19:20 through 25).

One can only imagine the scene on the third day, as the awesome power of God was revealed on Mount Sinai in thunder, lightening, earthquake, and a heavy cloud, without which the Israelites may have been blinded. One can only imagine a God so mighty that His voice sounded like a trumpet blast (Exodus 19:16), so holy that, if His people had merely touched the base of the mountain on which His presence rested, or tried to gain a glimpse of Him, they would have been struck dead instantly (Exodus 19:21).

The Law Given

Sanctification completed, the Lord gave His people His Law, by which they could be protected from sin as they grew to perfection. This was not the first Law God had given. As early as in the Garden of Eden, God had established His rule of law (Genesis 2:16 and 17). Then, when that law was broken, in grace, He made the first sacrifice to atone for and cover sin (Genesis 3:21). In addition, most of the covenants God made with the early patriarchs contained conditions which had to be obeyed if the contract was to be enforced. Noah received regulations for boat-building and animal-gathering which had to be followed exactly if he and his family were to be saved (Genesis 6:14 through 22). Abraham had to leave his ancestral home if he wanted his children to inherit Canaan (Genesis 12:1 through 7). Lot had to flee Sodom to realize the rescue God's angels promised (Genesis 19:15 through 17). Then, God had given His people the Passover provisions which had to observed if they were to avoid certain death (Exodus 12:1 through 28). And, He had given them the law of the manna which had to be obeyed to the letter if they were to be fed (Exodus 16:4 through 28).

Clearly, God has always had laws to which He expected His people to conform their conduct. Never before, however, had God placed His various ordinances, statutes, and laws into one, concise statement of His standards. God's children had become the citizens of His kingdom when His grace and mercy freed them from bondage in the kingdom of Egypt (Exodus 20:2); the Law was merely the legal code or constitution of that kingdom. It was practical, providing rules of conduct for every area of human life; it was timeless and would never become outdated; and it was permanent and would never be recalled for revision. Jesus Christ, Himself, confirmed in Matthew 5:17 and 18:

> *Think not that I am come to destroy the law, or the prophets: I am not come to destroy, but to fulfil. For verily I say unto you, Till heaven and earth pass, one jot or one tittle shall in no wise pass from the law, till all be fulfilled.*

That Law is contained in the Mosaic Covenant (Exodus 20:1 through 31:18) and was given in three distinct parts: the Law or the Ten Commandments, the judgments or statutes (Exodus 21:1 through 24:11), and the ordinances or sacrifices (Exodus 24:12 through 31:18). Each revealed a different aspect of God's legal system:

1. **The Law.** The Ten Commandments expressed the will of a righteous God to govern the moral conduct of the Israelites on their wilderness journey and in the land He had promised them. It has two divisions. The first four commandments (Exodus 20:1 through 11), govern man's behavior before God. The last six commandments (Exodus 20:12 through 17), were designed to govern man's moral conduct with all of his fellowmen. In the commandments, God is the Lord of Law and order and of discipline, the God who desires to be the Father of mature children. Just as He drew the line in Eden, commanding the tree be off limits, so He drew the line in the Law, declaring certain conduct prohibited. In both instances, the penalty was spiritual death.

According to Paul in Galatians 3:24, the Law of God also served another, very special purpose, *"Wherefore the law was our schoolmaster to bring us unto Christ, that we might be justified by faith."* God's Law was designed to show man his moral weakness, to cause him to seek forgiveness for his moral failures, and, thereby, to bring him to Christ. The God of the Law ordained it to point man in the direction of His Son. It was given to those saved by the first Passover lamb to turn them towards the last Passover Lamb. Then, His Son condensed the entire Law into two, easily remembered precepts in Matthew 22:37 through 40:

> *Thou shalt love the Lord thy God with all thy heart, and with all thy soul, and with all thy mind. This is the first and great commandment. And the second is like unto it, Thou shalt love thy neighbour as thyself. On these two commandments hang all the law and the prophets.*

Just after the Ten Commandments had been given, revealing their sinful natures to them, God's people reacted to the reality of the presence of God atop the mountain and made this very human request of Moses in Exodus 20:19: *"Speak thou with us, and we will hear: but let not God speak with us, lest we die."* The Law often causes the child of God to turn away from Him in fear, but this isn't God's intent. He gave the Law to help His people live in a way that would bring them into His presence and into a personal relationship with Him. This concept is even clearer under the covenant of grace. While the Law inspires fear and motivates man's desire for a mediator to stand between himself and God, grace inspires love and provides that personal Mediator, Christ Jesus.

At the end of the Law, God gave specific orders about building altars. They were to be made of earth or uncut stone. These substances had been made by God, not man, and were not to be improved upon by man. In Scripture, both substances were typical of an aspect of man. The earth was typical of man's body, which had been formed of the red dust of Eden (Genesis 2:7), the earth in which God's will in this world is to be performed (Matthew 6:10). The stone was symbolic of man's soul upon which God would one day write His laws (Deuteronomy 10:1 through 3; Jeremiah 31:33; Romans 2:15). In Scripture, it is the tree that typifies man's spirit, that part of man which is spiritually reborn at the moment of salvation, that part of man which communicates with God (Deuteronomy 20:19; Psalm 1:1 through 3; Proverbs 11:30).

Clearly, God meant for man to be His altar upon which the blood of the final Sacrifice could be poured out and who would willingly sacrifice the life of his flesh for life in the Spirit. Every mature child of God must strive to be such an altar, created by God, untouched by human improvements, dedicated to the service of God. Such an altar, such a believer, will have the very name of God placed upon him and will experience the blessings of God in every aspect of his life (Exodus 20:24).

2. **The Judgments or Statutes.** This codicil to the contract (Exodus 21:1 through 24:11) amplified and explained the Law by dealing with specific situations of everyday life. It was given to govern the social and business life of Israel, according to the legal, moral, and ethical standards of God. Every area of life was regulated, such diverse subjects as slavery, murder, disobedience to parents, kidnapping, assault and battery, injuries to others, the responsibilities of animal owners, larceny, carelessness with the property of others, borrowed property, rape, witchcraft, bestiality, idolatry, oppression of others, lending with interest, rebellion against government, sanctification of the firstborn and firstfruits, perjury, treatment of enemies, treatment of the poor, bribery of officials, the Sabbath, and faithfulness to God, etc. It is a legal system which has clearly stood the test of time. With the Ten Commandments, the judgments and statutes have provided the basis for many of the legal systems that still survive today. Through them, God is seen, not as a remote Deity unconcerned with the conduct of His creation, but as the hovering, overshadowing Creator, involved in every aspect of the lives of His people, interested in governing everything which touched their lives, the benevolent Master who set the standards and made the rules, but

only for the ultimate good of the people He loved so much. In addition, it is in the judgments and statutes that the three major feasts of Israel are listed for the first time and commands for their observance are given:

The Feast of Unleavened Bread or Passover (Exodus 23:15). This feast was to be held each year to celebrate the deliverance from Egypt on the first Passover night. It also foreshadowed another, future Passover when the final, perfect sacrificial Lamb would be slain to provide eternal deliverance for His children.

The Feast of Harvest, Firstfruits, or Pentecost (Exodus 23:16). Fifty days after Passover, God's people were to gather to praise God for the first of the wheat harvest. According to Jewish tradition, the Law was given on the fiftieth day of freedom, the fiftieth day after the first Passover, on Pentecost, which means, "fifty,"[1] It was originally called the Feast of Weeks (Deuteronomy 16:9 through 11) or First-Fruits (Numbers 28:26) and celebrated the beginning of the annual harvest. Later, it became a joint celebration of both the harvest and the giving of the Mosaic Law. The feast foreshadowed another Day of Pentecost on which God's people, the wheat of His fields, would be filled with His Holy Spirit. Among His many other tasks would be the conversion of that wheat, the life of the believer, into Bread, the life of Christ.

The Feast of Ingathering (Exodus 23:16). Later in the year, God's people were to celebrate the completed harvest of all crops and to recall the years of wandering when they had no fields to plant, no harvest to gather. It also looks forward to a final harvest when the Lord will return to reap His fields on earth, when all believers will end their wandering in this world and be gathered to Him forever.

These three significant and symbolic feasts were to be celebrated each year without fail, and Jews from all over world were to come God's center of worship (first, the tabernacle, later, Shiloh, and, finally, Jerusalem) to celebrate before God (Exodus 23:17).

The true child of God never forgets, never fails to celebrate, the three most important occasions in his spiritual life--the day he was born again, redeemed from sin and rescued from bondage by the Lamb (his personal Passover), the day he was filled with the Spirit of God (his personal Pentecost), and the day his Lord will return to receive him into Heaven (his personal Ingathering). No matter where he lives or where he goes, these three days serve as the major milestones of his life in God.

3. **The Ordinances or Sacrifices.** The Law, as given in the Ten Commandments and the statutes, was impossible for man to keep because of his sinful human nature. While the Law set the standard by which man was to live, it did nothing to alter man's nature or his heart, as Paul explained in Romans 8:3:

> *For what the law could not do, in that it was weak through the flesh, God sending his own Son in the likeness of sinful flesh, and for sin, condemned sin in the flesh.*

God knew man would break the Law and established a system of sacrifices in the ordinances to deal with man's sin and provide a basis for a personal relationship with God. There was a specific sacrifice designed to cover every situation, every sin. Where the Law showed man his moral failure and the judgments showed man his ethical failure, the sacrifices gave man a covering for his failures, an atonement for his sin, a route of approach to his God. They also foreshadowed the Messiah since every aspect of every sacrifice was an allegory of the Christ, the promised Redeemer. These are the sacrifices as detailed in the Book of Leviticus:

1. **Burnt Offering** - Leviticus 1:1 through 17. A male animal without blemish was used (Leviticus 1:5 and 11), its blood was sprinkled (Leviticus 1:8, 12, and 17) to make atonement for sin. It typifies Christ, who was without spot and was killed upon a wooden cross to make atonement for the sin of all mankind (Hebrews 9:13 and 14).

2. **Meat (meal) Offering** - Leviticus 2:1 through 16. This offering was composed of flour symbolizing the humanity of Christ, oil, typical of the Spirit, and frankincense, a metaphor for His priestly nature (Leviticus 2:1 and 16). It was to be made into unleavened cakes, typifying Christ, the Bread of Life (John 6:35).

3. **Peace Offering** - Leviticus 3:1 through 17. This offering was made using a male or female animal without blemish (Leviticus 3:1), which was to be killed (Leviticus 3:2, 8, and 13), its blood sprinkled (Leviticus 3:2, 8, and 13), and sacrificed upon wood (Leviticus 3:5). The need for this sacrifice typified the state of war between sinful man and God which is ended by Christ, our Peace with God, (Ephesians 2:12 through 16).

4. **Sin Offering** - Leviticus 4:1 through 35. This offering used a bullock without blemish (Leviticus 4:3, 23, 28, and 32) which was to be killed (Leviticus 4:4, 15, 24, 29, 33), its blood sprinkled (Leviticus 4:6 and 17) and poured out (Leviticus 4:7, 18, 25, 30, and 34), to make atonement for the sins of ignorance, sins committed unknowingly. It typifies Christ whose blood atones for the mistakes of the child of God (Hebrews 10:14).

5. **Trespass Offering** - Leviticus 5:1 through 6:7. This offering used a sheep without blemish (Leviticus 5:15, 18; 6:6) whose blood was to be sprinkled (Leviticus 5:9) and poured out (Leviticus 5:9) to make atonement for one's trespasses against others. This offering typifies the fellowship of believers in the shed blood of Jesus Christ which remains unbroken as slights one may commit against another are forgiven (1 John 1:7).

6. **Heave or Wave Offering** - Leviticus 7:28 through 36. This offering used the breast of the animal. It was not burnt, but lifted up before God, then given to the priest for his use, typifying Christ who was lifted up on the cross (John 8:28 and 12:32 and 33).

In the ordinances and sacrifices, God is revealed as the divine Originator who established a system whereby man might atone for his sin and come into the presence of God, a system allegorical of the offering of the final Sacrifice. It originated with God who loved so much that He gave. Having foreshadowed the final sacrifice, the day would come when He would give the final Sacrifice, too (John 3:16).

The Covenant Accepted

God stated His terms for the contract; then His people had to decide if they wanted to be His kings and priests enough to accept His terms and attempt to live by them. The way the contract was ratified was four-fold. First, came worship. Moses, the only one permitted to approach God; Aaron, the priest, and the elders, the judges chosen in Exodus 18:25, led in worship (Exodus 24:1 and 2). Worship, where man acknowledges who God is and pays homage, begins all transactions with God. Second, came acceptance of the terms of the contract, exactly as God had given them, as recorded in Exodus 24:3:

> *And Moses came and told the people all the words of the LORD, and all the judgments: and all the people answered with one voice, and said, All the words which the LORD hath said will we do.*

Based on acceptance, the contract was put in writing as Moses, God's legal representative, wrote it in a book. To be sure the people understood everything to which they were agreeing, Moses read the covenant aloud one last time and had them repeat their acceptance. He also built a monument of twelve pillars, one for each of the twelve tribes, as a permanent memorial (Exodus 24:4). Next, the contract was sealed in blood, the blood of sacrifices made by Moses on the altar he erected. This blood was sprinkled on the people as a permanent reminder of the contract to which they were now consenting parties with Jehovah God, Himself (Exodus 24:4 through 8). Then, the contract was concluded with a banquet at which Moses, Aaron, Nadab, Abihu, and the seventy elders of Israel saw God and were privileged to eat and drink with Him in Person (Exodus 24:10 and 11). This was according to Middle Eastern custom in which one never ate with his enemies; a peace treaty between friends, however, was concluded with just such a banquet. It also foreshadowed the New Testament provision of peace with God through acceptance of His Sacrifice, Christ, and observance of the commands of God (Romans 5:1). Finally, a permanent record was made of the contract. While Moses had written every command in a book, books can get lost or torn and their writing fades with time. To prevent such problems, God, Himself, would carve two tablets of stone and write His Law with His own hand (Exodus 24:12). In this permanent form, the Law would not be subject to the forgetfulness of man and it would always be there to provide guidance for God's people. Later, those tablets would be permanently stored in the Ark of the Covenant.

The Law Still Stands

God's Law was not addressed to the Jews, alone, nor was it lost to history. The Law is still the instructor which reveals man's sin and brings him to Christ for salvation (Galatians 3:24). God's Law is still a personal contract between the believer and his Lord, the only valid standard for holy living for every child of God. That's why God saw to it that His Law was recorded, preserved, and made a permanent part of His Word.

Grace, which was extended to the believer through Jesus, did not do away with God's moral Law, for He is an unchangeable God, as Jesus made crystal clear in Matthew 5:17. Salvation by grace simply enables the believer to live according to the Law. Under the Law, God's people obeyed out of fear--fear of God and fear of His judgment, but, under grace, the child of God now lives a holy life out of love--love of God and love of His Son who provides salvation (Exodus 20:6). Grace gave the believer a different sacrifice, too. Under the Law, millions of animals were killed to atone for sin and to foreshadow Christ. But, Jesus fulfilled the types contained in the offerings of the Law when He became the final Sacrifice to atone for the sins of all of God's children, for all time.

Today, most believers know from memory at least part of the moral Law of God, the part we have titled the Ten Commandments, but do we truly live according to this contract God has made with His people? Consider.

1. God has said His people must have no other gods before Him (Exodus 20:3). But, is it possible to make gods of family, friends, or even the pastor of the church? Consider.
2. God has said that His people must not have any idols (Exodus 20:4). But, can money, material things, even the church become idols in their lives? Consider.
3. God has said that His people must not take His name in vain (Exodus 20:7). Does this include the occasional slip or friendships with those who curse? Does it include watching movies, video tapes, TV programs, etc., which include such speech? Consider.
4. God has said that His people must keep His Sabbath (Exodus 20:8). But, does this include such activities as mowing lawns, washing cars, shopping, or attending or participating in sports contests and activities on the Sabbath? Does it include occupations which require work to be performed on the Sabbath? Consider.

5. God has said that parents must be honored (Exodus 20:12). Do today's Christian parents fulfill their responsibility to rear their children to know and love God? Do today's children respect their parents' God-given authority? How is the adult Christian to deal with his elderly parents? Consider.

6. God has said that His people must not kill (Exodus 20:13). Does this command cover "killing" the reputation of a brother in Christ through gossip? Does it include the endangering of life with such activities as speeding, etc? What about abortion? Consider.

7. God has said that His people are not to commit adultery (Exodus 20:14). If any kind of sex, except the loving sexual relationship between a husband and wife is forbidden by God, what must the believer's attitude be toward premarital sex or couples living together? What position must the believer take toward homosexuality? Consider.

8. God has said that His people must not steal (Exodus 20:15). Does this include things like library books, money, etc., which have been borrowed but not returned or items which may have been found but for which no attempt has been made to find the rightful owner? Does it include paper clips, pencils, etc., brought home from the office? Consider.

9. God has said that His people must not bear false witness (Exodus 20:16). Does this include passing along gossip which may or may not be true and which may damage a reputation? Does it include failing to correct a false impression? Does it include the "little white lie" meant to protect the feelings of others? Consider.

10. God has said that His people must not covet (Exodus 20:17). Does this prohibit envying the material possessions of others? Does it include the all-American desire to "keep up with the Joneses?" How could breaking this command lead the believer to break others? Consider.

[1]Pat Alexander, *The Lion Encyclopedia of the Bible*, p. 120.

Chapter 12
THE TABERNACLE OF GOD

The Sanctuary

Every child of God needs a sanctuary where he can get away from the terrible turmoil of life to be alone with the Lord. God knew His church in the wilderness would need a sanctuary, too. He had also promised He would dwell among His people. To keep that promise, He planned a place for His presence where He could approach them and they could approach Him. So, when Moses went to the mountain to receive the Law written in stone, God also gave him detailed directions for a Tabernacle, the place where His people could worship Him and make their sacrifices, the place where He could dwell among the children He loved so much. Those directions are recorded in chapters twenty-five through twenty-seven of Exodus and begin with this simple command of God to Moses in Exodus 25:8: *"And let them make me a sanctuary; that I may dwell among them."* "Sanctuary," is from the Hebrew root, *qadesh*, which means, "apartness, holiness, sacredness,"[1] often translated, sanctify or sanctification. Here, it's the Hebrew, *miqdash*, meaning, a holy place, a sanctuary, a chapel, or a hallowed place."[2] It was a meeting place set apart from the world and for God. It was also called the Tabernacle, from the Hebrew, *mishkan*, which meant a temporary, portable sanctuary, the tent that was the place set apart. Centuries later, when a permanent structure was built, it was known as the Temple, from the Hebrew, *hekal*, meaning, "a palace,"[3] also called a dwelling place from the Hebrew, *shebet*, which meant, "a seat or dwelling,"[4] indicating a fixed habitation.

The blueprints for the Tabernacle included plans for the structure, its furnishings, and the implements required for its functioning. No detail was omitted and not one aspect was left to man's logic (Exodus 25:9). Every part of the pattern was to be executed exactly since, aside from being the meeting place of God and man on earth and the place of sacrifice by which man approached God, each detail would carry two typological meanings important to all of God's people, then and now. First, the Tabernacle and everything in it was typical of Christ, as the writer of Hebrews noted in Hebrews 8:2 and 9:11 and 12:

> *A minister of the sanctuary, and of the true tabernacle, which the Lord pitched, and not man....But Christ being come an high priest of good things to come by a greater and more perfect tabernacle, not made with hands...not of this building; Neither by the blood of goats and calves, but by his own blood he entered in once into the holy place, having obtained eternal redemption for us.*

Clearly, only because Jesus willingly entered into a temporary Tabernacle, a human Body God had prepared for Him, could He offer the final sacrifice for sin and obtain redemption for all who accepted it. Every material from which the Tabernacle was constructed, every color, every design, spoke of Christ, His divinity, His humanity, and His sacrifice. Entire books have been written about the Tabernacle's symbolism, books profitable for the maturing believer. No single chapter of this work could duplicate all of the divine truths revealed in them. Here, however, is the briefest glimpse of some of the symbolism to be found in the Tabernacle, to whet the reader's appetite:

1. **The Tabernacle** (Exodus 25:8 and 27:9 through 21). It had three sections--the Outer Court, the Holy Place, and the Holy of Holies--just as Jesus was a Member of the Trinity,

the Father, Son, and Holy Spirit, and just as, in His incarnation, He was composed of three parts--body, soul, and spirit. The Outer Court is also symbolic of man's body. It is lit by natural light or life and is, according to Romans 12:1, the place of sacrifice:

> *"I beseech you therefore...by the mercies of God, that ye present your bodies a living sacrifice, holy, acceptable unto God, which is your reasonable service."*

Man's soul is symbolized by the Holy Place which is lit by the oil lamp (Exodus 27:20 and 21) and is the place of prayer and worship, just as the soul receives light from the Holy Spirit and is the part of man from which prayer and worship come, as seen in Luke 1:46: *"And Mary said, My soul doth magnify the Lord."* The Holy of Holies typifies man's spirit. With no provision made to light it, it would remain forever darkened unless lit by God, Himself, just as man's spirit remains dead until God lights it, as John 1:4 states, *"In him was life; and the life was the light of men."* And, this redeemed, reborn, and relit tabernacle of man is to be the Temple of the Holy Spirit, as 1 Corinthians 3:16 and 17 declares:

> *"Know ye not that ye are the temple of God, and that the Spirit of God dwelleth in you? If any man defile the temple of God, him shall God destroy; for the temple of God is holy, which temple ye are."*

In 1 Corinthians 6:19 and 20, he said, *"What? know ye not that your body is the temple of the Holy Ghost which is in you?"* Finally, in 2 Corinthians 6:16, we read, *"And what agreement hath the temple of God with idols? for ye are the temple of the living God...."*

You see, God created man in His own image (Genesis 1:27). Since God is a Trinity, He made man a trinity, too. Man's spirit was to commune with God and receive His commands; his soul, the seat of intellect, emotions, and will, was designed to make decisions based on that communion; and the body, the physical part of man which combines the five senses with mobility, was designed to carry out those decisions. In Eden, God communicated with man through spirit and commanded that he never eat of the tree of the knowledge of good and evil (Genesis 2:17). Man and Woman considered this command and decided to disobey it in their souls. Their bodies simply carried out that decision (Genesis 3:6). Now, God had already set a death penalty on sin (Genesis 2:17) and He did not lie or change His mind. Oh, man's body didn't die immediately; it lived on outside the garden (Genesis 3:23) where it still had five senses and the ability to move. Physical death would come later as a further result of sin for, although Adam and Woman had been prohibited from eating the fruit of the tree of the knowledge of good and evil, they were not refused access to the tree of life until after they committed sin (Genesis 3:22). Neither did man's soul die; he still possessed his intellect, his emotions, and his stubborn will. Eternal death of the soul only awaits unregenerate man, as his soul is forever separated from God and condemned to Hell for all the ages of eternity. But, man's spirit did die that day. Man could no longer have that close communion with God. At the moment of salvation, however, man's dead spirit is born again, personal communication with God is restored, he can make his decisions based on it, and he can live his life according to God's will. Death is defeated forever. Jesus told Nicodemus about this transformation in John 3:3 and 5 through 7:

> *Jesus...said unto him, Verily, verily, I say unto thee, Except a man be born again, he cannot see the kingdom of God....Jesus answered...Except a man be born of water and of the Spirit, he cannot enter into the kingdom of God. That which is born of the flesh is flesh; and that which is born of the Spirit is spirit. Marvel not that I said unto thee, Ye must be born again.*

A Scripture search, using the words, Tabernacle, Sanctuary, Temple, and Dwelling, shows just how God brings man, typified by the Tabernacle, from sin to maturity in Christ:

The tabernacle of the wicked.

a. Job 18:5 through 21 - man's need of salvation from sin and deliverance from bondage.
b. Psalm 79:1 through 9 - Satan in control; deliverance needed.
c. Ezekiel 44:7 and 8 - Satan in charge, polluting God's Sanctuary.
d. Psalm 74:3 - Satan doing wickedly in God's Sanctuary.
e. Isaiah 63:18 - God's Sanctuary trodden down by the enemy.
f. Leviticus 20:3 - God's Sanctuary given over to Satan and defiled.
g. Jeremiah 10:20 - God's Sanctuary spoiled by the enemy.
h. Psalm 78:58 through 60 - the defiled Tabernacle forsaken by God.
i. Lamentations 2:4 - God's judgment executed.
j. Isaiah 66:6 - God's enemies repaid.
k. Hosea 9:6 - the defiled Sanctuary left desolate.

The call to God.

a. Job 11:14 - call not to allow wickedness into the Tabernacle.
b. Job 22:23 - call to put iniquity out of God's Tabernacle.
c. Joshua 22:19 - call to come to God.
d. Zechariah 6:12 through 15 - Lord's promise to build His Temple--if man will obey.
e. Malachi 3:1 - the Lord will come to those who seek Him.
f. Ezekiel 37:23 - God promises to save and to cleanse.
g. Jeremiah 30:17 and 18 - God promises healing and mercy.

The transition from sin to salvation.

a. Psalm 43:1 through 3 - one's need and a cry for deliverance.
b. 2 Samuel 22:7 - the Lord hears the cry of distress.
c. Ezekiel 37:26 through 28 - covenant of peace made and Sanctuary created within.
d. Ezekiel 44:27 - the Lord enters in to minister.
e. Matthew 21:12 through 16 - Jesus cleanses and heals spiritual babes.
f. Psalm 68:21 through 24 - God seen in sanctuary and enemies wounded.
g. 2 Kings 11:10 through 16 - king's son crowned in the Temple, the Temple defended, and the adversary slain.
h. John 5:14 - the command to sin no more in the Temple.

The Christian life in God's Temple.

a. Job 5:24 - peace with God and free from sin.
b. John 7:28 and Matthew 26:55 - Jesus teaches in the Temple.
c. Zechariah 8:9 - the Temple built up by the words of the prophets.
d. Psalm 15:1 through 5 - God's criteria for abiding in His Tabernacle.
e. Psalm 61:4 - the choice is made to accept God's criteria and abide.
f. Psalm 84:1 and 2 - God's Tabernacle is a nice, amiable place to live.
g. Psalm 65:4 - God's Temple is a blessed dwelling.
h. Proverbs 14:11 - the upright will flourish.
i. Psalm 48:9 - the lovingkindness of God is in the midst of His Temple.
j. Acts 2:46 and 47 - one accord reaches the lost.

The Holy Spirit's activity in God's Temple.

a. Isaiah 6:1 - fills the Temple.
b. Isaiah 4:5 - lightens and defends.
c. Micah 1:2 - witnesses to the whole earth.
d. Psalm 46:4 - a river flowing out.
e. Ezekiel 47:1 - waters which issue forth.

Worship in God's Temple.

a. Psalm 29:9 - testifying of God's glory.
b. Psalm 150:1 - praising.
c. Psalm 118:15 - rejoicing.
d. Psalm 27:4 through 6 - safety and sacrifices of joy.
e. Psalm 134:2 - lifting hands (the universal sign of surrender).
f. Psalm 132:7 - worshipping.
g. Psalm 63:1 and 2 - seeing God.
h. Habakkuk 2:20 - earth (flesh) silenced.

Divine testing in God's Temple.

a. Psalm 11:4 and 5 - the Lord tries His own.
b. Joshua 22:29 - the choice is made not to rebel against God.
c. Psalm 20:2 - help and strength are sent.
d. Psalm 96:6 - the final state is strength and beauty.

Now, let's continue our examination of the various materials God ordered to be used in His Tabernacle:

2. **The Metals** (Exodus 25:3) - only three metals were permitted to be used:
    a. Brass - typical of judgment.
    b. Silver - symbolic of redemption.
    c. Gold - speaks of divinity.
3. **The Colors** (Exodus 25:4) - only three colors were permitted:
    a. Blue - typical of Christ's heavenly origins.
    b. Red or scarlet - typical of the blood of Christ.
    c. Purple - typical of the royal majesty of Christ.
4. **Fine Linen** (Exodus 25:4 and 26:1 through 6) - speaks of purity and righteousness.
5. **Animal Skins** (Exodus 25:5 and 26:7 through 14) - recalled the first sacrifices God made for Adam and Woman (Genesis 3:21), foreshadowing the future sacrifice of Christ.
6. **Shittim or Acacia Wood** (Exodus 25:5 and 26:15 through 27) - symbolic of the humanity of Christ.
7. **Oil** (Exodus 25:6) - typical of the Holy Spirit.
8. **Precious Stones** (Exodus 25:7) - represented the twelve tribes of Israel from which the Jesus came and over which He will reign.
9. **The Ark** (Exodus 25:10 through 16) - typical of the life of Christ.
10. **The Mercy Seat** (Exodus 25:17 through 22) - represented both Christ and Calvary.
11. **The Table of Shewbread** (Exodus 25:23 through 30) - typical of Jesus as the Bread of life (John 6:48).
12. **The Golden Candlestick** (Exodus 25:31 through 40) - symbolic of Christ, the light of the world (John 8:12), and of the enlightenment of the Holy Spirit, which Jesus promised all who believed (John 14:26).
13. **The Veil** (Exodus 26:36 and 37) - speaks of the incarnation of Christ in human flesh (Hebrews 10:20), the veil through which man must approach the holy presence of God.

14. **The Brazen Altar** (Exodus 27:1 through 8) - typical of the Jesus as both the Altar and the Sacrifice on it.

It is easy to see why God gave Moses such intricate instructions for the Tabernacle. No wonder God commanded His people to contribute the materials for building it willingly (Exodus 25:2 through 7), since God never forces His divine construction program on man; no wonder He reserved the right to act as divine Architect, setting the pattern and preparing the plans (Exodus 25:9), for only He knows how to build a sound structure within man. Paul noted these building principles in 1 Corinthians 3:9 through 15:

> *For we are labourers together with God: ye are God's husbandry, ye are God's building. According to the grace of God which is given unto me, as a wise masterbuilder, I have laid the foundation, and another buildeth thereon. But let every man take heed how he buildeth thereupon. For other foundation can no man lay than that is laid, which is Jesus Christ. Now if any man build upon this foundation gold, silver, precious stones, wood, hay, stubble; Every man's work shall be made manifest...because it shall be revealed by fire; and the fire shall try every man's work of what sort it is. If any man's work abide which he hath built thereupon, he shall receive a reward. If any man's work shall be burned, he shall suffer loss: but he himself shall be saved; yet so as by fire.*

So, God's children must build their tabernacles on the foundation He has laid, according to His divine plan, and using His building materials. No other foundation, no other plan, no other materials are acceptable; none will form a fit dwelling for His Spirit and none will make a Temple worthy of the blessings He promised in Exodus 25:8 and 22:

> *And let them make me a sanctuary; that I may dwell with them....And there will I meet with thee, and I will commune with thee.*

The Priest of God

Every sanctuary needs a priest to conduct worship. In chapters twenty-eight through thirty of Exodus, God gave instructions for the ordination, garments, and duties of His priests. This title comes from the Hebrew, *kohen*, which refers to the principal officer or chief ruler, the priest. While it seems an exalted title, from the outset, God ordained that the task of this principal officer, chief ruler, and priest, was to minister (Exodus 28:1), from the Hebrew, *sharat*, meaning, to serve. The priest is comparable to the modern pastor, whose title indicates a shepherd caring for sheep. While a church leader, he, too, is to serve, to minister--first, to God, then, to the sheep, the Christians in his care. Beware of the pastor-priest who wishes to make all decisions for every member of the congregation, who wishes to be served rather than to serve. As the first priest, God selected Aaron, the elder brother of Moses and his second in command. It was a hereditary office which would pass to his sons after him (Exodus 28:1). Although Aaron was to be in authority in the Tabernacle, he was still under the authority of Moses, the apostle of God to Israel and the man who was to ordain him, in all other things.

Next, God gave instructions for the priestly garments for Aaron (Exodus 28:2 through 43), garments that were holy--sanctified or set apart for this use alone, not the drab attire of mourning, but bright and beautiful clothes that would glorify God. And, there was a garment, a covering, for every part of the body, illustrating God's provision for every area of the priest's life. The watchword on the garments was "HOLINESS TO THE LORD" (Exodus 28:36), symbolizing the priests' separation for service to God.

God also prescribed a seven-day plan of ordination for His priests (Exodus 29:1 through 37). They were to be ceremonially bathed, a type of water baptism (Exodus 29:4; Acts 22:16) and dressed in their priestly robes, symbolic of putting on Christ (Exodus 29:5 and 6; Galatians 3:27). Next, the priests were to be anointed with oil, symbolic of the infilling of the Holy Spirit (Exodus 29:7; Acts 2:17 and 18). Specific sacrifices were to be offered, foreshadowing all aspects of the final sacrifice of Christ (Exodus 29:10 through 28; Hebrews 9:13 and 14). Finally, the priests were to be consecrated. This is not the same word usually translated, consecrate, sanctify, or hallow; the term translated, "consecrate," "consecration," and "consecrated" in this passage is the Hebrew, male, meaning, to fill or to be full. It is used to indicate filling, such as filling the hand, and signifying being filled or equipped for service (Exodus 29:29 through 37; Acts 1:8).

God's instructions for priests included a list of their duties (Exodus 29:38 through 42; Exodus 30:1 through 38). First and foremost was the task of making required sacrifices (Exodus 29:38 through 41), each pointing to Christ. They were also to serve continually (Exodus 29:42) in perpetual prayer, symbolized by the altar of incense (Exodus 30:1 through 10; 1 Thessalonians 5:17; Revelation 8:3 and 4); in perpetual ministry of redemption, typified by the collection of the ransom offerings (Exodus 30:11 through 16; Hebrews 9:12); in perpetual cleansing, seen in the brass laver (Exodus 30:17 through 21; Ephesians 5:26); in perpetual anointing, typified in the anointing oil (Exodus 30:22 through 33; Acts 2:4); and in perpetual praise portrayed in the incense (Exodus 30:34 through 38; Psalm 34:1).

Once the directions for priests were obeyed, God promised in Exodus 29:43 through 46, that blessings would be poured out since blessing always follows obedience. Then, God signed the contract. *"I am the LORD their God,"* Jehovah, their Elohim, He said.

> *And there I will meet with the children of Israel, and the tabernacle shall be sanctified by my glory. And I will sanctify the tabernacle of the congregation, and the altar: I will sanctify also both Aaron and his sons to minister to me in the priest's office. And I will dwell among the children of Israel, and will be their God. And they shall know that I am the LORD their God, that brought them forth out of the land of Egypt, that I may dwell among them: I am the LORD their God.*

This priesthood was to stand as type of three coming priesthoods, each ordained of God. First, it foreshadowed the Priesthood of Jesus, as Hebrews 8:1 records, *"We have such an high priest, who is set on the right hand of the throne of the Majesty in the heavens."* Christ, as our High Priest, was ordained by God, (Hebrews 1:1 through 3), just as Aaron was ordained by Moses; He ministered to the Lord (Hebrews 8:2), just as Aaron ministered to God. As Aaron was under the delegated authority of Moses, so Jesus, during His earthly ministry, exercised the delegated authority of God (Matthew 28:18). Also, just as Aaron had specific duties, so Jesus Christ came in the flesh to conduct worship, prayer, and praise (Matthew 6:9 through 13), to offer Himself as sacrifice (Hebrews 8:3 and 9:14), and to serve as the Shepherd of God's flock (John 10:11). The Aaronic priesthood also typifies the modern pastor-priest. As Aaron was ordained by God's apostle, so the pastor is ordained by a representative of God, ordained to minister to the Lord first, then to God's people. He exercises the delegated authority of Christ, as Aaron exercised the delegated authority of Moses in his absence (Exodus 24:12 through 14). He, too, like Aaron, must perform certain duties. He must conduct prayer, praise, and worship; he must offer sacrifice by presenting the final, perfect Sacrifice of Christ to his congregation; he must tend the flock of God which is placed in his care (Jeremiah 23:1 through 4), feeding them the nourishing spiritual food of God's Word (Jeremiah 3:15). Then, once he has placed the food before them, it is the responsibility of the sheep to eat, to apply the Word of God to their lives.

From the perspective of maturity, the most important type found in the Aaronic priesthood is of the believer, himself. Revelation 1:6 says Jesus has, *"Made us kings and priests unto God."* As His priests, believers are ordained by God's Apostle (Hebrews 3:1 and 2) to minister to him (2 Chronicles 29:11). Like Aaron, the believer-priest exercises the delegated authority of the Apostle in His absence and is to continue to do so until He returns, as He, Himself commanded in Matthew 28:18 through 20:

> *All power is given unto me in heaven and in earth. Go ye, therefore, and teach all nations, baptizing them in the name of the Father, and of the Son, and of the Holy Ghost: Teaching them to observe all things whatsoever I have commanded you: and, lo, I am with you alway, even unto the end of the world.*

Like Aaron, every believer-priest is sanctified, set apart, to worship and praise the Lord, as David instructed in Psalm 29:2, *"Worship the LORD in the beauty of holiness."* He is expected to offer certain sacrifices detailed in Scripture. For instance, in Psalm 141:2, David listed lifted hands as a sacrifice, *"Let my prayer be set forth before thee as incense; and the lifting up of my hands as the evening sacrifice."* In addition, all believer-priests are expected to offer the sacrifice of praise (Jeremiah 17:26). The writer of Hebrews also ordered this sacrifice in Hebrews 13:15, *"Let us offer the sacrifice of praise to God continually."* Romans 12:1 speaks of the believer-priest's own body as a sacrifice to God. In 1 Peter 2:5, Peter wrote of the believer-priest's duty to offer spiritual sacrifices, *"Ye also...are built up a spiritual house, an holy priesthood, to offer up spiritual sacrifices, acceptable to God."* Paul commends the believer-priest who gives temporal sacrifices, material gifts to help the less fortunate (Philippians 4:18). Then, in Acts 1:8 Jesus, in His final instructions to His disciples, called believer-priests to witness of His sacrifice:

> *But ye shall receive power, after that the Holy Ghost is come upon you: and ye shall be witnesses unto me both in Jerusalem, and in all Judea, and in Samaria, and unto the uttermost part of the earth.*

Here, the Lord commissioned all believer-priests to offer His sacrifice in Jerusalem (their homes), in Judea (their neighborhoods), in Samaria (to those against whom they hold prejudices), and to the whole world (wherever they may go). Finally, in John 21:15 through 17, Jesus asked the believer-priest who loves Him to be His pastor, feeding His sheep.

The priesthood was instituted for the mature. Aaron was a mature man when called to be the first priest and each of his descendants had to be thirty years of age before being permitted to enter the priesthood. It was not a calling for spiritual children. Still, it is the mature believer to whom the special privilege of priesthood is accorded--to be ordained by Christ, to minister to Him, to exercise the authority He has delegated, to worship Him, to offer Him sacrifices, to witness of Him, and to feed His flock. It is for this mature believer-priest for whom the special blessings of Exodus 29:43 through 46 are still reserved.

The Anointed Workers

God also gave Moses instructions for the Tabernacle workmen, men who possessed the many required skills--dyeing, sewing, weaving, metalwork, stonework, woodwork, etc. God already knew His workmen by name and had already commissioned and endowed them to perform the necessary tasks (Exodus 31:1 through 6). The primary requirement for positions in God's employ was that the workmen be filled with the Spirit of God (Exodus 31:3). Once selected, they were to make specific items for the Tabernacle, from the specific materials God ordered donated, according to the specific plans God had given (Exodus 31:4-11). And, they were to work within the confines of the Law (Exodus 31:12 through 17). That meant that, no matter what, no work was to be done on the Sabbath. God's work, performed according to His plan, could not be done in violation of His Law.

Again, these God-appointed workers stand as a double type. First, they are, of course, typical of the deacons of the church who, according to Acts 6:3, were also to be filled with the Holy Spirit, to be capable, and were to perform specific work for the Lord:

> *Wherefore, brethren, look ye out among you seven men of honest report, full of the Holy Ghost and wisdom, whom we may appoint over this business.*

But, these craftsmen symbolize believers, too, who have also been endowed with special talents and abilities and received a divine call, as 2 Timothy 1:9 says, *"Who hath saved us, and called us with an holy calling."* The mature child of God answers this call and dedicates his God-given talents to his Lord. These believers must also be filled with the Holy Spirit (Ephesians 5:18) and, according to Colossians 1:9 and 10, must be spiritually capable so they can perform the work God has for them:

> *That ye might be filled with the knowledge of his will in all wisdom and spiritual understanding: That ye might walk worthy of the Lord unto all pleasing, being fruitful in every good work, and increasing in the knowledge of God.*

The Law Written

To conclude this mountaintop conference, God gave the Law to Moses in written form just as He had promised, as Exodus 31:18 records, "And he gave unto Moses...two tables of testimony, tables of stone, written with the finger of God." Notice that the Law was written on two tablets, the Biblical number of fellowship and communion, the same fellowship and communion Moses had just enjoyed with his God for forty wonderful days. The tablets were made of stone for permanence, stone which is also typical of man's soul, upon which God desires to permanently inscribe His precepts and principles (Hebrews 8:10). Finally, the tablets were written with the very finger of God in God's own personal handwriting. This speaks of the personal touch of God upon the heart of the believer,

In all of this, one sees God beginning to build in the life of the believer, creating in him a tabernacle where he can worship God, calling him to be a priest before Him, entrusting sacred work to his care, and writing His Law in his heart. Through all of this divine construction work, the believer begins to grow and mature and become ever more perfect in the sight of his God.

But, even the most committed believer can fail God. What happens then? The next chapter has the answer.

[1]R. Laird Harris, Gleason L. Archer, Jr., and Bruce K. Waltke, *Theological Wordbook of the Old Testament*, p. 786.

[2]Ibid., p. 789.

[3]Ibid., p. 214.

[4]Ibid., pp. 411 and 412.

Chapter 13
WHEN A CHRISTIAN FAILS GOD

The Failure

Meanwhile, back at the ranch.... While the cat's away, the mice will play. These cliches perfectly suit the situation with which we are confronted in Exodus 32. During the forty days Moses was on Mount Sinai, receiving God's instructions, things were happening in the camp of Israel--and none of them were good, as noted in Exodus 32:1:

> *And when the people saw that Moses delayed to come down out of the mount, the people gathered themselves together unto Aaron, and said unto him, Up, make us gods which shall go before us; for as for this Moses, the man that brought us up out of the land of Egypt, we wot not what is become of him.*

Six weeks without a sign of Moses who had vanished on a mountain afire, smoking, and shaken with earthquakes (Exodus 19:18) was more than the Israelites could handle. They had no idea what was taking so long or even if Moses was still alive. If something had happened to him, what did that say about his God? In the vacuum, they wanted a new god, a tangible god, a god like those in Egypt. With their demand, they violated the very commandments God had just given and they had just agreed to observe (Exodus 23:3).

To the modern mind, it seems incredible. After all God had done for His people, after all He had done to the gods of Egypt, why would they seek such a substitute? Why did a brief period of waiting and wondering result in such failure? But, many an immature believer behaves in the same way when dealing with unexplained delay. While events may be moving according to God's timetable, they may not be moving fast enough to suit the young believer. "Why hasn't God answered my prayer?" "Why hasn't He healed me or saved my loved one yet?" These questions reveal the same crisis of faith seen at the foot of Mount Sinai. And, the Church may not do much better. As the days wax worse and worse, as many begin to wonder why Christ delays His coming, the faith of some will waver. Jesus foresaw and foretold this in Matthew 24:48 through 50:

> *But and if that evil servant shall say in his heart, My lord delayeth his coming; And shall begin to smite his fellowservants, and to eat and drink with the drunken; The lord of that servant shall come in a day when he looketh not for him, and in an hour that he is not aware of.*

Peter also predicted this phenomenon, warned believers, and provided the answer to all questions about it in 2 Peter 3:3, 4, 8 and 9:

> *Knowing this first, that there shall come in the last days scoffers...saying, Where is the promise of his coming? for since the fathers fell asleep, all things continue as they were from the beginning....But, beloved, be not ignorant of this one thing, that one day is with the Lord as a thousand years, and a thousand years as one day. The Lord is not slack concerning his promise...but is longsuffering to us-ward, not willing that any should perish, but that all should come to repentance.*

Man has a deep desire to control everything in his life, even though, he realizes his own inadequacy and seeks for a God to help him. Still, when he feels out of control, his faith is sorely tested and he is sorely tempted to take control of his life away from God and back into his own hands. Isaiah dealt with this very issue and forever settled the question of who is in control of circumstances in Isaiah 46:8 through 11:

> *I am God, and there is none else: I am God, and there is none like me. Declaring the end from the beginning, and from ancient times the things that are not yet done...yea, I have spoken it, I will also bring it to pass; I have purposed it, I will also do it.*

With all this doubt and delay, fear and uncertainty, the people turned from God, took back from Him control of their circumstances, and practiced some "do-it-yourself" religion. To help them, they turned to a man, Aaron, whom Moses had left in charge in his absence (Exodus 24:12 through 14). While the modern believer is incredulous at this, when facing similar doubts and fears, he often follows a similar path. For example, when afraid for his health, he may turn to a man, a physician, before he turns to his God. His emotional fears may drive him to another man, a psychiatrist or a psychologist, instead of his Lord. His financial worries may lead him to yet another man, a banker or a financial advisor, rather than to the One who owns the cattle on a thousand hills and the wealth in every mine. In his apprehension, he may turn to man after man for comfort in fear and direction in uncertainty. But, he may never turn to God or be willing to wait on Him.

Aaron collected the golden earrings, the Egyptian spoil which Jehovah had given His people, the very substance God wanted contributed to the building of His Tabernacle. Although they did not realize it, the children of Israel had just relinquished what was to be a major part of their personal meeting place with God just as He was about to move, just as Moses was about to return. Having surrendered some of the bounty God had bestowed on them, having placed at risk much of what God planned for them, they stood by as the man they trusted, Aaron, took the next step, as detailed in Exodus 32:4:

> *And he received them at their hand, and fashioned it with a graving tool, after he had made it a molten calf: and they said, These be thy gods, O Israel, which brought thee up out of the land of Egypt.*

Why Aaron agreed to be a participant, even a leader, in this sin is not known. Whatever his reason, he took no stand for God and made an idol which would lead his people even deeper into sin. His golden calf was a copy of the calf god, Apis, which the Egyptians believed controlled nature and which they worshipped at Memphis, very near the land of Goshen where the Israelites had lived. The children of Israel finally had a god they could see, touch, and control, as described in Psalm 106:19 through 22:

> *They made a calf in Horeb, and worshipped the molten image. Thus they changed their glory into the similitude of an ox that eateth grass. They forgat God their saviour, which had done great things in Egypt; Wondrous works in the land of Ham, and terrible things by the Red Sea.*

This was the very antithesis of walking by faith; it was, however, a path often pleasing to the immature believer. He wants to be able to pray and get immediate results, ask and receive instant answers. It is only as he grows in grace that he finds that God teaches patience in waiting and encourages spiritual exercise in a walk of faith.

Since the children of Israel had a new god, they needed new feasts and new sacrifices to worship it; gods, even false ones, require worship and believers, even deceived ones, are only too quick to give it. Aaron proclaimed just such a feast and ordered just such sacrifices for the very next day (Exodus 32:5). But, the worship of idols always has and always will cause man to commit sinful excesses, as Exodus 32:6 reports, *"And the people sat down to eat and to drink, and rose up to play."* The term, *"rose up to play,"* indicates that the children of Israel participated in the same perverted sexual rites which had always been associated with the worship of the Egyptian god, Apis. This digression of immature believers into the comfortable and controllable idolatry of the past brought God's children very low.

The believer can never afford to dabble in sin, for there is no such thing as a little bit of evil. Once involved, he will find his spiritual life deteriorating as he descends deeper and deeper into transgression. In the end, he finds himself deceived and defiled. Then, he will find that his sin, no matter how long-standing or well-hidden, will be discovered and dealt with by God. As Moses told the children of Israel in Numbers 32:23, *"Behold, ye have sinned against the LORD: and be sure your sin will find you out."*

Discovery of Failure

God knew precisely what was taking place on the plain below (Exodus 32:7 through 9). As He says repeatedly in Revelation 2:2, 9, 13, and 19 and Revelation 3:1, 8 and 15, *"I know thy works."* In His mercy, however, He didn't destroy them at the first sign of disobedience; instead, He gave them time to reconsider and repent. The Israelites didn't repent and, after their provocation had been progressive and prolonged, after His mercy had been extended and exhausted, God reacted in His wrath. He planned to consume His corrupted children and begin again with one obedient man, Moses (Exodus 32:10).

But, Moses was more concerned with God's reputation than his own. When he could have become the patriarch of a new nation, Moses, in the unselfishness and humility which mark the mature child of God, interceded for a people who, oblivious to their imminent danger, continued the raucous rites of their new idol (Exodus 32:11 through 13). Moses reminded God of His promise to take the Israelites safely into Canaan. If He failed to perform that promise, all who knew of it, the Egyptians included, would believe that He had been unable to do it. Moses also recalled that the promise had first been given to Abraham, Isaac, and Jacob, people who hadn't broken God's Law, people who hadn't worshipped idols, people who had believed in His promises and counted on Him keep them.

Was God testing Moses? Did He really intend to annihilate Israel and replace them with Moses' line? We'll never know the answers to these questions. It is enough to know that Moses set the example for the mature believer in dealing with the deficiencies of others. The mature child of God must be prepared to minister compassion, rather than condemnation, intercession, rather than invective, and restoration, rather than rejection.

Moses' intercession, based on God's reputation and God's promises, brought about God's action. God granted mercy, instead of dispensing destruction (Exodus 32:14).

With the stone tablets containing the Law in God's own handwriting, Moses went down the mountain to see for himself what was going on (Exodus 32:15 and 16). On the way, he met Joshua who had been camped on the hillside, waiting to serve him. As they descended together, they heard strange sounds which seemed to be of battle, sending a shiver of concern along the spine of the general, Joshua (Exodus 32:17). But, although a spiritual battle was certainly in progress and well on its way to being lost, Moses knew the sound was that of his sinning people singing to their newfound god (Exodus 32:18). Moses was certainly bringing the Law into a sinful situation which needed it badly.

Imagine the scene which met the man who had just spent forty days in the perfect presence of the Lord! Even though God had told him what was happening, he could hardly have been prepared for what he saw. There were the very people whom God had rescued less than four months before, singing, dancing, and defiling themselves before a copy of one of the very gods Jehovah had defeated to obtain their freedom. In his righteous anger, Moses threw down the tablets, shattering them to dust, to signify the breaking of the Law of God by people who had so recently vowed never to violate it (Exodus 24:3). Here, Moses stands again as a type of Christ, but, this time, as a type of the Christ, who, in His righteous indignation, will one day judge sin (John 5:22). Here, the Israelites represent the spiritually immature who, having once met God and been redeemed by Him, are then content to dabble in sin and spiritual adultery with whatever idols might appeal. They are oblivious to the danger which draws ever closer; they are unaware of the judgment to come.

The Results of Failure

In a master stroke only God could have inspired, Moses planned a punishment to fit the crime Israel had committed. He took their calf, melted it, ground it to powder, mixed it with water, and forced the people to drink it. This was both an appropriate penalty and a symbolic act with great spiritual significance. Moses showed that sin has inevitable consequences which cannot be foreseen; he also showed that those consequences are not just external, but internal, reaching into the very body and soul of the sinner.

As a result of his personal failure, Aaron had to answer for his construction of the idol and account for the conduct of his stewardship in Moses' absence (Exodus 32:21). Indeed, every child of God will one day face just such an accounting. It is the mature believer who knows that day is inevitable and lives accordingly. Notice that Aaron resorted to the defense of so many who are immature, both emotionally and spiritually--he blamed others for his failures. Aaron swore it was all the fault of the people; they made him do it (Exodus 32:22 through 24). Of particular note are his words recorded in Exodus 32:24:

> *And I said unto them, Whosoever hath any gold, let them break it off. So they gave it me: then I cast it into the fire, and <u>there came out this calf</u>.*

To hear Aaron tell it, there was no melting or molding, fashioning or carving, as indicated in Exodus 32:4. No, indeed! Aaron had simply tossed the gold into the fire and out walked the calf, all ready to worship. Even though Aaron, along with everyone else, had agreed to obey the spoken Law of God, even though he had acted of his own free will without duress, even though the time required to make the idol had given him space to reconsider, even though he had been left in authority and should have been setting an example, Aaron failed God miserably. Then, to top it all off, he tried to blame that failure on others, refusing to accept the responsibility for or the consequences of his own actions.

Such is the immature. When he fails to live up to the light already shed on his path, he's quick to blame others and slow to admit his own responsibility or accept the consequences of his actions. It is only as one grows in grace and matures in the Lord that he learns to handle failure, that he follows the example of David as given in Psalm 51, that he admits his sin against God (Psalm 51:4), that he pleads for mercy (Psalm 51:1), that he asks for forgiveness (Psalm 51:2 and 7), that he prays for restoration (Psalm 51:10 through 12). It takes a bigger person to do it this way; it takes a mature man (or woman) of God.

The question arises why Aaron wasn't more severely punished for his sin? While Scripture doesn't explain, some possible answers suggest themselves. For instance, while the Law of God had been spoken; it had not yet been written in stone and formally delivered to the congregation. The mercy of God must not be discounted, either; this was, after all, Aaron's first mistake and the Law was new to him, too. In addition, God knew Aaron's heart and He knew that the calf really wasn't Aaron's idea. Also, while Aaron made the calf, there is no evidence that he ever worshipped it. In his heart, he may have felt as much disgust as Moses exhibited; he simply chose to give the people over to their sinful desire (Exodus 32:25). But, when the time came to stand on the Lord's side, Aaron, as a son of Levi, took that stand (Exodus 32:26). God knew the hearts of the people, too. He knew that the idol had been their idea. They had willingly offered their wealth for its construction, sacrificed to it, worshipped it, and engaged in sinful sexual practices before it. Then, when the time of separation came, they refused to be counted for God.

But, Scripture isn't silent about the fate which nearly befell Aaron or the intervention which had prevented it. Aaron was skating on the thin edge of disaster and only persistent prayer saved him. In Deuteronomy 9:20, Moses gave this account of the event, *"And the LORD was very angry with Aaron to have destroyed him: and I prayed for Aaron."*

The result of sin is always death. It follows as the rainbow follows rain and would not be long in coming. As the Apostle Paul declared in Romans 6:23, *"For the wages of sin is death; but the gift of God is eternal life through Jesus Christ our Lord."*

Moses observed that Aaron had left the people naked, undressed and unarmed, before their enemies (Exodus 32:25), probably the Amalekites who may have been watching the whole sordid scene from the nearby hills. This is typical of the position of vulnerability before his enemy, Satan, in which the believer is placed when he strays into sin and occasions a break in his hedge of divine protection. As Ecclesiastes 10:8 declares, *"He that diggeth a pit shall fall into it; and whoso breaketh an hedge, a serpent shall bite him."* If the Amalekites weren't going to do anything about the defenseless position of Israel, Moses, as God's judge, was. Again, it was a punishment that fit the crime. Moses ordered a separation, as the Lord will one day separate the sheep from the goats and the wheat from the tares, before His judgment falls. Those who stood for God, including all of the sons of Levi, were commanded to execute God's death penalty against all who refused (Exodus 32:26 and 27). Three thousand fell that day (Exodus 32:28). It was a terrible penalty, but one can also see God's mercy even in the midst of judgment. The entire congregation of Israel was not killed, as God had first thought to do (Exodus 32:10). While the most rebellious ringleaders of the revolt were probably executed, many others were left alive, to learn from the experience, to teach others its lessons, and to be restored to God.

There was, indeed, spiritual restoration. Moses ordered immediate re-consecration or sanctification of the survivors (Exodus 32:29). In addition, a fresh sacrifice was made and its atonement appropriated to cover the sin of God's people (Exodus 32:30). Then, an intercessory prayer for forgiveness was offered (Exodus 32:31). Moses even stood with his sinful countrymen, offering to have his own name erased from the Book of Life, rather than see any of them lost (Exodus 32:32). Still, God made clear that no one is ever excluded from eternal life because of the sin of another (Deuteronomy 24:16); one is only blotted out of God's book based on his own sin (Exodus 32:33; Ezekiel 33:13).

Yes, there will be punishment following failure, but, God is still merciful, even as He chastises. Once the discipline has been dispensed, the mature child of God will determine to learn from his unhappy experience, to teach those lessons to others who are younger in the Lord, and to be completely restored to his God. It will require sanctification, appropriation of Christ's atonement, and forgiveness, but it will come.

The mature child of God will also note another fact of spiritual life, too. While God forgave His people, placed them back on the road to Canaan, and promised that His Angel would accompany them, they would have to live with the consequences of their sin (Exodus 32:34 and 35). The mature believer will realize that forgiveness and restoration do not automatically mean removal of the natural consequences of one's sin. While a smoker may be saved and set free of his bondage, he may, in the future, contract lung cancer, the natural consequence of his sin. While an alcoholic may be forgiven, he may still suffer cirrhosis of the liver, the natural result of his sin. While a drug abuser may find Christ, he may also find his brain cells or genes damaged, the natural results of his addiction. While the sexually promiscuous may be born again, they may also experience unwanted pregnancy, venereal disease, even AIDS, as consequences of their behavior. As the believer grows in God, he learns that the natural consequences which are a natural result of disobedience are not necessarily reversed at the moment of spiritual rebirth. Those consequences may continue to plague. This may be an unhappy truth--but truth just the same. There may even be consequences to those yet unborn, as Exodus 20:5 warns:

> *Thou shalt not bow down thyself to them, nor serve them: for I the LORD thy God am a jealous God, visiting the iniquity of the fathers upon the children unto the third and fourth generation of them that hate me.*

As Exodus 32:33 insures, the penalty and punishment of sin fall only upon the sinner, but the word translated, "iniquity," is the Hebrew, *awa*, which means, "bend, twist, distort, warp."[1] This word indicates an inclination or bent to commit similar sin which may span the generations and accounts for the hereditary predisposition to alcoholism, violence, sexual promiscuity, and other types of sin observed even by secular professionals. It also accounts for the case of Jeroboam I who came to the throne in about 930 B. C., over four hundred and fifty years after the events recorded in the thirty-second chapter of Exodus. When he became fearful of losing the loyalty of his people if he permitted them to travel to Jerusalem to worship at the Temple there, he followed his hereditary and historic inclination toward a particular form of iniquity, as recorded in 1 Kings 12:28:

> *Whereupon the king took counsel, and made two calves of gold, and said unto them, It is too much for you to go up to Jerusalem: behold thy gods, O Israel, which brought thee up out of the land of Egypt.*

Life After Failure

Yes, Christians do fail God. They do commit sin. They may even have idols, those things which they place before their God. There is also that dark night when God punishes the sin in their lives and chastises them as any father would correct his dear children. But, after that midnight hour, a bright and glorious morning comes. There is forgiveness to be found in the Lord who loves His own so much, that He was willing to make the final atonement for their sin; there is restoration for the truly repentant heart.

Still, the saint must not trifle with sin, for there are consequences that naturally flow from even the slightest contact with sin, consequences which cannot even be imagined at the time, consequences which can even destroy future generations. One does, after all, reap a full crop for every seed he sows. As Paul said, in Galatians 6:7 and 8:

> *Be not deceived; God is not mocked: for whatsoever a man soweth, that shall he also reap. For he that soweth to the flesh shall of the flesh reap corruption: but he that soweth to the Spirit shall of the Spirit reap everlasting life.*

It is the mature child of God who has learned this vital lesson and determines to live lawfully before the God he loves, every day of his life.

[1]R. Laird Harris, Gleason L. Archer, Jr., and Bruce K. Waltke, *Theological Wordbook of the Old Testament*, p. 650.

Chapter 14
FACE TO FACE WITH GOD

The Covenant Renewed

In Exodus 3:8, God had given Moses an important covenant for His people.

And I am come down to deliver them out of the hand of the Egyptians, and to bring them up out of that land unto a good land and a large, unto a land flowing with milk and honey; unto the place of the Canaanites, and the Hittites, and the Amorites, and the Perizzites, and the Hivites, and the Jebusites.

At that time, God had identified Himself to Moses as *"I AM THAT I AM,"* the ever-living, ever-present, self-existent One.[1] Clearly, if God was forever, so was His promise. Still, God reiterated and expanded His covenant in Exodus 6:6 through 8:

I will bring you out from under the burdens of the Egyptians, and I will rid you out of their bondage, and I will redeem you with a stretched out arm, and with great judgments: And I will take you to me for a people, and I will be to you a God: and ye shall know that I am the LORD your God....And I will bring you in unto the land concerning the which I did sware to give it to Abraham, to Isaac, and to Jacob; and I will give it you for an heritage: I am the LORD.

Jehovah, the covenant-making, covenant-keeping God, signed the contract. But, after the Israelites deliberately violated the Law He had just given with their idolatry, Jehovah God would have been well within His rights--legally, ethically, morally, and spiritually--to dissolve His covenant with them. In His overriding and overwhelming love and mercy, however, instead of revoking it, He renewed it as we see in Exodus 33:1 through 3:

The LORD said unto Moses, Depart and go up hence, thou and the people... unto the land which I sware unto Abraham, to Isaac, and to Jacob....And I will send an angel before thee, and I will drive out the Canaanite, the Amorite, and the Hittite, and the Perizzite, the Hivite, and the Jebusite: Unto a land flowing with milk and honey: for I will not go up in the midst of thee; for thou are a stiffnecked people: lest I consume thee in the way.

At first glance, the covenants seem the same and a close comparison reveals important similarities. First, God's plan remained the same. He intended to fulfill His promises to Abraham, Isaac, and Jacob, by taking their descendants into the land He had sworn to give their seed. People, no matter how disobedient, cannot alter God's will at all. God will carry out every plan, perform every promise, and fulfill every prophecy He ever made, in spite of people. Second, God's land grant was the same. Third, the identity of the inhabitants occupying that land were the same, as was God's promise to drive them out so that His people could safely dwell there. Fourth and finally, God's promise of prosperity was the same. The land was still abundant and would still provide plenty.

The covenants seem identical, but they aren't. There is a definite difference because sin costs, and the price must be paid--in full. In each previous version of the covenant, God had promised His personal presence to lead His people into their land. In Exodus 33:3, however, God refused to travel with them. Instead, He would send His Angel (Exodus 33:2). Many believe this Angel to be the Lord Jesus Christ, Himself, in His pre-incarnate state. Others believe Michael or another of God's created beings was assigned the task.

Whatever the identity of the Angel, the fact remains that, because of their spiritual adultery, God's people had lost God's presence, a high price for a few moments of pleasure. But, every believer must understand the high cost of sinning. One not only risks pain and punishment; he risks the personal presence of God in his life. Is anything worth that price?

God summed up His sinful people in a single word--stiffnecked (Exodus 33:3 and 5). Not mere pride, the term is from the Hebrew, *q sheh-orep*, which indicates the arrogance of a slave to his king, not only rebellion, but treason. The picture is that of an all-powerful Monarch whose lowly slave dares to defy Him. Such defiance is seen as rebellion against the King and treason in His kingdom, God's view of any who dare to sin against Him and His Law. There is only one fit penalty for such a slave and it is only through the mercy of God and the sacrifice of His Son that it is not instantly exacted in every case.

The Ultimatum Issued

As God delivered His verdict, His people were still standing before Him in the elegant clothes and ornate jewelry they had worn to revel before their golden god. The Lord took one look and issued an ultimatum; they must remove the symbols of their sin or He'd destroy them (Exodus 33:5). There was no insolence this time; they removed their ornaments immediately (Exodus 33:6). When one comes to God for pardon, one does not walk away the same, internally or externally. God can and does insist upon some external changes to reflect the internal transformation. These may include changes in dress, hairstyle, make-up, behavior, etc. One cannot belong to God and look like the world for long. With their ornaments removed, the children of Israel were, in effect, in the plain clothes of mourners, those who had suffered a great loss and were grieving as a result.

Meeting God in the Tabernacle

Sin having defiled the camp, Moses moved the tabernacle outside the camp. This was not the Tabernacle for which God gave Moses the pattern in Exodus 25 through 27 since that one was not even begun until Exodus 35. This temporary tent was the place Moses met with God and it had to be separated from sin. Note, he didn't just put it as close as possible to the camp without allowing it to become tainted by the sin. Moses took it far away, where it was sure to remain free of contamination, where the truly dedicated would have to leave home, family, friends, and possessions and to take the long walk to meet God.

Placing the temporary Tabernacle outside of the camp carried a two-fold significance. First, it spoke of Christ who, in His temporary human Form, suffered and died outside of the walls of Jerusalem. It also symbolizes the humble beginnings of the believer, separating from the contamination of the world, worshipping in a human tabernacle which is not yet built according to God's plan, but which is visited by God until His building pattern can be completed. Both of these types are seen and explained in Hebrews 13:12 and 13:

> *Wherefore Jesus also, that he might sanctify the people with his own blood, suffered without the gate. Let us go forth therefore unto him without the camp, bearing his reproach.*

Each time Moses went to the new location, thousands of eyes followed him (Exodus 33:8); thousands of eyes watched as he entered the Tabernacle (Exodus 33:8); thousands of eyes widened as the very presence of the Lord, in the form of a cloud, met him at the door (Exodus 33:9); and thousands of eyes closed in worship in their own tents, knowing they were excluded from the Tabernacle (Exodus 33:10). Also, each time Moses met God there, thousands of Jewish hearts knew what they had lost because of their sin. Oh, the soul-deep sorrow of the spiritually immature who never realize what they risk losing until it's too late! Oh, the bountiful blessing of the mature children of God who are welcomed into His precious presence and permitted to meet Him face to face!

So, there in a humble tent outside a contaminated camp, God had a face-to-face, friend-to-friend meeting with Moses (Exodus 33:11). Joshua was so impressed, so lost in the presence of God, that, when Moses left to go back to his tent, he stayed behind. Here, we begin to learn the secret of Joshua's faith, his strength, his spiritual growth.

In one of their Tabernacle meetings, Moses, still concerned about the loss of God's presence, again interceded for himself and his people, based on his status as a friend of God, one whose name was known by God, a recipient of the grace of God (Exodus 33:12). This indicates that successful intercession can only be made by friends of God who have kept themselves free of sin, whose new names are known to God, who have received His redeeming grace. Moses reminded God of the great burden He had placed upon his eighty year-old shoulders and of the impossibility of carrying it without His help (Exodus 33:12 and 13). In their exchange in Exodus 33:14 and 15, we hear God's answer:

> *"My presence shall go with thee, and I will give thee rest. And he said unto him, If thy presence go not with me, carry us not up hence.*

While God's presence had left Israel, God promised to remain with Moses all the way to Canaan. But, like Abraham interceding for believers in the soon-to-be-destroyed cities of Sodom and Gomorrah, Moses wanted more; he wanted the presence of God restored to all since it was only God's presence that distinguished Israel from other nations (Exodus 33:16). Indeed, the child of God endures all of the tests, trials, and temptations, all of the pains, problems, and predicaments to which all humanity is subject. There is only one difference; because of the presence of God in the life of the believer, he deals with those circumstances differently. It is the presence of God, then, which distinguishes the saved from the world. Based on his request and through the grace of God, Moses' petition was granted according to Exodus 33:17, *"And the LORD said unto Moses, I will do this thing that thou has spoken: for thou hast found grace in my sight, and I know thee by name."*

Seeing God's Glory

Moses had one last request, one the heart of every child of God knows. In Exodus 33:18, Moses said, *"Shew me thy glory."* In response, God pointed out that His glory is revealed to His own in many ways often missed. It is clearly seen in His goodness, His grace, and His mercy (Exodus 33:19). Each time a sinner is spared, God's glory is seen in His mercy; each time a soul is saved, God's glory is seen in His grace; and each time a believer is blessed, God's glory is seen in His goodness. The evidence is abundant. But, God knew the need of Moses and moved to meet it immediately. Explaining the divine principles involved, God honored Moses' request as seen in Exodus 33:20 through 23:

> *And he said, Thou canst not see my face: for there shall no man see me, and live.... Behold, there is a place by me, and thou shalt stand upon a rock: And it shall come to pass, while my glory passeth by, that I will put thee in a clift of the rock, and will cover thee with my hand while I pass by: And I will take away mine hand, and thou shalt see my back parts: but my face shall not be seen.*

Indeed, in his flesh, man cannot look upon God and survive. The fire of God's holiness would consume him in a moment (Deuteronomy 4:24; Hebrews 12:29). But, safely standing upon the Rock, Christ Jesus (Colossians 3:3), the believer begins to see just enough of God to put his flesh to death while allowing his spirit to soar. Isaiah experienced this during his own encounter with God, as recorded in Isaiah 6:1 and 5:

In the year that king Uzziah died, I saw also the Lord sitting upon a throne, high and lifted up, and his train filled the temple....Then said I, Woe is me! for I am undone; because I am a man of unclean lips, and I dwell in the midst of a people of unclean lips: for mine eyes have seen the King, the LORD of hosts.

Every believer realizes his flesh cannot see the face of his Lord and live. Still, the mature believer has decided to seek God's glory anyway, allowing his flesh to be crucified in the process and freeing his reborn spirit to live the life of a new creation in Christ.

Meeting God on the Mountaintop

There was still some unfinished business; the stone tablets Moses had shattered to symbolize the Law being broken by his people, would be restored the next day when God met Moses on the mountain. The mountaintop was God's ground, a type of spiritual victory. After a spiritual defeat, the mature believer must not surrender or quit; he must, instead, return to God on God's ground for some time alone with his Lord to begin the restoration process. He may even need to travel once again some of the same spiritual ground he had already traversed in the past (Revelation 2:5). In this mountaintop meeting, the written Law would be restored, but there were important differences. In Exodus 31:18 the first meeting is described this way, *"And he gave unto Moses... two tables of testimony, tables of stone, written with the finger of God."* A careful examination of this second meeting as described in Exodus 34:1, 4, 27 and 28 indicates some significant differences:

And the LORD said unto Moses, Hew thee two tables of stone like unto the first: and I will write upon these tables the words that were in the first tables, which thou breakest....And he hewed two tables of stone like unto the first...and took in his hand the two tables of stone....And the LORD said unto Moses, Write thou these words....And he wrote upon the tables the words of the covenant, the ten commandments.

Note the contrasts. The first set of stone tablets was cut by God (Exodus 24:12; 31:18), but Moses had to cut the second (Exodus 34:1 and 4). While God wrote the first tablets (Exodus 31:18), Moses had to carve the writing into the second set (Exodus 34:27).

There were, however, significant similarities between the two sets of tablets. First and foremost, both contained the same words (Exodus 34:1, 27 and 28) for God's Law never changes. Society's mores, morays, and morals may change, people's standards, ethics, and principles may change, even believers' commitment, dedication, and obedience may change; God's Law, however, never changes. Second, both sets were carved in stone, previously seen as symbolic of man's soul, his heart of hearts upon which God desires to write His Law (Hebrews 8:10 and 10:16). So, God's goal does not change. He still plans to place His Law upon man's inward parts where it can never be forgotten. Yet, once the Law has been broken, typified by Moses' crushing of the first tablets, and it isn't easy to regain what has been lost. Moses had to cut and carve; God did not simply deliver another copy. So, one must often labor long and hard to restore all that sin has cost him. Finally, the penalty for breaking the Law remained the same as in Exodus 20:5.

Thou shalt not bow down thyself to them, nor serve them: for I the LORD they God am a jealous God, visiting the iniquity of the fathers upon the children unto the third and fourth generation of them that hate me.

When God restored His Law, He also restored the penalty for breaking it, as seen in Exodus 34:7:

Visiting the iniquity of the fathers upon the children, and upon the children's children, unto the third and to the fourth generation.

Moses cut the new tablets and left for the mountaintop the very next morning (Exodus 34:4). A trip to God's mountaintop of spiritual victory always brings a new revelation of God; this trip was no exception. As soon as Moses arrived, God descended, His glory shrouded in a protective cloud, and kept the promise He had made in Exodus 33:20 through 23, to permit Moses to glimpse His glory (Exodus 34:6). He also gave His obedient servant a new revelation of His character in a new revelation of His name, just as He promised in Exodus 33:19. That revelation is recorded in Exodus 34:6 and 7:

> *And the LORD passed by before him, and proclaimed, The LORD, The LORD God, merciful and gracious, longsuffering, abundant in goodness and truth, Keeping mercy for thousands, forgiving iniquity and transgression and sin, and that will by no means clear the guilty; visiting the iniquity of the fathers upon the children, and upon the children's children, unto the third and to the fourth generation.*

In this brief passage, God revealed eleven aspects of His nature, characteristics which are important for every child of God to recognize:

1. **LORD** - Jehovah, the covenant-making, covenant-keeping God who swears by His own name as the self-existent One because there is nothing higher by which to swear.
2. **LORD God** - Jehovah El, the self-existent, strong, almighty One.
3. **Merciful** - He not only extends mercy, He is mercy personified.
4. **Gracious** - He gives as a free gift what man can neither earn nor ever hope to merit.
5. **Longsuffering** - His patience with His children cannot be exhausted.
6. **Abundant in goodness** - He never runs out of good things and blessings for His children, even when they disappoint and disobey Him.
7. **Abundant in truth** - His truth can never be exhausted.
8. **Keeping mercy** - He extends His mercy to those who do not deserve it.
9. **Forgiving iniquity, transgression, and sin** - Since all sin because of the predisposition or bent to sin with which all are born, the only hope for man is God's forgiveness.
10. **Not clearing the guilty** - God is merciful but He is also just. He will not ignore nor automatically wipe away the sin of those who do not ask His forgiveness.
11. **Visiting iniquity upon future generations** - God does not place either the sin of the fathers or its penalty upon the children (Exodus 32:33), but permits children to inherit the predisposition to sin in the same manner, perhaps so the fathers can experience what He endures when His children sin against Him.

In light of this new revelation of God, Moses immediately made intercession for his sinning countrymen (Exodus 34:8 and 9). In his prayer, Moses acknowledged their failure, pleaded for their forgiveness, and requested their reinstatement as God's inheritance. This same recipe--confession, a plea for forgiveness, and a request for restoration--was later followed by Daniel (Daniel 9:11 through 17) on behalf of Israel when her people were in bondage once again, this time in Babylon, because of their idolatry. The experienced child of God may also adopt this tried and true recipe of intercession which brings restoration.

As a result, the covenant was renewed, as God promised anew to deliver Israel from her enemies in Canaan (Exodus 34:11). But, a new preamble was added to the promise in which God vowed to perform marvelous miracles in behalf of His people, miracles never before seen by man, miracles greater than He had performed in freeing them from Egyptian bondage (Exodus 34:10). There were also new warnings, new conditions on the promise of God, warnings about the sin of idolatry, and conditions based upon the reinstated Law, statutes, and sacrifices (Exodus 34:12 through 26). First, God warned His people to stay separated from the world, its idols, and its lusts (Exodus 34:12 through 16) so that they would not be contaminated by the Canaanite worship of Baal as they had been by the Egyptians' worship of the calf god.

The principles expressed are serious ones; in fact, Paul left nearly the same instructions for the mature saint in 2 Corinthians 6:14 through 18, making it clear that the object is not to see how close one can come to the shore without wrecking on the rocks; the idea is to see how far away from the rocks one can stay every day of his Christian life.

> *Be ye not unequally yoked together with unbelievers: for what fellowship hath righteousness with unrighteousness? and what communion hath light with darkness? And what concord hath Christ with Belial? or what part hath he that believeth with an infidel? And what agreement hath the temple of God with idols? for ye are the temple of the living God; as God hath said, I will dwell in them; and I will be their God, and they shall be my people. Wherefore come out from among them, and be ye separate, saith the Lord, and touch not the unclean thing: and I will receive you. And will be a Father unto you, and ye shall be my sons and daughters, saith the Lord Almighty.*

In addition, God restated some of the provisions of the Law, provisions directly related to the failure of His people, provisions which would lead to spiritual success:

1. **Law of Monotheism** (Exodus 20:3 and 4 and Exodus 34:14 and 17) - Only God, no idol, was to be worshipped. This was the basis of the whole Law since, if Jehovah is not acknowledged as the one, true God, He is not accepted at all.
2. **Law of Passover** (Exodus 12:1 through 28 and Exodus 34:18) - Passover, typifying redemption through the blood of Christ, was to be kept every year, just as the believer is to reckon his life from the moment of his redemption.
3. **Law of Redemption** (Exodus 13:1 through 13 and Exodus 34:19 and 20). God's people must celebrate their own redemption by dedicating their first and their best to God.
4. **Law of the Sabbath** (Exodus 20:8 through 11 and Exodus 34:21) - God's people must observe a time of rest and worship before Him, a time which acknowledges Him as Creator.
5. **Law of the Feasts** (Exodus 23:14 through 17 and Exodus 34:22 through 24) - The three major feasts celebrated God's redemption and provision. So long as these feasts were kept, God promised His protection upon His obedient people and their possessions.
6. **Law of the Sacrifices** (Exodus 23:18 and 19 and Exodus 34:25 and 26) - Sacrifices must be made according to God's plan. No other sacrifice would be honored or accepted.

In the re-instituted provisions of the Law, the mature believer's life is symbolized, a life dedicated to one God, a life based on the sacrifice of the Lamb, a life redeemed by and for God, a life which recognizes and celebrates the Creator, a life which rests in and worships Him. It is, at one and the same time, a life lived on God's blessings and provisions while sacrificing the flesh. This is the life which grows to perfection in God.

Once the Law was repeated, re-established, and reinstated, it had to be rewritten. As God dictated, Moses wrote (Exodus 34:27 and 28) for forty days, working non-stop and without food or drink. When he was finished, God's covenant with His people was restored and renewed. Again, we see that, even when a believer fails, there is hope. Intercession can be made, forgiveness can be granted, the covenant can be renewed in Christ. So long as the believer is willing, he will find that God is willing, too.

The Aftermath and the Afterglow

Any personal experience with God is going to leave one changed. The changes produced in Moses are detailed in Exodus 34:29 through 35:

"Moses wist not that the skin of his face shone while he talked with him. And when Aaron and all the children of Israel saw Moses, behold, the skin of his face shone; and they were afraid to come nigh him. And Moses called unto them; and Aaron and all the rulers of the congregation returned unto him: and Moses talked with them. And afterward all the children of Israel came nigh: and he gave them in commandment all that the LORD had spoken with him in mount Sinai. And till Moses had done speaking with them, he put a veil on his face. But when Moses went in before the LORD to speak with him, he took the veil off, until he came out. And he came out, and spake unto the children of Israel that which he was commanded. And the children of Israel saw the face of Moses, that the skin of Moses' face shone: and Moses put the veil upon his face again, until he went in to speak with him."

The mature child of God will be different after a personal encounter with Christ. There will be an inevitable glow, a spiritual glow that shows. He will have something to share with the world, too, and people will listen because they'll know he has been with God. The world will react, even the nominal Christian world, to the mature child of God who has spent time in the Lord's presence. He'll be changed and people will notice; some will even fear. As a result, one's true spirituality, one's most precious experiences with God must often be veiled from the world. According 2 Corinthians 3:13 through 16, this occurs whenever a person or a nation fails to recognize Christ due to spiritual blindness and fear:

And not as Moses, which put a veil over his face, that the children of Israel could not steadfastly look to the end of that which is abolished: But their minds were blinded: for until this day remaineth the same veil untaken away in the reading of the old testament; which veil is done away in Christ. But even unto this day, when Moses is read, the veil is upon their heart. Nevertheless when it shall turn to the Lord, the veil shall be taken away.

But, praise God, the mature child of God needs no veil in His presence. He need not hide. God sees him as he is, knows him as he is, and loves him anyway. He can be unfettered, unencumbered, uninhibited in the presence of His Lord. He is free to glow with God's glory and to reflect that glory back in praise and worship. This is the joy of God's growing saint.

[1]Finis Jennings Dake, *Dake's Annotated Reference Bible*, p. 67.

Chapter 15
BUILDING GOD'S DWELLING

The Tabernacle Prepared

Complete instructions for the building of God's Tabernacle and for the selection and consecration of His priests had been given in Exodus 25 through 31. The Tabernacle would be typical of the coming Saviour; the priesthood typical of His Priesthood. The Tabernacle would also symbolize the triune nature of man, while the priesthood symbolized his role as a king and priest before his God. But, sin had entered the camp and delayed the project. Finally, after the violation of God's Law had been prosecuted, the idolatry purged, and the people punished, it was time to begin. The first step was the decision to build according to God's Law, so, from the outset, Moses ordered that no work be done on the Sabbath (Exodus 35:1 through 3), no matter what. When one wants to become a tabernacle in which he can meet with God and worship Him, he must build in accord with God's Law. He cannot live in sin and expect God to enter his tabernacle or dwell with him. God sets the rules; those who want His presence must build spiritual lives in accord with them.

Next came the donation of building materials. God could have miraculously dropped a completed Tabernacle out of Heaven, just as He rained down manna. Instead, God gave man the privilege of sharing in it. There was no coercion or coaxing. All were <u>invited</u> to participate, not <u>commanded</u> to do so, and they were to give only what they were willing to give. Here is an important key to spiritual maturity. God wants every believer to be a tabernacle of continuing communion with Him, but He will never compel compliance. He wants obedience freely given, not forced conformity, external obedience which merely masks internal rebellion. He wants believers who are truly willing to build of their lives a home where He can dwell with them. This voluntary giving from a willing heart illustrates man's triune nature working as God had originally intended. In man's spirit, particularly that of God's leader, Moses, God communicated His will concerning the materials needed; then, a decision was to be made in the soul--the mind, emotions, and <u>will</u>--of each individual to give <u>willingly</u>; finally, the body was to carry out the decision to contribute to the project. Not just any construction materials would do; those who wished to contribute had to use God's "shopping list" in Exodus 35:4 through 19. Only the things He had chosen were acceptable. The building materials began to pour in as Exodus 35:21 records:

> *And they came <u>every one whose heart stirred him up, and every one whom his spirit made willing</u>, and they brought the LORD's offering to the work of the tabernacle of the congregation, and for all his service, and for the holy garments.*

Stirred, is the Hebrew, *nasa*. Its root means, to lift or carry. The noun form could mean, the load or burden carried, or "a swelling, uprising, uplifting, exaltation."[1] These definitions indicate a swelling or uplifting within man's spirit which made him willing to lift and carry his share of the burden. This is precisely what happened within God's people.

After so much wealth had been used to create the golden calf, where had all the necessary materials been found? There's only one answer: Everything these former slaves had was given to them by God through the spoiling of the Egyptians. Knowing in advance exactly what would be required, God had, in advance, already supplied and protected it.

For some among the Israelites, these materials may have merely been an offering, but for others they must have been a real sacrifice. Some of the more costly materials could only be contributed by wealthier members of the congregation, the rulers (Exodus 35:27), illustrating the principle given by Jesus in Luke 12:48, *"For unto whomsoever much is given, of him shall much be required."* Also, some of the materials--metals, wood, and skins--had to be given in their raw form, while others, such as fabrics, required the skilled work of the contributors (Exodus 35:22 through 29). Whatever, the word of the Lord in the spirit had caused a desire in the soul to share the burden and the body did the work, as God's commands were carried out. So it is with the building of one's own tabernacle. God knows just what offerings are needed and what sacrifices must be made and has already provided His child with the ability to do it. But, all must be built according to the instructions received in the spirit which engender a desire in the soul that results in a decision of the will that is carried out by the body, all in accord with God's Law and His commands. Sometimes, obedience will be an easy offering to give, but, often, obedience to God's personal building plans will involve sacrifice of self. Each command obeyed, each instruction followed, each offering given, each sacrifice made will add to the perfection and the beauty of the tabernacle which the mature child of God desires to build for his Lord.

To execute the plan, God chose two skilled craftsmen (Exodus 35:30 through 36:4). The first was Bezaleel (Exodus 35:30) whose name meant, "under God's shadow,"[2] indicating the protection of those who work under God's Law. His work, which probably suited his talents, was with wood, precious metals, and jewels (Exodus 35:33). His assistant was Aholiab (Exodus 35:34) whose name meant, "the father's tent,"[3] particularly fitting since he would build the tent or Tabernacle of the Heavenly Father with the fabrics required to create the curtains and veil (Exodus 35:35). These men and their helpers, like the contributors, were wise-hearted and stirred up, willing to help carry the burden of the project. In addition to any materials they gave, they also contributed their time and God-given talents to this God-ordained work (Exodus 35:35 through 36:2). In their dedication, one sees that everything--not just material offerings--must be given to the Lord. He has given each saint certain talents and skills and requires that these talents and skills, along with time and service, be dedicated to Him by all who would become His Tabernacles.

So, God's workmen received God's offerings...and received...and received. Soon, it was clear that these eager Israelites were actually giving too much and had to be stopped. While their giving was commendable, it also illustrates an important lesson to the young in the Lord. The same Spirit who stirred up the desire to give was also quite capable of deciding how much to give--if He were obeyed. Often, though, baby believers get caught up in the emotion of the moment and give more than they can really afford, more than the Lord asks, until their own families suffer. They may give to unworthy groups using carefully-crafted emotional appeals and may even be deceived into giving all earthly possessions to them. They may give their time and service until they neglect necessary work or become exhausted. While God desires that God-given talents be dedicated to Him and His use, He does not want families neglected. While He expects generosity and concern for the poor, He does not require one to make himself or his family poor to do it. God, left clear counsel in such matters in 1 Timothy 5:8, *"But if any provide not for his own, and specially for those of his own house, he hath denied the faith, and is worse than an infidel."* Since the Spirit of God would never lead contrary to the will of God, then all deviations from the pattern of giving He ordained must be of the flesh and emotions, and, as such, are unacceptable to God and must be restrained. Often, the more mature believer can offer godly guidance to the spiritually immature in such matters, just as Moses did (Exodus 36:5 through 7) since the one thing God wants of His maturing believers more than any other is obedience. If He commands the donation of one dollar, it would be just as wrong to give ten as to give none. If He commands a fast of one day, it would be just as wrong to fast for ten days as not to fast at all. Only perfect obedience to each of God's commands is acceptable. As Samuel told King Saul, in 1 Samuel 15:22, *"Behold, to obey is better than sacrifice, and to hearken than the fat of rams."*

The Tabernacle Produced

It was in this spirit of obedience that the building of the Tabernacle went forward. Exodus 36:8 through 39:43 reveals that, under the direction of Bezaleel and Aholiab, every detail of the Tabernacle was done exactly as ordered in Exodus 25 through 27. Every material, every color was used just as God had instructed; every pattern, every item was completed just as God had said. This was not inexpensive. In the financial statement, given in Exodus 38:24 through 31, the precise price of the Tabernacle is calculated and recorded. We see that it cost God's people a great deal to be entirely obedient to Him. As each believer begins to build a personal tabernacle for his Saviour, he must answer the question Jesus asked in Luke 14:28, *"Which of you, intending to build a tower, sitteth not down first, and counteth the cost?"* Obeying God's commands completely and building a tabernacle fit for Him will cost the believer much, but God has already provided whatever may be necessary and has already promised to dwell with His obedient servant.

Once the Tabernacle was completed, the priests' garments had to be made. Again, every detail of the pattern God had given in Exodus 28 and 29, every fabric, every color was reproduced exactly as God had conceived it (Exodus 39:1 through 41). Nowhere is this attention to detail more evident than in a comparison of Exodus 28:36 and Exodus 39:30:

> *And thou shalt make a plate of gold, and grave upon it, like the engravings of a signet, HOLINESS TO THE LORD....And they made the plate of the holy crown of pure gold, and wrote upon it a writing, like to the engravings of a signet, HOLINESS TO THE LORD.*

The believer-priest's garments can be made only one way, God's way. Neither the individual nor society can set the pattern. God, and God alone, has designed the fashion statement for every true child of His, the white robes of righteousness he will wear now and forever. Those garments, that uniform, one's visible life of holiness, must be made according to God's pattern or one cannot be a priest in His temple or a soldier in His army.

Once God's workers had completed God's work, it was up to Moses to inspect and approve it. There were only two criteria to be considered--conformity to God's pattern and obedience to God's plan. What he found is recorded in Exodus 39:42 and 43:

> *According to all that the LORD commanded Moses, so the children of Israel made all the work. And Moses did look upon all the work, and, behold, they had done it as the LORD had commanded, even so had they done it: and Moses blessed them.*

The children of Israel had learned valuable lessons which the maturing child of God must learn, as well. There is only one way to please God--obedience. There is only one way to build His tabernacle in one's life--obedience. There is only one way to receive God's blessing--obedience. To obey truly is better than any amount of sacrifice.

The Tabernacle Erected

On the first day of the first month (Exodus 40:1) in 1445 B.C., on the first anniversary of the escape from Egypt, after nine months at Mount Sinai and about six months of work, the Tabernacle was finally erected. It was done at God's command, not before or after; it was done in God's perfect time, not early or late (Exodus 40:1 and 2). And, it was done in accord with God's building plans (Exodus 40:3 through 11), in obedience to His construction program (Exodus 40:16 through 30). The children of Israel had finally learned to build a place of worship God's way, just as every believer must.

The Priests Consecrated

Once the Tabernacle was pitched, the priests were consecrated to God's service according to His directions (Exodus 40:12 through 15) and His commands (Exodus 40:31 through 33). This ceremony of ordination involved four specific procedures. Each was typical of some aspect of the consecration of the believer to be a priest before God:

1. **Washing or cleansing** (Exodus 40:12 and 31). This symbolizes the cleansing of salvation and the subsequent progressive work of sanctification done by the washing of water by the Word of God (Ephesians 5:26).
2. **Dressing** (Exodus 40:13). This signified that sin had been taken away (Zechariah 3:1 through 5), and that righteousness had been conferred by God (Revelation 3:4 and 5).
3. **Anointing** (Exodus 40:13). This was typical of the anointing of the Holy Spirit without which no believer-priest can minister effectively to God or others (Acts 1:8).
4. **Sanctification** (Exodus 40:13). This is symbolic of the sanctification of the believer, when he is set apart from the world and sin (John 17:15 through 19 and Romans 6:6 and 7) and set apart to God and for His use (Romans 6:11 and Hebrews 2:11).

It was only after all of these procedures had been followed that the priest was ready to minister in the Tabernacle of the Lord. It is only after each of these steps of consecration has been accomplished in the life of the believer-priest, that he is prepared to fully worship the Lord and minister to Him from his human tabernacle.

The Construction Completed

The commands of God for the construction of His Tabernacle and the consecration of His priests had been followed exactly (Exodus 40:16). As a result, the building was completed and the Tabernacle erected according to God's plan (Exodus 40:33). Since the Tabernacle in the wilderness, for which God gave such specific commands, is typical of that human tabernacle which is to be fashioned by each believer according to God's plan and used to worship and minister to Him, Scripture must include specific commands for the construction of these tabernacles. Indeed, it does. Those instructions may be found in 1 Peter. Study them carefully, child of God. In that small epistle, the maturing believer will find all the directions necessary to construct within himself a worthy tabernacle, a dwelling God can inhabit, a temple where God may be worshipped and the world touched.

[1]R. Laird Harris, Gleason L. Archer, Jr., and Bruce K. Waltke, *Theological Wordbook of the Old Testament*, p. 600.

[2]Herbert Lockyer, *All the Men of the Bible*, p. 76.

[3]Ibid., p. 42.

Chapter 16
FILLED WITH THE SPIRIT

The Spirit-Filled Tabernacle

The Tabernacle had finally been built according to God's exact specifications and erected in the midst of the camp. Now, God's presence could inhabit it (Exodus 40:34). Here, we see a type of man, the tabernacle of God (1 Corinthians 3:9), the temple of the Holy Spirit (Exodus 3:16 and 17 and 6:19). The Holy Spirit, Himself, is symbolized by the cloud which descended upon the Tabernacle, typifying the Day of Pentecost when the Holy Spirit descended again to fill tabernacles dedicated to God and built according to His commands. The comparisons are numerous. This chapter will examine some of them.

When God first gave Moses the plans for the Tabernacle, He also gave him the promise recorded in Exodus 25:22, *"There I will meet with thee, and I will commune with thee."* In the same way, God promised to meet with believers through His Holy Spirit and to commune with them in dreams, visions, and prophecy, as recorded in Joel 2:28 and 29:

> *I will pour out my spirit upon all flesh; and your sons and your daughters shall prophesy, your old men shall dream dreams, your young men shall see visions.*

Jesus made similar promises to His disciples. In John 14:16, 17, and 26, He predicted that they would enjoy the same kind of communion Moses had once had in the Tabernacle:

> *And I will pray the Father, and he shall give you another Comforter, that he may abide with you for ever; Even the Spirit of truth; whom the world cannot receive, because it seeth him not, neither knoweth him: but ye know him: for he dwelleth with you, and shall be in you....But the comforter, which is the Holy Ghost, whom the Father will send in my name, he shall teach you all things, and bring all things to your remembrance, whatsoever I have said unto you.*

God kept His promise to Moses as His presence filled the Tabernacle with His abiding glory, as explained in Exodus 40:33 and 34, *"So Moses finished the work. Then a cloud covered the tent of the congregation, and the glory of the LORD filled the tabernacle."* The word, "glory," is from the Hebrew root, *kabed*, which meant, "to be heavy."[1] It indicated glory which is so weighty and heavy that man cannot stand in its presence. Indeed, this was exactly the case, as God's glory came to rest upon the Tabernacle, as described in Exodus 40:35, *"And Moses was not able to enter into the tent of the congregation, because the cloud abode thereon, and the glory of the LORD filled the tabernacle."* The promises made, both by God and His Son, to the believer were kept on Sunday, June 1, A.D. 32 at dawn, according to Acts 2:l through 4:

> *And when the day of Pentecost was fully come, they were all with one accord in one place. And suddenly there came a sound from heaven as of a rushing mighty wind, and it filled all the house where they were sitting. And there appeared unto them cloven tongues like as of fire, and it sat upon each of them. And they were all filled with the Holy Ghost, and began to speak with other tongues, as the spirit gave them utterance.*

These promises were also kept as a result of total, complete, and unquestioning obedience to the commands of the Lord, as explained in Acts 1:4, 12 and 14:

And, being assembled together with them, commanded them that they should not depart from Jerusalem, but wait for the promise of the Father, which, saith he, ye have heard of me....Then returned they unto Jerusalem....These all continued with one accord in prayer and supplication.

The fulfillment of these promises was accompanied by three evidences of God's glory, the **sound** of a rushing, mighty wind (Acts 2:2), the **sight** of cloven tongues like fire (Exodus 2:3), and the **speech** as they spoke with other tongues (Acts 2:4). Every believer whose tabernacle is filled with the Holy Spirit experiences these same evidences. As a result, he hears things differently because he hears from the Lord and sees things differently because he sees them from the Lord's perspective. He also speaks a new language (Mark 16:17) since his old vocabulary is changed and supplemented by his new heavenly tongue. That presence of the Holy Spirit is still so heavy, so weighty, so glorious, that man still has difficulty standing in His presence. Notice that the disciples who were filled with the Holy Spirit at dawn on the Day of Pentecost were still basking in His glory about three hours later, at 9 A. M., when the crowd that had gathered thought they were drunk because they were still "operating under the influence" of the Spirit and reeling under His power (Acts 2:5 through 13). Ever since, the glory of God has been entering into tabernacles prepared for His presence according to His plan. But, since man could not stand to enter into the Holy Spirit for the heaviness of His glory, He enters into man, confining His glory to that earthen vessel (John 14:17; Acts 2:4; 2 Corinthians 4:6 and 6).

The Spirit-Filled Church

Once the glory of God had come down to fill the Tabernacle His people had prepared for Him, He meant to lead them as Exodus 40:36 through 38 explains:

And when the cloud was taken up from over the tabernacle, the children of Israel went onward in all their journeys: But if the cloud were not taken up, then they journeyed not till the day that it was taken up. For the cloud of the LORD was upon the tabernacle by day, and fire was on it by night, in the sight of all the house of Israel, throughout all their journeys.

The Church in the wilderness (Acts 7:38) was led by a cloud, which provided shade from the desert sun during the day (Exodus 13:21 and 22; 14:19; and 40:36) and a pillar of fire, which gave light and heat in the chill of the desert at night (Exodus 13:21 and 22; 14:20; and 40:38). Both provided God's people with His divine guidance. In the Church, God wants to lead, guide, and direct all whom His Spirit fills, both by day and by night, in good times as well as bad. This is the message of Ephesians 1:22 and 23, *"And gave him to be head over all things to the church, Which is his body."* As the Head or brain of His Church, Jesus Christ does the thinking and the directing. As the human body obeys the brain, so the Church must obey the Lord's direction. If the Lord is the Head and the Church is the Body, the Holy Spirit is the Heartbeat, energizing and empowering the Church (Acts 1:8).

The Spirit-Filled Life

The Israelites, under the leading, protecting, and abiding presence of God, are a perfect illustration of the believer's life in the Spirit. As they were transformed by the presence of God, so the lives of believers are transfigured by the Holy Spirit, first internally, through the Fruit of the Spirit listed in Galatians 5:22 and 23, *"But the fruit of the Spirit is love, joy, peace, longsuffering, gentleness, goodness, faith. Meekness, temperance...."* While fruit usually refers to what is produced by trees, fields, the earth and through the inherent energy of a living organism, here, it is used metaphorically of that which is produced in the life of the believer by the inward working of the inherent power of the Holy Spirit. These Fruit of the Spirit are for the edification of the individual believer to enhance his Christian life. With the believer's cooperation, the Holy Spirit cultivates these fruit from small buds into an abundant crop as the believer grows and matures in the Lord:

1. **Love.** The Greek language had no less than twenty words for various kinds of love. (Nineteen are in the Greek New Testament.) The particular one used for love as a Fruit of the Spirit is agape which is the sacrificial love of God for man. No believer can have this kind of love in and of himself; it can only be exhibited <u>through</u> the believer as a Fruit of the Spirit, enabling him to love others sacrificially, just as God loves mankind.
2. **Joy.** Joy is not the same as happiness. While happiness is determined by external stimuli, joy is the result of an internal quality. The saint may not always be happy when confronting the circumstances of life, but he can always have, as a Fruit of the Spirit, an inner joy which is not dependent on circumstances.
3. **Peace.** Like joy, this peace is not dependent on external circumstances; it is the result of the harmonious relationship which exists between God and the believer and can continue to exist even in the presence of external strife, trouble, or spiritual warfare, etc.
4. **Longsuffering.** This fruit is that internal control which enables the believer to suffer wrong with patient forbearance, without losing his temper or returning evil for evil.
5. **Gentleness.** This is that quality of character which immediately moves to meet the needs of others in a kind and gentle spirit.
6. **Goodness.** This fruit enables one to reach for God's good himself and look for and find it in others.
7. **Faith.** While some translate this as faithfulness, the Greek New Testament does not use the word construction for the passive quality of faithfulness, but the word construction for the active quality of confidence and faith in God.
8. **Meekness.** According to Numbers 12:3, *"Moses was very meek."* This fruit enables the believer to bear with others as Moses bore with the often rebellious and constantly complaining children of Israel, without pride, but in an even tempered and tender way.
9. **Temperance.** While this term has historically been applied only to abstention from alcohol, the New Testament presents it in a much broader sense as the quality of mastery and self-control which the Spirit of God enables the believer to exercise in every area of his life. All things are to be done in moderation by the mature follower of God.

While the internal Fruit of the Spirit transform the character of the individual believer, the external Gifts of the Spirit are given <u>to</u> the believer to be ministered <u>through</u> him and <u>by</u> him to the Body of Christ. They are to be shared, not kept, or they are useless. They are free gifts of grace, freely given, freely received, to be freely shared so that all the needs of all may be met. They are listed and explained in 1 Corinthians 12:7 through 10:

> *But the manifestation of the Spirit is given to every man to profit withal. For to one is given by the Spirit <u>the word of wisdom</u>; to another <u>the word of knowledge</u> by the same Spirit; To another <u>faith</u> by the same Spirit; to another <u>the gifts of healing</u> by the same Spirit; To another <u>the working of miracles</u>; to another <u>prophecy</u>; to another <u>discerning of spirits</u>; to another <u>divers kinds of tongues</u>; to another <u>the interpretation of tongues</u>.*

Most times, gift, in the New Testament is a variation of the Greek, *doron*, which referred to a gift or offering given to a god. But, this isn't the word used of the Gifts of the Spirit. That's the Greek, charisma, which refers to a gift of grace. It always indicates a gift given by the grace of God, even though the recipient may not deserve it and cannot earn it. These gifts are divided into three groups:

The Knowing Gifts:

1. **The Word of Wisdom.** The Word of Wisdom is one spoken by man but prompted by the Holy Spirit who rightly applies spiritual knowledge to the human situation. The individual believer exercising the gift need not be wise in his own right because the wisdom is not his; the wisdom is given by the Holy Spirit and the believer merely vocalizes it.
2. **The Word of Knowledge.** The Word of Knowledge is spoken by the believer, not out of any special knowledge of his own, but out of knowledge given by the Holy Spirit. It often comes as just as much of a surprise to the speaker as it does to the hearers.
3. **Discerning of Spirits.** This is the God-given ability to recognize evil spirits by their manifestations and is designed by God to protect His people from deception. The believer need not accept every supernatural manifestation as an operation of God; through the Gift of Discerning of Spirits, he is given the ability to know the difference.

The Doing Gifts:

4. **The Gift of Faith.** "Faith" is the very same word used for faith as a Fruit of the Spirit. In the Gift of Faith, it is the Holy Spirit which implants the firm persuasion, the conviction which denies what is seen and is able to believe what God promised in His Word.
5. **The Gifts of Healing.** These gifts (plural) are unmerited, unearned gifts of completed cures which God bestows through the believer exercising the gift. This includes physical healings but may also include the spiritual, emotional, and mental healing so many need.
6. **The Working of Miracles.** Not restricted to healing, this may be any miracle which is accomplished by the active power of God working through the Spirit-baptized believer.

The Speaking Gifts:

7. **The Gift of Prophecy.** While prophecy is often seen as foretelling, the Greek word used actually means forthtelling, speaking forth a message from God. While the Gift of Prophecy may be predictive, it is not limited to that. The forthtelling which the Holy Spirit performs through the believer may give the mind and the counsel of God on any subject. One difference between the Gift of Prophecy and the Gift of Tongues followed by the Gift of Interpretation of Tongues is the language in which the message comes. While the message may be exactly the same, the Gift of Prophecy comes forth in the language of the speaker and the people present while a message brought forth by the Gift of Tongues comes in an unknown language which must then be interpreted.
8. **Divers Kinds of Tongues.** In the Greek New Testament, there are two kinds of tongues mentioned. The first, *dialektos*, refers to a language spoken by a people or province, a human language. It appears in Acts 1:9, 2:8, 21:40, 22:1, and 26:14 to indicate a language of men. The second, *glossa*, refers to a gift of language and is used of the supernatural gift of speaking in another language without having learned it. This word is used in Acts 2:3 and 4, 2:11, 10:46, 19:6; 1 Corinthians 12:10, 28, 13:1, 8, and in 1 Corinthians 14 to denote a heavenly language. Tongues, as a Gift of the Holy Spirit, is *glossa*, the supernatural ability to speak in a heavenly language. Since it has never been learned, it cannot be translated. Instead, the Holy Spirit provides the Gift of Interpretation.
9. **The Interpretation of Tongues.** This interpretation is not an exact translation as might be given in the United Nations. It is, rather, an explanation of the sense of a message received in an unknown tongue. Of course, not all words given through the Gift of Tongues are unknown. There are recorded cases of messages given in a language which, though unknown to most, may be the mother tongue of a single individual who is from another

country or has studied that language. This message is instantly understood by the one who knows the language, the one for whom it is meant, but must be interpreted for everyone else. There are also cases, reported by Spirit-baptized missionaries, in which the Holy Spirit has operated through the Gift of Tongues to bring a message in the language of the native people present, a language unknown to the missionary used to bring the message. Entire sermons have been preached in this mode, just as occurred in Acts 2:4 through 11.

So, when the presence of the Lord filled the Tabernacle in the wilderness, He foreshadowed much of His ministry in and through His Church. It is His express will that each believer become a tabernacle filled with His Holy Spirit, a temple of the Holy Ghost so he may live a Spirit-led life. Once filled, God desires that all of the Fruit of the Spirit grow in his life, so that the life of Christ may be reproduced in him. God also wants each Spirit-baptized believer to use the Gifts of the Holy Spirit given to him, to share those gifts with the Body of Christ, to minister those gifts to His Church. Then, all Christians are to work together at the Holy Spirit's direction, to operate all of their gifts whenever they may be used to meet the needs of the Body. Only when all of these instructions are obeyed completely, can all believers grow up together to full maturity in the Lord.

[1]R. Laird Harris, Gleason L. Archer, Jr., and Bruce K. Waltke, *Theological Wordbook of the Old Testament*, p. 426.

Chapter 17
LEARNING LIFE'S LESSONS

One Year Later

It had been just one short year since the Israelites had been freed from Egypt. During that brief time, they had gone from bondage to blessing, from groaning to glory, from slavery in sin to freedom in the Spirit. Think of it! They had also grown and matured in the Lord they had come to love. But, there were many more of life's lessons to be learned. Let's look at some of them.

The Lesson of Nadab and Abihu

The sacrifices God required had just been carefully detailed (Leviticus 1 through 7). The priests--Aaron and his sons, Nadab, Abihu, Eleazar, and Ithamar (Exodus 28:1)--had just been consecrated in a week-long ceremony which had become a prayer and praise service graced by the very glory of God, Himself (Leviticus 8 and 9). Yet, right on the heels of this spiritual mountaintop experience, for reasons which at first seem obscure, Aaron's two eldest sons, Nadab and Abihu, met with disaster in Leviticus 10:1 and 2:

> *And Nadab and Abihu, the sons of Aaron, took either of them his censer, and put fire therein and put incense thereon, and offered strange fire before the LORD, which he commanded them not. And there went out fire from the LORD, and devoured them, and they died before the LORD.*

God meant for His commands concerning worship to be executed exactly, nothing omitted and nothing added. But, in the emotion of the moment, Nadab and Abihu did indeed add something, their offering of incense in a way God had not instructed. As a penalty for this strange fire, God kindled His own fire which devoured the young priests.

At first reading, one wonders why this happened. One hint is found in the names of Nadab and Abihu, since the meanings of names then carried clues to character. For example, Nadab meant, "of one's free will."[1] The fact that Nadab was so named would indicate that he always had a tendency to do his own thing. This attitude and the willful action which resulted had a high price tag. Abihu's name meant, "he is my father."[2] This might mean that Abihu wasn't a priest by choice or because of commitment to God; it may have been just because his father was Aaron and their Heavenly Father had chosen his family for the priesthood. His lack of commitment to God and His commands was fatal.

Still, priests they were and, as such, they certainly couldn't plead ignorance. They knew the Law of God better than most. With knowledge, they became accountable and responsible to God. The lesson is clear. No matter what one's character may have been before salvation, once God has redeemed him, once he has knowledge of God's Law, he is expected to comply with it. Deliberate violations will be punished.

Another clue to this mystery is found in the term, *"strange fire."* They hadn't used the fire which God had kindled on the brasen altar (Leviticus 9:24). Instead, they used some other, human source. But, fire in Scripture is typical of the Holy Spirit. The Holy Spirit's fire in man must be kindled and controlled by God (1 Corinthians 12:11). Man simply yields to Him. Strange fire is symbolic of both the satanic counterfeits for the activity of the Holy Spirit and those activities of the flesh which are commonly called "wildfire." Neither are tolerated by God or in His name and could consume the practitioner.

In addition, the fire was not commanded by God (Leviticus 10:1). This speaks of do-it-yourself religion in which one seeks his own salvation apart from God's provision, or self-improvement techniques such as "turning over a new leaf." Man's methods done in man's strength are unacceptable to God. He has only one way and He must be obeyed.

As a result, three things happened. First, Nadab and Abihu were destroyed by the fire of God (Leviticus 10:2), typical of the spiritual destruction of those involved in spiritual counterfeits of any kind. Second, their bodies were ordered removed from the camp to a place of refuse and uncleanness (Leviticus 10:4 and 5), symbolizing the necessary elimination of such counterfeits from the church so that it cannot contaminate others. Finally, mourning for them, which may have indicated God's judgment was wrong or unfair, was forbidden (Leviticus 10:6 and 7). Instead, all Israel was to lament the fact that such judgment had been necessary (Leviticus 10:6). While this may seem cold and callous, it was essential that sin be eliminated; God won't permit counterfeits to contaminate His Church or His people. In addition, the Lord requires that His people not question His divine decrees; they must trust His justice and fairness, knowing that, if they could see the human tapestry from His viewpoint, they would echo the words of the redeemed observing the events of the Great Tribulation in Revelation 19:2a, *"true and righteous are his judgments."*

Still, the question remains: Why did Nadab and Abihu offer their strange fire in the first place? Scripture suggests two possible explanations for their behavior.

First, the two had just seen the glory of the Lord come down in such a spectacular way it actually ignited and consumed the sacrifice on the altar (Leviticus 9:22 through 24). They would naturally be in a state of spiritual ecstasy. But, like many who are spiritually immature, in their spiritual ecstasy, they allowed their flesh to creep into their worship. There is a vital lesson here. After a spiritual victory, one tends to feel invincible; but, at that very moment, he may be most vulnerable, presenting a welcome target to an enemy who is seeking any opportunity to entice with one of his counterfeits, especially his religious-looking counterfeits. It is at just such a time that the spiritually mature must be certain that they are moving only at the leading of the Lord and only under the anointing of His Holy Spirit. Nadab and Abihu did not possess that spiritual maturity and they paid dearly. The second clue to their failure is indicated in Leviticus 10:8 through 10:

> *And the LORD spake unto Aaron, saying, Do not drink wine nor strong drink, thou, nor thy sons with thee, when ye go into the tabernacle of the congregation, lest ye die: it shall be a statute throughout your generations. And that ye may put difference between holy and unholy, and between unclean and clean.*

Since God gave this order just after Nadab and Abihu died, it would seem they may have been drunk when they made their strange offering. Alcoholic intoxication probably produced then the same results it produces now--clouded thinking, lowered inhibitions, and the inability to distinguish between right and wrong--effects attorneys might term, "diminished capacity." In this state, they were even more vulnerable to deception. To insure that this never happened again, the Lord commanded that no priest ever consume alcohol before entering into the Tabernacle. Should a maturing Christian ever wonder if this injunction extends to him, Scripture is clear. First, in Revelation 1:5 and 6, every blood-washed believer is called to the priesthood of Christ, *"Unto him that loved us, and washed us from our sins in his own blood, And hath made us kings and priests unto God and his Father."* This call to the priesthood is reiterated and reaffirmed in 1 Peter 2:9, *"Ye are a chosen generation, a royal priesthood."* To these priests, this command is given in Ephesians 5:18, *"Be not drunk with wine, wherein is excess; but be filled with the Spirit."* Lest any think that this command applies only when entering the Tabernacle, one need only recall that he is the tabernacle of God, the temple of His Holy Spirit. From the example of Nadab and Abihu, the mature child of God learns that alcohol renders him spiritually vulnerable, defiles his personal temple of the Holy Spirit, and endangers his spiritual life. Strong drink is forbidden by God, Himself, and may bring His judgment. Therefore, the mature child of God will never permit alcohol in any form into his tabernacle.

The Lesson of Miriam and Aaron

Miriam and Aaron, the elder sister and brother of Moses, had been with him from the beginning. Then, something happened, as recorded in Number 12:1 and 2:

> *And Miriam and Aaron spake against Moses because of the Ethiopian woman whom he had married: for he had married an Ethiopian woman. And they said, Hath the LORD indeed spoken only by Moses? hath he not spoken also by us? And the LORD heard it.*

Miriam and Aaron had each been called by God to ministries; she was the prophetess (Exodus 15:20) who led the women of Israel and he was the ordained, anointed, and consecrated priest. Yet, on this occasion, both spoke against Moses, challenging his position as prophet of Israel, the one who spoke for the Lord (Numbers 12:2). They used the pretext of a marriage to an Ethiopian woman (Numbers 12:1). Two possibilities exist for this accusation. First, they may have been referring to a traditional story that, while commander of Pharaoh's forces in Ethiopia, Moses married an Ethiopian princess named Tharbis. There is, however, no Scriptural evidence that this marriage took place or that it continued. She may have died, refused to leave Egypt with him, or divorced him after he left. In any event, even if Moses had once been married to an Ethiopian princess, there is no reason why such a marriage would have disqualified Moses from serving as God's prophet to Israel. Second, Miriam and Aaron may have been referring to Zipporah, daughter of Jethro, priest of Midian. Some of the land of Midian lay on the east bank of the Jordan River and the Dead Sea, but much it was in the southern and eastern parts of the Sinai Peninsula, belonged to the descendants of Cush, and was the property of neighboring Ethiopia. Both Jethro and Zipporah were descendants of Midian, a son of Abraham by his second wife, Keturah (Genesis 25:1 and 2). Though they may have lived in a land owned by Ethiopians, they were the descendants of Abraham and ethnic Hebrews. But, once again, even if the accusation were true, even if Zipporah were an ethnic Ethiopian, there is still no reason why marriage to her would disqualify Moses in any way.

In any event, God knew how many times Moses had been married and to whom. Still, God called him as prophet. That stamp of approval, the only one that counted, should have satisfied Miriam and Aaron. So, if the nationality of Moses' wife was not the real issue, what was? From their own words, in Numbers 12:2, it would appear they were jealous of Moses' unique status with God, jealous that he was the only one to and through whom God had chosen to speak since they struck, not at his marriage, but at his ministry.

"Suddenly" (Numbers 12:3), God called Miriam and Aaron by name and defended His special relationship with Moses (Numbers 12:6 through 8). Then, He asked, *"Wherefore then were ye not afraid to speak against my servant Moses?"* Clearly, God considered any attack on Moses a personal attack on Him that He would personally handle. (Many years later, God reiterated this principle in 1 Chronicles 16:22, *"Touch not mine*

anointed, and do my prophets no harm.") God's defense of His impugned prophet was swift and sobering. Notice that the pretext, Moses' supposed marriage to an Ethiopian, was totally ignored by God, a further indication of its falsity. Instead, God strongly reaffirmed His sovereignty; He would speak to whom He chose, in the manner He chose, and any criticism of His choice would be considered a criticism against Him. Then, judgment fell; God struck Miriam with leprosy (Numbers 12:9 and 10), the most dreaded disease in the ancient world. Leprosy was a curse or plague, the judgment of God on sin (Deuteronomy 24:8), usually resulting in pain, disfigurement, and a long, slow, tortuous death. Once diagnosed, one was considered unclean and separated from everyone, even family and friends (Leviticus 13:45 and 46), symbolizing the fact that one who challenges God's authority or rebels against Him is spiritually unclean and is to be separated from fellowship.

It was more than Miriam could bear and Aaron instantly begged Moses to intercede for her (Numbers 12:11 and 12). Once again, intercession followed the already established pattern. First, came confession (Numbers 12:11), then prayer for restoration (Numbers 12:12). Based on this intercession (Numbers 12:13), God responded (Numbers 12:14 and 15). Miriam would be healed. First, though, God ordered her separated from everyone, to the place outside the camp where refuse and unclean things were disposed of (the ancient equivalent of a landfill or garbage dump), far from family, friends and human contact for seven long days. During those days, the Israelites were not permitted to travel.

The lessons are apparent. The mature child of God never criticizes God's chosen or envies their spiritual gifts, ministries, or positions. Such attacks, such jealousies are always wrong, are always the work of the flesh or the enemy, and will always be taken personally by God. The results can be painful and will halt forward progress.

The Lesson of the Spies

After about a year and a half, the Israelites came to the very border of Canaan at Kadesh-Barnea. It is interesting that this name was from the same Hebrew root which meant holiness and sanctification, and typified the place of holiness or sanctification from which the Lord's conquests can begin. Only later was it called Meribah (Numbers 20:1 and 13), meaning strife or contention, symbolizing the problems which often delay the conquests of God. Because His people had never seen Canaan and because God wanted them to know that it was indeed a land worth fighting for, He had Moses send twelve spies, one from each tribe (Numbers 13:1 through 16), to explore the length and breadth of Canaan for forty days to see what it was like, the number and military might of its inhabitants and the fortifications of its cities (Numbers 13:17 through 20). This information was to be used, not to discourage, but to help plan the upcoming military campaign of conquest.

The spies found it a good land, just as God had promised (Numbers 13:21 through 25), with pomegranates, figs, and grape clusters so large it took two men to carry them. Unfortunately, they also found cities with high, thick, impenetrable walls, and citizens of unusual size, descendants of the giant, Anak, who caused them to feel like grasshoppers by comparison (Numbers 13:28 and 29, 31 through 33). For the child of God, there is always fruit to feed upon and an inheritance to be claimed. But, there is always an enemy to be confronted, too, an enemy who seems frighteningly large. Remember, he can only make the believer feel like a grasshopper if he is willing to crawl before him.

At this news from ten spies, the people began to speak against Moses and Aaron, and wish that they had died in Egypt or the wilderness (Numbers 14:1 through 3). Some even tried to organize a return trip to Egypt (Numbers 14:4). This is often the response of the weak and immature in the kingdom of God. At the first sign of trouble, they speak out against God, murmur against His chosen leaders, and are ready to return to lives of sin and slavery. But, two of the spies, Caleb and Joshua, courageously countered the unbelief of their countrymen (Numbers 13:30). Rather than dwelling on the negatives, the obstacles, they saw the positive side, the good land (Numbers 14:6 and 7). They believed that, if God had promised them the land, He could and would give it to them. After all, God was clearly on their side (Numbers 14:8). To believe anything else was, in their minds, rebellion against God (Numbers 14:9). This must always be the stand of the mature child of God.

About to stone Caleb and Joshua, the people were halted only by the glorious presence of God entering the Tabernacle (Numbers 14:10). The Lord's patience with His people was nearly exhausted. Again, He considered wiping out the entire congregation of Israel and starting a new nation with Moses (Numbers 14:11 and 12).

What a man Moses proved himself to be! Once again, he and his descendants could have had everything for themselves, but, once again, Moses refused because God's reputation among the nations would have been damaged (Numbers 14:13 through 16). Moses begged God to forgive his unworthy countrymen (Numbers 14:17 through 19). The mature believer also realizes that God's reputation is more important than his own self-interest, His victory is more critical than personal gain or glory.

God honored the prayer of Moses and forgave the people (Numbers 14:20), but their unbelief could not go unpunished. Because those who had left Egypt and had seen His miracles in their behalf refused to believe Him, none of them over the age of twenty, believed by many to be the age of accountability, none of the supposedly mature adults could enter Canaan. They were defeated by their own doubt, as Hebrews 3:19 states, "*They could not enter in because of unbelief.*" Beginning the very next morning, they were to go back into the wilderness where they would wander until they died (Numbers 14:22 through 30). Only faithful Joshua and Caleb were exempted (Numbers 14:24). God would raise up a new generation, one which had never known Egypt and had no longing for it, one composed of the very children for whom their parents feared so much. With these faithful young people, God would conquer Canaan (Numbers 14:31 and 32). This process would require forty years, one year for each day the doubting spies had spent in Canaan (Numbers 14:33 through 35). In addition, God sent a plague, typical of the spiritual death which descends on all who doubt Him, a plague which came into the camp and killed all ten of the faithless spies (Numbers 14:36 and 37) while Caleb and Joshua survived (Numbers 14:38). Their faith based on God's promise had saved them! Such faith will always be the salvation of the mature believer.

Every child of God faces spiritual battles to claim the good things of God. He may contend with fleshly desires to claim God's holiness or have to defeat depression to claim the joy God has decreed for him. Perhaps he must fight fear to find the peace God has promised him or he may battle physical illness to obtain the healing already won in Jesus. How often in this warfare does he begin to doubt that God is really able to keep the promises He has made? How often does he retreat in fear, failing to claim God's promise, defeated by his own faithlessness. No wonder God's patience often wears thin! No wonder the faithless are left to face His anger and punishment! But, there is a lesson to be learned by the mature believer. There is an antidote to this poison of unbelief. It's called faith, faith so strong that doubt doesn't stand a chance, faith so constant that fear is unable to penetrate, faith that God will do it simply because He is God and He said He would. That kind of faith is like a muscle; it must be continually exercised or it becomes weak and could eventually atrophy and die. Those muscles of faith can only be exercised by trusting God, by believing His every word and reaching out to claim everything God has.

The Lesson of Korah's Rebellion

The most serious challenge to the God-given authority of Moses was instigated by four members of the congregation who should have been mature enough to learn by the experiences of Nadab and Abihu and of Miriam and Aaron. Unfortunately, they hadn't. Their rebellion is detailed in Numbers 16:1 through 3:

> *Now Korah, the son of Izhar, the son of Kohath, the son of Levi, and Dathan and Abiram, the sons of Eliab, and On, the son of Peleth, sons of Reuben, took men: And they rose up before Moses, with certain of the children of Israel, two hundred and fifty princes of the assembly, famous in the congregation, men of renown: And they gathered themselves together against Moses and against Aaron, and said unto them, Ye take too much upon you, seeing all the congregation are holy, every one of them, and the LORD is among them: wherefore then lift ye up yourselves above the congregation of the LORD?*

Once again, spiritual truth can be found in the names of the ringleaders. First, came Korah, whose name meant, "baldness,"[3] indicating that he was not under appropriate spiritual authority. Of the tribe of Levi, he was not of the priestly family of Aaron. Korah's family, the Kohathites, had been assigned by God to care for, pack, move, unpack and set up the furnishings of the Tabernacle (Numbers 3:29 through 31). Did Korah think this task unimportant or beneath his dignity? The name, Dathan, meant, "fount,"[4] but, as is clear from James 3:11, fountains can bring bitter water, as well as sweet. Abiram meant, "father is the exalted one."[5] Perhaps Abiram, Dathan's brother, sought the exaltation of his father's house, instead of his Heavenly Father's. On's name was from the word for pharaoh and meant, "sun,"[6] a possible clue to his own feelings of superiority. These three came from the tribe of Reuben which had absolutely no right to the priesthood at all.

Korah and his associates believed everyone was sanctified, set apart for the Lord's use, and was, therefore, worthy to be a leader or priest. It was true that they were of equal value and worth to God who had, after all, paid the same price for and loved each equally. It was also true that all were sanctified, set apart, as God commanded in Leviticus 20:7 and 8. But, equal value, equal worth, even equal spirituality does not imply equal function. As Sovereign, God reserves the right to choose whom He will to occupy the offices in His kingdom and those who intrude into those offices will face the wrath of that Sovereign.

Moses and Aaron did not try to assert their authority, secure their positions, or defend themselves. They realized that God had placed them in their offices, that only God could remove them, and that it was up to God to defend them. Moses and Aaron simply prayed (Numbers 16:4). Then Moses issued a challenge to his challengers. Since they wanted to be priests, Moses called on them to come the next day with censers for burning incense (Numbers 16:5 through 7). Moses promised that God would be there to defend His true priests (Numbers 16:8 through 11). In their rebellion, the conspirators first refused to come (Numbers 16:12 through 14), but, finally, at Moses' insistence, Korah and his cohorts agreed. All two hundred and fifty-four arrived at the Tabernacle with their censers (Numbers 16:18), the congregation following close behind (Numbers 16:19).

Again, God prepared to destroy them all, as soon as Moses and Aaron moved aside (Numbers 16:20 and 21) and, again, Moses had to intercede for his countrymen (Numbers 16:22). In reply, God ordered a division. Those who separated themselves from the conspirators would be spared (Numbers 16:23 through 27); those who didn't would be consumed with them (Numbers 16:28 through 30). The earth opened beneath the feet of the four conspirators, swallowing them alive, a judgment which symbolizes the way rebellion can pull one back into the world. Then, the fire of God devoured the other two hundred and fifty men who had dared to burn incense before Him, a punishment which illustrated the principle that one can be badly burned by unholy associations (Numbers 16:31 through 35). Only the offering of acceptable incense by an acceptable priest prevented further destruction (Numbers 16:36 through 40). The next day, many who still had not learned the lesson God was determined to teach, spoke out against Moses and Aaron, holding them responsible for the deaths of the rebels (Numbers 16:41). For their own rebellion, they were killed by a plague of God (Numbers 16:42 through 45) which was only halted by the further intercession of Moses and Aaron (Numbers 16:46 through 50).

Through the tragedy of this rebellion, the mature child learns that no one can take authority God does not want him to have or hold an office God does not wish him to occupy. He realizes that the God who placed him in his position is the same God who defends him there. He has the great security of knowing that God has put him in whatever office he may hold and, if God put him there, it is only God who can remove him. He finds no need to defend himself against human challengers by human means.

The Lesson of Moses' Sin

After thirty-eight wasted years of wandering in the wilderness, most of the older generation had passed into history, just as God had said (Numbers 14:26 through 35). Miriam had died (Numbers 20:1) and Aaron would not be far behind (Numbers 20:23 through 29). The new generation was back at Kadesh-Barnea (Numbers 20:1), the door of entry into the promised land. There, the people found no water and, even after all the years of God's provision, even after all the miracles they had witnessed, even after all of the lessons they should have learned, they began to complain against their God-appointed leaders (Numbers 20:2 through 5). Again, those leaders prayed for the provision to meet the need and, again, the Lord ordained a rock to be the answer, just as He had in Exodus 17:1 through 7. This time, however, there was one important difference in the directions. While, previously, God had told Moses to take his rod of authority and strike the rock (Exodus 17:5 and 6), on this occasion, He ordered that Moses take the same rod but merely speak to the rock (Numbers 20:8). The result, however, would be the same. Instead, in his human anger and frustration, in his unbelief in the efficacy of his new instructions (Numbers 20:12), he did what he knew had worked before, as recorded in Numbers 20:9 through 11, "*Moses lifted up his hand, and with his rod he smote the rock twice.*" While water came, there was no mercy for Moses, who had obtained God's mercy for so many so many times before. In Numbers 10:12, God set this penalty, "*Because ye believed me not...ye shall not bring this congregation into the land which I have given them.*" In addition, the site was renamed (Numbers 20:13). God called it "Meribah," which means, "strife and contention,"[7] because it was there that the Israelites, in fighting against Moses, had actually fought against God.

Many perceive the penalty God placed on Moses' failure as unfair, unmerciful. After all Moses had done, after all his years of faithfulness, after all of the maturity he had attained in God, they cannot understand why God refused to allow him to complete the journey, to lead into the promised land the people he had guided for so long. The reason behind the terrible price paid by Moses for one moment's disobedience is perhaps the most important lesson of all for the maturing child of God. It was essential that God's commands be obeyed precisely and completely for the symbolism of this situation was crucial to God's plan. You see, in 1 Corinthians 10:4, the Rock is identified:

And did all drink the same spiritual drink: for they drank of that spiritual Rock that followed them: and that Rock was Christ.

The first time the water of life was needed, it was necessary that the Rock be struck, foreshadowing the crucifixion of Christ. But, striking the Rock again was tantamount to crucifying Him anew, a sin from which there is no return as Hebrews 6:4 through 6 asserts:

For it is impossible for those who were once enlightened, and have tasted of the heavenly gift, and were made partakers of the Holy Ghost, And have tasted the good word of God, and the powers of the world to come, If they shall fall away, to renew them again unto repentance; seeing they crucify to themselves the Son of God afresh, and put him to an open shame.

And, Jesus, Himself, stated a similar principle in Matthew 7:13 and 14:

Enter ye in at the strait gate: for wide is the gate, and broad is the way, that leadeth to destruction, and many there be which go in thereat: Because strait is the gate, and narrow is the way, which leadeth unto life, and few there be that find it.

When one chooses to follow God, he embarks upon that narrow road. Then, as he grows and matures in God, the road becomes ever narrower, as illustrated in the life of Moses. Early in his walk, the murder of an Egyptian had been excused by God (Exodus 2:11 through 14). But, late in his walk, after he had traveled with God for many years, after he had seen the high premium God placed on precise obedience, after he had grown and matured in his relationship with God, Moses was not permitted to commit the seemingly less serious offense of striking a rock rather than speaking to it. For that spiritually significant sin, full as it was of momentous spiritual symbolism, Moses paid a high price indeed. His life's work and ministry were left unfinished, his life's goal left unattained.

Those who would come to maturity in God must soberly consider the seriousness of their decisions and carefully count the cost of their choices. God demands complete and unquestioning obedience from the mature of His kingdom, and especially those who would serve as His appointed leaders in that kingdom. He will accept nothing less and He will severely punish anything else. The closer one walks to God and the more mature he becomes, the narrower the path he must follow and the greater the penalty for any breach.

The End of the Road

The journey was almost over. Soon, Moses, too, would become a part of history. Lest any wonder about his spiritual condition after his failure, lest any question his salvation at the time of his death, one need only read the account of his final days. Just before he died, God allowed him to see Canaan for himself (Deuteronomy 34:1 through 4). Then, the death of Moses is recorded in Deuteronomy 34:5 through 7:

So Moses the servant of the LORD died there in the land of Moab, according to the word of the LORD. And he buried him in a valley of Moab, over against Beth-peor: but no man knoweth of his sepulchre unto this day. And Moses was an hundred and twenty years old when he died: his eye was not dim nor his natural force abated.

After his death, God, Himself, buried Moses and appointed that his body be protected by His own warrior angel, Michael, as Jude 9 explains:

Yet Michael the archangel, when contending with the devil he disputed about the body of Moses, durst not bring against him a railing accusation, but said, The Lord rebuke thee.

Then, God brought Moses to the Mount of Transfiguration, along with Elijah, to meet with Jesus to discuss His own approaching death, as Luke 9:30 and 31 records:

And, behold, there talked with him two men, which were Moses and Elias: Who appeared in glory, and spake of his decease.

Although he walked a difficult path, although he made more than one mistake along the way, Moses was ever the faithful servant of God and, at the end of the journey, laid his life in God's omnipotent hand.

It had been a long trip. Still, there would be much more to do, much more to learn, as the children of Israel conquered the land of Canaan. But, the maturing believers who stood on the brink of the promised land, were not the same spiritually immature children who had left Egypt forty years before. This generation had grown greatly and matured much along the way. All of that growth, all of that maturity, all of their faith, and all of their strength would be tested in the days and weeks, the months and years ahead. Part Two of "Coming to Maturity" will carry us along as the journey continues.

[1]Herbert Lockyer, *All the Men of the Bible*, p. 250.

[2]Ibid., p. 24.

[3]Ibid., p. 214.

[4]Ibid., p. 89.

[5]Ibid., p. 26.

[6]Ibid., p. 264.

[7]Merrill C. Tenney, *The Zondervan Pictorial Bible Dictionary*, p. 526.

PART TWO
JOSHUA--COMING INTO INHERITANCE

INTRODUCTION

A Look Over

Just before the death of Moses in the spring of 1406 B.C., God permitted him to look into the land of Canaan, the land God was about to give His people, the land He had been promising to their ancestors for more than half a millennium, the land He had reserved for them, alone (Deuteronomy 34:1 through 4). What a wonderful view that must have been! It was a view which only God could have given Moses. Only God could have led Moses to the perfect site from which the entire length and breadth of Canaan could be seen, whisked away the clouds from the sky so that his view would be completely unimpeded, preserved the eyesight of the one hundred and twenty year-old Moses so that he was able to see the entire scene, from the snow-capped mountains of Lebanon to the Judean desert, from the wide expanse of the glittering Mediterranean Sea to the land beyond the meandering Jordan River, from north to south, from east to west.

While Moses must have been saddened at his exclusion from entering in because of a moment of unbelief (Numbers 20:12), he must have also been gratified to know that his appointed task was almost done. He had safely brought the millions he led to the edge of an abundant land all their own. He had finished his course, kept the faith, and was ready to go to another land to be with the Lord he had followed for eighty years of his life.

A Look Into

Physical vision, however, could not provide a complete picture; the spiritual view had to be considered, too. Canaan was more than just a place to live, a place to grow food and rear children; Canaan was also the God-given spiritual inheritance of Israel. Did God open Moses' spiritual eyes to see this reality as well? One can only guess. How sad that so many end their days with their spiritual eyes unopened, never having seen or understood the inheritance they have in God! How unfortunate that many of those who do, never come to that state of spiritual maturity where they can claim all that is theirs in Christ!

There is a vast difference between inheritance and possession; the terms are not synonymous. The <u>inheritance</u> of the believer includes all the things available to him, God's blessings, His free gifts of grace given to His own. The <u>possession</u> of the believer, however, is that portion of the inheritance which he has already claimed and made his own. While the entire inheritance is available and he has a right to all of it, he will receive only as much as he claims. The concept is similar to that of an heir left a bequest in a will. The bequest may include a bank account, a home, stocks, jewels, etc. All this may be his by inheritance right, but he will never have access to his money until he goes to the bank and claims it, never own the home until he has the deed transferred into his name, never own the stocks or the jewels until he takes possession of them.

Canaan was the inheritance of the children of Israel, given to them by God, Himself. It was theirs by right, but it was presently occupied by others and was not yet in their possession. So, after Moses passed into history, it was the task of his God-ordained successor, Joshua, to take them into Canaan, to lead them into their inheritance and direct them as they struggled to make that inheritance their possession. It would be a difficult task, filled with obstacles and battles but resulting in mastery and conquest. Still, at the end of Joshua's life, much of the inheritance would not yet be possessed, ordained by God to be owned by Israel, but never yet claimed (Joshua 13:1).

There are those who view Canaan as typical of Heaven, a place of rest, residence, and reward at the end of life's long journey through the wilderness of this world. Many cherished Christian hymns are based on this idea. But, Scripture does not present Heaven as a place of warfare where the saint must overcome obstacles, battle besetting enemies, or fight for the reward God has already decreed is his. If this were the case, Heaven would not be very heavenly. Rather, this is more descriptive of the Christian's spiritual life on earth. Here, there is an enemy to be fought, an enemy whose aim is his eternal defeat, an enemy scheming to prevent the child of God from possessing any or all of the spiritual inheritance meant to be his. In addition to the enemy without, the maturing believer finds that there are also enemies within--enemies even harder to defeat. There are those perplexing habits which simply refuse to be broken, those complex character traits which will not yield to transformation into the image of Christ, and that dirty old man named Flesh who keeps trying to climb down off the cross on a regular basis. To claim one's full spiritual inheritance, all those enemies--inside and out--must be confronted, contested, and conquered. There's no other way to win total victory in Christ.

A Look at the Battle Plan

Once Canaan is recognized as typical of spiritual warfare in the Christian life, the Book of Joshua can be seen as God's battle plan for winning it. The promised inheritance Joshua fought to possess symbolizes the spiritual blessings already promised but not yet claimed. The enemies, both the Canaanite tribes and the renegades in the camp, can be compared to the foes, both internal and external, the Christian must fight for those blessings--even for his very life. The intrigues that deceived Joshua can be seen as similar to those deceptions that blind the believer. The battle strategies Joshua found successful can be adapted to today's spiritual warfare. In the end, the ownership, abundance, security, and rest of Canaan can finally be found to be the mature believer's conquest of self, his possession of all God has for him, and his position of victory in his Lord. God is able to deliver on His promises; through Him, the believer can conquer and claim his entire inheritance; and, through the tragedies and triumphs of the battles, God will develop His people into mature men and women capable of possessing all He has for them.

A Look Ahead

In the Book of Exodus, we walked our way from redemption from bondage, through those initial experiences which taught us our first crucial lessons in spiritual growth, and on to the very brink of spiritual maturity. In the Book of Joshua, we will march into spiritual warfare, confronting enemies without and within, and claiming our inheritance in Christ. Along the way, there will be even more lessons to learn, even more advancement to be accomplished, even more victories to be won. But, the Captain of the Lord's host walks with us. So, let us continue...

Chapter 1
THE COMMAND TO POSSESS

The Man Commanded

Joshua, who succeeded Moses as leader of the Israelites had been born in Egyptian bondage in about 1500 B.C. Perhaps as an indication of their faith, his parents chose to name him, Oshea, which means, "salvation,"[1] by which he was identified in Numbers 13:8 and 16. It was Moses who changed it, in Numbers 13:16, *"And Moses called Oshea the son of Nun Jehoshua."* With the addition of a single syllable, Jeh, Oshea, "salvation," became Jehoshua (or Joshua), "he by whom Jehovah will save."[2] This may have been done to honor Joshua, who had already been successful in leading the Israelites in battle against the Amalekites at Rephidim (Exodus 17:8 through 13). It is also possible that, even at the early point when the spies were chosen, Moses knew Joshua would be his eventual successor, the man God would use to save Israel in the battles ahead. It must also be noted that this was the very name given to the Saviour by divine decree (Matthew 1:21 and 25). *"JESUS"* is simply the Greek transliteration (phonetic equivalent) of the Hebrew, Joshua. It is, in part, for this reason that Joshua stands as a type of Christ, the Saviour.

Joshua was the son of Nun, whose name meant, "continuation,"[3] suggesting that Joshua would continue the work of his spiritual father, Moses. He was a member of the tribe of Ephraim (Numbers 13:8), an ancestral name meaning, "doubly fruitful,"[4] and descriptive of the life of Joshua which was doubly fruitful, having two distinct phases, in the wilderness and in Canaan, and two separate ministries, as servant and saviour.

Joshua was at least forty when called to leave all he had known in Egypt, to find either death or freedom in a land he had never seen. It took courage to answer that call, the courage he exhibited all of his life and for which he became famous in Israel's history. For the next forty years, Joshua endured all the hardships and frustrations of wilderness wandering. For example, although there is no evidence that he ever had formal military training, he was chosen by Moses to command Israel's army (Exodus 17:9 through 13), but served only under the direct authority of Moses, himself (Exodus 17:11), who had had previous training and experience in Egypt. Though freed from servitude, Joshua later acted as the servant of Moses (Exodus 24:13; Joshua 1:1), which might be considered a demotion after having held commanded. But, Joshua never revealed a trace of resentment or joined with those who rebelled against the leadership of Moses. Then, Joshua was selected to represent his tribe as one of twelve spies sent to explore Canaan (Numbers 13:8), and, in characteristic courage, was one of only two who showed true faith in God's promises, pledges, and plan. He was richly rewarded for that faith (Numbers 14:30).

As he entered Canaan, Joshua, by that time nearing ninety and probably the oldest man in Israel, entered the second phase of his life and ministry. Having been called and ordained the successor of Moses and anointed with the spirit of wisdom to act prudently as leader (Deuteronomy 34:9), Joshua finally stepped out of the shadow of obscurity and received full authority over God's people upon the death of Moses in 1406 B.C. He was commissioned by God, Himself (Joshua 1:5), and accorded the recognition of God's people (Joshua 1:16). Joshua had served an apprenticeship of no less than forty years and he had served all of it faithfully. He had never challenged the authority over him, but had waited patiently for God to advance him even though he was fast becoming a senior citizen. While he stands as a type of Christ, who served faithfully as an apprentice Carpenter before being revealed in His full authority, he also stands as a type of the mature believer. It is the immature Christian, who often seeks position and recognition in ministry before he is ready, before God's time arrives. On the other hand, the mature saint is willing to learn, willing to sacrifice self, to serve others, and to submit to God's appointed authority until God calls, anoints, equips, and commissions; it is the mature child of God who realizes that, only then and only in God's strength, does he have any hope of success in ministry.

God's Command

As the children of Israel paused on the brink of Canaan to mourn the death of Moses, the only leader they had ever known, God interrupted their reverie to issue some clear commands to get on with the business at hand, beginning in Joshua 1:2 and 3:

> *Moses my servant is dead; now therefore <u>arise, go over this Jordan</u>, thou, and all this people, <u>unto the land which I do give to them, even to the children of Israel</u>. Every place that the sole of your foot shall tread upon, <u>that have I given unto you, as I said unto Moses</u>.*

God acknowledged that Moses was gone, but then, called on His children to stop living in the past. It was time to go forward into the future God had already planned. Although Moses was a part of the past, the promises of God were not. While men are mortal, God's promises are immortal. As the child of God grows to maturity, he learns that he cannot live in the past, on past memories, past glories, or past victories, no matter how precious, or he can have no present or future conquests. Instead, he must recognize that, no matter what his age or position, so long as he lives, God has a future for him--future accomplishments, future conquests, and future possession. The mature believer must never stop to rest on his laurels; he must go forward, resting on the promises of God, alone.

God promised that every place His people set foot, from Lebanon to the Euphrates to the Mediterranean, would be theirs (Joshua 1:3 and 4). Not one of the warrior tribes of Canaan, would be able to stand against their advance (Joshua 1:5). As God summed up in Joshua 1:5, *"As I was with Moses, so I will be with thee: <u>I will not fail thee, nor forsake thee</u>."* God still promises the mature believer possession. He will not take him to territory he cannot claim and, if the Lord calls him there, it is his to own. God does, however, set specific boundaries as He sees fit. While one may possess what God has prepared for him, he may not intrude into the territory of another. So long as the believer walks according to God's instructions and respects the limits God has set, he is assured of victory.

There were, however, conditions on the promises of God, as most of God's promises are conditioned upon obedience. First, the Lord required Joshua to *"be strong,"* a phrase repeated three times (Joshua 1:6, 7, and 9) to assert its significance, according to the principle enunciated in Ecclesiastes 4:12 where a threefold cord (or a threefold command) is not easily broken. "Strong," is the Hebrew, *hazaq*, which indicates that strength and hardness one needs to prevail against the attacks of the enemy. This command does not refer to physical strength alone. The mature child of God must also be emotionally strong against the frights and fears, the deceits and deceptions the enemy would generate in his mind; he must be socially strong against the pull of peer pressure; and he must be spiritually strong against the temptations and trials the enemy would use to defeat him.

In addition, Joshua was told to have *"good courage,"* a command also issued three times (Joshua 1:6, 7, and 9) and referring to the strength previously ordered. It is the

Hebrew, *ames*, and indicates alertness to the devices of the enemy and boldness in dealing with them decisively. Again, this is not physical courage alone. One must also be mentally and emotionally alert to the snares of Satan and spiritually strong to avoid or withstand those devices designed to lead to his destruction. In short, he must be courageous and confirmed in the faith, in order to engage and overcome the enemy of his soul. Joshua also had to be fair (Joshua 1:6) when he divided the conquered territory among all the tribes of Israel. This could not be done selfishly, but selflessly, according to the plan, purpose, and will of God for His children. Joshua, like the Saviour he typified, was to minister, not to seek to be ministered to. To obey this command completely, to see the snare of selfishness and turn from its temptation, Joshua would need all of the strength of soul and courage of character he possessed. Such generosity and grace must govern the decisions of the mature in God's kingdom, too. The family of faith must also be treated with fairness and equity; only then, will they see the image of Christ in and through us. Joshua also had to set an example for others by speaking the Law, thinking about it, and being governed by it (Joshua 1:8). Only then, could he avoid the snare of Satan seen in the old maxim, "Power corrupts and absolute power corrupts absolutely." Only then, would he be blessed with the success and prosperity God had promised (Joshua 1:8). This, too, must be the commitment of the maturing child of God as noted in 2 Timothy 2:5, *"And if a man also strive for masteries, yet is he not crowned, except he strive lawfully."* Those who seek to mature, to assume authority in the Body of Christ, must recognize this principle. One does not win a heavenly crown simply by achieving success, especially if it's achieved improperly. In God's kingdom, the end does not justify the means. Success must be attained according to God's Law, the rules of conduct He has set to receive a crown of conquest.

But, there were two things Joshua could **not** do, things which could have caused defeat. First, he mustn't be afraid (Joshua 1:9), the Hebrew, *aras*, the terror that could cause one to break and run before the enemy. Neither could he be dismayed (Joshua 1:9), the Hebrew, *hatat*, the panic that breaks down one's defenses against the enemy. The mature believer is in spiritual warfare in which the enemy will try to terrify him until his spiritual defenses are shattered and he breaks and runs. Such fear and dismay are Satan's devices designed to bring defeat and must be vanquished to gain victory. Conformity to these commands of God will always bring the spiritual consequences which naturally flow from obedience, as God promised Joshua in Joshua 1:9, *"For the LORD thy God is with thee whithersoever thou goest."* Any child of God who wishes to experience this same result must obey the same commands. Scriptural principles will always bring Scriptural results.

The Saviour's Commands

Based on faith in the commands and promises of God, Joshua, a type and symbol of the Saviour who leads His own in conquest and possession, had some commands and promises of his own to present to God's people (Joshua 1:10 through 15). First, the Israelites were told to prepare food to sustain them in the taxing time ahead (Joshua 1:11). Like manna, this food is typical of the Word of God which feeds and nourishes the growing saint for all the battles ahead. It was this very Word of God which Jesus used with such effectiveness to defeat the enemy (Matthew 4:4, 7, and 10). The food referred to here, however, was not manna. Literally, the term used indicated game gotten by hunting. These children of God had clearly developed beyond milk and beyond manna; they were ready for meat and they were finally able to find it for themselves. This must be the goal of every growing believer. To advance, he must come to the level of spiritual maturity where he stops sucking spiritual milk, proceeds past spiritual manna, and seeks out spiritual meat within the pages of the Word of God, as Hebrews 5:13 and 14 teaches:

> *For every one that useth milk is unskillful in the word of righteousness: for he is a babe. But strong meat belongeth to them that are of full age.*

God also told His people to be ready to cross the Jordan River in three days (Joshua 1:11). Their circuitous route through the wilderness brought them to Canaan from the east, on the other side of the Jordan, instead of from the southwest where Egypt lay. The Jordan, swollen from the spring rains, symbolizes sanctification, setting one's self apart from sin and for God's use, the *"washing of water by the word"* (Ephesians 5:26). Indeed, no matter what one endeavors for God, he must first be sanctified to succeed. Crossing the Jordan also foreshadows the baptism of Christ, and through Him, the believer's baptism, signifying death to this world and eternal life in Him, as explained in Romans 6:3 and 4:

> *Know ye not, that so many of us as were baptized into Jesus Christ were baptized into his death? Therefore we are buried with him by baptism into death: that like as Christ was raised up from the dead by the glory of the Father, even so we also should walk in newness of life.*

Finally, the three days preceding the crossing of the river foreshadow the three days of the Lord's burial as explained in Romans 6:6 through 8:

> *Knowing this, that our old man is crucified with him, that the body of sin might be destroyed....For he that is dead is freed from sin. Now if we be dead with Christ, we believe that we shall also live with him.*

In all these types, the mature find the same message. To conquer, to take possession, one must be sanctified and separated, dead to the world and alive to Christ.

Possession was Joshua's very next command. God's people were to enter Canaan to possess the land (Joshua 1:11), not to be frightened by their enemies or defeated by their adversaries; they were to enter in to conquer and possess what God had given them. This can be the only aim of the growing saint engaged in spiritual warfare. He must dedicate his every effort to the eventual goal of full freedom and ownership in God.

In order to be able to obey these commands, Joshua had three instructions which would be crucial to success. First, God's people must remember His promises (Joshua 1:13). Both the ability to conquer Canaan and to rest securely in God's protection afterward were rooted in those promises, the same ones made by the same God in which the mature child of God still conquers and rests. Second, all soldiers were to enter Canaan well armed (Joshua 1:14). The mature child of God, too, must put on the whole armor of God to conquer effectively. That armor, which will be examined in detail later, and the adversaries against whom it is used are described in Ephesians 6:11 through 17:

> *Put on the whole armour of God, that ye may be able to stand against the wiles of the devil. For we wrestle not against flesh and blood, but against principalities, against powers, against the rulers of the darkness of this world, against spiritual wickedness in high places. Wherefore take unto you the whole armour of God, that ye may be able to withstand in the evil day, and having done all, to stand. Stand therefore, having your loins girt about with truth, and having on the breastplate of righteousness; And your feet shod with the preparation of the gospel of peace; Above all, taking the shield of faith, wherewith ye shall be able to quench all the fiery darts of the wicked. And take the helmet of salvation, and the sword of the Spirit, which is the word of God.*

Finally, Joshua ordered that there be no rest until the conquest was complete (Joshua 1:15) since only complete conquest would provide them with security in the future. Facing such enemies as Paul listed in Ephesians 6:11 and 12, the mature child of God must keep battling for his spiritual survival until the day of total triumph. Spiritual rest and spiritual enjoyment of all that has been possessed will follow fast on the heels of victory.

Of course, some do not wish to enter into their inheritance or possess all God has for them, such as the tribes of Reuben, Gad, and half of Manasseh. The land outside Canaan looked good and was acceptable to them. They chose it without ever seeing Canaan or viewing all of it. After forty years of wilderness wandering, after coming to the very coast of Canaan, they were satisfied with second best and struck a deal for this land with Moses (Numbers 32). But, comfort instead of conflict are not to be the hallmarks of God's people. So, Moses put strict conditions into the contract. These, too, had to prepare (Numbers 32:16), pass over Jordan (Numbers 32:21), and live on God's promises, until the conquest of Canaan was complete (Numbers 32:21 and 22). These tribes are typical of many in the kingdom of God who choose the easy life on a spiritual plane which looks and feels good, which demands little but gives even less. They seek a life with no battles, never realizing that, without conflict, there can be no conquest, and without vying, there can be no victory. They will never enter into the fullness of their inheritance rights, never know the delights of Canaan, never possess all God promises. Still, the commands are the same for all. All must prepare by feeding on the Word of God or meet defeat at Satan's first temptation. All must live a sanctified life, without which no one can see God (Hebrews 12:14). All must live on God's promises or face failure at the first sign of adversity. All must put on all of God's spiritual armor or go down to defeat at the attack of the enemy. None must ever rest until the conquest is complete or they risk remaining vulnerable.

The People's Promises

In Joshua 1:16, the people responded, *"All that thou commandest us we will do,"* and, in verse 18, they continued, *"Whosoever he be that doth rebel against thy commandment...shall be put to death."* This must be the answer the mature believer gives to God--to obey His every command and go wherever He sends, as He leads on to victory. In no case may the mature saint rebel against his Lord or even listen to those who counsel rebellion, knowing that the only penalty ever placed on spiritual rebellion is spiritual death.

The People's Possessions

Clearly, the mature believer has been led to the coast of Canaan and commanded to possess all before him, but just what does that inheritance contain? It is in the whole body of Scripture where the answer may be found. First, the children of Israel were to conquer the land. Since man was originally made of the dust of the earth (Genesis 2:7 and 3:19), land is typical of man. Before one can conquer anything else, he must first conquer himself. He can do this only as he submits to God's will, as was clearly indicated by Jesus in Matthew 6:10, *"Thy kingdom come. Thy will be done in earth, as it is in heaven."* The reward promised those who gain the victory over self is revealed in Isaiah 57:13, *"He that putteth his trust in me shall possess the land, and shall inherit my holy mountain."* Next, the children of Israel were to conquer their enemies. As we saw in Ephesians 6:11 and 12, that enemy is Satan, himself, but, in Genesis 22:17, the child of God is promised that, *"Thy seed shall possess the gate of his enemies."* The child of God can control the gates or openings through which Satan attacks. Some of those gates, the strongholds of Satan from which he seeks to wage spiritual warfare, are listed in 2 Corinthians 10:3 through 5:

...(For the weapons of our warfare are not carnal, but mighty through God to the pulling down of strong holds;) Casting down imaginations, and every high thing that exalteth itself against the knowledge of God, and bringing into captivity every thought to the obedience of Christ.

Fighting that good fight of faith, defeating the thoughts and fantasies the enemy would use to entice, the mature child of God will find that he wins the very same victory and possesses the very same abundance described in Nehemiah 9:25:

And they took strong cities and a fat land, and possessed houses full of all goods, wells digged, vineyards, and oliveyards, and fruit trees in abundance: so they did eat, and were filled, and became fat, and delighted themselves in thy great goodness.

Having won the battle, the child of God can rule and reign over the temptations and habits once used by the enemy to enslave him, as foreshadowed in Isaiah 14:2, *"And the people shall take...them captives, whose captives they were; and they shall rule over their oppressors."* He must also take control of his own body, the desires of his flesh, through sanctification, as 1 Thessalonians 4:3 and 4 declares, *"For this is the will of God, even your sanctification, that...every one of you should know how to possess his own vessel in sanctification and honour."* The mature must also control his own soul, his own mind or intellect, his own emotions, and his own stubborn will. This is the clear command of Christ, as given in Luke 21:19, *"In your patience possess ye your souls."* Note that, at no time, is the believer told to possess or take control of his spirit which belongs to God who gave it (Ecclesiastes 12:7). Apart from the new birth, it is destined to remain forever dead; following the new birth, the spirit is forever alive, but only unto God and under His personal control as His vehicle of communication with His child. Next, in Daniel 7:18, the saint is urged to possess the kingdom, *"The saints of the most High shall take the kingdom, and possess the kingdom for ever."* The kingdom of God to be possessed in this world is identified by Jesus in Luke 17:21, *"The kingdom of God is within you."* That is the abode of the Lord within, the throne of the believer's life which must be surrendered to Him. So, here is a paradox: In order to possess this kingdom, one must be possessed by its King and, in order to gain control, one must relinquish it to Christ. Finally, the Lord wants His children to possess all good things. In Proverbs 28:10, this promise is given to the mature and upright child of God, *"The upright shall have good things in possession."*

All of these things, then, are the inheritance of the mature believer and God desires him to possess every one in its entirety. As we follow the children of Israel on the path to possession of their inheritance, we must never forget the spiritual parallels, the spiritual possessions we are promised, the spiritual inheritance we are commanded to take.

[1]Arthur W. Pink, *Gleanings in Joshua*, p. 16.

[2]Ibid., p. 16.

[3]Herbert Lockyer, *All the Men of the Bible*, p. 261.

[4]Ibid., p. 112.

Chapter 2
THE WORLD IS WATCHING

A New Commission

It had taken over thirty-eight years, but the older generation had finally faded into history and the younger generation had grown into mature warriors. The time had come to conquer Canaan, beginning with Jericho. Jericho is believed to have been the oldest city in the ancient world. Its name meant, "moon city,"[1] indicating that Jericho was a center of occult moon worship. Built on a hill, it was the perfect place from which to celebrate the nightly moon rise. As such, Jericho is typical of a world under the influence and occult deception of the light bearer, Lucifer or Satan. Jericho was also the dominant city on the Plain of Jericho, controlling access to much of Palestine. It had an outer wall six feet thick and an inner wall twelve feet thick, with fields between to grow food during a siege. It was the fortress neighboring smaller, less protected cities trusted as their defense against invaders. If Jericho could be taken, those smaller cities would fall like dominoes. How could inexperienced soldiers with few weapons hope to conquer what professional armies had failed to take? It could only happen with God's help. The fortress of Jericho symbolizes those diabolical defenses of Satan which may seem impregnable and against which the child of God would appear to have no chance. But, appearance is not always reality, especially in spiritual warfare.

Joshua sent two trusted spies to search out Jericho (Joshua 2:1). Here, Joshua, standing as a type of Jesus is seen issuing commands designed to begin to prepare God's people for the conquest of Satan's territory, just as Jesus did in Mark 16:15 through 18:

> *And he said unto them, Go ye into all the world, and preach the gospel to every creature. He that believeth and is baptized shall be saved; but he that believeth not shall be damned. And these signs shall follow them that believe; In my name they shall cast out devils; they shall speak with new tongues; They shall take up serpents; and if they drink any deadly thing it shall not hurt them; they shall lay hands on the sick and they shall recover.*

These are the marching orders of mature believers, as they wrest helpless sinners from the grip of Satan. They can witness to a waiting world, be baptized with the Holy Spirit evidenced by speaking in tongues, minister healing to a hurting world, and wage spiritual warfare against the devil, his demons (symbolized by the serpents) and all of the habits, temptations, deceptions, and occult practices which build his fearful fortress.

Probably in an effort to avoid the public panic caused by the report of the first faithless spies, Joshua ordered his spies to operate secretly (Joshua 2:1). This speaks of living in the secret place of God that David, the warrior king, described so well in Psalm 91:1, *"He that dwelleth in the secret place of the most High shall abide under the shadow of the Almighty."* There, the believer finds, not only security and safety, but victory over Satan and his snares. Deliverance from the devil, all of his demons, and their diverse deceptions, begins when the truth of God, His Word, becomes the believer's shield.

Jericho's defeat began as Joshua sent his secret spies to look over the land, the earth, again, typical of man, fashioned from the dust of the earth by the hand of God. Before the mature believer can hope to free anyone from the deadly grip of Satan, he must understand the nature of that grip. It is through the Gift of the Discerning of Spirits, a Gift of the Holy Spirit (1 Corinthians 12:10), that this is possible. Through it, the Spirit-baptized believer may receive insight into the devilish defenses Satan has built within the life of man and may also learn the divine plan for bringing them down and defeating Satan.

Carrying Out the Commission

The spies entered a house of lodging or inn (Joshua 2:1) strategically located on Jericho's wall (Joshua 2:15). In many ancient cities, inhabited houses were built against or into their walls and some walls were composed of what might be called "row houses," with no back doors or windows. The residents, like canaries in coal mines, gave early warning of invasion. Note the Lord's plan of spiritual warfare, as given in Mark 3:27, *"No man can enter into a strong man's house, and spoil his goods, except he will first bind the strong man; and then he will spoil his house."* The spies had infiltrated a house of the strong man, typical of Satan. There, through Rahab, meaning, "breadth or width,"[2] symbolizing the wide way leading to destruction (Matthew 7:13), they would learn secrets for spoiling his city. Although the Jewish historian, Josephus, presents Rahab as a mere innkeeper, Scripture calls her a *"harlot,"* a prostitute (Joshua 2:1; 6:17 and 25), the Hebrew, *zana*, which refers to one who commits fornication or plays the harlot. Both may be correct. In any event, hers was the one house unknown men could enter without suspicion being aroused.

Power is often held with spies who seem to be everywhere, reporting everything. Soon, Jericho's king knew men of Israel had penetrated the city and entered a certain hotel (Joshua 2:2 and 3) and he instantly took action, sending men to capture them. Satan always knows of any threat to his kingdom. He hears the witness, reads the book, hears the audio tape, watches the video tape, attends the church service, or listens to the lesson. Whenever the word of freedom goes forth to set his captives free, he is aware and will act to keep his slaves in bondage. But, God acts, too, and His people are everywhere, as well. Rahab may have been on the broad road, but she took a detour. She chose to risk her life to hide Joshua's spies (Joshua 2:4) and to send the king's men on a wild goose chase, allowing the spies to escape (Joshua 2:4 and 5). It's interesting that she hid her guests under the flax on her roof (Joshua 2:6). These thick stalks were the raw material for linen, such as was used to make the priestly robes (Exodus 39:27 through 29), the swaddling clothes of the infant, Jesus, and His burial shroud (Luke 23:50, 52 and 53). Just such linen is also used in the white robes of righteousness of every saint of God (Zechariah 3:3 through 5).

Satan, too, pursues God's people to capture them, as 2 Timothy 2:25 and 26 warns, *"That they may recover themselves out of the snare of the devil, <u>who are taken captive by him at his will</u>."* Satan, too, tries to intercept the secrets by which conquest might be assured and victory obtained. Jesus left a clue to this enemy strategy in Mark 4:3 and 4, 14 and 15:

> *There went out a sower to sow: And...as he sowed, some fell by the way side, and <u>the fowls of the air came and devoured it up</u>....The sower soweth the word. And these are they by the way side, where the word of God is sown; but...<u>Satan cometh immediately, and taketh away the word that was sown in their hearts</u>.*

The efforts of the king's men, like Satan's, were in vain (Joshua 2:7). Although they knew the land, and its inhabitants served as their eyes and ears, they failed. Using Rahab, God protected His spies, just as He will always protect His own.

A World Watches

As important as the defensive secrets of a military target may be to invaders, so is the state of mind of its defenders. Rahab revealed this secret in Joshua 2:8 through 11:

I know that the LORD hath given you the land, and that your terror is fallen upon us, and that the inhabitants of the land faint because of you. For we have heard how the LORD dried up the water of the Red sea for you, when ye came out of Egypt....And as soon as we heard these things, our hearts did melt, neither did there remain any more courage in any man because of you: for the LORD your God, he is God in heaven above, and in earth beneath.

The Canaanites had seen everything God had done for His own, every obstacle He had removed, every victory He had given. Rahab revealed that everyone knew He had already given them Canaan, too. They realized that the God of Israel was the true God and that they were powerless before Him (Joshua 2:9 through 11). Although Satan won't admit it, he, too, has seen similar conquests by God's people in spiritual warfare. And, according to Luke 4:33 and 34, he recognizes the Lord responsible for those victories:

And in the synagogue there was a man, which had a spirit of an unclean devil, and cried out with a loud voice, Saying, let us alone; what have we to do with thee, thou Jesus of Nazareth? art thou come to destroy us? I know thee who thou art; the Holy One of God.

Satan knows that God has already given His mature followers the right to recover any territory he holds in bondage, as Luke 9:1 declares, *"Then he called his twelve disciples together, and gave them power and authority over all devils."* Satan quakes before that power and authority, as James 2:19 assures, *"The devils also believe and tremble."* He also recognizes those God has sent to defeat him. In Acts 19:13 through 15, we read, *"And the evil spirit answered and said, Jesus I know, and Paul I know; but who are ye?"* He also knows that God will give victory in spiritual warfare, as He promised in Micah 5:9, 11, and 12:

Thine hand shall be lifted up upon thine adversaries, and all thine enemies shall be cut off. And I will cut off the cities of thy land, and throw down all thy strong holds: And I will cut off witchcrafts out of thine hand; and thou shalt have no more soothsayers.

Finally, Satan knows that, against God's spiritual warrior, he is powerless and his demons are destined for defeat. In Acts 16:16 and 18, one such victory is recorded:

And it came to pass...a certain damsel possessed with a spirit of divination met us, which brought her masters much gain by soothsaying.... But Paul, being grieved, turned and said unto the spirit, I command thee in the name of Jesus Christ to come out of her. And he came out the same hour.

Those in this world should see similar sights as they watch the Church of the Lord Jesus Christ. They should witness His conquests, both in His believers and through them. They should see His victories over the devil and all of his devices, victories in His own, in the world, and in Satan's own kingdom. As a result, they should have no more courage to resist the wooing of the Holy Spirit. Like Rahab, they should cry out for salvation, a cry which will always be answered instantly and affirmatively.

A Life Changed

Wiser than her people, Rahab cast her lot with God. She avoided what she knew was certain death and made a covenant in the Lord's name for the salvation of herself and her entire family (Joshua 2:12 through 20), much like the Philippian jailer of Acts 16:30 through 34. Her covenant is symbolic of the salvation of the sinner who has recognized the Lord, witnessed His power, and understood that eternal death can be escaped only by salvation through His name, according to Acts 4:12, *"There is none other name under heaven given among men, whereby we must be saved.*" Salvation is sought, according to the terms of Acts 2:21, *"Whosoever shall call upon the name of the Lord shall be saved."* That request for salvation is immediately granted, as guaranteed in John 3:16, *"Whosoever believeth in him should not perish, but have everlasting life."* Through the grace of God, Rahab's cry for salvation was answered on the word of those who promised, *"Our life for yours,"* (Joshua 2:14), just as Jesus willingly gave His own life to save others.

The evidence of Rahab's rescue was the same red rope by which she lowered the spies over the wall on which her house stood (Joshua 2:18 and 21). That scarlet thread was reminiscent of the blood of the Passover lamb on the doorposts and lintels which provided protection during the dark night of the final plague. It also foreshadowed the blood of the Lord Jesus Christ, shed to save all who will but trust in it.

The Spies Report

The king's agents were unable to take Israel's spies (Joshua 2:22). Because of the covenant they had struck with Rahab, they returned safely to bring Joshua the report he awaited (Joshua 2:23). The child of God is assured of safety in his God-appointed mission. Satan and his demons are unable to capture the mature Christian who is waging spiritual warfare under the authority of the Saviour. Despite Satan's threats, despite the activity of his diabolical agents, he is destined to fall before the believer obeying Christ.

There was no negative report from these spies, who gave this account in Joshua 2:24, *"Truly the LORD hath delivered into our hands all the land; for even all the inhabitants of the country do faint because of us."* God's people will always have a good report to bring back to their Commander, for the Lord has delivered the land, the earth symbolizing man made of earth, to mature believers who are willing to wage spiritual warfare to take it. Then, all of the trespassers on that land, Satan and his demon hordes, faint and tremble and melt away because of God and the authority His people have in Him. Jesus' disciples brought Him a similar report in Luke 10:17 and 19:

> *And the seventy returned again with joy, saying, Lord, even the devils are subject unto us in thy name. And he said unto them...Behold, I give you power to tread on serpents and scorpions, and over all the power of the enemy: and nothing shall by any means hurt you.*

It is important to note that the enemy has power; but the Lord bestows on believers power over that power, power which can defeat that power. Such power may be possessed by any who have accepted Him as Lord and Saviour and are willing to fight the good fight of spiritual warfare at His command. The exploits accomplished by the believer using that power will be witnessed by the entire world--and it will change lives.

[1]Merrill C. Tenney, *The Zondervan Pictorial Bible Dictionary*, p. 413.

[2]George Barr, *Who's Who in the Bible*, p. 138.

Chapter 3
PREPARING FOR BATTLE

Follow the Lord

The Israelites, maybe a million or more strong, must have wondered why God had brought them to the Jordan River just when the spring rains and the melting snows of Mount Hermon made it a swollen torrent that overflowed its banks. They must have also wondered how Joshua, whose leadership had not yet been tested, would get them across.

Three days after his spies returned from Jericho, Joshua had his officers issue directions (Joshua 3:2 through 4). The priests, with the Ark, would go first. The people would follow about half a mile behind, keeping their eyes on the Ark to guide them into new territory. The Ark was the visible symbol of God's presence, as seen in 1 Samuel 4:22, "*The glory is departed from Israel: for the ark of God is taken.*" It was the visible symbol of His Law and His miracles, as shown in Hebrews 9:4, "*The ark of the covenant...wherein was the golden pot that had manna, and Aaron's rod that budded, and the tables of the covenant.*" The Ark was also the visible symbol of God's victory, as clearly revealed in 1 Samuel 4:3, "*Let us fetch the ark of the covenant of the LORD out of Shiloh unto us, that, when it cometh among us, it may save us out of the hand of our enemies.*" There are lessons to be learned through the Ark. God, not human logic, must be followed into all new spiritual territory. His presence may lead into new fields of labor or ministry; His Law, into new areas of obedience; His miracles, into new areas of faith; and His victories may lead into new territory. Still, these new areas are only conquered as the mature believer follows God.

Joshua told his people they were about to see a miracle. First, though, they had to sanctify themselves anew (Joshua 3:5). The Ark, the symbol of God, might lead, but it must be followed by a sanctified and set apart people, a cleansed and consecrated congregation, for victory to be achieved. The same requirement is set before today's soldier of Christ, in 2 Timothy 2:4, "*No man that warreth entangleth himself with the affairs of this life; that he may please him who hath chosen him to be a soldier.*" The spiritual warrior must be cleansed from all filthiness of the affairs of the world, prepared to follow his Commander's orders in the battle ahead. This is, after all, the will of God for all of the soldiers in His army in 1 Thessalonians 4:3 and 4, "*For this is the will of God, even your sanctification....That every one of you should know how to possess his vessel in sanctification and honour.*" The mature soldier of God knows he can't conquer sin until he is first set apart from it. He knows God can't use him in spiritual warfare until he is set apart for that use.

Once sanctified, the Israelites were called to follow their new commander. Joshua, typical of Jesus leading and directing His own, commanded the priests to lift the Ark of God and start across the river (Joshua 2:6). They obeyed without question, carrying Israel's most prized possession, the tangible symbol of God, toward the wild water. Then, the people, now led by the Ark instead of the pillar of fire and the column of cloud, followed. Notice the maturity, faith, and obedience the Israelites and their priests had achieved during their wilderness days, an example of growth and maturity for every child of God.

Even Joshua must have wondered what would happen next, but, after forty years of preparation, he was given this pledge in Joshua 3:7, "*This day will I begin to magnify thee in the sight of all Israel, that they may know that, as I was with Moses, so I will be with thee.*"

Often, the immature believer becomes impatient as God proves and prepares him. He may seek his own advancement or intrude into positions before he is ready. The results can be disastrous. But, the mature believer knows the necessity of God's testing. He understands that he must be found faithful in small things before he is trusted with greater responsibility and must serve under authority before being placed in authority. Once he's passed the tests, he knows God will exalt him at just the right time and in just the right way.

God told Joshua to tell the priests carrying the Ark to go to the edge of the river and simply stand in the water (Joshua 3:8). Next, God promised that, as proof He was with them to defeat their enemies and give them the land He had promised, He was going to stop the Jordan River, leaving a clear path to conquest, when the priests' feet touched the water (Joshua 3:9 through 13). The names of the Canaanite tribes to be conquered in Joshua 3:10 contain clues to the land of self one must conquer as he grows in grace.

1. **Canaanites.** This general name of all descendants of Noah's grandson, Canaan (Genesis 9:18), meant, "low,"[1] a type of the low or immoral traits one can conquer in Christ.
2. **Hittites.** The Hittites were descendants of Canaan through Heth (Genesis 10:15) whose name meant, "terrible,"[2] pointing to the fears and terrors one can overcome in Christ.
3. **Hivites.** The Hivites', also descendants of Canaan, name meant, "villagers,"[3] and speaks of those walled and protected secret sins, which are guarded from the approach of the Lord. They must be opened to Him, submitted to Him, and conquered in Him.
4. **Perizzites.** These seem to have been a collection of people from no particular tribe, although Genesis 13:7 indicates they were related to or perhaps neighbors of the Canaanites. Their name meant, "unwalled, open,"[4] and refers to the areas of the personality unguarded against the attack of the enemy. In Christ, these unprotected areas must be girded up, hedged in, protected, and defended against Satan if one is to have victory.
5. **Girgashites.** Also descendants of Canaan (Genesis 10:15 and 16), their name meant, "those who dwell in clay or soil."[5] As such, they would typify the flesh of man, flesh which was fashioned from the soil, flesh whose appetites and habits must be crucified in Christ.
6. **Amorites.** More descendants of Canaan (Genesis 10:15 and 16), their name meant, "mountain dwellers,"[6] representing the spiritual mountains which seem impossible to climb, spiritual problems which seem insurmountable, but which can be scaled in Christ.
7. **Jebusites.** The name of these descendants of Canaan through his son, Jebus (Genesis 10:15 and 16), meant, "a place trodden down,"[7] and speaks of the areas of the personality which have been trodden down by the enemy for years. They must be conquered in Christ, dedicated to Him, and filled with His Holy Spirit.

These Canaanite tribes were mortal enemies of Israel, just as the traits they typify are mortal enemies of the believer's spiritual life. The mature child of God must combat these occupants in his land and conquer them in Christ. Just as there was a plan to follow if the Israelites were to pass all obstacles, enter into the promises of God, and conquer Canaan (Joshua 3:8 through 13), God has a plan for His children that will remove every obstacle, release the promises of God, and result in victory in the battles ahead.

Trusting God's promise, the Israelites proceeded to strike their tents and follow the Ark (Joshua 3:14). They weren't disappointed. The instant the priests' feet touched the water, God made a road through the river (Joshua 3:15 and 16). There are many theories to explain it, all improbable. However God did it, He did do it, miraculously, just as He had said. It's significant that God confirmed Joshua's authority by dividing the Jordan River as the first miracle under his leadership, an obvious parallel to dividing the Red Sea, the first miracle under Moses' leadership. For any who had doubts about the authority of

Joshua, this was proof that the torch had been passed and that God was with the man who carried it. In the same way, God reveals to the maturing believer the authority of Christ as the Leader to follow, the Commander to obey, and the General who leads on to victory.

The priests went to the center of the river and, on dry ground, waited while the people crossed (Joshua 3:17). The obstacle had been overcome, Canaan had been entered, the march to conquest had begun, all because God's plan was obeyed. The mature believer, obeying the same God can see the same results. He can witness miracles, have the promises of God fulfilled in his life, and conquer the enemies of his spiritual growth.

Testify to Victory

After a spiritual victory, the child of God must pause and reflect, testifying to the victory and memorializing the triumph. So, before the priests left the Jordan, Joshua told twelve men, one from each tribe, to retrieve a rock from the dry riverbed. At the first campsite in Canaan, those rocks became a monument to remind everyone who saw it of this miracle (Joshua 4:1 through 8). Then, Joshua erected a second set of twelve stones at the place in the midst of the river where the priests had stood (Joshua 4:9 and 10). Long after the water flowed back into place, the monument would jut from the river as a permanent memorial to God's power; long after those who witnessed it passed into history, the testimony of that day would reach generations yet unborn. These monuments typify the necessity of recalling and recounting God's past victories, both to honor Him and to build faith for the future. Note that they were made of stone, a permanent material which signifies the soul of man--his mind, emotions, and will--indicating that past spiritual victories must be given a permanent place in his memory and retold often to encourage himself and others. One monument was erected at the site of the miracle, (Joshua 4:9 and 10).

There probably isn't a child of God alive who doesn't remember where he was born-again or healed or filled with the Holy Spirit. Each time that place is revisited, the memory comes alive once more, to be savored and shared. The second monument was at the place of lodging (Joshua 4:3). It is not enough just to recall the victories of God on rare occasions when one visits the scene of a past triumph; one must keep alive the warmth of those memories in the very place he lives, to reflect on them and to share them with others. Such monuments to past victories are a sign to the believer who had witnessed them (Joshua 4:6), building faith for future battles. When faced with an imminent spiritual struggle, the mature child of God is wise to look back at all of the monuments behind him. He'll find that the same God who won those past victories will defeat present foes. The monuments of the mature are also to be a sign for the children (Joshua 4:6), the spiritual babes in Christ and newcomers to spiritual warfare, to encourage them in the battles they still face. The monuments were a sign to the nation of Israel, too (Joshua 4:7), typical of the entire Church which confronts conflict from time to time and is encouraged by the testimony of past conquests. Finally, the monuments were to last forever and never be removed (Joshua 4:7). In good times and bad times, in the present and in the future, the testimony of past victory can sustain the child of God and spur him on to ever greater conquests in Christ.

By following God's plan and God's leader, God's people were in Canaan. What a contrast to their parents who had died in the wilderness because of their disobedience and doubts! There, on the other side of Jordan stood God's presence in the form of His Ark, His people, and His priests (Joshua 4:11). There, too, were the soldiers of the Lord, armed and ready for combat against the Lord's chosen target, Jericho (Joshua 4:12 and 13). The mature child of God involved in spiritual warfare must also live in the presence of God with the people of God, allowing Christ, his High Priest, to lead him. But, after a spiritual victory, that mature believer remains a soldier of God, armed with the spiritual weapons listed in Ephesians 6:11 through 17 and ready for whatever warfare may lay ahead.

As promised, God magnified Joshua in the sight of all Israel (Joshua 4:14). They would forever reverence him, just as they had respected Moses. Since Joshua stands as a type of Christ, one sees that God desires His Son to be exalted through the miracles He performs for His people, and the mature child of God will always praise and worship the Lord who gives the victory. But, as glorious as the miracle was, the Israelites were still forbidden to live in the past (Joshua 4:15 through 18). They had to go forward, past the Jordan River, to receive all the future blessings God had for them. Long after the river returned to its place and the monuments were built, the children of Israel were to remember the miracle and the God who performed it, but they were not to continue to live in it (Joshua 4:18). They had to move on to future miracles (Joshua 4:19 through 24).

The Jordan River stands as a type of death, death to self in sanctification, death to the old life in crossing over to the new. Coming up out of Jordan, coming into Canaan, speaks of the resurrection life of the believer. This death to the old life and resurrection to the new, may be seen in water baptism, as seen in Romans 6:3 through 5 and 11:

> *Know ye not, that <u>so many of us who were baptized into Jesus Christ were baptized into his death</u>? Therefore <u>we are buried with him by baptism into death that like as Christ was raised up from the dead by the glory of the Father, even so we also should walk in newness of life</u>. For <u>if we have been planted together in the likeness of his death, we shall be also in the likeness of his resurrection</u>....Likewise <u>reckon ye also yourselves to be dead indeed unto sin, but alive unto God through Jesus Christ our Lord</u>.*

But, that new resurrection life usually involves some cutting, some pruning, some circumcision. The new life in Canaan of the children of Israel was no exception.

Be Circumcised

Having seen the God of Israel miraculously bring His people across Canaan's last defensive barrier, the Canaanites were more consumed by fear (Joshua 5:1). In human logic, it was the perfect time to strike, to go forward, to conquer. To pause would seem to leave Israel vulnerable, inviting the attack of the enemy. But, man's logic is not always (or even usually) God's logic. During the days of Abraham, God had initiated the covenant of circumcision between Himself and His people in Genesis 17:10, "*<u>This is my covenant, which ye shall keep between me and you and thy seed after thee; Every man child among you shall be circumcised</u>*." Clearly, God meant circumcision to be the outward sign of an inward covenant between man and Himself. Uncircumcision was, therefore, an outward sign of an inward break in that covenant, the penalty for which was death. Nowhere is this more evident than in Exodus 4:24 through 26, where Moses was nearly killed because he had not circumcised one of his sons and could not go forward until this failure had been corrected. But, Israel hadn't kept the covenant of circumcision, as revealed in Joshua 5:7:

> *For the children of Israel walked forty years in the wilderness....And <u>their children</u>, whom he raised up in their stead, them Joshua circumcised: <u>for they were uncircumcised, because they had not circumcised them by the way</u>.*

By this failure, God's people had broken the covenant with Him. God had been patient, but it was necessary that they, like Moses, renew the covenant relationship before they could go forward to conquer. The mass circumcision of all males born in the wilderness was performed at Gilgal, whose name signified the removal of the reproach of their previous enslavement in Egypt, as well as the reproach of their uncircumcision. For the next four days, during which healing took place (Joshua 5:8 through 10), God honored their obedience and kept them safe from attack at a time when they were most vulnerable.

Paul ordered circumcision for every mature saint. It isn't performed in the flesh, however, but in the hearts of those who want a covenant relationship with Christ, as noted in Romans 2:28 and 29, *"Neither is that circumcision, which is outward in the flesh....But he is a Jew which is one inwardly: and circumcision is that of the heart, in the spirit...."* As that circumcision of the heart is accomplished, the believer becomes a spiritual Jew, one of God's chosen people. The glorious effects are revealed in Philippians 3:3, *"For we are the circumcision which worship God in the spirit, and rejoice in Christ Jesus, and have no confidence in the flesh."* This circumcision of the heart and the joyous new covenant relationship it brings also prepares one for spiritual warfare in which the victory is not man's, but God's. The child of God cannot go on to full conquest over self and sin until this heart circumcision is complete.

Feed on the Promises

The pain of circumcision past, it just happened to be the fourteenth day of the first month, the very date the Passover was to be kept (Exodus 12:6). Having sanctified themselves, having forded the Jordan River, typical of death to the past and resurrection to a new life, and having renewed the covenant of circumcision, the Israelites celebrated their first Passover in their new land of promise. Obedience in such things as sanctification, death to self, resurrection life in Christ, and personal circumcision of heart brings the maturing child of God into a similar position of living in the promises of his Lord.

Since God's people were now in the promised land, they could begin to feed on its abundance, while the miraculous manna, that had fed them during the wilderness years, stopped, as noted in Joshua 5:12, *"And the manna ceased on the morrow...neither had the children of Israel manna any more; but they did eat of the fruit of the land of Canaan."* The manna represented Jesus, the Bread of life broken for all (John 6:32 through 35), the Bread upon which all can feed, the Bread which brings life to all who come to Him, the crucified Christ. But, once the land of promise has been entered, the mature believer no longer need feed on salvation alone; he is ready to receive the fruit to be found in the risen Christ who is typified by the abundance of Canaan. Like the Israelites, the believer can enter the land of the Lord's promises and feed on the good things of God. Even as he prepares for the battlefield, he can enjoy the abundant blessings of life in the kingdom of God.

Follow the Captain

But, this land of promise was already occupied by those pesky Canaanites; God's people were going to have to fight to take it, and the first battle would be for the double-walled and heavily defended dominant city of Jericho. As Joshua paced, pondered his situation, and prayed for the Lord's help to take what must have seemed impregnable, Joshua suddenly saw something which must have made even the hairs on the back of his neck stand at attention. Joshua 15:13 through 15 records the scene:

> *And it came to pass, when Joshua was by Jericho, that he lifted up his eyes and looked, and, behold, there stood a man over against him with his sword drawn in his hand: and Joshua went unto him, and said unto him, Art thou for us, or for our adversaries? And he said, Nay; but as captain of the host of the LORD*

am I now come. And Joshua fell on his face to the earth, and did worship, and said unto him, What saith my lord unto his servant? And the captain of the LORD's host said unto Joshua, Loose thy shoe from off thy foot; for the place whereon thou standest is holy. And Joshua did so.

This was not an angel. An angel would never have accepted Joshua's worship or considered the place where he stood to be holy. Rather, this was a theophany, a visible manifestation of a Member of the Trinity. This particular Member was none other than the Lord Jesus Christ, Himself, the Commander of Heaven's armies (Revelation 19:11 through 14). This Captain of the Lord's host stood with Joshua, His sword drawn, ready to fight for God's children. It is significant that the Lord chose this moment, just before Joshua was to go into battle, to approach him using the very same words He had used when He approached Moses in Exodus 3:5, just before he was to go into spiritual warfare in Egypt. Again, the Lord reassured Joshua that He was indeed with him, just as He had been with Moses. This same Captain stands beside the mature child of God. Although he may face seemingly implacable enemies in spiritual warfare, the Captain has His sword drawn, ready to lead on to triumph. With that Captain for us, who can stand against us?

Preparations Complete

The children of Israel had come a very long way, but all of it was only preparation for what lay ahead. They had not yet faced a single adversary nor won a single battle. They had completed their preparations in perfect obedience, according to God's perfect plan. Now, at last, they were ready to go forward to their first victory.

Prudent preparation always precedes perfect victory and that preparation still includes sanctification, death to self, resurrection to new life in Christ, circumcision of heart, feeding on the Lamb of God and on the abundant blessings of the kingdom of God, and a personal introduction to the Captain who commands in spiritual warfare. It is only when all of these preparations have been accomplished in perfect obedience to Christ that the mature believer can go on to win the victory in the spiritual battles he will surely face.

[1]C. I. Scofield, *The Scofield Reference Bible*, Proper Name Index, p. 12.

[2]Herbert Lockyer, *All the Men of the Bible*, p. 145.

[3]Scofield, Proper Name Index, p. 22

[4]H. D. M. Spence and Joseph S. Exell, *The Pulpit Commentary*, Volume 3, The book of Joshua, p. 43.

[5]Scofield, Proper Name Index, p. 20.

[6]Merrill C. Tenney, *The Zondervan Pictorial Bible Dictionary*, p. 36.

[7]Scofield, Proper Name Index, p. 25.

Chapter 4
GOD'S PLAN BRINGS VICTORY

A Stronghold to be Conquered

The great fortress of Jericho was probably visible from the camp of Israel about a mile and a quarter away. There was no way around it; it dominated the whole Plain of Jordan and the entire region of the Jordan River and the Dead Sea. There was no way through it; it was protected by two stone walls, an inner wall twelve feet thick and an outer one six feet thick, each thirty feet high. It was a formidable obstacle on the path to possessing the promises of God. But, any city is only as good as its citizens and Joshua's spies had discovered that the people of Jericho had heard of the miracles of Jehovah God in behalf of His people and were already defeated in their hearts (Joshua 2:9 through 11).

Here is a classic confrontation between good and evil, a supernatural showdown between God and Satan. On one side is Jericho, whose very name meant, "moon city,"[1] indicating moon worship, an occult practice. On the other side, were God's chosen people, Israel, which meant, "a prince of God,"[2] or "one who rules with God."[3] It was a spiritual standoff. The forces of Satan seemed safe inside their fortress (Joshua 6:1), while, on the outside, God's people were preparing to prevail and rule with God. The maturing child of God will face such clashes in spiritual warfare, battles between good and evil, the flesh and the spirit, as described in Romans 8:6 through 8, *"For to be carnally minded is death; but to be spiritually minded is life and peace....they that are in the flesh cannot please God."* In order to grow in the Lord, it is necessary to fight the good fight of faith to bring down the stronghold of flesh and build the strongholds of the spirit. Then, one may be a God-ruled man, one who prevails and rules with his Lord, a mature soldier of the King.

The Battle Plan Given

Outside the impregnable fortress of Jericho, God had a message for Joshua, in Joshua 6:2, *"See, I have given into thine hand Jericho, and the king thereof, and the mighty men of valour."* God's promise is in the past tense. To God, it was already an accomplished fact and the outcome was never in doubt; Jericho already belonged to His people and their total victory was promised before the battle even began. Notice that God meant for His children to take the city, a type of Satan's stronghold, the king of the city, a type of Satan, himself, and all of the city's soldiers, typical of Satan's demonic hordes. God saw the spiritual implications of the battle and He meant to win it completely.

God had a unique plan that defied all military strategy of all time. A parade--Israel's soldiers, seven priests with rams' horn trumpets, and the priests carrying the Ark of the Covenant--was to march around Jericho once a day for six days in total silence, except for the sound of the trumpets (Joshua 6:3). Finally, on the seventh day, the parade was to make seven circuits of the city with trumpets blaring (Joshua 6:4). Then, as the trumpets sounded a sustained note, all the people of Israel were to shout. At that shout, the walls of Jericho would fall down flat (Joshua 6:5). The Septuagint, the Greek translation of the Hebrew Scriptures says, "The walls of the city will fall of their own accord."

A clue to this strategy lies in the order of march in Numbers 10:14, *"In the first place went...Judah...."* Judah, whose name meant, "praise,"[4] led all other tribes on any march or into any battle. Next, came seven priests armed only with trumpets, traditionally used to herald the arrival of a king (2 Kings 9:12 and 13) or call to worship or war (Numbers 10:1 through 9). They were followed by the Ark, the visible symbol of God's presence. The secret of this odd order of march is explained by David, Israel's greatest war hero, in Psalm 22:3, *"But thou art holy, O thou that inhabitest the praises of Israel."* The tribe of Judah, typifying the praises of God's people, had to come first. Then, according to King David, God would inhabit that praise and His presence would come upon the scene where the Lord God who fights for Israel (Joshua 10:42) would make short work of her enemies.

In spiritual warfare, the mature child of God must follow the same order of march in his battle plan. Rather than allow a spiritual attack to plunge him into depression or despair, he must praise the God who is his King, who fights for him, and who has promised victory. Success will soon follow. The presence of the Lord will enter the tabernacle built by praise. In that presence, there can be no defeat. The psalmist caught a vision of praise as a key to the defeat of enemies. In Psalm 149:6 through 9, he said,

> *Let the high praises of God be in their mouth, and a two-edged sword in their hand; To execute vengeance upon the heathen....To bind their kings with chains, and their nobles with fetters of iron; To execute upon them the judgment written: this honour have all his saints, Praise ye the LORD.*

On each circuit of the city, the soldiers could merely march silently, indicating that the battle is not man's and would not be won by man's strength or strategies. Then, the sounding of the trumpets would herald the arrival of the Warrior-King, whose battle it was. The mature soldier of the King must recognize that the spiritual battle is not his and cannot be won in his strength or strategies; the victory belongs to God, who will, in response to the praises of His child, enter the fray and defeat the foe. Praise, then, becomes one of the most effective weapons wielded in spiritual warfare.

The Battle Plan Followed

As ridiculous as the plan might have seemed to the logical mind, Joshua did not hesitate or question; he carried it out, just as God had given it to him. (Joshua 6:6 and 7). His people didn't hesitate or question, either, even though there is no hint that Joshua ever relayed God's promise to them. In immediate response to Joshua's orders and in faith alone, the parade prepared for its first procession around Jericho (Joshua 6:8 through 10).

Note the spirit of one accord which unified the people of God. Gone was the petty bickering and complaining of the previous generation which had paralyzed their progress. When a nation, a people, a family, or a single mature believer is in perfect unity with the Lord, anything can happen, as God, Himself, observed in Genesis 11:6, *"Behold, the people is one...and now nothing will be restrained from them, which they have imagined to do."* Such unity brings the Lord into any situation, as illustrated in the upper room on the Day of Pentecost, as Acts 2:1 and 4 records, *"And when the day of Pentecost was fully come, they were all with one accord in one place....And they were all filled with the Holy Ghost."*

So, once a day for six days, the procession circled the city in silence, except for the trumpets, and returned to camp. Imagine the unnerving effect this strange strategy must have had on the already unnerved inhabitants of Jericho. The very sight of their enemies circling their city without attacking must have inspired the same terror as Indians surrounding the circled wagons of the pioneers. The ear-splitting trumpeting of the rams' horns must have had the same effect as the incessant beating of jungle drums. By the end of the sixth day of this psychological warfare, the armies of Jericho would probably have welcomed an attack. The seventh day, with its seven circuits of the city going on for hours, must have brought them to the breaking point. Their torture was almost over.

Just before the seventh circuit on the seventh day, Joshua reminded his warriors that Rahab and her family were to be spared (Joshua 6:17), as his spies had promised in Joshua 2:18 and 19. He also gave specific orders regarding the spoils of war (Joshua 6:17 through 19). In Deuteronomy 20:13 through 15, Moses had left clear commands concerning the spoils of those cities outside Canaan which refused to surrender:

> *Thou shalt smite every male thereof with the edge of the sword: but the women, and the little ones, and the cattle, and all that is in the city, even all the spoil thereof, shalt thou take unto thyself; and thou shalt eat the spoil of thine enemies, which the LORD thy God hath given thee. Thus shalt thou do unto all the cities which are very far off from thee, which are not of the cities of these nations.*

But, the same standards did apply to the inhabitants of the cities within Canaan land or to their possessions, as Moses declared in Deuteronomy 20:16 through 18:

> *But of the cities of these people, which the LORD thy God doth give thee for an inheritance, thou shalt save alive nothing that breatheth: But thou shall utterly destroy them; namely, the Hittites, and the Amorites, the Canaanites, and the Perizzites, the Hivites, and the Jebusites; as the LORD thy God hath commanded thee: That they teach you not to do after all their abominations, which they have done unto their gods; so should ye sin against the LORD your God."*

The rules were clear. Foreign cities could choose to surrender peacefully and become tributaries of Israel; if they refused, the men would be killed, the children would be taken as servants, and the material possessions would belong to the finders. But, there could be no mercy for the cities of Canaan, no peace offered, no unconditional surrender accepted. Every person, regardless of age or gender, was to be executed and all valuables, many of which were Canaanite idols or religious relics, were to be destroyed.

Many wonder how God could order such slaughter and how His people could coldly carry it out. But, during the four hundred and thirty years of Israel's bondage in Egypt, God had patiently tolerated the Canaanite religion with its idolatry, prostitution, and human sacrifices. God told Abraham of His mercy for the Canaanites, specifically the Amorites, in Genesis 15:16, *"For the iniquity of the Amorites is not yet full."* God's long-suffering continued throughout the forty years of Israel's wilderness wandering when, according to the Canaanites' own testimony, they had witnessed God's miracles in behalf of the Israelites, realized that He would soon give them Canaan, and recognized Him as the one, true God (Joshua 2:9 through 11). Yet, the Canaanites refused to accept Jehovah as their God. They continued in their idolatry and their walled fortress was still called Jericho, the moon city. To illustrate the great grace God granted the Canaanites, note that, from the time Israel as a nation began to dabble in idolatry during Solomon's reign, until Judah was taken captive to Babylon as punishment, less than four hundred years elapsed. God extended more mercy to the Canaanites, who had not known a personal relationship with Him, than He did to His own people who had. Now, the account of the Canaanites had come due. In addition, God was protecting His children from contamination by the Canaanite religion (Deuteronomy 20:18), and the only way to stamp it out was to stamp out the Canaanites.

So, everyone, with the exception of Rahab and her household, was to be slaughtered (Joshua 6:17). All spoils were to be considered *"accursed,"* (Joshua 6:18) meaning devoted.

Just about everything in Jericho had been devoted to idols; now it was all devoted by God to utter destruction. Only raw ores--silver, gold, brass, and iron which had never been fashioned into an idol or anything devoted to one--were to be gathered up, dedicated to the Lord, and placed in the Tabernacle treasuries to make additional implements for worship.

This lesson is a difficult but necessary one. For the mature spiritual warrior, there can be no compromise with Satan and no dabbling with the occult since there is no Biblical recipe for redeeming the accursed thing dedicated to Satan. So, for the child of God, certain books, jewelry, art objects, music, movies, tapes, and television programs, etc.--any with Satanism, witchcraft, or the occult as their theme--are forever forbidden. There is no other way to victory in Christ. Paul repeated this requirement for separation from the unclean thing, in 2 Corinthians 6:16 through 18:

> *And what agreement hath the temple of God with idols? for ye are the temple of the living God; as God hath said, I will dwell in them, and walk in them; and I will be their god, and they shall be my people. Wherefore come out from among them and be ye separate, saith the Lord, and touch not the unclean thing: and I will receive you, And will be a Father unto you, and ye shall be my sons and daughters, saith the Lord Almighty.*

The Battle Plan Brings Victory

There was only one more step, one more order to be obeyed. The execution of that command and its results are recorded in Joshua 6:20:

> *So the people shouted when the priests blew with the trumpets: and it came to pass, when the people heard the sound of the trumpet, and the people shouted with a great shout, that the wall fell down flat, so that the people went up into the city, every man straight before him, and they took the city.*

At the end of the seventh circuit on the seventh day, the rams' horns blew their sustained note and the people shouted, just as God had decreed (Joshua 6:5). Notice that the shout of victory came before the reality of victory. This act of faith is recalled in Hebrews 11:30, "*By faith the walls of Jericho fell down.*" Notice, too, that God's commands performed in God's way brought the results God had predicted; the walls of Jericho, the walls in which her defenders had trusted, fell down flat. The Hebrew word used, *tahat*, literally meant, "from underneath."[5] There is evidence that those ponderous walls were miraculously undermined from beneath and went straight down into the ground like an elevator, leaving the city totally exposed and leaving a clear path for God's conquerors. The fate of the woman who believed in God is recorded in Joshua 6:25:

> *Joshua saved Rahab the harlot alive, and her father's household, and all that she had; and she dwelleth in Israel even unto this day; because she hid the messengers, which Joshua sent to spy out Jericho.*

In an interesting sidelight of history, Rahab later married Salmon, a prominent man of Judah, and gave birth to Boaz, the husband of Ruth and great-grandfather of King David (Matthew 1:5 and 6). According to Josephus, Rahab was given a grant of land within Canaan and was held in high admiration by her new countrymen.[6] Rahab, the former harlot of Jericho, became one of God's people and a direct ancestor of both King David and the Lord Jesus Christ. James 2:25 reports that she was also saved, "*Was not Rahab the harlot justified by works, when she had received the messengers...?*" Her salvation may have resulted in works, but it was born of faith, as Hebrew s 11:31 asserts, "*By faith the harlot Rahab perished not with them that believed not, when she had received the spies with peace.*"

Everything and everyone in the city of Jericho was to be destroyed that day, just as God ordered (Joshua 6:21 and 14), but there was a single exception to complete obedience. That deviation from God's design and its disastrous results will be considered next.

Jericho was taken that day because God's people had faith in Him and followed His plan for victory. This is still the only way that God's children can hope to succeed against the adversary--through complete and total obedience to God and to His commands for waging spiritual warfare. In this way, they, too, can overcome any obstacle to conquest, bring down any fortress of the enemy, and gain absolute victory over any adversary. In this way, too, they can touch the lives of others and win them to the Lord.

The Stronghold Cursed

As a parting gesture to the paganism of Jericho, Joshua placed a curse upon anyone who would dare to try to rebuild it, as recorded in Joshua 6:26,

> *Cursed be the man before the Lord, that riseth up and buildeth this city Jericho: he shall lay the foundation thereof in his firstborn, and in his youngest son shall he set up the gates of it.*

Over five hundred years later, during the days of evil King Ahab, someone actually did dare to defy that curse. His name was Hiel and he was from Bethel, a city which had been devoted to the worship of a golden calf by King Jeroboam (I Kings 12:28 and 29). I Kings 16:34 records the high price he paid for this foolhardy decision:

> *In his days did Hiel the Bethelite build Jericho: he laid the foundation thereof in Abiram his firstborn, and set up the gates thereof in his youngest son Segub, according to the word of the LORD, which he spake by Joshua the son of Nun.*

The mature child of God is never permitted to rebuild any accursed thing. It is never spiritually safe to return to an old habit, give in to an old temptation, or dabble in an old occult practice. The price for such reckless behavior is always high, risking the spiritual lives of those loved most and threatening the fruit of one's own life and ministry.

The Servant of God Exalted

The fall of Jericho, the fortress city in which all of the inhabitants of the plain trusted, insured the personal prestige of Joshua, Israel's commander. In Joshua 6:27, the local news report is recorded, *"So the LORD was with Joshua; and his fame was noised throughout all the country."* The world will still stand in awe of the mature believer who engages in spiritual warfare at the direction of his Lord, who wins the victory against the adversary, and who claims everything he has been promised by the word of his God.

[1]Merrill C. Tenney, *The Zondervan Pictorial Bible Dictionary*, p. 413.

[2]George Barr, *Who's Who in the Bible*, p. 80.

[3]Herbert Lockyer, *All the Men of the Bible*, p. 161.

[4]Tenney, p. 453.

[5]H. D. M. Spence and Joseph S. Exell, *The Pulpit Commentary*, Volume 3, The Book of Joshua, p. 98.

[6]Flavius Josephus, *The Complete Works of Josephus*, Antiquities of the Jews, Book V, Chapter 1, Verse 7.

Chapter 5
MAN'S PLAN BRINGS DEFEAT

Sin in the Camp

Among Israel's soldiers was Achan, whose name, appropriately, meant, "trouble."[1] Despite Joshua's instructions about spoils (Joshua 6:18), after Jericho fell, Achan picked up some of the accursed things (Joshua 7:1), devoted to idols by their owners and devoted to destruction or to the tabernacle treasuries by God (Joshua 6:19). He had disobeyed the God's direct orders, violated the Ten Commandments by coveting, and stolen things God reserved for Himself. In Joshua 7:21, Achan gave a complete inventory of the items:

> *When I saw among the spoils a goodly Babylonish garment, and two hundred shekels of silver, and a wedge of gold of fifty shekels weight, then I coveted them, and took them.*

The *"goodly Babylonish garment"* was literally, "a mantle of Shinar," a gorgeous robe which was usually decorated with brilliantly colored depictions of popular deities. The silver coins either carried the image or inscription of an idol or constituted an offering to one. The bar or, literally, "tongue" of gold was likely an idol with a grotesquely exaggerated mouth and tongue, consistent with pagan deities. Both the silver and gold were precious metals to be donated to the Tabernacle, not kept by the finder (Joshua 6:19). The child of God must avoid accursed things. Clothing, coins, and jewelry which have Satanic or occult themes are prohibited. Idols and images which have become a part of modern culture, often as souvenirs of trips to foreign countries and native areas of America, are likewise forbidden and can carry a spiritual curse.

The result of Achan's action is noted in Joshua 7:1, *"The anger of the LORD was kindled against the children of Israel."* God knew, He was angry, and His anger extended to everyone in Israel. At first glance, this may seem unfair, but look again. First, God had given fair warning that disobedience would affect the entire congregation, in Joshua 6:18:

> *And ye, in any wise keep yourselves from the accursed thing, lest ye make yourselves accursed...and make the camp of Israel a curse, and trouble it.*

Also note that precious metals are heavy. It was physically impossible for Achan alone to carry two hundred and fifty shekels of silver and a bar of gold. Others must have helped him carry his ill-gotten gains, and, therefore, shared his complicity and his penalty. The spiritually immature contend their sin hurts no one but themselves. Achan's example proves otherwise. The mature saint realizes his actions affect others, particularly his loved ones, and will obey God's commands to spare all involved. The code of the immature commands that one never inform on a friend. The case of Achan, however, shows that those who know of sinful action and do nothing to stop or expose it, bring the wrath of God upon themselves, too. Legally, this is "aiding and abetting" and one guilty of it is "an accomplice." These crimes can carry penalties as severe as those for the act itself. The mature child of God knows that, under God's Law, the same rules apply.

In addition, Israel, as *"the church in the wilderness"* (Acts 7:38), represents the modern church. When one member sins, especially if others know and overlook it, God's judgment may fall upon an entire congregation, particularly when a church leader is involved.

Effects of the Sin

Meanwhile, Joshua was planning the battle of Ai, a fortress on a conical mount about ten miles west of Jericho. It must have seemed an easy target after Jericho, so Joshua didn't pray, seek God's direction, or obtain God's battle plan. His very human attitude seemed to be, "Thanks, God, for your help at Jericho, but we can take it from here." Joshua had fallen into the same trap which destroyed Nadab and Abihu. On the heels of a great spiritual victory, during which he had conquered the greatest obstacle in Palestine and after which he had operated in the Gift of Prophecy (Joshua 6:26), he, like Nadab and Abihu, had acted rashly and proceeded without consulting God. Joshua had begun to believe his own press notices, as written by the local inhabitants (Joshua 6:27) and failed to acknowledge his total dependance on God. At a moment of spiritual triumph, even a mature believer can become conceited, complacent, and over-confident, tendencies that can turn triumph into tragedy. When coming down from the spiritual mountain-top, he is wise to move only as God directs and never take a single step in his own strength.

Rather than seek God, Joshua used his own logic and the same plan that had worked before. First, as he had done prior to his conquest of Jericho, he sent spies to report on the fortifications, armaments, and defenders in Ai (Joshua 7:2). They were so certain of Israel's military might, they advised Joshua to send only two or three thousand men, instead of the entire army, to take Ai (Joshua 7:3). Still ignoring God, Joshua took the advice of his spies, mere mortal men (Joshua 7:4). Some still fail to consult God when faced with a spiritual battle, especially if they have had past victories. The result is still the same. Man's plan, using man's logic, and dependent on man's strength is doomed to fail for, *"We wrestle not against flesh and blood,"* (Ephesians 6:12) so, the battle can't be won by flesh and blood. A spiritual battle must be waged with spiritual weapons at the direction of the spiritual General. The mature believer will seek God's advice in spiritual warfare (Psalm 1:1 and 2). Then, through the Holy Spirit's Gift of Discernment (1 Corinthians 12:10), God will reveal the foe and the strategy needed to defeat him.

What if Joshua had consulted God? No doubt, He would have revealed Achan's sin <u>before</u> the battle and judged it <u>before</u> it could cause defeat. Then, God would have given a battle plan guaranteed to bring victory. Instead, the first battle of Ai ended in discouragement and defeat (Joshua 7:4). Thirty-six innocent men died and the congregation became paralyzed in fear as, *"the hearts of the people melted and became as water,"* (Joshua 7:5). Joshua tore his clothes and he and Israel's elders sprinkled dust upon their heads, the Middle Eastern signs of sorrow and mourning. Finally, Joshua prayed (Joshua 7:6 and 8). Meanwhile, the same locals who had brought news of Moses' disgrace of the Egyptians and Joshua's defeat of Jericho, were spreading the story of Israel's rout at Ai. Israel would no longer be seen as invincible, damaging both the reputation of Israel and her Lord, just as Joshua feared most (Joshua 7:9). All of this was the result of one man's sin. If Achan ever thought what he did was no one's business but his own, if he ever believed it couldn't hurt anyone but himself, he was very wrong. So is anyone else who takes that view.

Be Sure Your Sin Will Find You Out

In response to Joshua's prayer, God finally spoke. What He had to say was neither gentle nor comforting; it was brusque, blunt, and to the point, as Joshua 7:10 through 13 records:

> *And the LORD said unto Joshua, Get thee up; wherefore liest thou thus upon thy face? <u>Israel hath sinned</u>, and <u>they have also transgressed my covenant</u> which I commanded them: for <u>they have even taken of the accursed thing</u>, and <u>have</u>*

also stolen, and dissembled also, and they have put it even among their own stuff. Therefore the children of Israel could not stand before their enemies, but turned their backs before their enemies, because they were accursed: neither will I be with you any more, except ye destroy the accursed from among you. Up, sanctify the people, and say, Sanctify yourselves against to morrow: for thus saith the LORD God of Israel, There is an accursed thing in the midst of thee, O Israel: thou canst not stand before thine enemies, until ye take away the accursed thing from among you.

1. **All Israel had committed sin.** Clearly, God knew that Achan had not acted alone; others aided, abetted, or simply knew and did nothing. God held everyone equally guilty.
2. **God's covenant and His commandments had been transgressed.** Jehovah would excuse neither.
3. **They had taken the accursed thing.** They had kept things previously devoted to idols which should have been devoted to God and His Tabernacle (Joshua 6:19).
4. **They had stolen.** This was a violation of the Eighth Commandment (Exodus 20:15).
5. **They had dissembled.** They had lied or deceived, a violation of the Ninth Commandment (Exodus 20:16).
6. **They had put it among their own stuff.** Their sin had come into the camp.

According to God, this situation required action, not wallowing in self-pity. One does not deal with sin by dissolving in despair, but by an act of cleansing. Until then, Israel would fall before her enemies and forward progress would be stopped. Once sin has entered the believer's life, he is helpless before his enemies. As Solomon wrote in Ecclesiastes 10:8, *"Whoso breaketh an hedge, a serpent shall bite him."* God builds a protective spiritual hedge around His own. Satan saw it around Job in Job 1:10, *"Hast thou not made an hedge about him...?"* This protective hedge excludes Satan and his demons while it encircles the child of God and shields him from spiritual attack. Sin creates breaks in this hedge, permitting the enemy in and allowing the child of God to be defeated. There is only one way to fix the hedge. The believer must identify the sin in his life and come to Christ for cleansing. Then, his spiritual hedge will be rebuilt, he will be safe from his adversary, and he will be able to conquer in Christ. It is the mature child of God who has learned this lesson and this secret of victory in spiritual warfare.

God ordered Israel cleansed and sanctified (Joshua 7:13), and the source of the trouble discovered and destroyed (Joshua 7:15). To do it, God gave Joshua a foolproof plan for identifying the guilty party (Joshua 7:14). All would pass before God and Joshua, first by tribes, next, by families, then, individually. Imagine Achan's feelings as first his tribe, then his family, and then his household were selected! Imagine his horror when Joshua stood toe-to-toe with him and identified him as the man who had caused all of Israel's trouble! Achan had no choice but to admit his covetousness, a violation of the Tenth commandment (Exodus 20:17), acknowledge what he had taken, and confess that he had hidden it in his tent (Joshua 7:21), where Joshua's aides later found it (Joshua 7:22 and 23). Tent, here, is the same Hebrew word translated, "tabernacle," throughout much of the Old Testament, including many of the passages referring to God's Tabernacle. This signifies sin being taken into the tabernacle, the body and life of the believer. The fact that God knew exactly were it was and worked through Joshua to uncover it, shows that no sin is ever hidden from God and that He will do whatever is necessary through the Saviour to expose it so that it may be removed. Just as there was only one answer for sin hidden in the tent, so there is only one solution for sin in the life of the believer. There must be admission of guilt, repentance of sin, cleansing from corruption, and death to the flesh which so easily leads into iniquity. In it all, God must be glorified (Joshua 7:19).

It was Joshua, again standing as a type of the Saviour, who presided over Israel's cleansing from sin and pronounced death to the sinner. Notice his play on words in Joshua 7:25, where he asked Achan, whose name meant trouble, *"Why hast thou troubled us?"* Why, indeed? As Solomon observed in Proverbs 15:27, *"He that is greedy of gain troubleth his own house."* Achan and his whole family, all of whom undoubtedly knew of his sin, would pay with their lives (Joshua 7:24 and 25), to eradicate the sin and everyone involved in it. Over their graves, a monument of stones became a constant reminder of the penalty of sin. Even the name of the location was changed to the Valley of Achor or the Valley of Trouble (Joshua 7:26), as a testimony to all who even spoke of the place. God's justice was finally satisfied, His anger finally assuaged (Joshua 7:26). Here, we see God's terrible penalty for the sinner and all who take part in his sin. This signifies the death of one's beloved flesh, the only way sin can be obliterated from the life of the believer. In Numbers 32:23, Moses had declared, *"Be sure your sin will find you out."* Once it does, admission, repentance, cleansing, and death to self are the only acceptable options, so far as God is concerned.

Cleansing Brings Victory

The sin and sinners eradicated, God had a reassuring message for His people--Ai was theirs and, this time, they could even share the spoils (Joshua 8:1 and 2). God even gave Joshua a strategy based on the previous defeat. Thirty thousand of Israel's warriors would attack just as before, and, just as before, they would turn and run. Their foes would see another easy victory at hand and, when they pursued, a second company of Israel's soldiers would destroy Ai before its defenders could return (Joshua 8:3 through 8). In this unique plan, the mature believer learns that God does not always (or even usually) work in the same way. He reserves the right to determine strategy differently each time. Then, God's warriors are taught that they can never trust in themselves or in a plan which worked previously; they must remain dependent on God's direction in each new battle they face.

God's strategy succeeded beyond belief. As Ai's warriors followed hard on the heels of the Israelites, they looked back just in time to see the smoke of their devastated city rising skyward (Joshua 8:9 through 20). Then, they were ambushed (Joshua 7:20 through 22). Ai was conquered (Joshua 8:19), her defenders defeated and destroyed (Joshua 8:21 and 22), her king captured and killed (Joshua 8:23 and 29), her inhabitants exterminated (Joshua 8:26), and her kingdom spoiled (Joshua 8:27). Man's plan had brought defeat but God's strategy brought victory. Here, is a perfect picture of spiritual warfare. When waged by man in the strength of his own flesh, the result is defeat. But, when fought with spiritual weapons and the spiritual strategy devised by God, the only outcome can be victory. Satan's stronghold is conquered; its demonic defenders are routed; its king, Satan, is brought down and his kingdom is spoiled by Christ, as Colossians 2:15 declares, *"And having spoiled principalities and powers, he made a shew of them openly, triumphing over them in it."*

Here, too, is a perfect illustration of Romans 8:28, *"And we know that all things work together for good to them that love God, to them who are the called according to his purpose."* Joshua loved God and had been called according to His purpose. So, God devised a strategy which actually took advantage of the previous defeat to lure Ai's defenders into a trap. After the victory, any future adversary would conclude that the first skirmish had simply been a cunning scheme to lure Ai to destruction. This would have left the inhabitants of the land even more unnerved than before. The child of God may, in the past, have suffered a setback or two in spiritual warfare. But, he, like Joshua, loves God and has been called according to His purpose. His God can and will devise strategies which will turn those defeats into victories, unnerving victories, which will leave the adversary trembling with trepidation before the believer and his Lord.

Afterward, Joshua took three actions. First, just as he had erected a marker of stones over Achan and his family to remind others of the defeat of sin, Joshua built a monument of stones to God's victory (Joshua 8:29). As previously seen, such monuments put future enemies on notice and encourage the child of God. Next, Joshua built an altar of stones, symbolizing the soul of man, and offered upon it some of the cattle captured as spoils (Joshua 8:30 and 31). This action illustrates that the glory of any victory must be returned to God in worship. As God declared in Isaiah 42:8, *"My glory will I not give to another."* Finally, Joshua wrote a new copy of God's Law upon stones and read it aloud to reacquaint everyone with God's requirements (Joshua 8:32 through 35). Again, stones signify the soul of man--his mind, his emotions, and his will. As God said in Hebrews 8:10, *"I will put my laws into their mind, and write them in their hearts: and I will be to them a God, and they shall be to me a people."* The mature child of God understands that sin, the violation of God's Law, results in spiritual defeat; it is only obedience to the Law of God, permanently placed in the mind and will of the believer, which can lead to spiritual victory.

More Lessons Learned

In his book, *Joshua in the Light of the New Testament*, W. Graham Scroggie, lists lessons which must be learned from the battles faced and won by God's children thus far in the Book of Joshua. Those lessons bear repeating and thoughtful consideration by any who would seek to come to maturity in Christ. They are:[2]

1. "As long as sin lasts, conflict with it will be necessary."
2. "In the conflict, the alternatives are victory or defeat."
3. "In this fight with evil, we have a divine Captain to follow whom obediently and courageously makes us more than conquerors."
4. "No evil is so insignificant as to allow of partial measures in dealing with it."
5. "When we are defeated, the cause may be discovered by prayer, but...."
6. "It will take more than prayer to repair the damage."
7. "The work of subduing our enemies is not sudden, but gradual."
8. "Success in one battle does not win the campaign, and defeat in one battle does not mean that the whole campaign has been lost."
9. "Divine help and human exertion must go together; God uses our efforts to fulfil His ends, and fights for them who fight for Him."
10. "As the enemies of God are manifold, the method of dealing with them must be multiform."
11. "Trusting and trying are not contradictory, but complimentary."
12. "The Law of God is given, not for our admiration, but for our obedience."
13. "When extermination of foes is commanded, confederation with them is a sin."
14. "We should keep a record of spiritual victories for the glory of God, for our own encouragement, and for the instruction of others."

[1]Herbert Lockyer, *All the Men of the Bible*, p. 31.

[2]W. Graham Scroggie, *Joshua in the Light of the New Testament*, pp. 45 and 46.

Chapter 6
IN LEAGUE WITH THE ENEMY

Enemy Strategies

After their defeat by Germany in World War I, the French erected the Maginot Line, a series of heavy gun emplacements built into the hills facing Germany. The designers were certain they could never be overrun. They may have been right; we'll never know. The next time Germany invaded France, at the start of World War II, she went north through Belgium, bypassing the Maginot Line completely. Since the guns faced east and could not be moved, they were never even fired. France fell again. This bit of history illustrates the fact that the enemy may not always do the expected. One must be prepared for the expected attack; one must also be prepared for the unexpected.

Open Attack

The Israelites had chalked up another victory at Ai. The other inhabitants of the land knew it was only a matter of time until their cities fell, too. So, the kings of Canaan formed an alliance against Israel (Joshua 9:1 and 2) which included the Hittites, the Amorites, the Canaanites, the Perizzites, the Hivites, and the Jebusites--the very enemies God had promised to defeat (Joshua 2:10). They were united in their goal, as well--the obliteration of Israel (Joshua 9:2). When the mature believer begins to score victories in spiritual warfare, his enemies will unite for an open attack on him. In 1 Corinthians 10:12, God warns against complacency after a spiritual victory, *"Wherefore <u>let him that thinketh he standeth take heed lest he fall</u>."* The Bible is full of believers who faced the open attack of their adversaries. Here are just a few:

1. **Job** - Job 1:6 through 12; 2:1 through 7.
2. **David** - 1 Samuel 18:10 and 11.
3. **Gabriel** - Daniel 10:12 and 13.
4. **Jesus** - Matthew 4:1 through 11.
5. **Peter** - Luke 22:31 through 34.
6. **Paul** - 2 Corinthians 12:7.
7. **Michael** - Jude 9.
8. **The woman**, the nation of Israel - Revelation 12:1 through 9.

Deception

The enemy of the believer is, however, the great deceiver, so his attack will not always be an open one. Often, it will come in the form of deception. Both happen because Satan, who is the source of all attack against God's children, is both a roaring lion and a subtle serpent. It was the subtle attack which Satan, as the serpent, brought against Woman in the Garden of Eden (Genesis 3:1). The Woman was indeed deceived, as 1 Timothy 2:14 explains, *"<u>The woman being deceived</u> was in the transgression."*

Such a deceptive attack may occur when an open attack has already failed, as Saul, who had himself tried several times to kill David, attempted to have him killed by the Philistines (1 Samuel 20:20, 21, and 25). The deception of the enemy may also come in addition to an open attack, as when Job's wife encouraged him to curse God at the time he suffered under the open attack of Satan (Job 2:9 through 13). It was this two-fold attack which Joshua and the Israelites faced. Some enemies had openly united against them while, at that very moment, another of their enemies attacked through deception.

The Gibeonites, who were actually Hivite (Joshua 9:7) residents of Gibeon, a city just slightly northwest of Jerusalem, staked everything on the hope that the Israelites were not yet familiar with all of Canaan. They sent ambassadors wearing old clothes and carrying stale provisions, in an effort to convince Joshua that they had come from some distant place (Joshua 9:4 through 13). The mature believer knows that appearances can be deceiving and things are not always as they seem. Just when Satan may seem to be very far away, his ambassadors may be very close indeed. Neither he nor they state their true identity or intentions. He often comes as a wolf in sheep's clothing and has even been known to use those who appear to be devout Christians to attempt to deceive and destroy true believers. Paul warned against this sort of deception in Acts 20:28 through 30:

> *Take heed therefore unto yourselves....after my departing shall grievous wolves enter in among you, not sparing the flock. Also of your own selves shall men arise, speaking perverse things, to draw away disciples after them.*

Gibeon's envoys had created a clever false impression. Before Joshua could expose it, they requested *"a league,"* the Hebrew, *berit*, an agreement containing curses if broken. They weren't even satisfied with a simple peace treaty; they wanted a mutual-assistance pact obliging Israel to defend them if attacked by others. Many children of God have been deceived into believing, if they simply leave Satan alone and pose no threat to him, he will cause them no harm. Nothing could be further from the truth, as we will see.

Notice how easily the Israelites' initial suspicions (Joshua 9:7) were allayed when the Gibeonites promised servitude and spoke in reverent tones of the name and fame of the Israelites' God and His victories in their behalf (Joshua 9:10). This was a classic appeal to Israel's pride, both in her military might and her God. It was also a hypocritical ploy designed to gain what Gibeon wanted, a pact which would spare her the wrath of the most successful military power in the area and place that military power on her side if needed.

Satan may not try to tempt the child of God into open sin. Instead, he may flatter the believer's pride, his piety and power with God, reassuring him of his own invulnerability and the invincibility of his God. Then, comes a seemingly sensible request. For example, consider a believer whose fasting and praying for the salvation of a loved one is becoming successful. The devil knows that loved one will soon surrender to Christ. Satan doesn't entice the believer into theft or murder or adultery; he's smarter than that. He commends the Christian's faithfulness in fasting and praises his prowess in prayer. It's just what he wants to hear. Next, Satan tells the believer he might be better able to wage spiritual warfare if he were not weak from continual fasting. It's logical; it's sensible; and it's what the believer wants to do, anyway. He's listening. Then, Satan promises servitude. Food, he assures, will serve the believer's purpose, sustaining him in the conflict to come, just as Satan guaranteed Woman that the fruit would only serve to make her wiser (Genesis 3:5). Satan has cunningly convinced the believer that he is on his side in the future fight. But, there is no battle. No spiritual warfare is ever waged for the soul of the loved one, for the battle was lost when the believer gave up his position of spiritual strength for the natural strength to be found in a piece of bread. Satan, it must always be remembered, never comes to serve, only to destroy, as Jesus warned in John 10:10, *"The thief cometh not, but for to steal, and to kill, and to destroy."* Like Israel, the believer, no matter how mature or spiritual or gifted, can never trust his own judgment or he is sure to be deceived. He must seek God's guidance and proceed only on His word, if he is to defeat the deception of his enemy. Failure to pray signifies pride in one's own judgment and, as Solomon declared in Proverbs 16:18, *"Pride goeth before destruction, and an haughty spirit before a fall."*

Obviously, Joshua and his advisors had failed to learn the lesson of their defeat in the first battle of Ai or to obey the clear command of God in Exodus 34:12:

> *Take heed to thyself, lest thou make a covenant with the inhabitants of the land whither thou goest, lest it be for a snare in the midst of thee.*

The betrayal of Joshua and his men was sealed when, once again, they failed to consult with God before taking action. Joshua 9:14 and 15 says, they, *"asked not counsel at the mouth of the LORD."* They concluded their treaty by eating with the Gibeonites (Joshua 9:14), a Middle Eastern custom which signifies friendship and trust. But, the child of God cannot afford any friendship with his enemy, as James 4:4 declares:

> *Know ye not that the friendship of the world is enmity with God? whosoever therefore will be the friend of the world is the enemy of God.*

Then, while accepting enemies as friends, the Israelites rejected God and His counsel (Joshua 9:14). The league made, Joshua and all the princes of Israel, the entire authority structure of the congregation, were obligated to the provisions of the pact (Joshua 9:15).

One may wonder why God did not simply sovereignly intervene to prevent this pact. The answer is both simple and sobering. There are some things God is not honor bound to do, even though He could. He won't intrude where His people haven't invited Him and He won't force His counsel on those who haven't asked for it. There are some things God will do. He will wait to see how His people handle such situations and He will let them learn their lessons, even if they must learn them the hard way. Had He been asked, God would certainly have revealed the deception of the Gibeonites and given clear counsel to defeat it. He was not consulted, however, and His people made their terrible treaty.

Deception Discovered

Three days later, the deception was discovered (Joshua 9:16 and 17) too late. The treaty, though fraudulent, stood. Jehovah expects His people to honor their vows because He is the covenant-making, covenant-keeping God who is party to their pledges. Failure violates the principle of Psalm 15:4 where praise and promises await he who, among other things, *"sweareth to his own hurt, and changeth not."* The seriousness with which God treats commitments is seen nearly half a millennium later, during David's reign, as a three-year famine struck Israel. When David prayed and asked the reason, God, in 2 Samuel 21:1, said "*It is for Saul...because he slew the Gibeonites*." Seven of Saul's sons had to die (2 Samuel 21:4 through 6) to end the dearth. The mature believer carefully considers the contracts he makes lest the fruit of his own life be endangered if he breaks them.

Since the Gibeonites couldn't be killed or cast out, Joshua could only enslave them (Joshua 9:20 through 27). Note that their work took them into the Tabernacle of God to deliver wood for sacrifices and water for the laver (Joshua 9:27). Their enemy could enter the one place set apart for the exclusive use of God and His people. When any believer makes a deal with the devil, his act has consequences. Satan is a legalist who'll demand his rights, even if he used deception to get them. Then, Satan will find subtle ways to creep into his life, God's tabernacle, the temple of His Holy Spirit. Any compromise will eventually bring death, just as it did for the seven sons of Saul. It is, therefore, essential that the maturing child of God make no pact with the enemy of his soul. He must remain ever watchful of deception and ever dependent upon God to expose it. Only then can he hope to keep his tabernacle free of the infiltration and influence of his enemy.

Attack Defeated

When the other Canaanite kings heard of Gibeon's traitorous treaty, they were furious (Joshua 10:1 and 2) and laid siege to the city (Joshua 10:3 through 5). The Gibeonites pleaded for the help their pact with Israel promised (Joshua 6). First, the enemy deceived; then, he forced God's people to fight for him. Compromisers often find themselves defending the devil's activity after allowing him into their lives. They lie and call it "a little white lie," or cheat and dismiss it with, "Everybody does it." They sin and excuse it saying, "I couldn't help it." Indeed, they may be unable to help themselves after granting the enemy right and residence within. They failed to ask God's counsel or allow Him to reveal all of the adversary's deceptions; they didn't permit Him to uncover the enemy's hiding places or yield to His power to cleanse the land of every last foe.

Even though the treaty was fraudulent, Joshua honored his word, given before God. Israel faced five furious Canaanite kings, claiming the victory God had promised (Joshua 10:7 through 9). God honored His word, too. With five armies under five commands, it was easy for Him to *"discomfit"* (Joshua 10:10) or confuse them, leaving them disorganized and vulnerable before the well-organized army of Israel. As they ran, God rained down huge hailstones, killing more Canaanites with hail than Israel killed with weapons (Joshua 10:11). It's clear God has no treaty with the adversary. He reserves the right to discomfit and confuse every enemy at every opportunity. He may use the mature child of God to wage spiritual warfare or He may take personal control of the conflict. But, working together, God and His dedicated warriors will defeat the enemy at every turn.

As sundown neared, more time was needed to achieve victory. This time, Joshua prayed first. Then, knowing total victory was God's will for His people, he took a giant leap of faith in full view of his astounded army. In Joshua 10:12 through 14, he said:

> *Sun, stand thou still upon Gibeon; and thou, Moon, in the valley of Ajalon. And the sun stood still, and the moon stayed, until the people had avenged themselves upon their enemies....So the sun stood still in the midst of heaven, and hasted not to go down about a whole day. And there was no day like that before it or after it, that the LORD hearkened unto the voice of a man: for the LORD fought for Israel.*

This miracle has often been debated and derided, even by Christians. But, Harold Hill, President of Curtis Engineering Company in Baltimore and consultant to NASA, gave this account in his tract, *The Missing Day*, through the International Bible Association:

> I think one of the most interesting things that God has for us today happened to our astronauts and space scientists at Greenbelt, Maryland. They were checking the position of the sun, moon, and planets out in space, where they would be one hundred years and one thousand years from now. We have to know this so we don't send a satellite up and in terms of the life of the satellite, and where the planets will be so the whole thing will not bog down. They ran the computer measurement back and forth over the centuries and it came to a halt. The computer stopped and picked up a red signal, which meant there was something wrong either with the information fed into it or with the results as compared to the standards. They called in the service department to check it out and they said, 'It's perfect.' The IBM head of operations aid said, 'What's wrong?' Well, we have found there is a day missing in space in elapsed time.' They scratched their heads. There was no

answer. One religious fellow on the team said, 'You know, one time I was in Sunday school and they talked about the sun standing still.' They didn't believe him, but they didn't have any other answer so they said, 'Show us.' So he got a Bible and went back to the book of Joshua where they found a pretty ridiculous statement for anybody who has 'common sense.' There they found the Lord saying to Joshua, *'Fear them not, I have delivered them into thy hand; there shall not a man of them stand before thee.'* Joshua was concerned because he was surrounded by the enemy and if darkness fell, they would overpower them. So Joshua asked the Lord to make the sun stand still! That's right! *'The sun stood still and the moon stayed...and hasted not to go down about a whole day.'* The space men said, 'There is the missing day!'....Isn't that amazing? Our God is rubbing their noses in His truth!

It happened! God stopped His universe for a mere mortal man because that man moved in accord with His will. Perhaps an even greater miracle occurred later, when God set it spinning again, at exactly the right speed. No wonder He asks in Jeremiah 32:27, *"Is there anything too hard for me?"* The reason for this miracle is given in Joshua 10:14, *"For the LORD fought for Israel."* God is on the side of His people and His side will always win.

Israel's third victory left the inhabitants of Canaan speechless (Joshua 10:21). Joshua had his people put their feet on the necks of the five captured Canaanite kings (Joshua 10:15 through 25). Since the neck symbolized strength and power (Song of Solomon 4:4; 7:4; Isaiah 48:4), this proved Israel had broken the power of her adversaries and put the strength of her enemies under her feet (Genesis 49:8; Psalm 18:40). The mature child of God can do it, too (Matthew 12:26 through 29). Then, the Canaanite kings were executed and hanged on trees (Joshua 10:26), the penalty pronounced on the accursed of God (Deuteronomy 21:22 and 23). Finally, their bodies were entombed in the same cave in which they had hidden (Joshua 10:27). Their place of protection had become their grave and a monument to God's victory (Joshua 10:27). In the aftermath, Joshua promised them even more victories in Joshua 10:25, *"Fear not, nor be dismayed, be strong and of good courage: for thus shall the LORD do to all your enemies against whom ye fight."* This promise is for every mature child of God engaged in spiritual warfare, but, to claim it, he must not be afraid or dismayed; he must exhibit the strength and courage to stand and fight. If the child of God meets the conditions, the Lord will fulfill the promise.

In one extraordinary day, God had caused all things to *"work together for good"* (Romans 8:28). The Lord used the treaty with the Gibeonites to assemble the united armies of five Canaanite kingdoms, just so Joshua could defeat them all at one time, in one battle, on one miraculous day. Israel was closer than ever to the total conquest of Canaan.

God Still Fights for His People

No matter how imposing the enemies, if the mature believer asks God's guidance and remains in His will, He'll perform whatever miracle is needed to guarantee victory. Still, the keys to conquest remain the same. The believer must never permit fear to destroy his ability to fight and allow his foe to triumph over him; he must be strong and courageous in the Lord; and he must be willing to stand and battle the enemy of his soul. Using these keys, the believer can open the door to deliverance; he can trample his enemies under his feet and see them go down to everlasting destruction, just as God promised through Paul in Romans 16:20, *"And the God of peace shall bruise Satan under your feet shortly."* Then, he can erect in his memory one more memorial to the miracle-working power of his Lord.

Chapter 7
THE STRONGHOLDS FALL

Strongholds Falling

After nearly forty-eight hours of combat, one would think Joshua's men might be exhausted. Yet, before that miraculous sun set, Joshua led them against Makkedah, conquered it, killed its king, and obliterated its population (Joshua 10:28). Libnah, too, suffered the same fate on the same lengthened day (Joshua 10:29 and 30). In fact, Joshua and his army did not pause to make camp until they laid siege to Lachish (Joshua 10:31) which, along with Eglon, Hebron, and Debir fell the next day (Joshua 10:32 through 39).

Once Jericho had fallen, the major fortress in which all other cities trusted, once Ai had capitulated after first chasing Israel, and once the alliance of the five kings of Canaan had been defeated after presenting a united and seemingly unbeatable force against Israel, other, less fortified cities went down like dominoes. The spirit of their defenders had been broken and they fell before Joshua in short order, offering little or no resistance.

A clear pattern emerges in these conquests. In each case, an enemy stronghold taken, its king killed, its defenders destroyed, and its citizens crushed. No quarter was given and no mercy extended. Complete conquest of every city, complete destruction of every enemy, was the only acceptable outcome. This, too, must be the strategy of the mature child of God, as he wages spiritual warfare. He must lay siege to Satan's strongholds in his life using God's battle plan in James 4:4, *"Submit yourselves therefore to God. Resist the devil, and he will flee from you."* Soon, the child of God will find that even the most impressive stronghold crumbles like a house of cards. Then, Satan, the king of each stronghold, and his demons, its defenders, can be eliminated from the land, the life of the believer. Like Joshua, the mature believer must show no mercy. The enemy must be totally destroyed to prevent future attack. Joshua did it, as seen in Joshua 10:40 and 42:

> *So Joshua smote all the country of the hills, and of the south, and of the vale, and of the springs, and all their kings: he left nothing remaining, but utterly destroyed all that breathed, as the LORD God of Israel commanded....And all these kings and their land did Joshua take at one time, because the LORD God of Israel fought for Israel.*

God's tactics worked on all types of terrain. Joshua had total victory wherever he walked because God walked with him. The mature believer, too, can win on any spiritual plane. With God's battle plan, he is victorious over all. The reason for the believer's success is still the same. When the mature child of God wages warfare at God's command and according to God's instructions, God fights for Him, with him, beside him, and through him. Together, God and His child are a majority who can fight any foe and win any battle, no matter how big the enemy force, no matter how well defended his stronghold.

Resistance Broken

Once Satan begins losing, he will take the offensive, trying to regain territory already lost and to prevent any future failures. Then, he'll devise some new strategy for which the child of God may be totally untrained and unprepared. This happened in Canaan, too.

Having witnessed the complete capitulation of the strongholds in the south, the neighbors to the north formed a new alliance against Israel (Joshua 11:1 through 3). They planned a different kind of warfare with which Israel had no experience and for which they had no time to prepare. In all previous battles, siege warfare had been waged, but the northern alliance would use mobile warfare, an offensive rather than defensive strategy. Josephus, the Jewish historian, detailed the armies and armaments arrayed against Israel:[1]

> Now the number of the whole army was three hundred thousand armed footmen, and ten thousand horsemen, and twenty thousand chariots; so that the multitude of the enemies affrighted both Joshua himself and the Israelites.

Over a quarter million foot soldiers faced Israel, with ten thousand horsemen usually armed with javelins or lances they hurled with amazing accuracy and speed. The chariot, the forerunner of the tank, was built of wood overlaid with iron. It carried two to four men armed with bows, arrows, and flame-tipped darts they could fire from the security of the chariot's protective plating. Each chariot had long projections, some straight spears, some curved scythes, affixed to the axles to decimate infantry troops--and, Israel had only infantry troops, not a single horse, not a single chariot. This force was enormous and the expertise and capabilities were enough to terrify anyone. God, however, wasn't at all intimidated by this swarm of flies. In Joshua 11:6, He said, *"Be not afraid because of them: for to morrow about this time will I deliver them up all slain before Israel."* God even gave directions for the disposition of the spoils afterward. The outcome was never in doubt.

On God's word, Joshua launched a surprise attack with lightening speed. The northern Canaanite forces never had a chance against his "blitzkrieg." The attack may have come so suddenly that they never got to use their impressive weapons or climb into their imposing chariots. Their alliance was smashed, their quarter of a million soldiers were killed (Joshua 11:7 and 8), and their chariots became firewood for Joshua and his troops (Joshua 11:9). The lesson to be learned here is often heard on the football field, "The best defense is a good offense." The enemy need not be given time to muster his forces, devise his strategy, and mount his attack. The believer can take the offensive in prayer, wage warfare against Satan in the heavenlies, and defeat him before he ever has a chance to strike. His armies can be crushed, his weapons left in ruins, and his forces disabled, just as God promised in Isaiah 54:17, *"No weapon formed against thee shall prosper."*

Conquest Completed

For five to seven years, Joshua led his armies against one city after the other (Joshua 11:19). He was always victorious and, always, in obedience to the command of God (Joshua 11:12 and 15), all of the inhabitants and their heathen religious relics were destroyed. Except for the Hivites in Gibeon, none requested peace terms or surrendered (Joshua 11:19). This, too, was in accord with God's will, as revealed in Joshua 11:20:

> *For it was of the LORD to harden their hearts, that they should come against Israel in battle, that he might destroy them utterly, and that they should have no favour, but that he might destroy them, as the LORD commanded Moses.*

The immature child of God often wonders why there is constant conflict between his flesh and his spirit, between his desire to be a Christian and the temptations he faces. The mature believer, however, knows that this, too, is in God's plan. It is God's will that the enemy attack so that His child may gain the victory and claim his inheritance in Christ. Yet, the day will dawn when temptation no longer has the pull it once did, when, as in Joshua 11:23, the land, the life of the believer, rests from war.

One particular enemy faced by Joshua must be singled out for special attention. The Anakims were, according to Numbers 13:33, the descendants of Anak, giants who terrified ten of the original twelve spies sent into Canaan by Moses. There are many who believe that the origin of the Anakims is described in Genesis 6:4:

> *There were giants in the earth in those days; and also after that, when the sons of God came in unto the daughters of men, and they bare children to them, the same became mighty men of old, men of renown.*

These *"sons of God"* are thought by many to have been fallen angels, the offspring of their unions with mortal women, gigantic demons. Yet, the very Scripture used to advance this theory clearly contradicts it. Twice, these children are called *"men,"* never once demons or evil spirits. There are two other problems with this theory. First, satanic activity on earth begins in the third chapter of Genesis with the serpent's temptation of Woman. This was approximately two thousand years before the events of the sixth chapter of Genesis, so Satan and his demons predated the offspring of Genesis 6 by a couple of millennia. The offspring, then, could not have been the original demons. Second, *"the daughters of men"* and *"the children"* born to them, whatever they were, were wiped out in the flood of Noah's day. They could not have survived as demons or Anakims for Noah, his wife, their three sons, and their three daughters-in-law were the only survivors (Genesis 9:18 and 19). So, the Anakims, rather than being the offspring of fallen angels and mortal women, were some unusually large race of people which came into existence when the earth was repopulated following the flood. While they terrorized ten of the original spies, forty years later, one of the other two made short work of them, as seen in Joshua 11:21 and 22:

> *And at that time came Joshua, and cut off the Anakims....Joshua destroyed them utterly with their cities. There was none of the Anakims left in the land of the children of Israel: only in Gaza, in Gath, and in Ashdod, there remained.*

Gaza, Gath, and Ashdod, the three cities where Joshua allowed the Anakims to remain, would later belong to the Philistines. Joshua's mercy to the remnants of this race would one day rise up to haunt Israel. In 1025 B.C., approximately three hundred and seventy-five years later, a ten-foot tall giant from Gath, a descendant of the Anakims spared by Joshua, Goliath by name, stood against God and His champion, David. He was defeated by a single stone from David's sling, but he had many relatives who would each take their turn opposing God and His people (1 Chronicles 20:4 through 8). The message is clear. There can be no mercy extended to Satan or his emissaries. All must be dealt the death blow in the life of the believer or they may attack him or his offspring in the future.

Joshua and his armies had taken all of the major fortresses of Canaan and it was time to rest in victory. There was still territory to be taken, small unwalled villages and uninhabited lands, but each tribe would be expected to conquer and hold the territory it inherited (Joshua 13:1 through 7). The twelfth chapter of Joshua contains a complete list of the cities conquered thus far. In the meanings of their names, the mature believer finds hints to the fortresses of Satan which must be conquered if he is to have rest in the Lord:

1. **Aroer** (Joshua 12:2) - "poor, naked, helpless,"[2] like those areas of one's life not yet brought under the covering and authority of God and, therefore, vulnerable to enemy attack. They can be reclaimed, put under God's covering, and protected from future attack.
2. **Bashan** (Joshua 12:4) - "smooth, fertile,"[3] symbolizing those areas of one's life which are fertile and could bring forth fruit but, because of the interference of Satan, lie fallow and unfruitful. They may be restored and become a fruitful vine in Christ.

3. **Jericho** (Joshua 12:9) - "moon city,"[4] typifies the occult influences which may touch one's life. Occult contamination can be cleansed through the true doctrine of Christ.

4. **Ai** (Joshua 12:9) - "a heap of ruins,"[5] those areas of one's life which have been completely devastated by past attacks of Satan. They can be restored in the Lord.

5. **Jerusalem** (Joshua 12:10) - "founded in peace,"[6] signifies those areas where Satan has stolen peace. True peace is still possible in Christ, who is the believer's peace. While the king of Jerusalem was slain during this initial phase of the conquest, neither Judah nor Benjamin were able to take the city itself, which lay over twenty-five hundred feet above sea level and was cradled between three mountain peaks. It was not taken until more than five hundred years later when the newly-crowned King David conquered it to be his new capital city and the permanent residence of, first, the Tabernacle, and, later, the Temple of God (2 Samuel 5:6 through 10). Only then did the nation of Israel begin to find peace.

6. **Hebron** (Joshua 12:10) - "league or confederacy,"[7] identifies the areas where one has made a league with his spiritual problems. That league can be broken in Christ.

7. **Jarmuth** (Joshua 12:11) - "height,"[8] speaks of one's pride or haughtiness which exalts itself against Christ. It can be brought in subjection to the Lord and freed from bondage.

8. **Lachish** (Joshua 12:11) - "impregnable,"[9] is Satan's most impregnable hold in one's life. It, too, can be conquered in Christ.

9. **Eglon** (Joshua 12:12) - "circle or chariot,"[10] those forces of Satan which enclose or encircle. That circle can be breached and those foes defeated by God in spiritual warfare.

10. **Gezer** (Joshua 12:12) - "precipice,"[11] signifies the position of spiritual danger into which Satan may place one. Rescue and safety are available in Jesus.

11. **Debir** (Joshua 12:13) - "a recess,"[12] speaks of the deepest recesses of one's personality which are bound by Satan. Those bonds can be broken and the recesses freed by the Lord.

12. **Geder** (Joshua 12:13) - "wall,"[13] typical of the walled fortresses, the strongholds, in which Satan hides. He can be exposed and evicted in spiritual warfare.

13. **Hormah** (Joshua 12:14) - "a devoted place laid waste,"[14] is one's temple of the Holy Spirit which has been laid waste by Satan. It can be rededicated and rebuilt in God.

14. **Arad** (Joshua 12:14) - "wild ass,"[15] are the attitudes of rebellion and stubbornness which bring defeat. Rebellion can be broken and stubbornness made subject to Christ.

15. **Libnah** (Joshua 12:15) - "whiteness,"[16] is typical of the areas that look good but still contain a few dead man's bones (Matthew 23:27). The bones can be resurrected in Christ.

16. **Adullam** (Joshua 12:15) - "justice of the people,"[17] are the areas of the mind which exalt man's law above the Law of God. Such thinking can yield to the mind of Christ.

17. **Makkedah** (Joshua 12:16) - "place of the shepherds,"[18] that place where Christ should dwell but which is usurped by Satan. Jesus can chase the usurper in spiritual warfare.

18. **Bethel** (Joshua 12:16) - "house of God,"[19] those areas which should be dedicated to God but are trampled by Satan. Jesus can drive him out as He did the money changers.

19. **Tappuah** (Joshua 12:17) - "apple,"[20] that which is the apple of one's eye, and which, through Satan, has become an idol in one's life. That idol can be brought down in God.

20. **Hepher** (Joshua 12:17) - "well,"[21] symbolic of the joy which should well up within but which Satan has stolen. That joy can be restored in Christ to become one's strength again.

21. **Aphek** (Joshua 12:18) - "strength,"[22] the seemingly unbeatable strength of Satan. But, God is stronger and can break Satan's might in spiritual warfare.

22. **Lasharon** (Joshua 12:18) - "of the plain,"[23] the place where the Rose of Sharon would grow were it not for Satan's weeds. His weeds can be pulled and the Rose replanted.

23. **Madon** (Joshua 12:19) - "contention,"[24] typifies the contention Satan causes in one's life. That contention can be forever calmed in Christ.
24. **Hazor** (Joshua 12:19) - "castle,"[25] the seat of Satan's rule and reign in one's life. In spiritual warfare, he can be evicted from his castle so that Christ can rule and reign instead.
25. **Shimronmeron** (Joshua 12:20) - "watchful,"[26] speaks of Satan watching for a weakness in one's life that he can exploit. In Christ, those weaknesses can become strong again.
26. **Achsaph** (Joshua 12:20) - "enchantment,"[27] is an interest in magic and the occult which may bind one's life. It can be banished and replaced with a desire for God.
27. **Taanach** (Joshua 12:21) - "battlement or defense of Anak,"[28] typical of the strongholds of the giant problems in one's life. As David defeated Goliath, these strongholds and the giants which inhabit them can be defeated in Christ.
28. **Megiddo** (Joshua 12:21) - "place of troops,"[29] speaks of Satan's demonic troops which fight in one's life. These demons may be beaten and banished in the Lord.
29. **Kedesh** (Joshua 12:22) - "sanctuary,"[30] is the internal sanctuary of God where Satan often trespasses. That trespasser can be evicted and that sanctuary set apart for God.
30. **Jokneam** (Joshua 12:22) - "possessed by the people,"[31] the areas of one's life which are influenced by others. These areas can be brought under the influence of Christ.
31. **Dor** (Joshua 12:23) - "dwelling,"[32] those areas of one's life where Satan dwells. Satan can be evicted from his dwelling so that Christ may take up residence there.
32. **Gilgal** (Joshua 12:23) - "circle of stone,"[33] typical of the soul of man encircled by Satan. In Christ, that circle can be broken and the soul freed.
33. **Tirzah** (Joshua 12:24) - "pleasantness,"[34] signifies the pleasure of sin for a season which brings death. Sin's pleasures can be replaced by the pleasures of God forever.

In this list of the cities conquered in Canaan, God left a message for every mature child of God to read and understand. It is the responsibility of each believer to identify the influences of Satan in his own life, to wage spiritual warfare to conquer and reclaim them, and to win the victory in Christ.

[1]Flavius Josephus, *The Complete Works of Josephus*, Antiquities of the Jews, Book V, Chapter I, Verse 18.

[2]Merrill C. Tenney, *The Zondervan Pictorial Bible Dictionary*, p. 73.

[3]Ibid., p. 99.

[4]Ibid., p. 413.

[5]C. I. Scofield, *The Scofield Reference Bible*, Proper Name Index, p. 5.

[6]Ibid., Proper Name Index, p. 27.

[7]Ibid., p. 345.

[8]Ibid., p. 403.

[9]Scofield, Proper Name Index, p. 30.

[10]Herbert Lockyer, *All the Men of the Bible*, p. 95.

[11]Scofield, Proper Name Index, p. 19.

[12]Ibid., Proper Name Index, p. 15.

[13]Ibid., Proper Name Index, p. 19.

[14]Ibid., Proper Name Index, p. 23.
[15]Ibid., Proper Name Index, p. 7.
[16]Ibid., Proper Name Index, p. 30.
[17]Ibid, Proper Name Index, p. 5.
[18]Tenney, p. 503.
[19]Ibid., p. 109.
[20]Scofield, Proper Name Index, p. 44.
[21]Tenney, p. 348.
[22]Scofield, Proper Name Index, p. 7.
[23]Ibid., Proper Name Index, p. 30.
[24]Tenney, p. 501.
[25]Scofield, Proper Name Index, p. 22.
[26]Ibid., Proper Name Index, p. 42.
[27]Ibid., Proper Name Index, p. 4.
[28]Tenney, p. 821.
[29]Scofield, Proper Name Index, p. 32.
[30]Ibid., Proper Name Index, p. 29.
[31]Ibid., Proper Name Index, p. 28.
[32]Ibid., Proper Name Index, p. 15.
[33]Tenney, p. 314.
[34]Scofield, Proper Name Index, p. 44.

Chapter 8
TAKING YOUR INHERITANCE

Division Ordered

Joshua had completed the conquest of Canaan, as Joshua 11:15 and 23 record, *"He left nothing undone of all that the LORD commanded....So Joshua took the whole land."* But, he was about a hundred years old and was experiencing the infirmities commonly associated with old age (Joshua 13:1), so God had a new command for him, in Joshua 13:7, *"Divide this land for an inheritance unto the nine tribes, and the half tribe of Manasseh."*

There's a big difference between inheritance and possession. Inheritance, in Joshua, is the Hebrew, *nahala*, which means, "inheritance, heritage," or to "give as property."[1] Possession is the Hebrew, *morash*, which means, to "dispossess, drive out, cast out, seize, gain control over."[2] Clearly, God had given the land to His people for their inheritance, but Israel had not yet taken full possession of it and driven out its occupiers. Israel had conquered, but had not yet possessed; she had inherited but not yet inhabited. The believer often finds himself in the same position. In Hebrews 9:15 through 17, we read:

> *And for this cause he is become the mediator of the new testament, that by means of death, for the redemption of the transgressions that were under the first testament, they which are called might receive the promise of eternal inheritance. For where a testament is, there must also of necessity be the death of the testator. For a testament is of force after men are dead.*

According to the writer of Hebrews, Jesus Christ made a last will and testament, naming every born-again believer as beneficiary of an eternal inheritance. When He died, that will went into effect. From that moment, every promise in the Book belonged to the believer. It is his by right of inheritance. Yet, how much of it does he presently possess?

To speed possession of Canaan, God commanded Joshua to divide it among the twelve tribes of Israel (Joshua 13:7). This division would accomplish three things. First, division would set defined, discernable, and defensible boundaries. Each tribe would recognize its area of responsibility and what belonged to others. Second, division would confer clear title to the land to its new owners. Third, once the division was completed, each tribe would move to take possession of their portion of the land and, all tribes working together, would take it all. Each child of God has a copy of his Lord's last will and testament--the Bible. It contains all of the bequests, promises, and inheritance rights which are his. It remains only for him to take possession of them in his own life in Christ. In addition, for each maturing child of God, the Lord has a prescribed area of responsibility, a defined ministry (not necessarily an office, but a capacity in which to serve Christ and others) which is his by inheritance right. Each and every mature believer is to fulfill that responsibility, to claim that ministry, and to move confidently in it.

The Inheritors Named

The list of the twelve tribes inheriting the land of Canaan also contains interesting and important lessons which God, Himself, teaches the mature believer. The patriarch, Jacob or Israel, the father of God's people, had been blessed with twelve sons (Genesis 35:22 through 26)--Reuben, Simeon, Levi, Judah, Dan, Naphtali, Gad, Asher, Issachar,

Zebulun, Joseph, and Benjamin. This list is not, however, the same as the list of the twelve tribes which were given inheritance rights in Israel in Numbers 1:4 through 17--Reuben, Simeon, Judah, Issachar, Zebulun, Ephraim, Manasseh, Benjamin, Dan, Asher, Gad, and Naphtali. Notice that Joseph and Levi have been replaced by Ephraim and Manasseh.

Joseph had been his father's youngest and favorite son (Genesis 37:3). Out of jealousy, his ten older brothers sold him into slavery in Egypt (Genesis 18 through 28). Still, even in Egypt, God was able to use Joseph to save his entire family from famine (Genesis 45:5 through 8). It would seem that, as a reward for Joseph's faithfulness and obedience, he was to be doubly blessed (Genesis 48:21 and 22). So, in Genesis 48:5, Joseph's father, Jacob, adopted his two sons, Ephraim and Manasseh, and Joseph's double portion of the inheritance was to be split between the descendants of these two boys. Joseph, himself, requested no inheritance in the land except a gravesite (Genesis 50:24 through 26).

God also ordered that the tribe of Levi receive no land (Joshua 13:14 and 33). While this seems unfair at first, there were four important reasons for this decision. First, if the tribe of Levi had received a portion of land, they would have had to conquer and hold it. This was impossible since the Law said the Levites could neither be numbered for warfare nor sent out to fight (Numbers 1:47 through 49). Second, they would have had to farm their land or raise animals on it so its abundance would not be wasted. This would have distracted them from the work God intended that they do. Third, they did not need land nor crops to meet their needs. According to the Law, the Levites were to receive the tithe, one tenth, of all the crops and animals raised by the other tribes (Numbers 18:21 and 24). Also, a designated portion of each sacrifice was to be given to the priests to provide them with meat (Leviticus 7:33 through 38). Finally, God, Himself, His blessings, and His presence were the true inheritance of the tribe of Levi. Who could ask for more? The needs of the modern minister of God are still met by the tithes, offerings, and, yes, sometimes even the sacrifices of the congregation. The mature in that congregation will be generous, realizing that, by giving to the minister and the ministry, they are truly giving to God. Still, the Lord, Himself, His blessing, and His presence are the precious inheritance the minister of God has the privilege of possessing.

In the names of the twelve tribes given an inheritance in the land, the mature believer learns that God reserves special blessings, special promises, and special possessions for those who serve Him in faith and obedience. But, God has blessings and possessions for all of His children. God also honored Moses' commitment to the tribes of Reuben, Gad, and half of the tribe of Manasseh (Numbers 32), further confirmation that God has a specific inheritance, area of responsibility, and place of ministry for each of His children. There are other lessons hidden in the meanings of the names of the twelve inheriting tribes which will help the child of God come to maturity in Him and to claim all of His promises:

1. **Reuben** - "behold a son."[3] One cannot begin to grow until he has first seen the Son.
2. **Simeon** - "a hearkening."[4] To mature and claim promises, one must hearken to Him.
3. **Judah** - "praised."[5] One matures and claims God's promises through praise first.
4. **Dan** - "judge."[6] One matures as God judges and deals with the sin in his life.
5. **Naphtali** - "my wrestling."[7] Maturing causes a wrestling between flesh and spirit.
6. **Gad** - "a troop."[8] The mature believer is in the troop, the army of God which wages spiritual warfare to claim God's promised inheritance.
7. **Asher** - "fortunate, happy."[9] A mature relationship with God brings true happiness.
8. **Issachar** - "hire"[10] or reward. God rewards the mature who possess their inheritance.

9. **Zebulun** - "dwelling or wished-for habitation."[11] The mature child of God finds his dwelling place in God and his wished-for habitation in His promises.
10. **Benjamin** - "son of the right hand."[12] (He was first named Benoni, "son of my sorrow.")[13] As one matures, he is transformed from one who brought the Father sorrow, to a son who labors at the Father's right hand to reach out to claim his Father's promises.
11. **Manasseh** - "one who causes to forget."[14] Once one has matured in the Lord and fought to claim His promises, he forgets all the battles and remembers only victories.
12. **Ephraim** - "fruitful."[15] Once the believer has matured in Christ and taken possession of His promises, he can then be truly fruitful in the service of the Lord.

Note God's growth plan. The child of God matures from first beholding the Son to possessing all he is promised and becoming fruitful in his God.

One Who Failed to Inherit

Balaam had been a true prophet of God who heard His voice (Numbers 22:9 through 13). But, Balaam was corrupted by money (Numbers 22:7), by *"the rewards of divination,"* and tried to curse his own (and God's own) people to get it (Numbers 22:15 through 24:25; 2 Peter 2:15; Jude 11). He tried to sell his prophetic gift for money. When that failed, Balaam advised, Balak, the Canaanite king who was paying him, to entice Israel into idolatry to bring God's curse on them (Numbers 25:1 through 3; Revelation 2:14). As a result, Balaam was no longer considered a prophet of God but a common soothsayer. As God's judgment on his sin, Balaam fell by the sword of the very people he had tried to curse and bring to defeat, as recorded in Joshua 13:22, *"Balaam also the son of Beor, the soothsayer, did the children of Israel slay with the sword among them that were slain by them."*

One Who Inherited It All

Fifty or more years before, Caleb had been one of the twelve sent to spy out Canaan (Joshua 14:7) and one of only two (Joshua was the other) who had believed God was able to give His people the land He had promised them, advising them to go forward to take it (Joshua 14:8). For his faith, Caleb was promised by God (Numbers 14:24) and Moses that he and his family would possess the mountain where Hebron was located, the mountain he had walked upon, the very mountain which was home to the Anakims (Joshua 14:9 through 12). Half a century had passed, but Caleb's strength had not diminished (Joshua 14:11), his memory of God's promise had not faded, and his faith had not wavered. Caleb knew Hebron was his inheritance and he was determined to possess everything God had for him (Joshua 14:12). He believed that the God who had promised was able to deliver.

Joshua, symbolizing the Saviour, gave Caleb his blessing to claim the inheritance his faith and obedience had earned (Joshua 14:13 through 15). Joshua also set aside as the rest of Judah's portion, the land surrounding Caleb's claim (Joshua 15). So, the division of the land began with Judah, meaning, "praise," because praise begins any move of God. The first city assigned to Judah, was Maaleh-acrabbim (Joshua 15:3), whose name means, "ascent of the Mount of Scorpions,"[16] because it was, literally, a mountain full of scorpions. In Luke 10:19 and 20, Jesus gave this command to His disciples, typical of His mature child:

> *Behold, I give you power to tread on serpents and scorpions, and over all the power of the enemy: and nothing shall by any means hurt you. Notwithstanding in this rejoice not, that the spirits are subject unto you; but rather rejoice, because your names are written in heaven.*

The people of the tribe of Judah were not to praise God for the power He gave them over the scorpions, but because they were His chosen people. The mature believer, too, is not to praise God because he has been given the authority to trample Satan's kingdom underfoot; he praises God because he is a child of the King, for it is only that special relationship which confers upon him that special authority.

Eighty-five year-old Caleb went on to take possession of his promised mountain driving every giant off of it (Joshua 15:13 and 14). Then, when his daughter married his nephew, Othniel, he shared part of his possession with the newlyweds (Joshua 15:16 through 19), and the inheritance rights were passed to the new generation. But, Caleb's tribe, Judah, was unable to take full possession of all they had inherited. In Joshua 15:63, we read, *"As for the Jebusites the inhabitants of Jerusalem, the children of Judah could not drive them out."* Jerusalem was not taken nor the Jebusites annihilated until King David did it in 1003 B.C. (2 Samuel 5:6 and 7), approximately four hundred years later.

The Inheritance Divided

The division of the land of Canaan continued. Ephraim received its assigned inheritance (Joshua 16:1 through 9), but never took full possession because they failed to destroy the Canaanites who occupied it (Joshua 16:10). The mature believer will recall that the enemy always creates a stumblingblock between himself and his God. For this reason, God commands that he be driven out completely. It is God's responsibility to give the believer the promised inheritance; it is the believer's responsibility to take possession of it.

The other half of the tribe of Manasseh was given a separate portion of land on the western side of the Jordan River (Joshua 17:1 through 11). They, too, opted for man's money, rather than God's promises and allowed the Canaanites to live among them in return for tribute (Joshua 17:12 and 13). As a result, they were crowded and asked Joshua for a larger portion (Joshua 17:14). Joshua did not dispute their size nor their overcrowded conditions. He did, however, advise them to do as God had commanded and drive out the Canaanites if they wanted more living space (Joshua 17:15). This is still God's command to His maturing child. He must exercise full authority over the area of responsibility which God has already placed within his care before he can clamor for some greater rights or authority in the kingdom. As Jesus said in the parable of the talents (Matthew 25:21), *"Thou hast been faithful over a few things, I will make thee ruler over many things."*

Worship Begun

Before the division of the land ended, the Tabernacle was erected and the worship of the God who had given the land was begun (Joshua 18:1) at Shiloh, whose name meant, "rest."[17] It was located about twenty-five miles north of Jerusalem, about half way between Bethel and Shechem. Scripture contains no reason for this choice. Some say God selected the site. While Jerusalem was undoubtedly God's choice as the eventual place He would put His name (2 Kings 21:4), the tribe of Judah had been unable to take it from the Jebusites (Joshua 15:63). Shiloh, which stood on an isolated and easily defensible hill, was a logical alternative. It would remain the center of worship for about three hundred years, until about 1075 B.C. Shiloh illustrates the fact that God wants to be worshipped among His children. Before anything else can be accomplished, worship must be established.

The Division Completed

There were still seven tribes which had not received land for their inheritance (Joshua 18:2). Joshua could not understand why they made no request for land nor tried to claim any (Joshua 18:3). It was time to get on with God's business so Joshua ordered each of the seven tribes to select three men to survey the land and divide it into seven equal parts (Joshua 18:4 and 5). To insure fairness in the assignment of the parcels, Joshua would draw lots among the seven tribes for them (Joshua 18:6). This reminds one of the young mother of two whose children constantly squabbled over which received the largest dessert. She tried everything, but, no matter how she divided the dessert, both were certain that the other had received a larger share. Finally, she got a brilliant idea. She had the elder of the two divide the dessert, but she allowed the younger to select his portion first. Problem solved! Joshua avoided any such squabbles with his equally clever plan. The surveyors had to divide the land into equitable parcels since no one, including Joshua, had any idea which parcel would be drawn for which tribe. The men set to work immediately and recorded their findings in a book (Joshua 18:8 and 9). As soon as the survey was concluded, Joshua conducted the drawing (Joshua 18:10). The remainder of the land was fairly divided between the remaining tribes (Joshua 18:11 through 19:48), each of which was expected to take possession of all of the lands and cities assigned to them.

During all of the battles and divisions, Joshua had asked nothing for himself. Finally, after all of the land had been apportioned, the Israelites came together to award him the city God had promised him, Timnath-serah (Joshua 19:49 through 51). This small village was located in the land given to Joshua's tribe of Ephraim. Joshua, the type of Christ, rebuilt it and was eventually buried there. So often, the immature child of God gives the Saviour, not the first nor the best of his energy and talents, but whatever happens to be left. It is only through the grace and mercy of the Saviour that He receives whatever is dedicated to Him and rebuilds of it a shining city in which He dwells. The mature saint, on the other hand, will dedicate his life to his Lord and devote to Him the first and best of his time, his energies, and his talents. Then, the Saviour will build of his life a beautiful temple in which His Holy Spirit is pleased to dwell.

The Importance of One's Inheritance

How the believer uses his God-given inheritance is critical, as seen in a careful review of the list of the twelve tribes of Israel as they will be sealed to receive their final, heavenly inheritance in Revelation 7:4 through 8--Judah, Reuben, Gad, Asher, Naphtali, Manasseh, Simeon, Levi, Issachar, Zebulun, Joseph, and Benjamin. We see that the list has changed again. Joseph and Levi have been restored while Dan and Ephraim are missing. Why? How did Dan and Ephraim lose their final inheritance from God? The answer is significant and contains an important lesson God would teach His maturing children.

The key to this mystery lies in one wrong decision made over five hundred years after Joshua divided the inheritance among the twelve tribes of Israel. After the death of Solomon, David's son, Israel split in two. Solomon's son, Rehoboam, ruled over Benjamin and his own tribe of Judah, where Jerusalem and the Temple were located. Jeroboam became king of the remaining ten tribes. But, the Law commanded that Jews celebrate three sacred feast days at the place God placed His name (Exodus 23:14 through 17), and, by that time, that place was Jerusalem. Jeroboam had to make a decision. He could allow his subjects to go to Jerusalem for the feasts and risk losing their loyalty, or he could keep them home by establishing an alternative place of worship. The answer seemed obvious, it looked good, it was logical, and there seemed no other choice if Jeroboam wanted to keep his kingdom. His decision is described in 1 Kings 12:28 through 29, *"The king...made two calves of gold, and...he set one in Bethel, and the other put he in Dan."* Dan, a major city in northern Israel, was the capital of the tribe of Dan (Joshua 19:47). Bethel, a major southern city not far from Jerusalem, had originally been assigned to the tribe of Benjamin

(Joshua 18:21 and 22) and lay just inside of Benjamin's border with Ephraim (Joshua 16:1 and 2). When Benjamin couldn't take Bethel from the Canaanites, Joseph's descendants did. They gave it to the descendants of Joseph who lived nearest to it, the tribe of Ephraim. It was listed as their possession in 1 Chronicles 7:28.

The people of Israel had to make some decisions, too. They had to decide whether these golden calves, imitations of the one made by Aaron which had caused their ancestors so much trouble, could be placed in the territory they had inherited as their possession from God. Then, they had to decide if they would worship them. 1 Kings 12:30 records their fateful decision, *"And this thing became a sin: for the people went to worship before the one, even unto Dan."* For violating the Second Commandment by permitting the golden calves to be placed in their inheritance and for violating the First Commandment by worshipping them, Dan and Ephraim lost everything. They will lose their eternal inheritance in Heaven.

The mature child of God will learn the lesson of Dan and Ephraim. He will claim his inheritance in God, move to possess all of the promises of God, and will strive to hold them in holiness and obedience all of the days of his life. Only then, can he be assured of receiving that heavenly inheritance which awaits him.

[1]R. Laird Harris, Gleason L. Archer, Jr., and Bruce K. Waltke, *Theological Wordbook of the Old Testament*, p. 569.

[2]Ibid.

[3]C. I. Scofield, *The Scofield Reference Bible*, Proper Name Index, p. 39.

[4]Ibid., Proper Name Index, p. 42.

[5]Ibid., Proper Name Index, p. 29.

[6]Ibid., Proper Name Index, p. 14.

[7]Ibid., Proper Name Index, p. 35.

[8]Ibid., Proper Name Index, p. 18.

[9]Ibid., Proper Name Index, p. 8.

[10]Ibid., Proper Name Index, p. 24.

[11]Herbert Lockyer, *All the Men of the Bible*, p. 342.

[12]Scofield, Proper Name Index, p. 10.

[13]Ibid.

[14]Ibid., Proper Name Index, p. 31.

[15]Ibid., Proper Name Index, p. 17.

[16]Finis Jennings Dake, *Dake's Annotated Reference Bible*, p. 253.

[17]Scofield, Proper Name Index, p. 42.

Chapter 9
SAFETY IN GOD

Refuge Commanded

God's people were possessing the land He had given them. It was a wonderful time in Israel's history. But, the Lord knew that not every day was going to be wonderful just because God's people were living in God's land. There would be future problems, serious problems, problems to be resolved in a godly manner, even problems as serious as murder.

Murder, the taking of human life, was of great concern to the Lord, who had made man in His own image, but the killer's intent also concerned Him. He knew there would be some premeditated murders and other deaths which were accidental. Someone would have to decide which was which, mete out justice to the deliberate murderer, and minister mercy to the one who inadvertently caused a death. God also knew that, in either case, there would be grieving relatives who would want to take the law into their own hands and avenge the death. Someone would have to care for them and their concerns, too.

So, as the land was being divided, God reminded Joshua of His command to Moses concerning cities of refuge in Canaan, recorded in Numbers 35:10 through 15:

> *When ye be come over Jordan into the land of Canaan; Then ye shall appoint you cities to be cities of refuge for you; that the slayer may flee thither, which killeth any person at unawares. And they shall be unto you cities for refuge from the avenger; that the manslayer die not, until he stand before the congregation in judgment. And of these cities which ye shall give six cities shall ye have for refuge. Ye shall give three cities on this side Jordan, and three cities shall ye give in the land of Canaan, which shall be for cities of refuge. These six cities shall be a refuge, both for the children of Israel, and for the stranger, and for the sojourner among them: that every one that killeth any person unawares may flee thither.*

Refuge, here, is the Hebrew, *miqlat*, which refers to a strong, high, or inaccessible place of escape to which one may flee. There were to be six such cities, three on the east side of the Jordan River and three on the west bank. When a death occurred, the one responsible could go to the nearest city of refuge and find safety from avenging relatives. One would not escape justice there; in fact, he would find it. The city elders were to conduct a fair trial with justice rather than vengeance as their guiding principle.

The mature believer realizes that God's children still need a Refuge. Even though they are His people, living in His promises, they will still make mistakes because they are still human. God understands this, as Psalm 103:14 declares, *"For he knoweth our frame; he remembereth that we are dust."* Yet, God is still concerned about motivation, the intent of the believer's heart. He knows the difference between innocent errors in judgment which are to be forgiven and deliberate sins which must be punished. The mature believer also realizes there is still an avenger, one who would seek to take the Christian's life in either case. He accuses the child of God for the slightest infraction and he seeks any opportunity to exact vengeance and execute the death penalty pronounced in Romans 6:23, *"For the wages of sin is death...."* This avenger, this accuser, is identified in Revelation 12:9 and 10:

And the great dragon was cast out, that old serpent, called the Devil, and Satan, which deceiveth the whole world: he was cast out into the earth, and his angels were cast out with him. And I heard a loud voice saying in heaven, Now is come salvation, and strength, and the kingdom of our God, and the power of his Christ: for the accuser of our brethren is cast down, which accused them before our God day and night.

God still provides six refuges for His own. First, the mature believer finds refuge in God, Himself, as Psalm 46:1 declares, *"God is our refuge and strength, a very present help in trouble."* The second refuge is found in God's Son, as recorded in Colossians 3:3, *"For ye are dead, and your life is hid with Christ in God."* Third, refuge against Satan lies in the salvation of the Lord in 2 Samuel 22:2 and 3, *"The LORD is my rock, and my fortress, and my deliverer...my refuge, my saviour; thou savest me from violence."* The fourth refuge is the name of the Lord, as recorded in Psalm 9:9 and 10, *"The LORD also will be...a refuge in times of trouble. And they that know thy name will put their trust in thee."* The fifth refuge is in the shelter of the Lord's wings in Psalm 57:1, *"In the shadow of thy wings will I make my refuge."* Finally, the mature child of God finds his sixth refuge in the fear of the Lord in Proverbs 14:26, *"In the fear of the LORD is strong confidence: and his children shall have a place of refuge."* With these six "cities" of refuge provided, all the believer need do is trust them, just as the slayer trusted in the six cities of refuge Joshua set aside. The writer of the Book of Hebrews caught a glimpse of this in Hebrews 6:18, *"We might have a strong consolation, who have fled for refuge to lay hold upon the hope set before us."* The result of fleeing to the places of refuge God has established for the believer is recorded in Romans 8:1, "There is therefore now no condemnation to them which are in Christ Jesus."

Refuge With a Purpose

God gave clear commands regarding the use of the cities of refuge (Numbers 35:16 through 34; Joshua 20:3 through 6) which are similar to modern American homicide laws. Both note a difference between premeditated murder and manslaughter, both consider the intent of the heart of the slayer at the time, and both set the penalties accordingly. In American homicide law, manslaughter is defined as the taking of a human life without premeditation. This charge encompasses the loss of life through negligence, accident, or in the heat of passion. God also defined manslaughter in Numbers 35:22 and 23:

But if he thrust him suddenly without enmity, or have cast upon him any thing without laying of wait, Or with any stone, wherewith a man may die, seeing him not...and was not his enemy, neither sought his harm.

Then, in Joshua 20:3, the manslaughterer is further identified as, *"The slayer that killeth any person unawares and unwittingly...."* When such an accidental death occurred, the slayer could go to the nearest city of refuge (Joshua 20:3). There, he would get a fair trial before the city elders (Joshua 20:3; Numbers 35:24) where he had every opportunity to prove his innocence. The avenger acted as prosecutor and the elders were the jury. If the elders were convinced the death was accidental, the avenger could not exact retribution (Joshua 20:5; Numbers 35:25). Still, the slayer was not free to go. A life had been taken and the slayer, while not guilty of premeditation, had carelessly contributed to the death. A sentence involving loss of freedom was imposed. The slayer could not return to his family, his home, or his business. He had to remain in the city of his refuge for the current high priest's lifetime (Joshua 20:6; Numbers 35:25) with no early release or parole. If he left before that, he forfeited his protection, and the avenger could impose the death penalty

(Numbers 35:26 through 28). When the high priest died, the slayer was free to go and the avenger's right to execute the death penalty was forever lifted (Numbers 35:28).

Although Scripture gives no natural reason for the manslaughterer's penalty to be linked to the death of the high priest, for the mature child of God, this provision is a beautiful foreshadowing of the believer's safety in Christ. Having sinned, man comes under the penalty of spiritual death which the avenger will happily execute. But, man may flee to his refuge in Christ. The believer who makes an honest mistake may flee to this same Christ. In Him, both find the mercy and forgiveness of God, Himself, and safety from the avenger. Still, once refuge is obtained, these children of God are not permitted to return to their old lives of spiritual carelessness which resulted in sin and death in the first place. They must begin new lives and remain hidden in their Refuge until the death of the high priest. Here is an interesting twist. In Hebrews 6:20, Jesus is identified as, *"an high priest for ever after the order of Melchisedec."* But, this High Priest has already died and, when He did, He took the penalty with Him, as Colossians 2:14 and 15 declares, *"Blotting out the handwriting of ordinances that was against us...and took it out of the way, nailing it to his cross."* In Calvary, the avenger forever lost his right to execute the penalty of spiritual death against the believer. Now, this High Priest is alive forever to provide continuing security and continual intercession for His own, as Hebrews 7:24 and 25 states:

> *But this man, because he continueth ever, hath an unchangeable priesthood. Wherefore his is able also to save them to the uttermost that come unto God by him, seeing he ever liveth to make intercession for them.*

Sadly, there are those who depart from their refuge in Christ, those who choose to backslide. All who do, place themselves, again, in the hand of the avenger who will execute the death penalty for all of their past sins, as God decreed in Ezekiel 3:20:

> *Again, When a righteous man doth turn from his righteousness, and commit iniquity, and I lay a stumblingblock before him, he shall die: because thou hast not given him warning, he shall die in his sin, and his righteousness which he hath done shall not be remembered; but his blood will I require at thine hand.*

In the American law, murder is defined as the deliberate taking of a human life. In most states, there are at least two types of murder. Murder in the first degree is committed deliberately and with premeditation--forethought and planning. Murder in the second degree is committed without any premeditation or planning in advance. In God's Law, there were three types of premeditated murder, as defined in Numbers 35:16 through 21:

> *And if he smite him with an instrument of iron, so that he die, he is a murderer: the murderer shall surely be put to death. And if he smite him with throwing a stone, wherewith he may die, and he die, he is a murderer: the murderer shall surely be put to death. Or if he smite him with an hand weapon of wood, wherewith he may die, and he die, he is a murderer: the murderer shall surely be put to death. The revenger of blood himself shall slay the murderer: when he meeteth him, he shall slay him. But if he thrust him of hatred, or hurl at him by laying of wait, that he die; Or in enmity smite him with his hand, that he die: he that smote him shall surely be put to death; for he is a murderer: the revenger of blood shall slay the murderer, when he meeteth him.*

First, there was murder using a weapon (Numbers 35:16 through 19). It was assumed one would only have a weapon if he planned to use it. The second type of murder involved ambush. Clearly, one who lay in wait to ambush had time to consider his act, to premeditate. The third type of murder involved a past history of hatred (Numbers 35:20

and 21) and the presumption that the slayer was motivated by that hatred. Again, God dealt with the intent of the heart. One who committed any of these types of murder also received a fair trial and the testimony of at least two witnesses was required for a guilty verdict (Numbers 35:30). Once found guilty, there could be no satisfaction taken, no fine paid, no bribe accepted, no plea bargaining conducted. There was no other penalty possible but the one God had already set in Exodus 21:12 and 14:

> *He that smiteth a man, so that he die, shall be surely put to death....But, if a man come presumptuously upon his neighbour, to slay him with guile; thou shalt take him from mine altar, that he may die.*

No mercy was possible. One who deliberately took the life of another was found guilty and delivered to the avenger to execute the death penalty (Numbers 35:19 and 20). Here, is a difficult lesson the mature believer must learn for his own safety. When one clearly understands God's Law and its provisions in Christ and deliberately chooses to sin (not a mistake or error in judgment), no more mercy will be extended to him. He has murdered, he has done it deliberately, and his victim is none other than God's own Son, crucified anew. This hard truth is clearly set forth in Hebrews 6:4 through 6 and Hebrews 10:26 through 31:

> *For it is impossible for those who were once enlightened, and have tasted of the heavenly gift, and were made partakers of the Holy Ghost, And have tasted the good word of God, and the powers of the world to come, If they shall fall away, to renew them again unto repentance; seeing they crucify to themselves the Son of God afresh, and put him to an open shame....For if we sin wilfully after that we have received the knowledge of the truth, there remaineth no more sacrifice for sins. But a certain looking forward to of judgment and fiery indignation, which shall devour the adversaries. He that despised Moses' law died without mercy under two or three witnesses. Of how much sorer punishment, suppose ye, shall he be thought worthy, who hath trodden under foot the son of God, and hath counted the blood of the covenant, wherewith he was sanctified, an unholy thing, and hath done despite unto the Spirit of grace? For we know him that hath said, Vengeance belongeth unto me, I will recompense, saith the Lord. And again, The Lord shall judge his people. It is a fearful thing to fall into the hands of the living God.*

Such a person is judged guilty by God, Himself. There can be only one penalty. He must be delivered to the avenger, who will execute the sentence of eternal spiritual death.

Refuge Found

These principles of murder and manslaughter shed an interesting new light on the first recorded murder case, Cain and Abel in Genesis 4:3 through 15. Cain had repeated the error of his parents (Genesis 3:7) by trying to cover his sin with produce from the field (Genesis 4:3). But, God required a blood sacrifice, as He had shed the blood of animals to make coverings for Adam and Woman (Genesis 3:21). The wrong sacrifice was sin (Genesis 4:7) and was unacceptable (Genesis 4:5). Cain was upset (Genesis 4:5), but he was upset with God for refusing his sacrifice (Genesis 4:5). He didn't express hatred for his brother, one of the criteria for premeditation (Numbers 35:21). Nor is there any record that Cain had a weapon, the second criterion for premeditation (Numbers 35:16 through 18). Then, the murder occurred as the two were talking (Genesis 4:8); Cain had not lain in wait to ambush his brother, the third criterion for premeditation (Numbers 35:20).

Cain was judged by God, Himself, whose judgment and justice are beyond reproach. He was sentenced to be forever separated from his family and his agricultural business since the ground would no longer produce for him (Genesis 4:12). God did not, however, sentence Cain to death. In fact, He placed a protective mark on Cain to shield him from any avenger who might execute the death penalty (Genesis 4:15). Since God never violates His own principles and laws, one can conclude that Cain's killing of Abel was manslaughter, committed in the heat of passion (1 John 3:12), and was not a case of premeditated murder, for which the only acceptable punishment would have been death.

Refuge Appointed

Joshua appointed six cities of refuge, three on the east bank and three on the west bank of the Jordan River (Joshua 20:7 through 9). In the names of the selected cities, the mature child of God can learn about the Refuge in whom he trusts:

1. **Kadesh** - "be holy."[1] The believer's Refuge requires that those who hide in Him be holy, and He promises to make them holy (Leviticus 20:7 and 8).
2. **Shechem** - "back, shoulder."[2] The back or the shoulder bore burdens. The burden of the believer's sin has been borne by his Refuge. It was also the back of Christ upon which the stripes for healing were laid. In the believer's Refuge, there is healing.
3. **Kirjath-arba** - "a city;"[3] also known as **Hebron** - "a league, a confederacy,"[4] "an alliance."[5] In Christ, the believer may have an alliance, a real relationship with Him.
4. **Bezer** - "strong."[6] Of the believer's Refuge, Proverbs 18:10 says, *"The name of the LORD is a strong tower: the righteous runneth into it, and is safe."*
5. **Ramoth** - "high."[7] Psalm 144:2 refers to the believer's Refuge as, *"My high tower, and my deliverer; my shield, and he in whom I trust."*
6. **Golan** - "exultation, joy."[8] In the believer's Refuge is exultation and joy forever.

Of these six cities of refuge, A. B. Simpson, in his book, The Land of Promise, records the following historical information:[9]

> These six cities were set apart in all sections of the land of Canaan as places of refuge for the manslayer when pursued by the Goel, or avenger of blood. They were within easy approach of every part of the land. Public roads were provided leading directly to them, kept constantly open and in good repair at the expense of the government. Every torrent was bridged and every obstacle removed; and wherever the cross-roads might render the way uncertain, finger-posts were erected, opening to the refuge and preventing all possible mistake. Ample provision was made within the city for the supply of all wants of the fugitive; the gates were ever open, and no weapon was permitted within the inclosure. There the unhappy man could rest in perfect safety until his case was formally adjudicated upon or until the death of the high-priest, when he was free to return to his home in perfect safety, and no one dared molest him.

For the mature believer, God has appointed a Refuge. He is holy in justice and in mercy; His is the back which bore the believer's sins and the stripes for his healing; He is the One in whom the believer's relationship with God is founded; He is strong to protect the believer from the avenger; He is the believer's High Tower and his High Priest; and He is the Source of the believer's everlasting and overflowing joy. Finally, the way to that Refuge is ever open and never difficult to find, as Isaiah 35:8 assures:

And an highway shall be there, and a way, and it shall be called The way of holiness; the unclean shall not pass over it; but it shall be for those: the wayfaring men, though fools, shall not err therein.

In Christ, the mature child of God finds a place of eternal safety from all harm. If he should happen to make a mistake, so long as he repents and runs into his Refuge, he is sheltered and shielded from the avenger. So long as he remains in his Refuge, he has a High Priest who will live forever to protect him from Satan's vengeance. Christ is the believer's divinely-appointed City of Refuge. Psalm 46 says it all:

God is our refuge and strength, a very present help in trouble. Therefore will not we fear, though the earth be removed, and though the mountains be carried into the midst of the sea; Though the waters thereof roar and be troubled, though the mountains shake with the swelling thereof. Selah. There is a river, the streams whereof shall make glad the city of God, the holy place of the tabernacles of the most High. God is in the midst of her; she shall not be moved: God shall help her, and that right early. The heathen raged, the kingdoms were moved: he uttered his voice, the earth melted. The LORD of hosts is with us; the God of Jacob is our refuge. Selah. Come, behold the works of the LORD, what desolations he hath made in the earth. He maketh wars to cease unto the end of the earth; he breaketh the bow, and cutteth the spear in sunder; he burneth the chariot in the fire. Be still, and know that I am God: I will be exalted among the heathen, I will be exalted in the earth. The LORD of hosts is with us; the God of Jacob is our refuge. Selah.

[1]Merrill C. Tenney, *The Zondervan Pictorial Bible Dictionary*, p. 461.

[2]C. I. Scofield, *The Scofield Reference Bible*, Proper Name Index, p. 41.

[3]Tenney, p. 469.

[4]Ibid., p. 345.

[5]Scofield, Proper Name Index, p. 22.

[6]Tenney, p. 114.

[7]Scofield, Proper Name Index, p. 39.

[8]Arthur W. Pink, *Gleanings in Joshua*, p. 384.

[9]A. B. Simpson, *The Land of Promise*, pp. 121 and 122.

Chapter 10
THE PRIEST IN RESIDENCE

The Priesthood Accommodated

Each of the tribes of Israel had received a land grant, except for Levi which was given another kind of inheritance in Joshua 13:33, *"But unto the tribe of Levi Moses gave not any inheritance: the LORD God of Israel was their inheritance."* Still, they needed places to live so, in Numbers 35:2, God ordered, *"Command the children of Israel, that they give unto the Levites of the inheritance of their possession cities to dwell in."* The Levites couldn't withdraw from the other tribes; they would be dispersed among them. Here, the priesthood is typical of Christ as High Priest, with Israel symbolizing believers. Clearly, one must make room in his life for the High Priest who wants to dwell, not confined only to the Church, but in every area of His child's life. He can only do so when a place is set aside for Him.

The Levites reminded Joshua and Eleazar, son of Aaron and high priest, of God's command; it was obeyed immediately (Joshua 21:1 through 3). The tribes were asked to donate cities in their inheritance which the Levites were to accept. This included the cities of refuge, also scattered throughout Israel to be easily accessible to fugitives. The Levites were given the suburbs or pastures surrounding the cities, too, in which to raise the cattle required for the sacrifices. In the same way, the mature believer must freely surrender a place within his land, his life, where his High Priest may reside. Then, the High Priest accepts and abides in any and all areas of the believer's life willingly set apart for Him.

The Priesthood in Residence

The tribe of Levi, meaning, "joined,"[1] contained three families named for Levi's sons, Kohath, Gershon, and Merari. The descendants of Kohath, meaning, "assembly,"[2] included Aaron's family, the priestly line. The other Kohathites cared for the most sacred furnishings of the Tabernacle (Numbers 3:27 through 32). The Kohathites were granted twenty-three cities, donated by five and a half tribes--Judah, Simeon, Benjamin, Dan, and the half tribe of Manasseh. Thirteen cities, donated by Judah, Benjamin, and Simeon, were designated for the Aaronic priests (Joshua 21:9 through 19), while ten more, donated by Ephraim, Dan, and half of Manasseh, were set aside for other Kohathites (Joshua 21:20 through 26). In the work of the Kohathites, we see a perfect picture of Christ in His divinity. The heavenly Christ, the Son of God, was assembled together with God (Philippians 2:6). As the Kohathites cared for the Tabernacle furnishings, each representing God, so Jesus personified the divinity of God tabernacled among men and represented Him to the world as John 1:18 declares, *"No man hath seen God at any time; the only begotten Son, which is in the bosom of the Father, he hath declared him."* Even the names of the two and a half tribes which contributed cities to the Kohathites and the names of the ten cities they gave, (Joshua 21:20 through 26) speak of the divine Christ and His divine ministries to His own:

1. **Ephraim** - "fruitful."[3] The divine Christ, representing God, was fruitful, producing many sons and daughters for the Father. Here are the cities Ephraim gave:

a. **Shechem** - "back, shoulder."[4] It is on the strong shoulder of the divine Christ that the believer's burdens are borne. In His strength, the believer may be fruitful.

b. **Gezer** - "precipice."[5] It is the divine Christ who came down from Heaven to rescue the sinner from the edge of the precipice of sin.

c. **Kibzaim** - "two heaps."[6] Here, we see the double ruin of sin, the ruin of the body in this life and the soul in the next. It is only the divine Christ who defeats both.

d. **Beth-horon** - "house of the hollow."[7] It is in the hollow of the hand of the divine Christ and the God He represents that the believer securely rests (John 10:28 and 29).

2. **Dan** - "judge."[8] The divine Christ has been designated by God to judge the world and will represent Him at the final judgment of all (John 5:22). Dan donated these cities:

a. **Eltekeh** - "whose fear is God."[9] In the judgment of God, as carried out by the divine Christ, there is fear only for the sinner.

b. **Gibbethon** - "a lofty place."[10] The judgment seat of the divine Christ will be a lofty place indeed.

c. **Aijalon** - "place of gazelles."[11] Gazelles are among the swiftest creatures on earth. The judgment of the divine Christ upon the sinner will be swift indeed.

d. **Gath-rimmon** - "winepress of pomegranates."[12] The winepress in Scripture always speaks of the judgment of God which will be administered by the divine Christ.

3. **Manasseh** - "one who causes to forget."[13] The divine Christ will bring His own to Heaven where they will forget all suffering, their tears will be wiped away (Revelation 7:17 and 21:4), and they will be judged for their rewards. Manasseh donated these two towns:

a. **Tanach** - "castle."[14] Heaven is the castle of God, the home to which the divine Christ will bring all who trust in Him.

b. **Gath-rimmon**, "the winepress of the gazelles," also known as **Bileam** (1 Chronicles 6:70) and **Ibleam** (Joshua 17:11) - "destruction."[15] Sinners will tread the winepress of God where they will be destroyed by the word of the divine Christ.

The names of the three tribes which contributed towns for the priests (Joshua 21:9 through 19) and the thirteen cities they gave are significant of the priestly aspect of Christ:

1. **Judah** - "praised."[16] It is Christ, the High Priest, the Offspring of the tribe of Judah, who made the final, perfect sacrifice for the believer's sin and who is to be praised.

2. **Simeon** - "a hearkening."[17] It is Christ, the Intercessor, who hearkens to the prayer of the believer and intercedes on his behalf before God.

The prayer and praise of the believer, as typified in the holy incense ascending up to God's throne (Revelation 8:3 and 4), are inseparable, just as the nine cities given by Judah and Simeon are listed inseparably (Joshua 21:9 through 16):

a. **Hebron** - "alliance."[18] The alliance between the believer's prayer and praise.

b. **Libnah** - "whiteness."[19] The righteousness of Christ enables the believer to lift up his prayer and praise to God in a white robe of righteousness.

c. **Jattir** - "excelling."[20] The divine Christ excels above all.

d. **Eshtemoa** - "obedience."[21] It was the obedience of Christ in going to the cross (Philippians 2:8) which enabled Him to be the believer's High Priest and Intercessor.

e. **Holon** - "sandy,"[22] as a beach or a safe harbor. Christ, the High Priest and Intercessor, is the safe Harbor of the child of God.

f. **Debir** - "a recess,"[23] Christ dwells in the recess of the spirit of the believer.

g. **Ain** - "an eye, or a fountain."[24] Christ, the High Priest, provided a fountain for the believer's cleansing. Now, His eye watches over the believer and intercedes for him.

h. **Juttah** - "extended,"[25] or enlarged. It is through Christ, the High Priest and Intercessor, that the land (spiritual life) of the believer is extended and enlarged.

i. **Beth-shemesh** - "house of the sun."[26] The divine Christ is the *"Sun of righteousness"* of Malachi 4:2 who has healing in His wings for those who trust in Him.

3. **Benjamin** - "son of the right hand,"[27] first called **Benoni**, "son of my sorrow."[28] Christ, as High Priest, was first the Son of sorrow, bearing the sin of the world. As Intercessor, He's now the Son who sits at the right hand of God. The four cities Benjamin gave are:

a. **Gibeon** - "pertaining to a hill."[29] The "altar" where Christ, the High Priest, offered His final sacrifice for sin belonged to the hill of Golgotha or Calvary outside Jerusalem.

b. **Geba** - "hill."[30] This points to the hill of Calvary, itself, upon which Christ, the High Priest, made His sacrifice.

c. **Anathoth** - "answers to prayer."[31] It is through the intercession of Christ, the Intercessor, that the prayers of the believer are answered.

d. **Almon** - "hidden."[32] After His sacrifice, Christ, the High Priest, was hidden in a tomb for three days.

The name of Gershon, the eldest son of Levi, meant, "a stranger there."[33] His descendants cared for all of the soft materials in the Tabernacle, including the Tabernacle, itself (Numbers 3:25 and 26). The Gershonites were given thirteen cities donated by three and a half tribes--Issachar, Asher, Naphtali, and the other half of the tribe of Manasseh (Joshua 21:6). In the Gershonites and their work, we see Christ in His humanity, a Stranger here, the divine Son of God tabernacled in soft, human Flesh (John 1:14). In the names of these tribes and the cities they donated the humanity of the God-Man is seen:

1. **Issachar** - "he is hired,"[34] or "there is hire or reward."[35] Jesus was hired or appointed by God to come to earth to be man's Kinsman-Redeemer and pay the price or reward for man's sin. The four cities given by Issachar (Joshua 21:28 and 29) are:

a. **Kishon** - "tortuous."[36] After living in Heaven, life on earth must have been tortuous for Jesus, not to mention the tortures inflicted upon Him at His death.

b. **Daberah** - "pasture."[37] Jesus, in His humanity, was *"the good Shepherd"* who gave His life for His sheep (John 10:11) and still provides pasture for them.

c. **Jarmuth** - "height."[38] It was Christ, in His humanity who had to be lifted up upon the heights of the mount of Golgotha in order to draw all men to Himself.

d. **En-gannim** - "fountain of the garden."[39] In the Garden of Gethsemane, the humanity of Jesus was seen in perspiration like a fountain of drops of blood.

2. **Asher** - "fortunate, happy."[40] In His humanity, Jesus found happiness in doing the will of His heavenly Father. The four cities donated by Asher (Joshua 21:30 and 31) are:

a. **Mishal** - "prayer."[41] It was in prayer that Jesus maintained His relationship with His Father. In prayer, the child of God can find that same relationship.

b. **Abdon** - "servile."[42] In His humanity, Jesus was the Servant of His Father, just as the believer is to be the servant of Christ.

c. **Helkath** - "a portion."[43] The earthly life of Jesus was only a portion of His eternal existence. The believer's brief portion on earth is overshadowed by eternal life to come.

d. **Rehob** - "street."[44] Christ, in His humanity, was *"the way"* to Heaven.

3. **Naphtali** - "my wrestling."[45] In His humanity, Jesus wrestled in prayer in the Garden of Gethsemane. The three cities Naphtali gave (Joshua 21:32) are:

a. **Kedesh** - "sanctuary,"[46] and "to be holy."[47] In His humanity, Jesus occupied the sanctuary or tabernacle of human flesh, yet remained holy, just as the believer must.

b. **Hammoth-dor** - "warm springs of the dwelling."[48] All during the years of His human life, Jesus poured forth from the spring of living water within Him.

c. **Kartan** - "double city."[49] In His humanity, Jesus was a double city with a doubly-fruitful life, one lived here on earth and one lived in eternity as the Christ, the Son of God.

4. **Manasseh** - "one who causes to forget."[50] In His humanity, Jesus gave His life so that all who believed in Him could forget the sin of the past and live new lives in His salvation. The two cities ceded by the other half of Manasseh (Joshua 21:27) are:

a. **Golan** - "exultation, joy."[51] The pain and sorrow of the human existence of Jesus were lost in the joy and exultation of His triumphant return to His Father's side.

b. **Beesh-terah** - "house or temple of Astarte."[52] In His humanity, Jesus lived in a world steeped in heathen worship, yet He brought the truth of God to all who believed.

Levi's third son was Merari meaning, "bitter."[53] His descendants cared for the framework and structural supports of the Tabernacle (Numbers 3:36 and 37). In the name and work of Merari, we see the bitter sacrifice of Christ on a wooden cross nailed with metal spikes, as the structural support of man's salvation, as 1 Corinthians 3:11 declares, *"For other foundation can no man lay than that is laid, which is Christ Jesus."* The mature believer builds on this foundation the tabernacle designed in 1 Corinthians 3:12 through 17:

> *Now if any man build upon this foundation gold, silver, precious stones, wood, hay, stubble; Every man's work shall be made manifest...because it shall be revealed by fire; and the fire shall try every man's work of what sort it is. If any man's work abide which he hath built thereupon, he shall receive a reward. If any man's work shall be burned, he shall suffer loss; but he himself shall be saved; yet so as by fire. Know ye not that ye are the temple of God, and that the Spirit of God dwelleth in you? If any man defile the temple of God, him shall God destroy; for the temple of God is holy, which temple ye are.*

The names of the three tribes--Reuben, Gad, and Zebulun--and the twelve cities they gave tell of the sacrifice of Christ and the foundation it provides the mature believer:

1. **Zebulun** - "dwelling or wished for habitation."[54] The sacrifice of Jesus provides the foundation of the wished for habitation of the child of God. The four cities given by Zebulun (Joshua 21:34 and 35) are:

a. **Jokneam** - "possessed by the people."[55] The sacrifice of Jesus was made for *"whosoever will,"* (John 3:16) and may be possessed by any who will accept their inheritance.

b. **Kartah** - "city."[56] A walled city, strong enough to withstand any attack of the enemy, may be built upon the foundation of this sacrifice.

c. **Dimnah** - "dunghill,"[57] or a place of refuse. The sacrifice of Jesus can transform the life of the believer from a place of refuse to a walled city of God.

d. **Nahalal** - "a pasture."[58] The Good Shepherd gave His life a sacrifice for His sheep. Now, they are permitted entry into His sheepfold, His pleasant pasture.

2. **Reuben** - "behold a son."[59] In John 1:29, John the Baptist introduced the Son of God saying, *"Behold the Lamb of God which taketh away the sin of the world."* One sees salvation when he beholds the Son. The four cities given by Reuben (Joshua 21:36 and 37) are:

a. **Bezer** - "strong."[60] The sacrifice of Jesus provides a strong foundation upon which the child of God may build his life, a fit temple of the Holy Spirit.

b. **Jahazah** - "a place trodden down."[61] The sacrifice of Jesus was made outside Jerusalem, a place Jesus predicted would be trodden down by the Gentiles (Luke 21:24). One's life, too, is trodden down by his enemies until he accepts the sacrifice of his Lord.

c. **Kedemoth** - "eastern parts."[62] The hill of Golgotha or Calvary, where the sacrifice of Jesus was made, was located outside of the eastern wall of Jerusalem.

d. **Mephaath** - "beauty."[63] While the cross of Jesus may have been a thing of horror at the time, it is a thing of beauty to the child of God who has accepted His sacrifice.

3. **Gad** - "a troop."[64] A troop of Roman soldiers carried out the sacrifice of Jesus, after a troop of Jews sought His death. The four cities given by Gad (Joshua 21:38 and 39) are:

a. **Ramoth-gilead** - "heights of the hill of witness."[65] The sacrifice of Jesus was witnessed on Calvary. It is now witnessed to by all who have accepted it.

b. **Mahanaim** - "two camps."[66] When confronted with the sacrifice of Jesus, people may choose one of two camps, those who reject His sacrifice and those who accept it.

c. **Heshbon** - "counting,"[67] as in counting the cost. In the Garden, Jesus counted the cost of His sacrifice. Each one who comes to Him must count the cost of accepting it.

d. **Jazer** - "whom God aids."[68] Jesus could have called twelve legions of angels for aid, but He made the sacrifice through which God now aids the sinner with eternal life.

Each tribe gave no more than five cities, with most giving four for a total of forty-eight. This loss would not be too great for any tribe, but each would have its inheritance graced by the Levites in residence. As the Levites possessed their cities, the mature child of God can see his High Priest, Jesus Christ, dwelling with him and living in his land. There, the High Priest can minister to his needs day by day as he grows to full maturity.

The Priesthood in Possession

The inheritance of Israel had been equitably divided. God had kept every promise, as seen in Joshua 21:43 and 45:

> *And the LORD gave unto Israel all the land which he sware to give unto their fathers; and they possessed it, and dwelt therein. There failed not any good thing which the LORD had spoken to Israel; all came to pass.*

Yet, even though God had given Israel all the land He had promised, they had not taken every city, nor had they driven out every enemy. In too many cases, they allowed their Canaanite enemies to remain, paying tribute. Their materialism got the better of their spirituality--and they'd live to regret it. The mature believer can possess his full inheritance. He can live in every promise in the Book, as Jesus told Satan in Matthew 4:4, *"Man shall not live by bread alone, but by every word that proceedeth out of the mouth of God."* This message is reiterated in 2 Peter 1:3 and 4, *"According as his divine power hath given unto us all things....Whereby are given unto us exceeding great and precious promises."* The mature believer can also have rest in his land, as Jesus vowed in Matthew 11:28 through 30:

> *Come unto me, all ye that labour and are heavy laden, and I will give you rest. Take my yoke upon you, and learn of me....and ye shall find rest unto your souls. For my yoke is easy and my burden is light.*

The believer's victory is assured in 1 Corinthians 15:57, *"But thanks be to God, which giveth us the victory through our Lord Jesus Christ."* Isaiah 54:17 promises every enemy weapon will fail, *"No weapon that is formed against thee shall prosper."* God will deliver all enemies over to the believer so that he may have complete victory in Christ, as David sang in Psalm 18:40, *"Thou hast given me the necks of mine enemies; that I might destroy them that hate me."* The Lord will also give all good things to the mature believer, as He promised in both Psalm 68:19 and Psalm 84:11, *"Blessed be the Lord, who daily loadeth us with benefits....no good thing will he withhold from them that walk uprightly."* Finally, not one promise will fail, as assured in 2 Corinthians 1:20, *"For all the promises of God in him are yea, and in him Amen."* This is the inheritance, the promised possession of the mature child of God because he has set aside in his land, his life, a place where his High Priest may dwell. To any who would be mature men and women of God, He calls in Revelation 3:20:

Behold, I stand at the door and knock: if any man hear my voice, and open the door, I will come in to him, and will sup with him, and he with me.

Those who would come to maturity in Christ must answer that call, open the door, feed on his truth, and a provide a place of residence for their High Priest.

[1]Herbert Lockyer, *All the Men of the Bible*, p. 217.

[2]Ibid., p. 214.

[3]C. I. Scofield, *The Scofield Reference Bible*, Proper Name Index, p. 17.

[4]Ibid., Proper Name Index, p. 41.

[5]Ibid., Proper Name Index, p. 19.

[6]Ibid., Proper Name Index, p. 29.

[7]Merrill C. Tenney, *The Zondervan Pictorial Bible Dictionary*, p. 110.

[8]Scofield, Proper Name Index, p. 14.

[9]Ibid., Proper Name Index, p. 17.

[10]Ibid., Proper Name Index, p. 19.

[11]Ibid., Proper Name Index, p. 5.

[12]Tenney, p. 301.

[13]Scofield, Proper Name Index, p. 31.

[14]Ibid., Proper Name Index, p. 43.

[15]Ibid., Proper Name Index, p. 9.

[16]Ibid., Proper Name Index, p. 29.

[17]Ibid., Proper Name Index, p. 42.

[18]Ibid., Proper Name Index, p. 22.

[19]Ibid., Proper Name Index, p. 30.

[20]Ibid., Proper Name Index, p. 25.

[21]Ibid., Proper Name Index, p. 18.

[22]Ibid., Proper Name Index, p. 23.

[23]Ibid., Proper Name Index, p. 15.

[24]Ibid., Proper Name Index, p. 5.

[25]Ibid., Proper Name Index, p. 29.

[26]Ibid., Proper Name Index, p. 11.

[27]Ibid., Proper Name Index, p. 10.

[28]Ibid.

[29]Ibid., Proper Name Index, p. 19.

[30]Ibid.

[31]Ibid., Proper Name Index, p. 6.

[32]Ibid.
[33]Lockyer, p. 126.
[34]Scofield, Proper Name Index, p. 24.
[35]Lockyer, p. 161.
[36]Scofield, Proper Name Index, p. 30.
[37]Ibid., Proper Name Index, p. 14.
[38]Ibid., Proper Name Index, p. 25.
[39]Ibid., Proper Name Index, p. 17.
[40]Ibid., Proper Name Index, p. 8.
[41]Ibid., Proper Name Index, p. 33.
[42]Ibid., Proper Name Index, p. 3.
[43]Ibid., Proper Name Index, p. 22.
[44]Ibid., Proper Name Index, p. 39.
[45]Ibid., Proper Name Index, p. 35.
[46]Ibid., Proper Name Index, p. 29.
[47]Tenney, p. 461.
[48]Scofield, Proper Name Index, pp. 15 and 21.
[49]Ibid., Proper Name Index, p. 29.
[50]Ibid., Proper Name Index, p. 31.
[51]Arthur W. Pink, *Gleanings in Joshua*, p. 384.
[52]Scofield, Proper Name Index, p. 10.
[53]Lockyer, p. 237.
[54]Ibid., p. 342.
[55]Scofield, Proper Name Index, p. 28.
[56]Ibid., Proper Name Index, p. 29.
[57]Ibid., Proper Name Index, p. 15.
[58]Ibid., Proper Name Index, p. 34.
[59]Ibid., Proper Name Index, p. 39.
[60]Tenney, p. 114.
[61]Scofield, Proper Name Index, p. 25.
[62]Ibid., Proper Name Index, p. 29.
[63]Ibid., Proper Name Index, p. 33.
[64]Ibid., Proper Name Index, p. 18.
[65]Ibid., Proper Name Index, pp. 20 and 39.
[66]Ibid., Proper Name Index, p. 31.
[67]Ibid., Proper Name Index, p. 22.
[68]Ibid., Proper Name Index, p. 24.

Chapter 11
WORSHIP WHEREVER YOU ARE

The Altar Erected

The general invasion of Canaan had been successfully concluded. The task of continuing the conquest, taking full ownership of the land and eradicating all enemies would now be the responsibility of each tribe acting within its own borders to possess its inheritance. There comes the time in the life of each mature child of God when he must claim the promises of God for himself, on his own, and in his own life. As he comes to maturity in Christ, he will find that he must stand on his own to claim and possess the full inheritance God has given him. He will discover that the most precious promises and sweetest victories are obtained at those times when he stands alone with God.

So, Joshua demobilized the army and sent his soldiers home, beginning with Reuben, Gad, and half of the tribe of Manasseh. Their land, which lay on the eastern side of the Jordan River (Joshua 22:1), had been taken first, but, according to the commands of Moses and Joshua, they had continued to serve for about seven years to conquer all of Canaan. They had served with distinction for which Joshua commended them (Joshua 22:2 and 3). Now that the land west of the Jordan had been taken, their countrymen also had possession of their inheritance, and there was rest from war, they, too, could go home to enjoy the blessings of the Lord (Joshua 22:4). The mature believer must also serve his commanding General with dedication and distinction, following the commands in His Word, yielding to His will, and obeying His voice at all times and in all situations. He will enlist in the army of God, never leaving his brethren to fight the good fight of spiritual warfare alone. He will keep the charge and perform the ministry the Lord has given him, serving faithfully until he is relieved by his Commander. When the army of God is eternally demobilized, may each mature believer hear the commendation of his Lord, recorded in Matthew 25:21:

> *Well done, thou good and faithful servant: thou hast been faithful over a few things, I will make thee ruler over many things: enter thou into the joy of thy Lord.*

While the soldiers of Reuben, Gad, and half of Manasseh were released from military service and any further obligation to those west of the Jordan, they were not released from the Law of God. Joshua's last order to them was to continue to obey the commandments of God and to serve the Lord who had given them their inheritance (Joshua 22:5). While ministry obligations may end and duty stations change from time to time, no child of God is ever freed from his duty to obey the commandments of God and to serve his Lord. Having commended them for their faithful service, Joshua released the men of Reuben, Gad, and Manasseh to return to their homes and pronounced his blessing on them and their future endeavors (Joshua 22:6). To reward their outstanding service, they were given a generous portion of the spoils of war (Joshua 22:8). They had crossed the Jordan River as lowly soldiers; they would return to their homes as wealthy landowners. Their rewards are typical of the blessings the mature child of God may receive:

1. **Much riches** - typical of the spiritual riches of a relationship with the Lord.
2. **Much cattle** - typical of the spiritual meat and milk one finds in the Word of God.
3. **Silver** - typical of redemption with which the child of God is crowned.

4. **Gold** - typical of divine character as one is changed into the image of Christ.
5. **Brass** - speaks of humanity approaching God, as one approaches God in prayer.
6. **Iron** - used to make weapons for war and implements for work; typical of the mature believer's weapons of spiritual warfare and the implements of his service to God.
7. **Much raiment** - typical of the white robes of righteousness given to the saints.

The discharged soldiers of Reuben, Gad, and half of Manasseh departed from Shiloh, the home of the Tabernacle and the altar of God (Joshua 22:9). Just after they crossed the Jordan on their way home, they paused to construct an altar in their territory (Joshua 22:10). This altar was large and easily visible from a great distance. There was no attempt to be secretive or deceptive; the altar was out in the open for all to see.

The Altar Discovered

Soon, news of the altar reached the Israelites living in the west (Joshua 22:11). They were instantly incensed and met at Shiloh to propose an immediate civil war to wipe out their brethren on the east bank (Joshua 22:12). It would appear that the meeting was conducted before an investigation into the facts and before the three tribes involved could even be asked about their altar. Also, the congregation came to this decision without first going to prayer and consulting the Lord, without even consulting their own leaders. One can see the adversary at work here. He always knows just where the child of God worships, how he worships, and what form his worship takes and he'll always try to create a breach between worshippers in any way he can. All too often, the immature in the kingdom of God will fall into the adversary's trap; but the mature believer knows that the adversary can be defeated with careful inquiry into the facts coupled with concerned prayer and consultation with the Lord and His appointed leadership to resolve the rift.

In this case, cooler heads finally prevailed. Instead of sending warriors to annihilate their brothers to the east, the Israelites sent a delegation of elders led by Phinehas, the son of the high priest, Eleazar, and the grandson of Aaron, a man who had proven himself zealous in defense of the Law in the case of Peor, an Israelite who had consorted with a Canaanite woman in violation of God's clear command (Numbers 25:6 through 8). With him went the heads of the other nine and a half tribes (Joshua 22:13 and 14). Together, they went to Gilead to confront their brothers and negotiate a resolution of the problem (Joshua 22:15). While there are divine standards which must be scrupulously observed in all spiritual matters, God wants His children to worship Him, not to go to war with each other over how that worship is to be conducted. Here, God is represented by His chosen elders, men He appointed to lead His children in conforming to His standards, not men commissioned to eradicate them at the first hint of failure.

This mission must not be trivialized. The elders had serious spiritual and legal concerns about a second altar appointed by man rather than God (Joshua 22:16 through 20). God had given clear commands to His people. When some broke His command to remain separated from the Canaanites, twenty-four thousand people died (Numbers 25:9). On another occasion, when God's orders regarding spoils were violated by one man, his entire family and thirty-six of Israel's soldiers died (Joshua 7:5, 24 and 25). The elders reminded their countrymen of these past tragedies (Joshua 22: 17 and 20), for they had learned from these painful experiences that one could not afford to trifle with God. Just as clearly, God had designed the Tabernacle to be the one place where He would meet with His people (Exodus 25:8) and He had ordained that the brazen altar within it be the one place where sacrifices could be made for their sin (Leviticus 1:3 and 8). That

Tabernacle and altar were presently located in Shiloh. Deliberately disobeying this command could result in yet another tragedy (Joshua 22:18).

The seriousness of this matter must also be understood in the light of typology. The altar was a place of sacrifice and approach to God. As such, it symbolized the cross of Christ where the final sacrifice for the sin of the world was offered and where sinners may approach God to receive salvation. The elders could not tolerate a substitute altar any more than God would tolerate a substitute cross. They realized that a surrogate would be an act of rebellion against God and His ordained place of sacrifice and worship which could result in judgment upon all Israel. Had the altar been built as a replacement for the brazen altar of the Tabernacle, the elders would have been quite correct in their assessment of the risk the situation posed for the entire nation. The golden calf had brought the wrath of God upon Israel and nearly resulted in the destruction of the entire congregation. The twin golden calves of Jeroboam would lead Israel into idolatry and eventually result in their captivity among their enemies. No mature child of God is willing to incur such risk.

Rather than have such a thing happen, the nine and a half tribes west of Jordan even offered to share their land with the two and a half tribes of the east so that they could be closer to the Tabernacle in Shiloh (Joshua 22:19). This was clearly a generous offer, made in the interest of brotherhood and to avert the wrath of God.

The Altar Explained

In response to the elders, the men of Reuben, Gad, and Manasseh were quick to bring God into their situation. They called Him, *"the LORD God of gods, the LORD God of gods,"* which is the Hebrew, "*El Elohim Yehovah*," the strong God, the Creator-God, the eternal God. Using these three principal names of God, they reaffirmed their belief in Him and no other. Then, they placed their case before Him, knowing that only He understood the motive of their hearts (Joshua 22:22 and 23). Here, the mature believer finds further clues for dealing with disputes and disagreements between believers. If all concerned are quick to affirm their belief in the same God, to place their cases before Him, and to trust Him with the outcome, matters can soon be resolved. It is, after all, only God who can fairly judge the intents of all hearts and bring a solution which will satisfy each.

The men of Reuben, Gad, and Manasseh explained that their altar was not meant to be a substitute for the brazen altar, nor a worship site to rival the Tabernacle. No offerings were ever even made there (Joshua 22:23), their tacit recognition that sacrifices could only legally be offered on the brazen altar in the Tabernacle. Their altar had been built just to prevent future religious disunity and disharmony because of the geographical separation of the two groups of Israelites (Joshua 22:24 and 25). It would be an ever-present visible reminder of the singleness of belief which united the groups, a witness and monument to them and their children of the unity of worship between them all (Joshua 22:26 and 27). It had even been patterned after the altar in the Tabernacle (Joshua 22:28) to point their children there, their way of signifying to all generations that the Israelites in Gilead were just as sincere in their worship of Jehovah as those in Canaan and had just as sure a right to enter the Tabernacle of God. The altar was meant to tie the two divisions of the nation together in unity, never to signal rebellion against their God (Joshua 22:29).

This illustrates the differences between public and private worship, as well as the unity between them. The mature believer engages in public worship in the tabernacle, the particular church in which God has placed him, with other members of the Body of Christ. He finds that certain spiritual activities can only take place as a part of corporate worship.

For example, the sacrifice of Christ, as typified in Communion, is a part of public worship. One's spiritual gifts can also be offered for the edification of all in Body ministry as a part of public worship, all in conformity with Hebrews 10:25, *"Not forsaking the assembling of ourselves together, as the manner of some is."* But, one may engage in private worship anywhere, in any part of one's territory and possession, in any activity of one's daily life. In private worship, the mature believer prepares a place for God in his own personal life, maintains his close personal relationship with God, and is sustained in that relationship between public services. It is also outside of the public worship service that the mature child of God witnesses to others, teaches his children, and directs his family in Christian living day by day. Private worship, then, never becomes a substitute for public worship in the church. Instead, private worship becomes an important addition to public worship which enhances the daily life of the believer and all with whom he comes in contact.

The Altar Accepted

Once Phinehas and the elders understood the godly intent of their countrymen, they were rather pleased at the idea (Joshua 22:30). They were even more pleased that God had kept them from going to war against their brothers in the east on the basis of a misunderstanding (Joshua 22:31). They returned home to report to the waiting Israelites who were happy that civil war had been averted (Joshua 22:33). To prevent any future misconceptions, the Israelites in Gilead gave their altar a name which identified the purpose of its existence to all who might wonder, as recorded in Joshua 22:34, *"And the children of Reuben and the children of Gad called the altar Ed: for it shall be a witness between us that the LORD is God."* Bible scholars don't know how long the altar called Ed stood as a silent witness between God's people on both shores of the Jordan. For as long as it remained, it was a unifying bridge between the Israelites of Canaan and Gilead. Like the Israelites, the mature child of God is pleased whenever a misunderstanding can be prevented from causing a breach in the Body of Christ. Often, such a schism can be averted by simply adopting the same methods used to resolve this dispute:

1. **Avoid haste.** Don't jump to conclusions based on incomplete information.
2. **Ask questions.** Investigate and get enough information for an informed decision.
3. **Wait for answers.** Listen attentively to both sides in the dispute.
4. **Achieve understanding.** Be certain all parties clearly understand the position of all others. Attempt to achieve a solution which is fair, equitable, and acceptable to all.
5. **Conform.** Once a decision is made based on the Word of God, all parties to the dispute should be willing to conform to that decision.
6. **Avoid disunity.** Attempt to end the dispute in harmony and unity. Disharmony and disunity tear God's people apart; harmony and unity cement them together.

God's instructions regarding public worship, as found in 1 Corinthians 14, rest upon two paramount considerations. The first is recorded in 1 Corinthians 14:12, *"Even so ye, forasmuch as ye are zealous of spiritual gifts, seek that ye may excel to the edifying of the church."* Each member of the Body must use his spiritual gifts to build up all other members. The second primary consideration is found in 1 Corinthians 14:40, *"Let all things be done decently and in order."* To do that, all aspects of public worship must exalt God rather than any individual. Obedience to these commands will prevent much dissension in the church as believers learn to lift their gaze from each other and the mundane problems around them, to Him, and Him, alone. Then, their corporate worship will touch the very throne of God and release His power to work in their midst, resolving all problems.

God's commands for private worship are just as clear and just as exacting. The mature child of God must observe them just as strictly for his private worship to enhance his personal relationship with his Lord. The first rule of private worship is recorded in Psalm 96:9, *"O worship the LORD in the beauty of holiness: fear him, all the earth."* Before the children of Israel were permitted into the presence of God, they were always instructed to sanctify themselves. In the same way, the mature child of God must set himself apart **from** the world and all of its concerns and set himself apart **to** commune with God. The second principle of private worship was given by Jesus, Himself, in John 4:23 and 24:

> *But the hour cometh, and now is, when the true worshippers shall worship the Father in spirit and in truth: for the Father seeketh such to worship him. God is a Spirit: and they that worship him must worship him in spirit and in truth.*

True worship is not found in words, no matter how religious-sounding they may be.

The mature believer realizes that true worship takes place only when one is communicating with God spiritually, man's spirit communing with God's spirit. There may be no words at all, for none are needed. He may find that it is in moments of quiet contemplation and silent adoration that he is truly able to touch his Lord in worship. The mature child of God also knows that true worship is honest and truthful. High-sounding phrases and feigned praise have no place in this exchange. God only accepts truth--a true acknowledgment of one's humble status before the King, a true recognition who God is, a true expression of one's adoration of him. Once these conditions of private worship are met, the mature believer will discover that his personal relationship with God is continually growing, continually becoming even closer and more fulfilling. Then, he will find that it is indeed possible to worship God anywhere, at any time, and in any situation.

Chapter 12
NO PLACE FOR COMPROMISE

The Leaders Called

Between the end of chapter twenty-two and the beginning of chapter twenty-three of Joshua, about a quarter century elapsed. For those twenty-five years, Israel had enjoyed rest from war (Joshua 23:1) and the benefits and blessings of life in the abundant land God had given her. But, God's people had also become comfortable, content, and complacent. Homes had been erected, farms cultivated, and businesses built. Children were born and grew to adulthood knowing nothing of Egyptian bondage, wilderness wandering, or conflict and conquest. They were living the good life. While comfort and contentment are nice, they can also be risky to the child of God if they lead to complacency. The Israelites were so comfortable and content and complacent, that they allowed the remnants of the Canaanite nations they had displaced to remain among them in mutual tolerance, many in a state of virtual servitude while others willingly paid tribute. But, they were still there and, as long as they were there, their idolatry was there, too. Israel was so comfortable, she had lost the determination to completely exterminate them as God had commanded.

Now, there's much to be said for comfort and contentment, but it's only profitable for the believer when he is able to keep God on the throne of his comfortable, contented life. Paul linked the two in 1 Timothy 6:6, *"But godliness with contentment is great gain."* Too much comfort and contentment and too little godliness, however, can be downright dangerous for any child of God. Little development takes place, since continuing spiritual growth requires continuing spiritual exercise. There is the tendency to lose the strong spiritual muscles one gained during periods of pressure and progress. These times can be particularly perilous if the child of God allows himself to become complacent, accepting of the sin he sees around him, and tolerant toward the adversary of his soul.

Joshua saw this hazard endangering Israel and, even though he was nearing one hundred and ten years old (Joshua 24:29) and experiencing the decline of health and strength associated with advanced age (Joshua 23:1), he wanted to use his great influence to warn against complacency and to encourage complete conquest. So, Israel's venerable leader called a meeting of the representative national council, composed of the elders, the seventy judges, the military officers, and the heads of the twelve tribes (Joshua 23:2). Although Scripture does not name the location of the meeting, it logically would have been held either at Joshua's home in Timnath-Serah or at the Tabernacle in Shiloh.

It's a good idea for the maturing believer to periodically evaluate his own spiritual situation, where he has been, where his is, and where he is going. It is useful to consider areas of complacency and contemplate action. It is also beneficial to evaluate possible future problems and prepare for them. This is just what Joshua had in mind.

The Past Recalled

Joshua opened the meeting reminiscing about past victories, all gained only because God had fought for His people (Joshua 23:3). Then, he recalled the division of the land (Joshua 23:4) which provided the comfort and contentment they were enjoying so much and which should have been fully possessed by this time.

An occasional look at the past can be a positive step into the future for the mature child of God. It's good to look over one's shoulder at the monuments which grace the landscape, each commemorating a battle hard fought and a victory hard one, each there only because the Lord fought for His own. It's good for the believer to see how far God has brought him along the road to full maturity and how much is still available to him in the spiritual realm. It is also good to consider just how much he has already possessed and how many good things remain to be gained in God. Such reflection can be a perfect "launching pad" for future action, future possession, and future growth. There are, however, two dangers. First, one must not live in past victories, "the good old days" syndrome. One should never be so content with past conquests that they become a substitute for future actions. The second danger is allowing past failures and defeats to become a barrier to future efforts. A look at the past is only valuable when used to plan for future progress.

The Future Envisioned

Joshua understood this and soon ended his remembrances of the past with a discussion of the future. Using strong language, he promised that God would still eject all adversaries from the land He had given Israel (Joshua 23:5). Expel, is the Hebrew, *hadap*, generally used of the complete obliteration of an enemy, and, to drive out, is the Hebrew, *yaresh*, which means disinheriting, dispossessing and destroying. This was just what God had in mind for Israel's enemies and, when those enemies were expelled, their heathen religion would be expelled with them so it would no longer have any influence on God's children. God did not even want the Canaanites within sight of the Israelites (Joshua 23:5), in servitude or not, paying tribute or not. There could be no compromise. In return, God would give His people the land still occupied by their adversaries. It would be theirs to possess because, according to Genesis 15:18 and Psalm 24:l, it was God's to give and He desired to give it to them. God still desires that His children make no compromises with the enemy of their souls or with the sin he offers. Even if he isn't on the offensive at the moment, he and all his influences are to be driven out of the believer's life in their entirety. They are not even to be within sight through art work, books, television, or movies, etc. For the mature child of God, no compromise with Satan's kingdom is possible. In return, God still offers His child possession of all that He promises. But, to receive the promises, the children of God must relinquish their complacent lifestyle and act on God's word.

In this regard, Joshua called on Israel to use the courage they had always shown in battle to totally fulfill God's commands in the Law (Joshua 23:6). Then, Joshua pointed out where God's people were dangerously close to breaking that Law. In the interest of peace with their neighbors, in the course of governing their servitude and collecting their tribute, the Israelites were engaging in more and more contact with them. They were curious about the various deities the Canaanites served in their very midst and the religious practices the Canaanites conducted amongst them. This familiarity with sin had to end. It was bad enough that the Israelites allowed the Canaanites to be among them; they must not allow themselves to be among the Canaanites. Through their representatives, Joshua called on all Israelites to separate themselves from these evil influences (Joshua 23:7). To God, attending the services of these deities, adopting their customs, or speaking or swearing by their names was forbidden. All such contacts were violations of God's Law, particularly the First and Second Commandments, as given in Exodus 20:3 and 4.

At first glance, these rules seem needlessly strict, but an examination of the Joshua's words sheds new light on these commands and explains the need for them. Mention, is the Hebrew, *zakar*, which indicates meditating upon or confessing the name of the heathen deity in a way one is only to meditate upon and confess the Name of God. Swear, is the Hebrew, *shaba*, which refers to the binding of one's soul by an oath. Serve, is the Hebrew, *abad*, which indicates worship, obedience, and enslavement. Finally, bow, is the Hebrew, *shaha*, and means to prostrate one's self in worship. Clearly, Joshua wasn't referring to the mere mentioning of the name of a Canaanite deity, as one might do in conversation or in teaching about and against it; he was warning against meditating on, confessing, binding one's self by an oath to these gods, or to worshipping or prostrating one's self before them. Paul issued a similar warning which went to the very heart of the problem idolatry presented for the believer in 1 Corinthians 10:19 through 21:

> *What say I then? that the idol is any thing, or that which is offered in sacrifice to idols is any thing? But I say, that the things which the Gentiles sacrifice, they sacrifice to devils, and not to God: and I would not that ye should have fellowship with devils. Ye cannot drink the cup of the Lord, and the cup of devils: ye cannot be partakers of the Lord's table, and the table of devils.*

All idols are identified by Paul as manifestations of Satan's kingdom, empowered by his demons, and all contact with them is fellowship with the demons behind them. Once the mature believer knows this, he can begin to understand the deadly danger involved. To meditate upon a heathen deity is to meditate upon Satan; to confess it is to accept citizenship in Satan's kingdom; to swear by it or call on its name is to invoke the demon behind it; to worship it is to worship the demon which empowers it; to prostrate one's self before it is to worship that demon. There is infinite power, power the child of God cannot even begin to comprehend, power loosed in the believer's behalf when he speaks the Name of Jesus. But, there is also power, power the child of God often does not take seriously, demonic power which may be loosed against him in the spiritual realm if he invokes the name of a pagan god. This is not mere superstition as so many nowadays believe and in which so many nowadays become innocently involved; according to the Word of God, this is Satan's own fire which must not be played with if one wants to avoid being burned.

Joshua called Israel to rededicate herself to God, to love Him and no other (Joshua 23:8 and 10), to separate herself from all of the influences of the Canaanites around her and to return to her first love. Jehovah will not share the love and intimacy of His people with another. In His sight, anything else is spiritual adultery. If she did as required, Joshua had a precious new promise for Israel, in Joshua 23:9, *"One man of you shall chase a thousand: for the LORD your God, he it is that fighteth for you, as he hath promised you."* This promise was, of course, conditional upon obedience to God's command to separate from sin and come into close relationship with Him, but it contains the key mathematical equation of spiritual warfare which every mature child of God would do well to memorize. He can put one thousand of the enemy to flight, not because of any power he possesses, but because his God fights for him. Imagine it! One thousand demons, one thousand of the temptations they bring, one thousand of the fears they inspire, one thousand of the oppressions they create--all banished from the believer's life by his God!

Disobedience Cautioned Against

Joshua also wanted the representatives to relay to the entire congregation important warnings which could mean the difference between spiritual life and spiritual death. First, he cautioned against clinging to the Canaanite gods in that special way they were to cling to God, alone (Joshua 23:12). This was a warning against integrating heathenism into the worship of Jehovah God as He had ordained it. It's symbolic of God's caution to the believer against integrating anything of the kingdom of Satan into his spiritual life. He may not, for example, consult a horoscope and pray for God's guidance at the same time.

Joshua also warned the Israelites against marrying Canaanites. To God, there could be no unions between the two and Joshua predicted serious problems resulting from them (Joshua 23:13). First, the Israelites would cease to be successful in warfare because God would cease to fight for them. Then, their heathen mates and associations would ensnare and entrap them until they, too, were brought into subjection to heathenism, as symbolized by the scourges, or whips, and thorns, or restraints, mentioned by Joshua.

God often warns against such marriages--and for good reason. Consider King Solomon, the world's wisest man. He wasn't too wise in his choice of wives or in the effect he permitted them to have on his spiritual life, as seen in 1 Kings 11:1 through 3:

> *But king Solomon loved many strange women....Of the nations concerning which the LORD said unto the children of Israel, Ye shall not go in to them, neither shall they come in unto you: for surely they will turn away your heart after their gods: Solomon clave unto these in love....and his wives turned away his heart.*

Solomon chose to deliberately disobey the clear command of God with women of the very nations God had warned against. As a result, the precise consequence God had predicted occurred and Solomon's heart was turned away from his God. Paul issues the very same warning to the mature child of God in 2 Corinthians 6:14 through 18:

> *Be ye not unequally yoked together with unbelievers: for what fellowship hath righteousness with unrighteousness? and what communion hath light with darkness? And what concord hath Christ with Belial? or what part hath he that believeth with an infidel? And what agreement hath the temple of God with idols? for ye are the temple of the living God; as God hath said, I will dwell in them, and walk in them; and I will be their God, and they shall be my people. Wherefore come out from among them, and be ye separate, saith the Lord, and touch not the unclean thing; and I will receive you, and will be a Father unto you, and ye shall be my sons and daughters, saith the Lord Almighty.*

The mature believer must understand that, according to Ephesians 5:31 and 32, marriage symbolizes the mystical union between Christ and His Church. Therefore, the marriage of a believer to an unbeliever or an idolater symbolizes an unholy union between the Christian and Satan. Such a thing is no more acceptable to God now than it was then, and for the very same reason. The influence of sin which the unbeliever brings to the marriage will turn the heart of the believer away from the God he once loved supremely. The very fact that a Christian would even consider such a marriage is an indication that his heart has already begun to turn against God and His commands.

The Meeting Concluded

As Joshua brought the meeting to a close, he spoke of his impending death. He had lived a long and eventful life and he reminded the Israelites that, in all of that time, God had always kept His promises (Joshua 23:14). Well, God had one more promise for the children of Israel, and it was not a pleasant one. Joshua warned that, just as God had given them all the blessings He had promised as long as they obeyed Him, so He would allow all evil to break loose upon them if they disobeyed His commandments and turned to other gods. In the end, they, like the Canaanites who engaged in these pagan practices before them, would be removed from the land (Joshua 23:15 and 16) because their idolatry would cause the anger of the Lord to be kindled against them (Joshua 23:16). The word translated, *"anger,"* is the Hebrew, *anep*, which literally indicates flaming nostrils or snorting, like a bull ready to charge. This terrible anger would be kindled from a spark into a consuming flame which would destroy all of God's disobedient children. God, Himself, had issued a similar warning to His people in Deuteronomy 4:23 and 24:

> *Take heed unto yourselves, lest ye forget the covenant of the LORD your God, which he made with you, and make you a graven image, or the likeness of any thing, which the LORD thy God hath forbidden thee. For the LORD thy God is a consuming fire, even a jealous God.*

So, Joshua's first meeting with the national council of Israel ended in silence. What was there to say? God had put His mighty finger on an area of compromise with the Canaanites and their pagan religion, compromise which could result in the consumption of the entire nation. There was nothing to do but to take it to heart.

No Compromise Permitted

There can still be no compromise between the children of God and the kingdom of Satan. Jesus, Himself, repeated this warning to His followers in Matthew 7:13 and 14:

> *Enter ye in at the strait gate: for wide is the gate, and broad is the way, that leadeth to destruction, and many there be which go in thereat: Because strait is the gate, and narrow is the way, which leadeth unto life, and few there be that find it.*

As Jesus said, the broad road is easy to find and easy to walk. It's a comfortable, well-traveled highway with much companionship along the way. It's also the main thoroughfare of Satan's kingdom and always leads to the same end--complete destruction. The narrow road is more difficult to find and harder to walk. It is not as comfortable or well-traveled and there will be times when the child of God feels that he walks alone. But, this road is the main street of the kingdom of God and leads to only one place--Heaven. Jesus mentioned no middle road, for there can be no compromise with sin or Satan. One must travel God's highway of holiness which the prophet envisioned in Isaiah 35:8:

> *And an highway shall be there, and a way, and it shall be called The way of holiness; the unclean shall not pass over it; but it shall be for those: the wayfaring men, though fools, shall not err therein.*

That is the highway which leads to Heaven and to eternal life. John described it in Revelation 22:2:

> *In the midst of the street of it, and on either side of the river, there was the tree of life, which bare twelve manner of fruits, and yielded her fruit every month: and the leaves of the tree were for the healing of the nations.*

If one does not choose to walk that street, he is automatically on the broad road, Satan's road, as Jesus declared in Matthew 12:30, *"He that is not with me is against me; and he that gathereth not with me scattereth abroad."* There is only one destination for those on Satan's road. The map is found in Proverbs 16:25, *"There is a way that seemeth right unto a man, but the end thereof are the ways of death."* It is the responsibility of the mature child of God to check his Roadmap often and that Roadmap is the Word of God, the Bible. This Roadmap will direct the believer to the right road and guide him all along the way. This Roadmap will alert him to possible detours into compromise which would only lead him to the broad highway of sin. Finally, this Roadmap will bring him safely to his destination--the gates of Heaven.

Chapter 13
WE'VE COME THIS FAR BY FAITH

Israel Assembled

There is no record of time lapse between Joshua's first meeting with Israel's leading representatives and the second, though it seems this second assembly occurred just prior to his death (Joshua 24:29). His final meeting with his people took place at the ancient city of Shechem. Shiloh, about ten miles northwest of Shechem, was the site of the Tabernacle and the spiritual headquarters of Israel; Gilgal was the staging point of the invasion of Canaan and the military headquarters; but Shechem was Israel's political capital. It was Abraham's point of entry into Canaan and the place where Jacob bought a family burial ground and erected an altar to the Lord (Genesis 33:18 through 20). In fact, Joshua may have called Israel together there to conduct Joseph's funeral so that his bones, which had been brought out of Egypt some seventy years before and had been carried through the wilderness for forty years, could be laid to rest in the family plot (Joshua 24:32). When the land was divided among the tribes, Shechem was assigned to the descendants of Joseph's son, Ephraim. It was set aside by Joshua to be one of the cities of refuge (Joshua 20:7) and ceded by Ephraim to be one of the cities of the Levites (Joshua 21:20 and 21). Since it was a Levitical city, the Levites may have moved the Tabernacle or just the Ark of the Covenant there from Shiloh for this conclave, as indicated in Joshua 24:26.

Joshua summoned the entire nation to Shechem (Joshua 24:1). Then, Israel's representatives were singled out by Joshua to stand before God and receive a message from Him (Joshua 24:1). It was delivered by Joshua in the form of a prophecy which came directly from God. Note the use of the personal pronoun, *"I,"* seventeen times. The prophetic tone and divine origin of the message is also clearly established by its introduction in Joshua 24:2, *"And Joshua said unto all the people, <u>Thus saith the LORD God of Israel</u>...."*

Past Recalled

God's prophetic message consisted of a brief recitation of the past history of His people (Joshua 24:2 through 13), covering the entire period from Abraham's call out of Ur of the Chaldees in 2091 B.C. to the settlement of several million of his descendants in Canaan, the land God had promised him, in about 1400 B.C., a period of nearly seven hundred years. Joshua had begun his previous meeting with these same elders with a similar report (Joshua 23:3 and 4), but it appears he had been ignored. Now, God, Himself, forced those leaders to look at the past again, to remember how their nation had begun with one faithful and obedient man, to see how far God had already brought them, and to consider their future course. Since God knows that human beings learn best by example, He didn't appeal to the Law; instead, He selected some of the most illustrious examples in Israel's history and reviewed their lives, not from their perspective, but from His. Still, God did not recount every event in the long history of His people; He chose only those events which illustrated the spiritual danger in which Israel presently stood.

From time to time, the mature believer may be called aside by God to review his own spiritual life, to see where he has come from, where he stands, and where he is going. Since he, too, learns best by example, God may direct his attention to those who have gone before, to their victories and their failures. He may even give a glimpse of His omnipotent and omniscient perspective so that the child of God may see the work of God within the lives of His own, and the appropriate lessons may be learned.

God began with the example of Abraham, a man whose entire family had *"served other gods"* (Joshua 24:2). Yet, God had chosen Abraham, a former idolater, to be the progenitor of His people. Then, He had personally conducted him on a tour of the length and breadth of Canaan, showing him the land He would one day give to his posterity. Finally, God had miraculously blessed him with a son, Isaac, to preserve the line which would one day inherit it all (Joshua 24:3). Here, God gave a glimpse of the major spiritual events in Abraham's life as viewed from His side of the tapestry. An account of the same events from Abraham's perspective is recorded in Hebrews 11:8 through 10:

> *By faith Abraham, when he was called to go out into a place which he should after receive for an inheritance, obeyed...not knowing whither he went. By faith he sojourned in the land of promise, as in a strange country, dwelling in tabernacles with Isaac and Jacob, the heirs with him of the same promise: For he looked for a city which hath foundations, whose builder and maker is God.*

God saw Abraham's life from the perspective of the abundant grace He extended to him. Born and reared in idol worship requiring the sacrifice of one's own children, God called him out of idolatry well before that requirement could threaten the life of the son He would give him. Then, God showed him the legacy that son and his descendants would enjoy before the child was even born. Abraham saw the same events from a perspective of faith, obeying even when he didn't know where he was going, believing in a permanent home for his descendants even when he and his children were living in tents. God had also poured out His grace upon Israel, giving them the land He had promised Abraham, the land of Canaan, the land of their enemies. In response, they, too, were to reject the idolatry around them, even if they didn't always understand the danger posed to themselves and generations yet unborn. They must trust, as Abraham did, that God had a good reason for requiring His people to worship Him alone, a reason rooted in their ultimate good. As God had miraculously given Abraham a son to inherit the land of promise, so He would bless His people with many children whose inheritance would continue to be Canaan, a legacy they could pass from one generation to the next. Those generations would be preserved to inherit it by God, Himself, only if they remained faithful to Him.

Here is a lesson for the mature believer. He, too, must break all ties of compromise with the adversary which threatens his own spiritual life and that of his offspring, both his natural children and his children in the faith, so that he can inherit the promises of God. Those promises, that inheritance, will be his legacy to those children and they, in turn, will be preserved in the faith to receive God's promises, too. As Proverbs 22:6 vows, *"Train up a child in the way he should go: and when he is old, he will not depart from it."*

God's next example was Abraham's son of promise, Isaac (Joshua 24:4), to whom He gave twin sons, Jacob and Esau, and provided a separate inheritance for each. When famine later struck the land, however, Jacob and his family went to Egypt for food (Genesis 42:1 and 2) and were enslaved, while Esau and his family, it is implied, remained in the land, trusting God to sustain them. They were not only spared starvation, but the bondages of Egypt, too. Isaac's perspective on his sons is recorded with more brevity in Hebrews 11:20, *"By faith Isaac blessed Jacob and Esau concerning things to come."* Isaac had blessed his two sons, but Jacob, the younger, had defrauded his brother of the blessing reserved for the eldest son. His blessing included the promise of abundance, the homage of his brother and his descendants, a curse on all who cursed him and a blessing on all who blessed him (Genesis 27:28 and 29). Esau's blessing also included a promise of abundance, but it contained a provision that he would have to fight to regain what had been his, too (Genesis 27:39 and 40). From his perspective, Isaac could hardly have understood why God allowed the blessings of his sons to be reversed. All he could do was bless them in faith. From God's perspective, however, it was all quite clear. He had meant for the younger son to rule over the elder and for the offspring of both to have abundance. Esau's family may have enjoyed its abundance sooner because they remained in the land God gave them, while Jacob's family came to the abundance of Canaan by way of slavery in Egypt, but both were blessed by God, just as Isaac had said. It was all according to God's sovereign plan.

Isaac and his sons were an example to Israel. God would bless them with abundance in Canaan and there would be enough inheritance for all. But, they, like Jacob and Esau, had to make a fundamental decision. Would they stay in the land, remain faithful to God, and be sustained by Him? Or, would they seek their spiritual food from another source and find themselves in bondage as a result? The mature believer must make the same decision. The Lord has promised him many spiritual children as the fruit of his service. In God's promises, there is ample inheritance for all, a double portion of His Spirit, just as Elisha received from his spiritual father, Elijah (2 Kings 2:9). But, like Jacob and Esau, like Israel, the believer must decide if he will be faithful where God has placed him, or will instead seek some other source of spiritual sustenance and find himself in bondage to Satan as a result. It is a decision each child of God must make every day of his spiritual life.

Next, God spoke of Moses and Aaron (Joshua 24:5). He commissioned both men and, through them, brought ten plagues upon Egypt, showing His superiority over their gods (Exodus 12:12), resulting in the unconditional release of Israel along with much Egyptian spoil (Exodus 11:1 and 2). The message to Israel was clear. Their parents' freedom was gained, not because of the faith or spiritual strength of any man, but only because God had proven Himself more powerful than Egypt's gods. Then, God called their children to conquer Canaan and possess the inheritance God promised them. To do it, God promised to fight for them (Joshua 10:42) against the Canaanites and their gods (Deuteronomy 20:17 and 18). Would those very children now become involved with pagan gods proven inferior to their own? Each mature believer is commissioned to take his inheritance and possess all of God's promises. God will still fight for him and give him victory over any attack of his enemy. But, only he can decide if he will, instead, compromise with the enemy and permit his idols to stand between himself and his Lord.

Israel's forefathers provided the next example (Joshua 24:6 and 7). God had powerfully brought them out of slavery in Egypt and erected a barrier of protection between them and their enemies. Then, He had purposely permitted the Egyptians to follow the Israelites, not to destroy them, but only to show them His miracle-working power in their behalf as he executed His final judgment against the Egyptians (Exodus 14:3 and 4). Although the forefathers had seen the Red Sea part with their own eyes, they still disobeyed and disbelieved Him and spent the rest of their lives wandering in the wilderness, before their children could come into Canaan. Those children should have learned the lesson their parents' example taught. God was able to break any bondage, evict any enemy, and perform any miracle they needed. They had watched with their own eyes as God did mighty miracles for them during their conquest of Canaan; if that did not inspire total faith and obedience in them, they, too, might have to wander in a wasteland of their own sin and idolatry. The lesson for the mature believer is the same. God has also brought him out of bondage, protected him from attack, and performed mighty miracles in his behalf. But, if, after God has done all of this, His child has learned nothing of Him, of His love, and of His power, if what he has seen does not inspire unquestioning faith and unfaltering obedience in him, he, too, may be destined to die in a spiritual desert.

The people to whom God spoke, were His final example (Joshua 24:8 through 13). He had given all the victories He cited in Joshua 24:8 through 12. He had given them land, cities, and fruit for which they had not labored (Joshua 24:13). He had done it all!

Through these examples, God showed His people that, for centuries, He had been arranging the events which had brought them into the safety and security, prosperity and pleasures, comfort and contentment of Canaan land. They had done nothing in their own strength; God had done it all in His strength. Would His people now turn from Him and go after gods that had been helpless before Him? The mature child of God must look back at the events which have brought him this far. He will see that he has done nothing in his own strength; whatever spiritual blessings he may have received, whatever spiritual victories he may have attained, whatever spiritual progress he may have achieved, whatever spiritual maturity he may have developed--it was all accomplished through the power of God in his behalf. He will realize that, all along, it has been God who has been planning his life to bring him to the place of peace and prosperity where he now stands. He will acknowledge that God, and God alone, is his Source. After all God has done in his life, is really there anything Satan can offer that will entice him away from such a God?

Choices Offered

To conclude His prophetic message through Joshua, God called on His people to learn the lessons of the examples He had used. In Joshua 24:14, He said:

> *Now therefore fear the LORD, and serve him in sincerity and in truth: and put away the gods which your fathers served on the other side of the flood, and in Egypt; and serve ye the LORD.*

Sincerity, is the Hebrew, *tamim*, which refers to the state of being perfect, entire, and whole. These same words define perfection and maturity in the New Testament. God meant for the examples of their history and their own experiences to bring His children to maturity. In that maturity, they would abandon the searching of spiritual childhood and serve God completely, perfectly, and with their whole hearts. They must forever forsake the gods their fathers once served, the same sort of gods worshipped in Canaan and to which they seemed increasingly drawn. They must covenant to serve Jehovah God alone.

Today's mature believer is called upon to make a choice, too. He must end the searching of spiritual immaturity, knowing that Jehovah is God and that there is no other. He must recognize that it is possible to have idols in one's life--the idols of family, friends, materialism, even the church--anyone or anything which comes before God. Since God will not share the love and worship of His people with any of these things, one's personal idols must be forsaken forever and replaced with the single-minded worship of Jehovah, alone.

Joshua recognized these principles of spiritual life and, as God's prophetic message concluded, he placed the choice squarely before his people. In Joshua 24:15, Joshua stands as a type of the Saviour, calling to account, calling to decision:

> *And if it seem evil unto you to serve the LORD, choose you this day whom ye will serve; whether the gods which your fathers served that were on the other side of the flood, or the gods of the Amorites, in whose land ye dwell: but as for me and my house, we will serve the LORD.*

Joshua identified for Israel three choices, like those presented to the believer today. Israel could serve the idols of Ur of the Chaldees which Abraham's family followed before his call to Canaan or the gods of the Egyptians which had so influenced their parents. The modern believer may also choose the traditional religion of his forbearers, with little or no thought of the true God as presented by Scripture. But, it is not religion that saves, but relationship; while traditional religion may be comforting, it is not converting. It must be forsaken for a real relationship with the Lord. Israel's second choice was the gods of the land, the gods which hadn't been able to hold that land for the Canaanites, the gods Jehovah had defeated to give that land to His own. Today, there are the popular religions of heresy and humanism, cults and the occult, and the popular gods of wealth, power, and lust waiting to be worshipped. Without Scripture, which warns again and again against these "religions," one might choose to follow the crowd into these substitutes for worship of God. Finally, Joshua offered the Israelites the opportunity to choose Jehovah, the God behind all of the events of their history, the God who had personally brought them out of bondage in Egypt, the God who had given them possession of Canaan. But, this God must be worshipped with one's whole heart, forever dispossessing and replacing all idols in one's life. This worship of Jehovah, performed as Scripture commands, will not always comply with tradition and will never be popular. These were the three choices with which Joshua confronted Israel. They are the same three choices which confront believers today.

Choices Made

As Israel considered the choices, Joshua announced his own decision for all to hear. *"As for me and my house,"* he thundered, *"we will serve the LORD."* As prophet, priest, and king in his home, Joshua took responsibility for himself and for all under his authority. Such was the spiritual maturity Joshua had achieved during his long years of following God; such must be the spiritual maturity every child of God strives to attain. The people responded, *"God forbid,"* they said, *"that we should forsake the LORD, to serve other gods."* They had learned from the examples God had brought to memory (Joshua 24:17 and 18) and, based upon those examples, based upon all that the Lord had done for them and to their enemies, each person present made the personal decision to pledge allegiance to Jehovah God alone (Joshua 24:18). Making a decision based upon experience is a further sign of personal growth and development. While the immature may base decisions on emotion or peer pressure, the mature believer will base his choices on his own experience with God, the experiences of others as expressed in testimonies, biographies, etc., and the examples of the lives of those presented in His Word. Having found God faithful in all of these experiences and examples, the mature believer will make a firm decision to follow God alone, too.

Simply making a decision is not an end in itself; one must carry out that decision, and Joshua made certain his people knew it (Joshua 24:19 and 23). Their decision to serve God carried with it the responsibility to put away all the other gods they had previously permitted among them. Failure to do so was sin, sin against a holy God who requires holiness in His people, sin against a jealous God who will not share the love of His people (Joshua 24:19). Joshua also made sure everyone knew the penalty God has placed on those who refuse to reject spiritual adultery; the same God who had done so much good for them, would turn around and do them hurt (Joshua 24:20). Hurt, is the Hebrew, *ra'a*, indicating evil and distress which breaks or shatters. God would inflict this hurt on all who would not forsake idolatry to follow Him and it would destroy them. The mature child of God must adultery and will be punished by spiritual death. There is only one escape from this penalty--one must choose to put away all of his idols, all of the things which he may once have placed before God. Having made that choice, he must carry it out.

Again and again, Joshua called on God's people to be certain of their choice. Again and again, they reaffirmed their determination to serve God (Joshua 24:21, 22, and 24). At last, Joshua accepted it, but with the solemn warning found in Joshua 24:22:

> *And Joshua said unto the people, Ye are witnesses against yourselves that ye have chosen the LORD, to serve him. And they said, We are witnesses.*

Witnesses, is the Hebrew, *ed*, which is the name chosen by the two and a half tribes east of the Jordan River to identify their altar of witness (Joshua 22:34). This word conveyed the idea of returning, repeating, or doing over again, indicating that the words uttered by the children of Israel before Joshua could come back to haunt them if repeated by God in condemnation and judgment, should they fail to keep their commitment to Him. Here, another important mark of spiritual maturity is illustrated--the ability to consider and accept the consequences of one's actions. The mature believer must realize that, as a consequence of his decision to serve God, he will be condemned by his own lips if he fails to keep his word. It isn't enough to promise; one must fulfill one's promises to God. It is better never to have made a commitment to God than to fail to keep it. The consequences should be carefully considered before one speaks.

Finally, Joshua accepted the decision repeatedly reaffirmed by God's people. To conclude the meeting, he and his countrymen made a covenant to serve Jehovah (Joshua 24:25), a covenant considered a part of the Law of God and just as binding as the Ten Commandments, themselves. Then, a huge stone was placed under an oak tree near the Tabernacle as a permanent monument of the meeting and the momentous decision made there (Joshua 24:26 and 27). The Septuagint, the Greek translation of the Hebrew Scriptures used by the New Testament believers, records that the patriarch, Jacob, once collected all of the gods of the residents of Shechem and buried them under a nearby oak tree (Genesis 35:4). Is it possible that Joshua set the stone of witness of the Israelites' commitment to forsake all idolatry under the very same oak tree? Whichever oak Joshua chose, the message remains the same. Just as surely as Jacob buried the idols of Shechem of his day, just as Joshua called Israel to put away all idols in his day, the mature believer of today must separate himself from anything which stands between him and his God.

Joshua sent his countrymen home to their inheritance (Joshua 24:28). No doubt, he hoped that they would return home different men, men with the burning determination to serve Jehovah to the exclusion of all other gods, to put away the Canaanite idols around them, and to possess all that they had inherited so many years before.

Leadership Passed

Shortly after this final meeting with his people, Joshua died at one hundred and ten years of age and was buried at Timnath-serah, a part of the personal inheritance he had fully possessed in obedience to the command of God (Joshua 19:49 and 50). One can only imagine the sadness as the Israelites gathered to bury their great warrior and leader, the man who had brought them into the land they now enjoyed.

In accord with his dying expression of faith (Genesis 50:24 through 26), Joseph, the son of Jacob and the "saviour" of the family line during the time of famine, was finally laid to rest in the family plot at Shechem (Joshua 24:32). Joseph had entered into the land of promise and received his inheritance, even after he was dead as far as this world knew.

What an example Joseph presents to the mature child of God! He, too, must wait to enter into the promises of God, to claim them as his personal inheritance, and to take them as his personal possession until after he is dead to sin and dead to this world. This is the message of Paul to the mature believer in Romans 6:11 and 14:

Likewise reckon ye also yourselves to be dead indeed unto sin, but alive unto God through Jesus Christ our Lord....For sin shall not have dominion over you: for ye are not under the law, but under grace.

Joseph is typical of the Christ, Himself. He took possession of His own, His people, and was accorded a place of permanent residence in and among them after He was dead as far as the world was concerned as Ephesians 1:20 through 23 declares:

Which he wrought in Christ, when he raised him from the dead, and set him at his own right hand in the heavenly places. Far above all principality, and power, and might, and dominion, and every name that is named, not only in this world, but also in that which is to come: And hath put all things under his feet, and gave him to be the head over all things to the church, Which is his body, the fulness of him that filleth all in all.

Finally, Joseph's dying faith in his inheritance in Canaan is an example of the truly mature child of God who has surrendered the famine of life in this world for the abundance of life in the kingdom of God. As Paul wrote in Colossians 2:20:

I am crucified with Christ: nevertheless I live; yet not I, but Christ liveth in me: and the life which I now live in the flesh I live by the faith of the son of God, who loved me, and gave himself for me.

Then, Eleazar, the son of Aaron and his heir as high priest, died and was buried on a hill in Ephraim near the Levitical city in which his son and successor, Phinehas, lived. This illustrates the permanence of the high priesthood, which Christ occupies now and forever in the life of every mature believer.

This Far By Faith

The children of Israel had come this far by faith. The progress they had made in less than a century was amazing. They had come:

1. Out of death, into life.
2. Out of bondage, into freedom.
3. Out of failure, into victory.
4. Out of captivity, into conquest.
5. Out of emptiness, into inheritance.
6. Out of being possessed, into possessing.
7. Out of immaturity, into maturity.

What lay ahead for the mature children of God who made that momentous choice for God in their final meeting with Joshua before his death? The writer who picked up the pen of Joshua and completed his book answered that question in Joshua 24:31:

Israel served the LORD all the days of Joshua, and all the days of the elders that overlived Joshua, and which had known all the works of the LORD, that he had done for Israel.

For the next few years, those who had experienced the miracles of God for His people and those who remained under their authority and influence would follow Jehovah. It is sad that, after these spiritually mature men and women of Israel passed into history, their children would once again slip back into idolatry, the spiritual adultery against which

Joshua had issued such a firm warning. The primary reason for this backsliding would be the continual influence of their Canaanite neighbors, whom, contrary to the clear command of God and of Joshua, Israel never completely expelled from their inheritance. For their spiritual adultery, their descendants would be forced to endure seventy years of captivity, a fate they may have been spared if their ancestors had only fully followed God. Only after this captivity, would Israel, as a nation, forsake idolatry and follow God forever.

The mature child of God has also made much spiritual progress as he has come along the road to full spiritual maturity. He, too, has come:

1. Out of spiritual death, into eternal life.
2. Out of spiritual bondage, into spiritual freedom.
3. Out of past failure, into present victory.
4. Out of Satan's captivity, into conquest with Christ.
5. Out of the emptiness of sin, into his spiritual inheritance.
6. Out of being possessed, into possessing the promises of God.
7. Out of spiritual immaturity, into spiritual maturity.

Where will the mature believer go from this place? Will he continue to serve God, or will he slip back into spiritual adultery before the idols of this present world? Will he continue to allow the enemy of his soul to live in his midst, or will he expel him once and for all? Will he continue in the liberty of the Lord, or will he suffer captivity before he learns the last and most important lesson of all--that Jehovah God must always come first in his life? Each mature believer must answer these questions for himself. Each must make his own decision. Each must choose.

In Summation

In this final chapter of the Book of Joshua, the believer learns much more about the nature and character of spiritual maturity. First, maturity is seen as the state of being perfect before God. But, this perfection is not godly perfection or angelic perfection, neither of which is attainable by man. This perfection is found in worshipping God wholly, completely, entirely, with one's whole heart and soul and mind (Matthew 22:36 and 37). This is full spiritual maturity. It is this measure of maturity which is commanded by Jesus in Matthew 5:48, "*Be ye therefore perfect, even as your Father which is in heaven is perfect.*" It's also the God's command through Paul, in 1 Corinthians 13:11, "*Be perfect, be of good comfort, be of one mind, live in peace; and the God of love and peace shall be with you.*" It is this standard of maturity to which Paul called Christians in Colossians 1:28 and 4:12, "*That we may present you perfect in Christ Jesus....that ye may stand perfect and complete in the will of God.*" This last chapter of Joshua also reveals that this spiritual maturity will be exhibited in the spiritual life and conduct of the mature child of God. For example, he will assume responsibility for himself and for those under his authority in the kingdom of God (Joshua 24:15). He will make his decisions based upon his previous experience with God (Joshua 24:17 and 18) and he will consider the spiritual consequences of each of those decisions (Joshua 24:19 through 22). Once he gives his word, he will faithfully keep it (Joshua 24:23). Finally, this mature man or woman of God will accept full responsibility for his actions and their consequences (Joshua 24:22). These, then, are the signposts along the road as one comes to maturity in God.

PART THREE
EPHESIANS: COMING INTO PERFECTION

INTRODUCTION

The History of the Period

After Joshua's death, until the end of the Old Testament, the nation of Israel would experience some of the most momentous events of its history. During the days of the judges, which lasted from about 1385 B.C. until about 1050 B.C., Israel fell into cycles of sin and idolatry, followed by the punishment of God in the form of oppression by Canaanite neighbors which still had not been completely driven out, followed by repentance, and concluded by deliverance by a God-appointed judge or deliverer. Then, from approximately 1050 B.C. until the fall of Jerusalem in 586 B.C., Israel experienced her golden age, the period of the monarchy. This time may logically be divided into two segments. The first was the united monarchy, which lasted from about 1050 B.C. until about 930 B.C. during which Saul, David, and Solomon reigned over the entire nation. The second was the divided monarchy, from 930 B.C. until 586 B.C., when the nation was divided into two independent countries, as Israel and Judah, each with its own king. Because of their idolatry during the monarchy, both Israel and Judah were punished with captivity. Israel's bondage began in 722 B.C. at the hands of the Assyrians, although many of her poorest inhabitants remained in their land under Assyrian occupation. Israel's sinful sister, Judah, fell captive to Babylon in 586 B.C.; her Temple was looted and burned to the ground, along with nearly all of the homes of her citizens. The return and restoration continued from approximately 539 B.C. until about 430 B.C. during which many Babylonian captives came back to Jerusalem, rebuilt their Temple, and re-established their nation.

As the Old Testament ended, Israel was still divided. Most of her people remained dispersed throughout the Persian Empire, which had replaced the Babylonian Empire, living more like colonists than captives. A small remnant, mostly from the tribe of Judah, had returned to the land of their forefathers with the permission of Cyrus the Great and his successors. Zerubbabel, a prince descended from David, and many survivors from the priestly line of the Levites went with them. They reconstructed the Temple of Jehovah God and reinstituted worship of Him. Under the leadership of Ezra and Nehemiah, a stable government ruled by a council of elders and priests, fashioned on the Mosaic pattern and a predecessor of the Sanhedrin of the time of Jesus and Paul, was formed. This council was known as the Great Synagogue and Ezra served as its first president. It was composed of one hundred and twenty members and acted much like an ecclesiastical court, interpreting the Law, teaching it, and compelling obedience to it. This body ruled religious life in Israel until the time of Simon the Just in approximately 292 B.C. Ezra and Nehemiah also established smaller synagogues in many towns, synagogues which conducted worship, established schools of instruction, and acted as local courts where causes of action under the Mosaic Law could be tried. Though sacrifices could only be offered at the Temple in Jerusalem, the synagogues became the centers of local religious life throughout Israel and in most of the cities of the world in which Israelites had taken up residence.

God's people had finally lost all interest in idolatry, although it continued to exist in the rest of the world and to influence the Jews who remained outside of Israel. The Jews of Israel knew what it had cost their ancestors and they were determined not to repeat the mistakes of the past. They wanted to know about their God and study His Law, making the new synagogues quite popular. It was during this period and as a result of this thirst for knowledge that the traditions, commentaries, and interpretations of the Law were composed. The Mishna and the Gemara, which formed the Talmud, and the Halachoth, the Midrashim, and the Kabbala soon so overshadowed the Law that, in many synagogues and for many people, they actually came to supersede it. It was also during this time that the major religious sects of the time of Jesus and Paul came into existence. To fully understand the religious world which influenced Paul, the writer of Ephesians, it is necessary to have some understanding of these sects.

The Persians, who had taken the Middle East from the Babylonians under Cyrus the Great, were finally defeated by the young Greco-Macedonian conqueror, Alexander the Great, in 331 B.C. Josephus wrote that a dream caused Alexander to treat the Jews with great favor,[1] permitting them to retain self-government and their own religion. Later, when Alexander built his namesake city, Alexandria, Egypt, he encouraged Jews to settle there, giving them equal rights with all of his other citizens. In fact, it was in Alexandria between 294 and 289 B.C. that seventy Jewish scholars translated the Old Testament into Greek. Known as the Septuagint, this was the Bible from which Paul quoted. But, Alexander died at the age of thirty-two, leaving no heir. As a result, his kingdom was divided among his four top generals. Cassander took Greece and Macedonia, Lysimachus took Asia Minor, Seleucus took Syria and Babylon, and Ptolemy took Egypt. Tiny Israel was once again in the middle, between Persia and Egypt, between the so-called anvil and hammer.

In response to the aggressive, forceful, and insulting Hellenizing of the Syrian Seleucid king, Antiochus Ephiphanes, a successor to Seleucus who then held Israel, the Jews of Palestine revolted in 168 B.C. Their leaders were Mattathias, of the tiny village of Modein, and his five sons. Although the family name was actually Hasmon, one of Mattathias' sons, Judas, was given the title, "Maccabee," or, "the hammer," in honor of his ferocious fighting style, and it is by this name that the entire family is known to history. To rally all devout Jews to his side, Mattathias issued a call for all who were zealous for the Law and lived according to its covenant to join with him and his family in the struggle against Hellenistic tyranny. All who answered that call became known as "the Hasidim," which means, "the pious ones."[2] The Hasidim had no interest in establishing a political party nor in achieving political power; their only interest was in obtaining the freedom to observe the Law of Moses. In the successful Maccabean revolt, they won that right.

About thirty years later, during the rule of John Hyrcanus, the grandson of Mattathias and the first of the Hasmoneans, the sect of the Pharisees, meaning, "the separated ones,"[3] emerged from the old Hasidic group. The title referred as much to their separation from the Hasidim as to their doctrine of separation from sin and their practice of separating from those considered to be Hellenizers or sinners. They were mostly from middle-class working families, not the exalted priestly class, and were, therefore, more acceptable to the masses in Israel. In fact, they became by far the largest and the most influential of the sects of Israel, although even at the height of their power, the Pharisees never claimed more than six thousand members. They were considered experts in the Law of Moses and, consequently, were accorded more than their rightful share of high government offices and positions on the Sanhedrin, the seventy-man ruling body of Judaism.

The Pharisees accepted as inspired the Old Testament canon, as determined by Ezra and the Great Synagogue of restoration days and wanted everyone to live according to it. So, the Pharisees mandated traditions which extended the Law well beyond the boundaries of Scripture, based on the so-called "oral law," which, according to the rabbis, God had given Moses in oral form at the same time He gave him the tablets of the Law in written form. These oral laws supposedly elaborated upon and explained the written Law and were then handed down from generation to generation of priests, finally becoming the property of the rabbis, a class of teachers which evolved during the captivity and restoration. While the written Law ordered that the Sabbath be kept holy, the Pharisees, using oral law, prescribed in great and burdensome detail, what comprised work and what could and could not legally be done on the Sabbath. They said a journey of more than one kilometer, the carrying of a package, the lighting of a fire, or the tying of an apron all constituted work and were, therefore, forbidden on the Sabbath. Piety had begun to verge on legalism. The Pharisees intent was good, in effect, to "build a fence around the Law," to protect the devout from accidently sinning. In practice, however, such minute intrusions into everyday life caused many to give up in frustration any attempt to keep the Law. The Pharisees believed in divine providence, predestination, the immortality of the soul, and an eternal destination where man received the punishments or rewards earned in this life. They also believed in a coming Messiah, although they viewed Him as the One who would bring national and political freedom, a twist on truth which kept many from recognizing Jesus, the Messiah of spiritual freedom, when He came. Nearly all of these beliefs stood in sharp contrast to those of the Greeks and the Pharisees resisted any and all attempts at Hellenization, maintaining their Jewish Law, Jewish traditions, Jewish customs, and Jewish way of life. But, for all their good intentions and beliefs, the passing years saw their sect deteriorate into legalism, self-righteousness, and spiritual contempt for all who were unable to fulfill the Law and the traditions according to their lofty standards. It was this tendency toward excess and hypocrisy against which our Lord cried out during His ministry.

Once the Maccabeans and Hasidim drove the Seleucid Syrians out, Hellenistic Jews found society most hostile to their views and began an underground movement, the sect of the Sadducees, meaning, "the righteous ones,"[4] so called presumably because most members were descended from the priestly line of Aaron. Their insecure existence continued until the reign of Alexander Jannaeus, son of John Hyrcanus, who was an outspoken defender and apologist for the Sadducees, even ordering the crucifixion of large numbers of the opposition Pharisees. The Sadducees accepted only the written law of Moses. In fact, as descendants of the Levitical priesthood, they saw themselves as the natural guardians of the Torah and rejected both the oral law and the Pharisaical traditions based on it. Favoring Greek thought, the Sadducees rejected belief in angels, demons, or other spiritual beings. They saw man as the master of his fate and, therefore, rejected any idea of predestination, divine providence, divine guidance, divine intervention in the affairs of men, life after death, Heaven, Hell, or eternal reward or punishment. While the working-class Pharisees were considered amiable, the wealthier Sadducees seemed arrogant and boorish by comparison.

The Hasidim of Maccabean days who did not join the emerging Pharisees, evolved into the sect of the Essenes, believed to mean, "the holy ones."[5] The Essenes saw Jewish society and worship as corrupted, calling the Pharisees, "givers of easy interpretations," while regarding themselves as the guardians of the true piety and religion which would usher in the age of Messiah. Never numbering more than four thousand, they separated from society and established their own communities, usually in remote desert areas of Palestine.

This probably explains why, while the Pharisees and Sadducees are mentioned often in the New Testament, the Essenes, cloistered in their communes, are not mentioned at all.

The Essenes saw asceticism and self-denial as the only means to holiness before God. They were vegetarians, rejecting the bloody animal sacrifices of the Mosaic Law in favor of their own bloodless rites. In addition, sexual intercourse was considered unclean and unholy, marriage was anathema, and the state of perpetual and lifelong celibacy was seen as especially virtuous and sanctified. In lieu of marriage and family, the Essenes perpetuated their sect by adopting the unwanted or orphaned children of others. The Essenes practiced complicated and continual purification rites and, once a new convert had endured a three-year probationary initiation period, he was required to swear to reveal nothing of these rites or life in the commune. Those accepted in the community wore white linen robes, indicating their purity and righteousness.

Presiding over these three, mutually exclusive and mutually antagonistic sects, as well as Jewish society, was the Sanhedrin whose name, according to the Mishna, meant, "house of judgment."[6] This governing body of Judaism traced its origins to Numbers 11:16 and 17 where God ordained a council of elders to assist Moses. While it seems this council did not survive the period of the judges, it was revived by Ezra during the restoration and continued until abolished by the Romans after their conquest and destruction of Jerusalem in A.D. 70. The Sanhedrin had seventy members presided over by the high priest. According to the New Testament, members were drawn from three classes, as Mark 14:53 records, "*And with him were assembled all the chief priests and the elders and the scribes.*" The chief priests were those who had already served as high priest or were in preparation for that office. The scribes, many of whom were Pharisees, were men who painstakingly hand-copied the Scriptures and were, therefore, considered experts in the provisions of the Law. The elders were the noble heads of the tribes and major families of Israel. The jurisdiction of the Sanhedrin extended to all matters of ceremonial and civil law along with many criminal matters, and all cases were decided using the Law of Moses.

As the sects and the Sanhedrin were evolving during the days between the Testaments, Alexander's kingdom was deteriorating into anarchy. Much of the third century B.C. was convulsed by wars between his four ambitious successors weakening their realms and paving the way for the rise of Rome. Unlike previous conquerors, the Romans were not primarily motivated by personal glory, empire building, or a quest for wealth. Their conquest had more to do with geography than economics. Rome, on the Italian Peninsula surrounded on three sides by the Mediterranean Sea and bordered on the north by the Alps, had the feel of an island, a centrally located island from which the Mediterranean Sea lanes could be controlled, but an island very vulnerable to the anarchy around it. Roman expansion provided a buffer zone of defensible frontiers behind which she felt secure. By 63 B.C., Rome's most famous general, Pompey, had completed his conquest of Greece, Asia Minor, Syria, and the entire Middle East. Later, he moved north through Gaul, now France, the Rhine River valley, and even Great Britain. Into these newly conquered territories, Rome extended her generally benign rule and justice, which was well in advance of most earlier justice systems. Rome would usually install indigenous leadership presided over by recognized national rulers and, so long as they were able to keep the peace, collect the taxes, and prevent rebellion, they kept their jobs, Rome kept the profits, and the Roman legions kept their distance. In most of her territories, this system maintained "the Pax Romanus," the peace of Rome, and was welcomed by most of her subjects, who saw it as a refreshing change from the tyrants which had previously ruled them (Acts 24:2 and 3).

It was in this spirit that Julius Caesar, in 47 B.C., gave John Hyrcanus and his heirs all rights to the high priesthood of Israel, along with many other benefits. At the same time, the actual political power was given to Antipater, an Idumean (or one from the land of Edom, the historic domain of Esau's descendants), who served as procurator or governor of Judea. Antipater's son, Herod, was also appointed governor of Galilee. Ten years later, Herod, with the help of the Roman legions, solidified his power and disposed of all rivals. Then, little by little, he sacrificed his Jewish heritage to Rome, cultivating Roman customs, fostering their immorality, corrupting the priesthood, and killing any who got in his way. At the time of the birth of Jesus, this same Herod ordered the murder of all children under two in order to rid himself of any threat to his own hold on power.

Rome maintained the Pax Romanus, comparative tranquility, throughout her empire for several centuries, to the relief of most of her subjects. In fact, where deification and worship of previous rulers was traditional, these subjects hailed the Roman emperors as gods. This folk custom, originally mocked by the emperors, was later adopted and, finally, commanded by their successors, leading to a cult which would constantly clash with the Christian Church of Paul's day. While most in Rome's empire may have found her rule beneficent and her emperors god-like, most Jews of Israel did not. They were scandalized by the sexual excesses of the Romans, offended by their multitheistic religion and the deification of their emperors, and disgusted by the complicity of their own king. They bristled under Roman rule and waited for the promised Messiah, who they were certain, would soon come to deliver them. It was the common belief that the Messiah would conquer Rome that caused most Jews, possibly including a young man named Saul, to miss Him when He finally appeared. It was the duplicity between conquered and conqueror, this threat to the delicate balance of the Pax Romanus, which would eventually cause their own Jewish leaders to put Him to death, the very death predicted so many centuries before, as seen in John 11:48, "*If we let him thus alone, all men will believe on him: and <u>the Romans shall come and take away both our place and our nation</u>.*"

If the Jewish leaders thought the death of one Man would kill the revolutionary spirit in their countrymen, they were mistaken. Small rebellions surfaced all over Israel, but they were no match for the Roman war machine and the seasoned Roman troops who drove it. This Jewish nationalism, along with the rise of a sect called "the Nazarenes" or "Christians" who followed their own King, brought the wrath of Rome against Jews of every political and religious persuasion. It would result in the systematic persecution of the early Church, the martyrdom of many of her shining stars, including a man called Paul, and the spreading of her Gospel to all the known world. Then, in A.D. 70, three years after the execution of Paul by the infamous Nero, the Jewish rebellion was crushed, their Temple sacked and burned once more, and their people scattered among the Gentile nations. They would not return to their land en masse until modern times, after the Nazi Holocaust and the re-establishment of a Jewish homeland in Palestine in 1948, a Jewish homeland called Israel.

This, then, was the religious and political maelstrom into which a Jewish child with Roman citizenship, a child known as Saul, a child also known as Paul was born. These were the turbulent influences which molded and shaped his early life and produced the zealot who grew up to fight, first for his religion, then for his Saviour, in a world where neither was welcome. These were the forces that would forge his character, test his courage, and, finally, take his life. This was the world of the first century A.D.

The Author of the Book

Some Bible scholars have expressed doubt that Paul was the author of the letter to the Ephesians, citing differences in the vocabulary and thought used. Most scholars, however, believe that it was indeed Paul who penned the letter which has been called, "the Queen of the Epistles." Just who was this man who revealed so many of the mysteries of the Gospel so clearly and beautifully for the mature in the faith? From where had he come and how had he reached the level of maturity indicated in his writings?

Down through the centuries, either because of dispersion, captivity, or business pursuits, Jews had traveled from Israel to all parts of the known world, taking their religion with them. Some found their way to Cilicia in Asia Minor, now Turkey. The geography of Cilicia was perfectly suited to protect her inhabitants from invasion, bounded on the north and west by the Taurus Mountains, on the east by the Amanus Mountains, and on the south by the Mediterranean Sea. It was divided into two parts, roughly similar in size but very different in topography. The western half, dominated by mountains and called Rough or Rugged Cilicia, was the geographical setting of the city of Ephesus. The eastern half, known as Flat Cilicia or the Plain of Cilicia, was a flat plain which was perfect for settlement and agriculture. At the western edge of the Plain of Cilicia, at the point where the Cydnus River carried the cold waters of the melting mountain snows, was the city of Tarsus. It was the capital of the province, a logical choice because of its central location, and, as Paul said in Acts 21:39, it was *"no mean* (average) *city."*

When Alexander the Great conquered the area several centuries earlier, he found its inhabitants to be barbarians. His influence would soon change that; by the time of Paul, the city had a distinctly Hellenistic flavor and was world famous for its Greek university, theatre, art school, gymnasium, and stadium. Greek domination of Cilicia had given way to control by the Seleucids after their defeat of the followers of Lysimachus, the general of Alexander's army who had taken Asia Minor after his death and governed the territory from their capital, Antioch. Cilicia first came under Roman rule in about 100 B.C. and had both its civil and military affairs reorganized by Pompey in 66 B.C. Politically, under Pax Romanus, Cilicia maintained its Greek identity while the Cilicians took advantage of every benefit of Roman rule. The residents of Tarsus, for instance, could hold Roman citizenship because their city was the capital of the province and they could vote. This was the province into which Saul was born in about A.D. 10.

From birth, Saul had a three-fold heritage evident in his later life, ministry, and writings. First, he was born to a Jewish family of the tribe of Benjamin, to a father who was a Pharisee (Acts 23:6). Second, because his city was the provincial capital, he automatically received Roman citizenship with all its rights and privileges. He would find this useful later (Acts 16:36 through 39). Third, Tarsus was very much a Hellenized city, contributing to Saul's fluency in Greek and his familiarity with Greek thought, expression, and philosophy. As a Jew, he would have learned Hebrew from infancy; as a citizen of Tarsus, he would have learned Greek from his youth. Since all of the Old Testament quotes in his writings came from the Greek Septuagint even though his later education under Gamaliel was conducted from the Hebrew Scriptures, he must have learned the Greek version first, at an earlier age.

In his writings, Paul never mentioned his mother, who may have died when he was young, but he did write of his father who was a Pharisee. So, although the family lived in Tarsus under Roman rule and Greek influence, their homelife would have been distinctly

Jewish, a conclusion supported by the fact that Saul was circumcised at birth, a command Jews often neglected when living outside of Israel and assimilating into their new homelands. At that time, he was named Saul, which meant, "asked of God."[7] He may have been named after his father, a common Jewish practice, or after King Saul, the historic hero of his tribe. His other name, Paul, which meant, "little,"[8] may have been a family pet name or the nickname given to a boy who was unusually small in size. Indeed, he may have been called by both names from youth, using his Hebrew name, Saul, at home and his Greco-Roman name, Paul, to facilitate acceptance in the larger world. It is significant that he began to be known exclusively by his Gentile name at just about the time he began his ministry among the Gentiles. In Tarsus, by its very nature, Saul had learned to be *"all things to all men, that* [he] *might by all means save some"* (1 Corinthians 9:22).

The social position and economic circumstances of Saul's family is uncertain. Some believe the family was wealthy based on the fact that they were Roman citizens, but they lived in a provincial capital, entitling them to such citizenship. In addition, citizenship was often conferred for services rendered, rather than purchased. Others are just as certain that Saul's family was poor because he was trained in the rather menial trade of tentmaking, but the Hebrew Talmud commanded every father of a son to, "circumcise him, teach him the law, teach him a trade." Saul may have been taught tentmaking because the haircloth used to make tents came from the goats of the province or because his father was also involved in this occupation, either as a tentmaker, as a herdsman of the goats, or as a seller of tents.

Saul's received his earliest education from his parents at home, in accord with Deuteronomy 6:7. Since Saul was the son of a Pharisee, he would not have been sent to one of the Hellenistic schools to learn Greek religion and philosophy. Instead, after young Saul was weaned, he probably received his formal education in the local synagogue from the resident rabbi. This seems clear since he later gained admission to the foremost rabbinical school of his day, a privilege reserved for those who had not only attended synagogue schools, but had a record of high achievement there.

Once Saul came of age, at twelve years-old, he could attend synagogue services and hear the Law read by the rabbi. He may even have traveled with his father to the Temple in Jerusalem for the three highest and holiest feast days of the Jewish calendar--Passover, Pentecost, and the Feast of Tabernacles--as God had commanded in Deuteronomy 16:16. This trip would have been a crash course in geography, going partly by sea, across the blue waters of the Mediterranean to one of the coastal ports, and partly by land, over the rocky countryside and up the mountains which surrounded and cradled the city of Jerusalem. As he arrived, Saul would have had that first breathtaking view of the city, as he crested the hilltops which held it like a jewel, and looked down on the city, itself. There, Saul would have received another crash course, this one in politics, religion, and sociology. There, he would have seen Roman centurions quartered in the holy city and Romanesque buildings dwarfing nearby Hebrew structures. He would have observed the priestly class, most of them Sadducees, and the members of the Sanhedrin faring quite well under Roman rule, while the common people lived in abject poverty.

Still rejecting the Hellenistic education easily available at the Greek university in Tarsus, Saul's parents eyed the two famous rabbinical schools of the time, the rival schools of Hillel and Shammai. Both were Pharisaical in outlook, but Hillel believed that tradition was often superior to the Law, while Shammai hated any tradition that contradicted or added to the Law. It was said that even Elijah the Tishbite would never be able to reconcile the disciples of Hillel and Shammai. Of the two, the school of Hillel was the most influential and its most eminent teacher was Gamaliel, grandson of Hillel, himself, and son of Rabbi Simeon. Although steeped in the Law, he was known to be without the prejudices of many, a fact supported by his tolerance for Peter in Acts 5:34 through 39. Gamaliel was known by the title, "the glory of the Law," and was the first of only seven rabbis to receive the title of Rabban or Honored Master. It was to this Jerusalem school and to this renowned teacher that Saul was sent at about eighteen for his continuing Hebrew education, comparable to today's college or university training. To study at the feet of Gamaliel, was to assume the humble position before a superior as advised in an old Jewish maxim, "Place thyself in the dust at the feet of the wise." At school, Saul learned the intricacies of the Law, the mysteries of the prophets, and the music of the poets. He was schooled in Jewish history, in accord with Deuteronomy 6:20 through 25, and memorized much Scripture, in accord with Deuteronomy 6:4 through 9. He was also taught to use what he learned, along with his own logic, to argue the truth of Scripture, a skill that would prove useful later. During this period, Saul developed the enthusiasm for the Law and for Judaism, itself, which made him a zealot for both. It was this zeal that quenched his human compassion at the stoning of Stephen, that caused him to pitilessly persecute the followers of a Nazarene Carpenter, believing he did God a great service, and brought him face to face with that same Nazarene Carpenter on the dusty road to Damascus. Saul's youth was over. He had been well-educated and well-trained to take his place in society. In fact, the goal of the school of Hillel was to produce classic Pharisaical rabbis worthy of future positions of honor as members of the Sanhedrin. But, the path which seemed so clear on graduation day, would take twists and turns no one could have foreseen. God had a very different life ahead for him than the one he and his noted teacher had planned.

By the time Saul completed his rabbinical training at about twenty-six, Jesus had died, risen, and ascended. The disciples, obeying His final command, waited in Jerusalem until they were baptized in the Holy Spirit. From that day on, the Church grew, adding new members as soon as they were saved. But, Saul had spent eight years studying Jewish Law; he was anxious to help enforce it. Witnessing the stoning of Stephen for supposed violations of that Law had probably only flamed his passion. Saul began his savage persecution of those who believed as Stephen had, those who recognized a lowly Galilean Carpenter as the long-awaited Messiah. By the account of Luke (Acts 9:1 and 2), an intimate of both the persecutor and the persecuted, and his own account (Acts 22:4), Saul zealously disrupted the early Church in every way he could, invading Christian converts' homes and having them tried, beaten, forced to blaspheme the very Name they held most dear, and executed. Saul even went after women, traditionally exempt except for the most infamous crimes. Saul's persecution, designed to obliterate Christianity, instead caused converts in Jerusalem, who feared for their lives, to disperse all over the known world. Wherever they went, they took their Saviour, their faith, and their Gospel with them, just as Jesus had predicted in Acts 1:8, *"And ye shall be witnesses unto me both in Jerusalem, and in all Judea, and in Samaria, and unto the uttermost part of the earth."* This must have filled Saul with absolute fury. No longer satisfied to confine his activities to Jerusalem, Saul determined to track down the perpetrators of this "heresy" and stamp them out forever (Acts 9:1). Having proceeded thus far with no recorded authority, Saul asked the Sanhedrin to give him letters of introduction to the synagogues in Damascus, where newly arriving Jewish Christians would logically go to discuss and propagate their beliefs, letters giving him permission to seek out, arrest, and return to Jerusalem for trial any he could find. Saul must have received the letters he sought for he set out for Damascus immediately.

Ironically, Jesus allowed Saul to come to the outskirts of Damascus (Acts 9:3), before He brought the tired traveler to his knees. Just when he could nearly taste victory, Saul suffered utter defeat. Suddenly, from Heaven, there came a light so bright, Saul later described it as eclipsing the midday Middle Eastern sun (Acts 26:13). Saul and those with him fell to the ground in terror, but it was Saul alone who heard a voice he had never heard before, a voice that called his name, a voice that spoke words only he could understand. In Hebrew, the voice said, *"Saul, Saul, why persecutest thou me?"* (Acts 9:4). Immediately, Saul knew he was in the presence of One who was superior and he knew that he had done something this Superior took very personally. In Acts 9:5, he asked, *"Who art thou, Lord?"* The answer came, *"I am Jesus whom thou persecutest."* Then, in a voice touched with compassion, this Jesus observed, *"It is hard for thee to kick against the pricks,"* a reference to the sharply pointed sticks used to keep oxen from rebelling against their masters. His rage gone, Saul surrendered to One who possessed greater power than he, greater power than the letters he carried. There was no long prayer, no carefully composed words; there was just a simple, *"Lord, what wilt thou have me to do?"* In that instant of recognition and surrender, Saul became a born-again Christian! By comparing Acts 9:6 with Acts 26:16 through 18, the Lord's complete instructions to Saul become clear:

> *Arise, and go into the city, and it shall be told thee what thou must do....for I have purposed, to make thee a minister and a witness both of these things which thou hast seen, and of those things in the which I will appear unto thee; delivering thee from the people, and from the Gentiles, to whom I now send thee. To open their eyes, and to turn them from darkness to light, and from the power of Satan unto God, that they may receive forgiveness of sins, and inheritance among them which are sanctified by faith that is in me.*

Saul's companions scrambled to their feet. Saul rose, too, but, when he opened his eyes, he was totally blind. The zealous defender of the Law who planned to terrorize every Christian in town, suffered the humiliation of being led by the hand into the city.

In Damascus, was a Christian called Ananias. He may have fled Jerusalem in fear of Saul or been a citizen of Damascus who had heard the reports of others. He knew Saul's reputation (Acts 9:13 and 14) and, as a believer, he had every reason to avoid him. But, God gave Ananias Saul's name and address, assured him he had nothing to fear, and sent him to minister to Saul's needs. The Lord also told him of His call on Saul's life, as Acts 9:15 records, *"...for he is a chosen vessel unto me, to bear my name before the Gentiles, and kings, and the children of Israel."* In one of the greatest acts of courage ever, Ananias obeyed the Lord, went to Saul, and greeted him with these words, *"Brother Saul."* Then, in Acts 9:17, he said, *"...the Lord, even Jesus, that appeared unto thee...hath sent me, that thou mightest receive thy sight, and be filled with the Holy Ghost."* In an instant, it happened!

Immediately after his conversion, healing, and baptism, Saul began witnessing right there in Damascus. In the very city where he had sought to bring death and destruction, he brought the life and love of Jesus Christ instead. He spent time with Damascus Christians, many of whom had probably come there to avoid the one they now aided and taught. There was much to learn, much to add to the education received from Gamaliel, much to master about his new Messiah. After a brief trip to Arabia (Galatians 1:7), Saul returned to Damascus once again and so enraged the Jews of the city, they plotted to kill him. They laid in wait near the city gates, waiting to ambush him, but the plot was known to Saul and other Damascus disciples who let him down over the wall in a big basket.

Three years had elapsed since Saul had been saved. It was time to go back to Jerusalem, back to the city where he had been educated, back to his beginnings so he could begin again. Imagine his memories as he traveled from Damascus to Jerusalem, probably along the same road he had traveled three years before. He must have passed by the site of his conversion and, as he approached the holy city, the site of Stephen's martyrdom. In Jerusalem, Saul found Peter (Galatians 1:18). While both had been in Jerusalem at the same time on previous occasions, there is no evidence that they had ever met. It's possible that the reputation of the big fisherman who had actually walked with Jesus and who now steadied the young Church in Jerusalem, had reached all the way to Damascus. Imagine their conversations during the fifteen days they spent together.

But, other disciples were not so open, so welcoming of Saul as Peter had been. Acts 9:26 records their reaction, *"And when Saul was come to Jerusalem, he assayed to join himself to the disciples: but they were all afraid of him, and believed not that he was a disciple."* All that the believers of Jerusalem knew of him was the reputation he had made for himself before he left for Damascus. They knew of his complicity in the death of Stephen, his persecution of the Church, and his request for permission to take his inquisition all the way to Damascus. As a result, Saul received only the coldest and most suspicious of receptions. It was Barnabas who finally got the Christians in Jerusalem to accept Saul. In the same generosity which had prompted him to sell his land and donate the proceeds to the young Church (Acts 4:36 and 37), Barnabas welcomed Saul as his new brother in the Lord, introduced him to other disciples, and testified to his conversion. This may indicate that Barnabas knew Saul prior to his trip to Jerusalem or heard him preach in Damascus. Saul was finally accepted to live and work among the disciples of Jerusalem. Acts 9:29 and 30 tells us that Saul preached boldly, with that same zeal he had once misused. He also entered into a debate with the Greek converts to Judaism. Not surprisingly, it wasn't long until Saul aroused so much attention that his murder was imminent. So, the disciples took him to Caesarea, a port city on the Mediterranean coast, and put him on a boat which would take him home to Tarsus. Saul wouldn't return to Jerusalem for fourteen long years.

In A.D. 46, Saul traveled to Antioch of Syria, where followers of Christ were first called Christians. Soon, Barnabas, arrived. About a year later, in response to God's call, the prophets and teachers at the Antioch church consecrated them to be His missionaries, to take the Gospel of Jesus Christ to the whole world, and sent them forth on their first missionary journey. In company with Barnabas, Silas, and others, Saul, soon to be known exclusively as Paul, would embark on at least three missionary trips which would take him all over the known world. Along the way, he would endure many persecutions and afflictions, as he detailed in 2 Corinthians 11:24 through 27:

> *Of the Jews five times received I forty stripes save one. Thrice was I beaten with rods, once was I stoned, thrice I suffered shipwreck, a night and a day I have been in the deep; In journeyings often, in perils of waters, in perils of robbers, in perils by mine own countrymen, in perils by the heathen, in perils in the city, in perils in the wilderness, in perils in the sea, in perils among false brethren; In weariness and painfulness, in watchings often, in hunger and thirst, in fastings often, in cold and nakedness.*

Finally, Paul was beheaded by the emperor, Nero, in approximately A.D. 67 along the Ostian Way in Rome. But, before that day arrived, there would be many days of trips and travels, of preaching and teaching and reaching the world with the Gospel of Christ. One of the cities Saul would visit along the way was known as Ephesus.

The Recipients of the Letter

At the time of Paul's visits to Ephesus, it was the most important city in the Roman province of Asia Minor. Due to its location at the mouth of the Cayster River where the western edge of Asia Minor touches the Aegean Sea, Ephesus stood as a natural bridgehead between East and West, a primary port, and the end of one of the main caravan routes through Asia. Ephesus was a beautiful city with wide streets paved with white marble, public baths, well-stocked libraries, a thriving market place, and a theatre which seated more than twenty-five thousand people. But, the citizens of Ephesus worshipped an old Anatolian fertility goddess called Artemis by the Greeks and Diana by the Romans. They even believed that their original statue of Diana, a grotesque monstrosity with a turreted head and many breasts, fell to them from the heavens. In her honor, the Ephesians had built a temple four times the size of the Parthenon at Athens and one of the seven wonders of the ancient world. Her cult drew pilgrims from all over the world, keeping local artisans busy making silver shrines, images, and talismans for the tourists to take home. But, God would not be mocked forever. The Ephesus Paul knew was a dying city. Its harbor was beginning to fill with the silt which washed down the Cayster River. In A.D. 65, a futile attempt was made to clear the silt away and improve the channel. In a few short years, its candlestick would be extinguished forever, just as Jesus predicted in Revelation 2:5. Today, nothing exists of Ephesus, the center of the cult of Diana, except its ruins.

It was on his second missionary journey that Paul, in company with Aquila and Priscilla, made his first brief stop in Ephesus. While he was there, he taught in the synagogue and received a fairer hearing than usual. Though invited to remain longer, he had to leave for a feast in Jerusalem. Just before he returned on his third missionary journey, which began in A.D. 53, Aquila and Priscilla, whom he left in Ephesus near the end of his previous trip, encountered another traveler, Apollos. He was an Alexandrian Jew who knew Scripture well and visited synagogues preaching all that he knew of salvation, those principles of repentance and water baptism he had learned from John the Baptist years earlier. When Aquila and Priscilla heard him preach, they befriended him and taught him all they had learned from Paul. Soon, he was proclaiming Jesus, the Messiah, and, in a short while, left for Corinth to share his new-found faith. When Paul arrived, he found a small group of believers in the city, possibly converts of Apollos, since they, too, had only the limited information John the Baptist had taught. Paul shared with them the truth of the Baptism in the Holy Spirit, laid hands on them, and saw them filled and speaking in tongues as the initial evidence of their experience. People were maturing in their faith.

As was his custom, Paul went to the local synagogue to share Jesus with the Jews. At first, he was allowed to teach, but, after about three months, a division arose when many who refused to believe Paul's message began speaking out publicly against his Gospel. There was no point in continuing. Paul left the synagogue and began teaching his disciples in the school of Tyrannus who, as a convert to Christianity through Paul's ministry, opened his facility for the apostle's use. Paul remained there for two years and his work was so successful that this is the report Luke recorded in Acts 19:10 through 12:

> *So that all they which dwelt in Asia heard the word of the Lord Jesus, both Jews and Greeks. And God wrought special miracles by the hands of Paul: So that from his body were brought unto the sick handkerchiefs or aprons, and the diseases departed from them, and the evil spirits went out of them.*

Paul and the Gospel he preached gained such a reputation in Ephesus that some attempted to capitalize on it. Among them were the seven sons of Sceva, the local chief priest. The boys made their living trying to cast out demons using the charge recorded in Acts 19:13, *"We adjure you by Jesus whom Paul preacheth,"* as though these were magic words. One day, they encountered a demon-possessed man. When they tried to cast out the demon using their "magic words," the demon shot back, *"Jesus I know, and Paul I know; but who are ye?"* They had learned too late that it wasn't the words which worked, but the personal relationship and personal authority flowing from it that brought results. The next thing they knew, all seven of them were stripped and beaten by one demonized man. The news spread like wildfire in Ephesus, causing the fear of the Lord to come on all who heard it. Soon, the Ephesians were accepting Jesus as Saviour, forsaking the occult and worship of Diana, and destroying all of their occult books and materials. Luke reported Paul's revival in Ephesus, in Acts 19:20, *"So mightily grew the word of God and prevailed."*

Of course, whenever the Lord is moving, the adversary will fight. Demetrius, a silversmith who earned his living making replicas of Diana for local worshippers and tourists, was suddenly out of business and he wasn't happy about it. The hostility he stirred up against the Christians threatened to overwhelm them all. Two Macedonian converts who accompanied Paul were taken by the crowd to that huge theatre for which Ephesus was famous for a town meeting. Paul wanted to go to there to speak in behalf of his fellow believers, but his friends wisely stopped him. In the theatre, the town clerk got the mob's attention and began to speak. He accepted their belief in Diana and her supposed heavenly origins, but he also reminded them of the Pax Romanus, which they were seriously violating, and counseled them to proceed according to the law if they wanted to avoid the wrath of Rome. Having calmed the group, he adjourned the meeting and sent everyone home safely.

Paul had remained in Ephesus for three years, but it was time to move on. He gathered his disciples, hugged them, and wished them farewell. Then, he was gone.

Paul had a brief meeting with the church elders of Ephesus at Miletus as he traveled to Jerusalem for the last time. After being acquitted at his first trial in Rome in about A.D. 64, Paul spent two years in Spain, then decided to make a circuit of all of the churches in Asia Minor. Paul found that various heresies had crept into the churches there. Greek philosophy, Oriental theosophy, the Jewish superstition, Kabbala, and Persian magic had all gained popularity. Paul must have never felt so disheartened or so needed.

His headquarters during this period seems to have been none other than Ephesus. Soon, however, he left Ephesus for the last time, headed for Rome with a stop at Corinth. Paul probably spent the winter of A.D. 66-67 in Nicopolis, in Greece, was arrested there by Roman magistrates who had had quite enough of this new sect, and was sent to Rome for trial. When he arrived, few friends remained close to him and he was not permitted to live under the conditions of house arrest he had previously enjoyed. Instead, he was confined as a common criminal to the dreaded Mamertine Prison, a cold, damp, dark place of incarceration which was totally underground, except for the ground level entrance and officers' quarters. In about A.D. 67, Paul was finally tried, found guilty, and sentenced to death. Because he had that precious Roman citizenship, he was spared crucifixion or any of the other forms of slow torture Nero reserved for Christians and slaves. John Foxe, in his famous book, Foxe's Book of Martyrs, described Paul's death:[9]

> Paul, the apostle, who before was called Saul, after his great travail and unspeakable labors in promoting the Gospel of Christ, suffered also in this first persecution under Nero. Abdias, declareth Parthemius, to bring him

word of his death. They, coming to Paul instructing the people, desired him to pray for them, that they might believe; who told them that shortly after they should believe and be baptised at His sepulcher. This done, the soldiers came and led him out of the city to the place of execution, where he, after his prayers made, gave his neck to the sword.

The Christians at the young church of Ephesus would never see their beloved Paul again, but they would always treasure the precious letter he had once written.

The Letter

In approximately A.D. 64, Paul wrote the letter which would come to be known as the Book of Ephesians. Many maintain that this letter was meant to have a wider readership and may have been intended to be circulated to some or all of the churches in Asia Minor. In fact, there are those who maintain that it was not sent to the Ephesians at all, but to the Laodiceans (Colossians 4:16), who gave a copy of it to the Ephesians after Paul's death. However the Ephesian Christians obtained the letter, it was still in their possession in the middle of the second century when Marcion made the first compilation of Paul's epistles.

In any event, the letter, though very similar to the one sent to the Colossians, goes much further. In chapters one through three, it presents the mature believer's position in Christ. Then, in chapters four through six, Paul detailed the mature believer's proper conduct in the world, as based on that position in Christ. In these chapters, Paul related the mature saint's conduct of Christian ministry, Christian marriage, Christian family, Christian work relationships, and Christian spiritual warfare. The guiding principle of such Christian conduct is expressed in Ephesians 5:20 and 21, "*Submitting yourselves one to another in the fear of God.*" The epistle of Ephesians stands as the handbook of victorious Christian living in relation to Christ and to all others. It is the handbook of every mature child of God. It is the handbook which provides the final lessons for those who would come to maturity in Christ.

[1]Flavius Josephus, *The Complete Works of Josephus*, Antiquities of the Jews, Book II, Chapter 8, Verse 4.

[2]Pat Alexander, *The Lion Encyclopedia of the Bible*, p. 133.

[3]William Smith, *Smith's Dictionary of the Bible*, Volume 3, p. 2471.

[4]Merrill C. Tenney, *The Zondervan Pictorial Bible Dictionary*, p. 740.

[5]Ibid., p. 261.

[6]Smith, Volume 4, p. 2838.

[7]George Barr, *Who's Who in the Bible*, p. 143.

[8]Tenney, p. 627.

[9]John Foxe, *Foxe's Book of Martyrs*, p. 4.

Chapter 1
THE POSITION OF THE BELIEVER

The Address

Paul, an apostle of Jesus Christ by the will of God, to the saints which are at Ephesus, and to the faithful in Christ Jesus.

While some argue the authorship of the letter known as Ephesians, such criticisms are not convincing since even the earliest versions of the epistle have carried Paul's name in the address. In it, as in the addresses of most of his other epistles, Paul identified himself as an apostle, from the Greek, *apostolos*, designating one sent forth as a messenger or ambassador. This refers back to that landmark day on the way to Damascus when Paul was called by Jesus, Himself, and sent to take the Gospel to the Gentiles (Acts 26:16 through 18). While it is a lofty and exalted rank, it also recognizes the supremacy of One who is loftier and even more exalted. Since an apostle is, by definition, one who is sent in the delegated power and authority of another, the title affirmed that all Paul accomplished was done by the power and authority of the Christ he served. Paul's early education is evident in this title. He had been trained to recognize and accept the supremacy of those in authority over him, first, the rabbi in his synagogue school, then, his teacher, Gamaliel, and, finally, the Sanhedrin who authorized his mission to Damascus. As a Christian, he simply recognized the supremacy of the Lord who had saved, called, and commissioned him.

Some also dispute the accepted belief that this letter was sent to Ephesus, saying it was originally sent to the church at Laodicea and is the writing mentioned in Colossians 4:16. They hold that the letter circulated among all the churches of Asia Minor and the epistle held so dear by the Ephesians was only a copy of the Laodicean letter to which they had added their name. For our purposes, it isn't necessary to resolve this dispute. There is, however, no dispute that the letter was addressed *"to the saints"* and *"to the faithful,"* the terms of interest to the maturing child of God. Saints, is the Greek, *hagios*, which identifies those who are sanctified, set apart from the world and sin, set apart to God and for His use. Faithful, is the Greek, *pistos*, which refers to believers who are firmly persuaded and confident in their Lord and who are faithful, trustworthy, and worthy of the confidence of others. Clearly, this describes the mature child of God who is secure in his sanctification and stable in his commitment to Christ, who has ended his wilderness wandering, entered into and claimed the promises of God, and is ready to go on to perfection, total maturity, in his Lord. This is the believer to whom the letter known as Ephesians is addressed.

The Believer's Position in Christ

This mature child of God need not wander in the wilderness of spiritual uncertainty, nor must he be unsure of the promises of God which are his inheritance and his possession in Christ. He can comprehend the depth and breadth of all of the spiritual mysteries of his position in Jesus. Here are some of those mysteries as explained in Ephesians:

1. **Grace.** First, the mature believer must understand that his position in Christ, indeed, everything he receives from Christ, is rooted solely in the grace of God (Ephesians 1:2). Grace is the free and unmerited love and favor of God. There is nothing one can do to deserve it or earn it; one can't even purchase it. It is for these reasons that God just gives

of His grace freely. It is grace, not faith or works, by which the believer is saved, as Paul explained in Romans 3:23 and 24, *"For all have sinned, and come short of the glory of God; Being justified freely by his grace through the redemption that is in Christ Jesus."* Then, in Romans 11:5 and 6, Paul continued his discourse on grace:

> *Even so then at this present time also there is a remnant according to the election of grace. And if by grace, then is it no more of works: otherwise grace is no more grace. But if it be of works, then is it no more grace.*

It is grace, the unmerited and undeserved favor of God, which offers salvation to fallen man when he is unable to do anything for himself. Faith can only reach out to accept that offer and works can do nothing whatever to facilitate the transaction. All that man has or ever hopes to have is his because of the divine grace of God.

2. **Peace.** Man is born in sin, and, since a perpetual state of war exists between God and sin, a perpetual state of war also exists between man and his Maker, as James 4:4 declares, *"Know ye not that the friendship of the world is enmity with God? whosoever therefore will be a friend of the world is the enemy of God."* But, through the saving grace of God and the Blood of Christ, man's sin is purged and he is at peace with God (Ephesians 1:2). The state of war is ended, the peace treaty is signed, and man is no longer the enemy of his God, as Paul explained in Romans 5:1, *"Therefore being justified by faith, we have peace with God through our Lord Jesus Christ."* Not only is the believer at peace with God, he is also given the peace of God which transcends the tribulation of this world, as Paul revealed in Philippians 4:7, *"And the peace of God, which passeth all understanding, shall keep your hearts and minds through Christ Jesus."* It is no wonder, then, that, above all else, Paul desired that the grace and peace of God be the possessions of the mature believers to whom he wrote for it is grace and peace that bring salvation and tranquility in the face of tribulation.

3. **Blessed.** It is generally assumed that the word, blessed, in Scripture invariably means, happy. Indeed, this is the meaning of blessed in the Beatitudes of Christ, for example. But, such is not always the case. The blessing with which the mature believer is blessed in Ephesians 1:3, is the Greek, *eulogia*, which literally means to speak well of or to praise. It can even carry the idea of bragging about. It was in this sense that God blessed or spoke well of Job to Satan in Job 1:8, *"Hast thou considered my servant Job, that there is none like him in the earth, a perfect and an upright man?"* Imagine it! The mature or perfect child of God may be spoken well of, praised, even bragged about by the Lord God of this universe. More, God will even brag about His own in the face of Satan. The *"heavenly places"* of Ephesians 1:3, are designated by the Greek, *epouranios*, the same Greek word translated, *"high places,"* in Ephesians 6:12 and referring to the abode of Satan's demonic powers. There can be no doubt that, like any proud Father, God will brag about His mature children and He will do it in Satan's own backyard.

4. **Chosen.** According to Ephesians 1:4, God chose each of His children before the foundations of the world were laid. Chosen, is the Greek, *eklego*, which identifies what one chooses for oneself or lays aside for one's own use. The mature child of God did not choose Christ. Rather, Christ chose him, just as He said in John 15:16, *"Ye have not chosen me, but I have chosen you."* When God chose or set aside the mature believer for Himself and His own use, He ordained that the believer be holy, sanctified, set apart for Him. The fact that this choice was made before the world was even created, leads to the next aspect of the believer's position in Christ--predestination.

5. **Predestinated.** Predestination is often misunderstood. God does not build plastic robots whose every thought and move are completely programmed before they are born. Predestination, is the Greek, *proorizo*, which designates that which is marked beforehand. A more complete explanation of predestination is given in Romans 8:29 and 30:

> *For whom he did foreknow, he also did predestinate to be conformed to the image of his Son, that he might be the firstborn among many brethren. Moreover whom he did predestinate, them he also called: and whom he called, them he also justified: and whom he justified, them he also glorified.*

The predestination of God is clearly based on His foreknowledge. Through His foreknowledge, God knew before He created the world who would accept His Son as Saviour and who wouldn't. Based upon His foreknowledge of the decision each will make, God marked those He knows will be saved. Then, each one who is born-again is continually changed into Christ's image, His likeness, His mirror reflection, an exact duplicate of Him (Romans 8:29). God has also foreordained that all who accept Jesus will receive certain predetermined benefits. First, he'll be called (Romans 8:30), invited into the service of the King. Next, he'll be justified, the legal verdict of acquittal in the court of Heaven, just as though he had never committed a single sin. Finally, he'll be glorified or recognized, honored, praised, made glorious. So, it is not man's decision about Christ which is predestined by God; only the consequences of that decision are foreordained (Ephesians 1:5). Although God, in His foreknowledge, already knows what man's decision will be, He permits man the freewill to make it.

6. **Adopted.** Another of the benefits God foreordained for the believer is adoption into His family. To understand it, one must understand the Roman adoption laws upon which Paul's use of the term was predicated. There is no better explanation than that given by William Barclay in his book, *The Letters to the Galatians and Ephesians*:[1]

> In the Roman world the family was based on what was called the patria potestas, the father's power. Under Roman law a father had absolute power over his children so long as he and they lived. A Roman father could sell his child as a slave, and could even kill the child. According to ancient Roman law, and that law still operated in Paul's time, a father had the right of life and death over his children. Dion Cassius tells us that the Roman law was that 'the law of the Romans gives a father absolute authority over his son, and that for the son's whole life. It gives him authority, if he so chooses, to imprison him, to scourge him, to make him work on his estate as a slave in fetters, even to kill him. That right still continues to exist even if the son is old enough to play an active part in political affairs, even if he has been judged worthy to occupy the magistrate's office, and even if he is held in honour by all men....' Under Roman law a child could not possess anything; and any inheritance willed to him, or any gift given to him, became the property of his father. It did not matter how old the son was, or to what honours and responsibility he had risen, he was absolutely in his father's power. In circumstances like that it is obvious that adoption was a very serious step. It was a serious step to take a child out of one patria potestas and to put him into another. It was, however, not uncommon, for children were often adopted to ensure that some family should not become extinct, but should continue to exist. The ritual of adoption must have been very impressive. It was carried out by a symbolic sale in which copper and scales

were used. Twice the real father sold his son, and twice he symbolically bought him back; finally he sold him a third time, and at the third sale he did not buy him back. After this the adopting father had to go to the praetor, one of the principle Roman magistrates, and plead the case for the adoption, and only after all this had been gone through was the adoption complete. But when the adoption was complete it was complete indeed. The person who had been adopted had all the rights of a legitimate son in his new family, and completely lost all rights in his old family. In the eyes of the law he was a new person. So new was he that even all debts and obligations connected with his previous family were cancelled out and abolished as if they had never existed.

Indeed, the change of state in adoption was so permanent and so all-encompassing that it created many an interesting case in Roman history. Here is just one: Because the emperor, Claudius, had no son, he adopted a youth called Lucius Domitius Ahenobarbus, the son of a vicious criminal, to be his heir. From the moment of adoption, he was, in the eyes of the law, the natural son of Claudius and the heir to his throne. Then, he sought to marry Octavia, the natural daughter of Claudius, to further insure his right to rule. Even though the two were not related by blood, they were brother and sister by adoption and were, thus, prevented by Roman law from marrying each other. A special exception had to be obtained from the Roman Senate for the nuptials to go forward. This adopted son took the name, Nero Claudius Caesar Germanicus, and is better known to history as Nero. Paul explained more about the adoption of the believer in Romans 8:14 through 17:

> *For as many as are led by the Spirit of God, they are the sons of God. For ye have not received the spirit of bondage again to fear; but ye have received the Spirit of adoption, whereby we cry, Abba, Father. The Spirit itself beareth witness with our spirit, that we are the children of God: And if children, then heirs; heirs of God, and joint-heirs with Christ.*

Using the analogy of the Roman adoption laws, Paul, in the single word, adoption, drew this detailed word picture of the child of God. The believer was once under the power, the patria potestas, of his father, Satan (John 8:44). At the moment of salvation, he is adopted into the family of God (Ephesians 1:5) and the power of his former father, Satan, is broken so that he no longer holds the patria potestas over the believer (Romans 6:18). The believer may take nothing from the old family of sin. By his adoption, ties to the old life, to the old lifestyle, etc., are broken forever (Romans 6:11). Even the old debts of sin are wiped out as though they had never existed (Romans 8:1). The believer now shares equally in all of the benefits and inheritance rights of Heaven--the Holy Spirit, eternal life, eternal riches, etc. Because God is his adoptive Father, the believer is a joint-heir with Christ and shares all things equally with Christ (Galatians 4:5 through 7). The believer has no brothers or sisters in the old family of sin; those relationships are broken (1 Corinthians 6:14 through 20). His brothers and sisters are now in his new family of faith. They minister to each other's needs and bear one another's burdens (Galatians 6:2). Though they may have disagreements, as any family might, they are to maintain their family unity, reconcile their differences, and love each other and their Father (1 John 4:7 and 8). The believer is now under the patria potestas, the complete power of his Father as long as He lives--forever. He will never outgrow his dependence on or his responsibility to his Heavenly Father (1 Corinthians 11:3). The believer's needs are now the responsibility of his adoptive Father who will faithfully meet them all (Philippians 4:19).

7. **Accepted.** As a further benefit of the grace of God, the believer is accepted into the beloved (Ephesians 1:6). There is an interesting play on words in the original Greek version of this verse. Grace, is the Greek, *charitos*, unconditional, unmerited favor, while the word, accepted, is the Greek, *charito*, made acceptable by grace. So, by *charitos*, the believer is made *charito*. This acceptance places the believer in the beloved, the Greek singular, *agapao*, indicating the One who is loved with the agape love of God. So, the believer is not simply accepted into the beloved, plural, the company of the saints; he is accepted into the beloved, singular, the One God loves with agape love; he is accepted into Christ, Himself. Paul expressed a very similar thought in Colossians 3:3, *"For ye are dead, and your life is hid with Christ in God."*

8. **Redeemed.** Redemption was an important principle of the Mosaic Law with which the young rabbinical student, Saul, would have been very familiar. The term, in both Hebrew and Greek, means to ransom or buy back. The legalities of redemption are recorded in Leviticus 25:47 through 49:

> *And if a sojourner or stranger wax rich by thee, and thy brother that dwelleth by him wax poor, and sell himself unto the stranger or sojourner by thee, or to the stock of the stranger's family: After that he is sold he may be redeemed again; one of his brethren may redeem him; Either his uncle, or his uncle's son, may redeem him, or any that is nigh of kin unto him of his family may redeem him; or if he be able, he may redeem himself.*

Often, in Old Testament times, poor people found it necessary to sell a possession, a house, a field, even a child. But, God had given the land and everything in it to specific tribes and families and He wanted it to remain the property of those tribes and families. So, when such a sale was necessary, God granted the right of redemption, the right to buy back, to the nearest relative who had the money or goods to make the purchase.

Adam sold the human family into sin to a stranger and trespasser called Satan. The right to return to God's family could only be bought back or redeemed by another Member of our human family whose life was perfect, untouched and unenslaved by sin--a Redeemer. There was only One who ever had the necessary qualifications to make the transaction--Jesus Christ. He came to earth in human form, for there was no other way He could become man's Kinsman in the human family. He lived a perfect, sinless life, free of man's bondage, so that He could buy man back out of that bondage. Then, Jesus freely offered the purchase price, His own life, His own blood, to redeem man, to buy him back into God's family, to make man free. Jesus not only paid the price of man's redemption, He actually became the price of man's redemption; He not only paid the ransom; He actually became the ransom, as 1 Timothy 2:5 and 6 makes clear, *"For there is one god, and one mediator between God and man, the man Christ Jesus; Who gave himself a ransom for all."* The transaction of redemption is accomplished in the believer's life at the moment of salvation when he is bought back into God's family through Christ's blood (Romans 3:25).

9. **Knowledgeable.** The mature believer need not be ignorant of the plans and purposes of God; he can have knowledge of spiritual things. In fact, the same Lord who takes such great pleasure in bestowing all of His benefits on His own, will also abound toward them in knowledge (Ephesians 1:8). Abound, the Greek, *perisseuo*, means to have over and above what is needed, to have more than enough. This is the abundance Jesus promised in John 10:10, *"The thief cometh not, but for to steal, and to kill, and to destroy: I am come that they might have life, and that they might have it more abundantly."* The particular abundance spoken of by Paul here is the abundance of wisdom and prudence. Wisdom, is

the Greek, *sophia*, the right use of knowledge, while prudence, is the Greek, *phronesis*, good sense and practical wisdom. The mature believer, then, can use his spiritual "common sense" to rightly apply his spiritual knowledge to his life and the decisions he makes.

This spiritual knowledge will include an understanding of some of the marvelous mysteries of God (Ephesians 1:9 and 10). Mystery, is the Greek, *musterion*, and indicates things which are known to those who have been initiated. This is knowledge which is beyond natural perception, can only be given by divine revelation, and is made known by God only to those who are illuminated by the Spirit of God. These are the initiated, the born-again, the Spirit-baptized, the mature children of God. The spiritual mysteries God will reveal to the mature and initiated include an understanding of His will, His purposes, and His plans for ordering events of this universe (Ephesians 1:9 and 10). While he may not always understand each individual event, as a mature saint initiated into the Body of Christ, he will be given revelation about the general design of God as He orchestrates the occurrences of this world. Many of these revelations are recorded in God's Word. Through continuous and systematic Bible study, the Lord will reveal His mysteries to His initiated child. Revelation in these mysteries is also one of the ministries of the Holy Spirit to the Spirit-baptized believer, as Jesus promised in John 14:26 and John 16:13:

> *But the Comforter, which is the Holy Ghost, whom the father will send in my name, he shall teach you all things, and bring all things to your remembrance, whatsoever I have said unto you....Howbeit when he, the Spirit of truth, is come, he will guide you into all truth: for he shall not speak of himself, but whatsoever he shall hear, that shall he speak: and he will shew you things to come.*

This revelation knowledge of the mysteries of God, whether accomplished by the Word or through the ministry of the Holy Spirit, enables the mature believer to begin to see the overall plan of God at work in the world. First, the believer learns that it is the ultimate will of God to save as many as will come to Him, as revealed in 2 Peter 3:9:

> *The Lord is not slack concerning his promises...but is longsuffering to us-ward, not willing that any should perish, but that all should come to repentance.*

Then, the glorious purposes of God become clear to the child of God, such as 1 John 3:8 reveals, *"For this purpose the Son of God was manifested, that he might destroy the works of the devil."* That destruction is accomplished by the grace of God through the salvation His Son came to bring. The purpose of God, as revealed through the mystery of the sacrifice of Christ, is recorded in 2 Timothy 1:9 and 10:

> *Who hath saved us, and called us with an holy calling, not according to our works, but according to his own purpose and grace, which was given us in Christ Jesus before the world began. But is now made manifest by the appearing of our Saviour Jesus Christ, who hath abolished death, and hath brought life and immortality to light through the gospel.*

It is through an understanding of these mysteries that the believer begins to receive revelation in the mystery of the nature of God, Himself. Far from being the terrifying Tyrant pictured by many, He takes great delight in giving salvation to all who will accept it, as seen in Psalm 149:4, *"For the LORD taketh pleasure in his people: he will beautify the meek with salvation."* It is also God's joy to grant to all who belong to Him dominion and authority in this world and in the world to come, as Luke 12:32 assures, *"Fear not, little flock; for it is your Father's good pleasure to give you the kingdom."*

But, there is another side to the mysteries of God, as shown by the word, dispensation, in Ephesians 1:10, the Greek, *oikonomia*, the management or administration of property or a household. This word does not refer to a period of time or an epoch of history, as often wrongly interpreted; rather, it refers to the laws or rules by which a household is administered. There are, of course, laws of God which are in operation in this world, laws which direct the attention of humanity back to God, the Author of those laws. For example, there is the divine law of sowing and reaping evident in the lives of all who inhabit this planet and detailed in Galatians 6:7 and 8:

> *Be not deceived; God is not mocked: for whatsoever a man soweth, that shall he also reap. For he that soweth to the flesh shall of the flesh reap corruption; but he that soweth to the Spirit shall of the Spirit reap life everlasting.*

There is, for all mankind, the divine law of life and death which confronts man with his own mortality so that he may choose where he will spend eternity. That law was given just after the first man sinned and lost his right to eat of the tree of life in Genesis 3:19, *"In the sweat of thy face shalt thou eat bread, till thou return unto the ground; for out of it wast thou taken: for dust thou art, and unto dust thou shalt return."*

In his knowledge of all of these mysteries and in God's revelation to him of their import, the mature believer comes to comprehend that it is His ultimate plan to bring *"whosoever will"* to salvation and to bring the entire universe back under His authority and into harmony and unity with Him at the end of time.

10. **Inheriting.** The mature believer is bequeathed certain inheritance rights in God's kingdom. It's God's will and purpose that he inherit and possess all things which He has set aside for him. In Acts 20:32, Paul said God would, *"Give you an inheritance among all them which are sanctified."* Scripture reveals some specific provisions of that inheritance. For example, what was only seen in type and allegory in Joshua is openly stated in Hebrews 6:12, *"That ye be not slothful, but followers of them who through faith and patience inherit the promises."* The believer is also entitled to inherit a blessing from the Lord, according to 1 Peter 3:9, *"That ye should inherit a blessing."* Then, there is the mature believer's heavenly inheritance, beginning with eternal life, as promised by Jesus in Matthew 19:29:

> *And every one that hath forsaken houses, or brethren, or sisters, or father, or mother, or wife, or children, or lands, for my name's sake, shall receive an hundredfold, and shall inherit eternal life.*

The mature believer will also inherit the kingdom of God, as Matthew 25:34 confirms, *"Then shall the King say unto them on his right hand, Come, ye blessed of my Father, inherit the kingdom prepared for you from the foundation of the world."* Finally, the mature child of God will, according to Revelation 21:7, inherit everything that his heavenly Father has prepared for him, *"He that overcometh shall inherit all things; and I will be his God, and he shall be my son."*

Of course, all of this inheritance is made possible to the believer because of the death of Christ Jesus, as explained in Hebrews 9:16 and 17:

> *For where a testament is, there must also of necessity be the death of the testator. For a testament is of force after men are dead: otherwise it is of no strength at all while the testator liveth.*

But, while these inheritance rights are eternally secure, Paul's declaration regarding inheritance in Ephesians 1:11 and 12 carries an even greater concept. Inheritance, here, is the Greek, *kleroo*, which indicates obtaining an inheritance. Here, however, it is not in the active voice, which would denote the receiving of an inheritance, but in the passive voice, which indicates being made an inheritance. By use of this passive voice, Paul meant to convey the concept that mature believers were predestined by God to be an inheritance of praise for Christ, who died to provide their salvation. What a magnificent thought!

11. **Sealed.** Finally, the mature believer is sealed by the Holy Spirit until he receives his full inheritance and he becomes part of the inheritance of Christ in Heaven (Ephesians 1:13 and 14). Sealed, is the Greek, *sphragis*, the impression of a seal or signet, such as stamped by an ancient king in letter wax or on his decree. It marked his ownership and possession, carried his authority as the signer, protected against undetectable infiltration by trespassers, and sealed his letter or decree until it was delivered to the addressee. By the seal of the Holy Spirit, the mature believer is uniquely marked as being owned and possessed by Jesus Christ. Although they did not comprehend this mystery seal, it was this mark of ownership which was sensed by those who heard Peter and John speak, in Acts 4:13:

> *Now when they saw the boldness of Peter and John, and perceived that they were unlearned and ignorant men, they marvelled; and* <u>*they took knowledge of them, that they had been with Jesus.*</u>

This seal places the mark of the Lord's authority upon His own as revealed in Matthew 28:18 and Acts 1:8:

> *And Jesus came and spake unto them, saying, All power is given unto me in heaven and in earth....But* <u>*ye shall receive power, after that the Holy Ghost is come upon you*</u>*: and ye shall be witnesses unto me both in Jerusalem, and in all Judaea, and in Samaria, and unto the uttermost part of the earth.*

The seal of the Holy Spirit also protects the mature believer against the attempted infiltration of the trespasser, Satan. This is assured in John 10:4 and 5:

> *And when he putteth forth his sheep, he goeth before them, and the sheep follow him: for they know his voice. And* <u>*a stranger will they not follow, but will flee from him*</u>*: for they know not the voice of strangers.*

This seal also protects the believer as the purchased possession of Christ until he is safely delivered to the heavenly Addressee, the Redeemer, the Lord Jesus Christ. Finally, this seal of the Holy Spirit is the *"earnest,"* the first installment, the surety, pledge, and guarantee of the full inheritance to come in 2 Corinthians 1:21 and 22; 5:1 through 5:

> *Now he which stablisheth us with you in Christ, and hath anointed us, is God;* <u>*Who hath also sealed us, and given us the earnest of the Spirit in our hearts*</u>*....For we know that if our earthly house of this tabernacle were dissolved, we have a building of God, an house not made with hands, eternal in the heavens. For in this we groan, earnestly desiring to be clothed upon with our house which is from heaven: If so be that being clothed we shall not be found naked. For we that are in this tabernacle do groan, being burdened: not for that we would be unclothed, but clothed upon, that mortality might be swallowed up of life. Now he that hath wrought us for the selfsame thing is God,* <u>*who also hath given unto us the earnest of the Spirit.*</u>

These, then, describe the mature believer's position in Christ Jesus, as revealed by the Apostle Paul in Ephesians 1:2 through 14. It is a position which the believer can come to understand through God's Word and the ministry of the Holy Spirit. It is a position in which he may rest assured in his Lord throughout his life on earth.

The Believer's Position Secure

In John 19:30, the final moment of the life of Jesus as He hung upon the cross is recorded, *"When Jesus therefore had received the vinegar, he said,* <u>*It is finished*</u>*: and he bowed* *his head, and gave up the ghost.*" At the very moment Jesus cried out, *"It is finished,"* He had completed His God-appointed assignment and had done all that was necessary to make the believer's position in Him available and secure. From that moment until this, from that day until the day the mature children of God meet at His heavenly throne, all of the following have been available and guaranteed to them:

1. The grace of God.
2. Peace **with** God and the peace **of** God.
3. The blessing of God.
4. Status as the chosen of God.
5. The predestination of God, as based on His foreknowledge.
6. Adoption into the family of God.
7. Acceptance by God.
8. Redemption.
9. Abundant knowledge and revelation of the mysteries of God.
10. Inheritance rights.
11. The seal of the Holy Spirit of God.

This position of the mature believer is forever guaranteed. There is nothing in this world or the next which can possibly separate the believer from the love of his Lord. This was Paul's message to the Romans in Romans 8:38 and 39:

> *For I am persuaded, that neither death, nor life, nor angels, nor principalities, nor powers, nor things present, nor things to come, Nor height, nor depth, nor any other creature, shall be able to separate us from the love of God, which is in Jesus Christ our Lord.*

Finally, in Romans 4:21, the mature believer has the personal guarantee of God, Himself, that all He has promised, He will do, *"And being fully persuaded that, what he has promised, he is able also to perform.*" What more marvelous position could the mature child of God every hope to occupy? And, all of it is his!

[1]William Barclay, *The Letters to the Galatians and Ephesians*, pp. 338 through 340.

Chapter 2
THE POSITION OF THE CHURCH

The People of the Church

For the first fourteen verses of the first chapter of Ephesians, Paul had been writing about the position of the believer, but, beginning in verse fifteen, he wrote to the whole Church. The Ephesian church had gained a reputation in first century Christianity. The balance of faith and love in the lives of believers there had been heralded throughout the early Church and had even come to Paul's attention. It would be wonderful if mature believers today cultivated and maintained this same balance in their lives and in their dealings with others, if their churches were so filled with love and faith that the reputation spread far and wide. This would, indeed, be the perfect and mature Church of Jesus Christ.

The faith Paul wrote of in Ephesians 1:15 is the Greek, *pistis*, a firm confidence and conviction based, not on sight or knowledge, but on hearing from God in His Word. It is this unshakable belief in Jesus Christ, the living Word of God (John 1:1) and in the written Word of God, which is the cornerstone of His Church. In Koine Greek, there were no fewer than twenty words translated, love, each expressing a different kind of love, making the Greek language much more precise than English in describing the various types of love. Nineteen of those words found their way into the Greek New Testament. (The only Greek word for love not there is *eros*, indicating erotic, lustful, sexual love.) It is important that, whenever the mature student of the Bible encounters love in the New Testament, he takes the time to discover which Greek word is being used so that he can gain a clearer understanding of the meaning conveyed. Here they are:

1. ***Agape*** - love of God for man (John 3:16).
2. ***Philagathos*** - love of goodness (Titus 1:8).
3. ***Philadelphia*** - brotherly love (Hebrews 13:1).
4. ***Philandros*** - love of a husband for a wife (Titus 2:4).
5. ***Philanthropia*** - love of all mankind (Titus 3:4).
6. ***Philarguria*** - love of money (Luke 16:14 and 2 Timothy 3:2).
7. ***Philautos*** - love of self (2 Timothy 3:2).
8. ***Phileos*** - love in friendship (John 21:15 through 17).
9. ***Philedonos*** - love of pleasure (2 Timothy 3:4).
10. ***Philotheos*** - love of God (2 Timothy 3:4).
11. ***Philologos*** - love of talk (Romans 16:15).
12. ***Philoneikia*** - love of strife (Luke 22:24).
13. ***Philozenia*** - love of strangers and hospitality (Romans 12:13 and Hebrews 13:1).
14. ***Philoproteuo*** - love of being first; love of pre-eminence (3 John 9).
15. ***Philosophia*** - love of wisdom (Colossians 3:8).
16. ***Philostorgos*** - love of family (Romans 12:10).
17. ***Philoteknos*** - love of children (Titus 2:4).
18. ***Philotimeomai*** - love of honor (Romans 15:20).
19. ***Philophoron*** - friendliness and kindness (1 Peter 3:8).

In Ephesians 1:15, *agape*, the love of God for man, is used. This is sacrificial love which gives expecting nothing in return because the one loved has nothing fit to give, the love which caused God to send His Son to the cross to provide the sacrifice for man's salvation even though man has nothing to repay the favor. Man, in and of himself, is incapable of this kind of love; only God can generate it in and through mature believers who are then able to love others with the sacrificial love of God.

Paul continually thanked God for the Ephesian church, for saving each soul and changing each life. He was also thankful for the Body ministry, motivated by faith and love, working through each member of the church. The mature child of God, too, should never forget to thank God for each soul saved, each life changed, and all of his brothers and sisters in Christ. Without them, living the Christian life would be lonely, indeed.

Paul also prayed perpetually for this church, and his prayers were not just repetitious phrases. The Greek word used, *proseuchomai*, indicates the kind of intercession or supplication where one literally pours out his heart before God in behalf of another. This is just the kind of intense prayer the mature believer should offer in behalf of his brothers and sisters in Christ for this was the Lord's command through Paul in Galatians 6:2, *"Bear ye one another's burdens, and so fulfill the law of Christ."* It was also Paul's personal request of his brothers in 1 Thessalonians 5:25, *"Brethren, pray for us."* This kind of prayer follows the example set for the believer by Jesus Christ, Himself, in John 17:19, *"I pray for them: I pray not for the world, but for them which thou hast given me; for they are thine."* It also follows the example of the Holy Spirit in Romans 8:26, *"The Spirit itself maketh intercession for us with groanings which cannot be uttered."*

The Need of the Church

There are few verses in Scripture where the entire Trinity appear; Ephesians 1:17 is one of them, *"That the God of our Lord Jesus Christ, the Father of glory, may give unto you the spirit of wisdom and revelation in the knowledge of him."* Here, Paul saw a need of the church which could only be met by the activity of all three Persons of the Trinity. The church needed the Spirit of wisdom and revelation in the full knowledge of her Lord. Wisdom, is the Greek, *sophia*, which refers to the rightly used wisdom of the Lord in spiritual matters. Revelation is the Greek, *apokalupsis,* which indicates an opening of the mysteries of God. Knowledge is, *epiginosko*, which means to study and observe so attentively that one may perceive and discern full knowledge of the subject. These words indicate that Paul knew the church to which he wrote needed the wisdom of the Lord in spiritual matters, wisdom which would reveal the mystery of God at work in the world, wisdom which would bring complete knowledge of the Lord and His purposes. This wisdom could only come through the ministry of the entire Trinity in the life of mature believers.

During His ministry, Jesus made clear that the Holy Spirit was given to the believer by His Father and could be received in no other way. For example, in Luke 11:11 through 13, He taught, *"How much more shall your heavenly Father give the Holy Spirit to them that ask him?"* God is also revealed as the Giver of His special spiritual wisdom to believers in James 1:5, *"If any of you lack wisdom, let him ask of God, that giveth to all men liberally, and upbraideth not; and it shall be given him."* While the Father would give the Holy Spirit, Jesus, Himself, would send Him to believers in His baptizing power. Jesus promised this to His disciples in John 16:7, *"It is expedient for you that I go away: for if I go not away, the Comforter will not come unto you; but if I depart, I will send Him unto you."* According to both Testaments, the Holy Spirit brings the revelation wisdom of God in spiritual matters. In Isaiah 11:1, we read, *"And the spirit of the LORD shall rest upon him, the spirit of wisdom."* Then, in the New Testament, special wisdom as a Gift of the Holy Spirit is promised to the believer in 1 Corinthians 12:8, *"For to one is given by the Spirit the word of wisdom; to another the word of knowledge by the same Spirit."* Mature believers still need the ministry of the Trinity and the activity of the Spirit of wisdom. Only then will the mature of the kingdom learn to uncover and understand those deep spiritual truths which will give them full and complete knowledge of the nature and purposes of their Lord.

Through the ministry of the entire Trinity, Paul promised that *"the eyes of your understanding being enlightened,"* the mature believer will see truths concerning the kingdom of God (Ephesians 1:18 and 19). Paul wasn't talking about physical sight, but about the believer's spiritual vision which sees spiritual things when acted upon by the Holy Spirit. This spiritual sight brings spiritual enlightenment, the Greek, *photizo*, which metaphorically means the spiritual enlightenment given only by the Lord (John 1:9). The Holy Spirit gives spiritual light, the spiritual eyes of the mature believer perceive that light, and, as that light dawns, the mind of the believer understands spiritual truth he didn't understand before. Through this spiritual understanding, mature believers find full knowledge of important spiritual matters and, through the understanding of such spiritual concepts, mature children of God will come to a more complete knowledge of their Lord.

For example, mature believers will understand *"the hope of His calling"* (Ephesians 1:18). Here, hope, is the Greek, *elpis*, which indicates the happy anticipation of something good. The mature members of the church must understand God, His Word, His plan, His will, and His methods, if they are to come to confidently expect all that their Lord has for them in this world. They must also understand the concepts of eternal life and heavenly reward, if they are to come to confidently expect all He has for them in the world to come.

Next, Paul promised that the Spirit of wisdom would reveal to the spiritual vision of mature believers *"the riches of the glory of his inheritance in the saints"* (Ephesians 1:18). As seen in the previous chapter, not only will the saints receive an inheritance of all that is promised them in Christ, a gloriously rich inheritance, they actually become the inheritance of Christ, and the glory of membership in that company is rich, indeed.

Finally, Paul promised that the ministry of the Trinity, through the Spirit of wisdom, would enable mature children of God to comprehend *"the exceeding greatness of his power"* (Ephesians 1:19). The words used here are powerful all by themselves. For instance, exceeding, is the Greek, *huperballo*, which originally signified throwing beyond a certain limit, but, through the pens of the New Testament writers, including Paul, came to mean surpassing or exceeding all limits or expectations. There is no limit to the power of God in this universe. That power is the Greek, *dunamis*, from which the word, dynamite, comes. It indicates the mighty strength of God which virtually explodes in behalf of believers whenever needed to defeat Satan. Satan may have power, but God is all-powerful. This is the power which raised Jesus from the dead (Ephesians 1:20) and, as Paul noted in Romans 8:11, will someday do the same for the mature believer:

> *But if the Spirit of him that raised up Jesus from the dead dwell in you, he that raised up Christ from the dead shall also quicken your mortal bodies by his Spirit that dwelleth in you.*

This power enabled Christ to assume a position of rest, seated at the right hand of His Father (Ephesians 1:20) on the day of His ascension, as described by Mark in Mark 16:19, *"So then after the Lord had spoken unto them, he was received up into heaven, and sat on the right hand of God."* It's the position in which the dynamic deacon, Stephen, saw Him standing to receive him just before he was martyred in Acts 7:56, *"Behold, I see the heavens opened, and the Son of man standing on the right hand of God."* It's the position He will occupy until the day He comes to rapture His saints, as recorded in Hebrews 12:2:

> *Looking unto Jesus the author and finisher of our faith; who for the joy that was set before him endured the cross, despising the shame, and is set down at the right hand of the throne of God.*

It's the position where there is nothing Satan's forces, implicit in the terms principality, power, might, and dominion in heavenly places (Ephesians 1:20 and 21) can do to disturb Him. Peter, also received this revelation and wrote about it in 1 Peter 3:22, *"Who is gone into heaven and is on the right hand of God; angels and authorities and powers being made subject unto him."* What a wonderful position! In chapter two of Ephesians, the mature child of God will find that this is a position he, too, can occupy, a position he, too, can share with Christ (Ephesians 2:6).

The Lord of the Church

It was because of the activity of the entire Trinity, working through the Spirit of wisdom, that Paul could comprehend the unique relationship between the Lord of the Church and the Church of the Lord and share it with those to whom he wrote in Ephesians 1:22 and 23, *"And hath put all things under his feet, and gave him to be head over all things to the church, Which is his body, the fulness of him that filleth all in all."* The Scriptures reveal to the mature child of God some of the things which have been placed beneath the feet of Christ. First, Satan is under the Lord's feet, just as God predicted in Genesis 3:15, *"And I will put enmity between thee and the woman, and between thy seed and her seed; it shall bruise thy head, and thou shalt bruise his heel."* The troubled sea, typifying the believer's tempests, turmoils, and tribulations, was also under the feet of the Saviour in Matthew 14:24 and 25, *"But the ship was now in the midst of the sea, tossed with waves: for the wind was contrary. And...Jesus went unto them, walking on the sea."* All of the Lord's enemies, and that includes all of the believer's enemies, too, were seen under Christ's feet by Paul in 1 Corinthians 15:25, *"For he must reign, till he hath put all enemies under his feet."* Finally, in Ephesians 1:22, we find that the Lord has *"all things"* under His feet.

Paul next revealed the position of the Lord as Head of His Church. The symbolism is clear. In the human body, the head or brain does the thinking, makes decisions, initiates movement, and controls the body. If the head were severed, the body would die. In the Church, Christ, the Head, must do the thinking, make every decision, initiate every action, and exercise supreme control. Without Him, His Body would surely die, too. The position of the Body, the Church, is also clear. In the human being, the body receives direction from the head or the brain and responds reflexively, obeying every order. If a body, for whatever reason, is unable to obey the brain, it is called handicapped, paralyzed, or crippled. How sad it would be if the Church, the Body of Christ, were handicapped in this world, paralyzed in her work, or crippled in her walk because she ignored the commands of her Head! The Body can obey the commands of her Head through the Holy Spirit, the Heartbeat of the Church, the energizing Force that empowers her to work for her Lord.

In this allegorical view of Christ and His Church, the mature believer receives the spiritual enlightenment to understand one of the great spiritual mysteries of God, the divine plan which summoned Jesus to leave this world and all of His children in it, so that He could rule His earthly kingdom from the throne room of Heaven. When Jesus lived in His earthly body, He could be in only one place at a time and He could accomplish only one task at a time. He was, in His human Form, finite, subject to the same limitations as all other human beings. For example, when Jesus was born in human Form, He had to grow and mature, as recorded in Luke 2:52, *"And Jesus increased in wisdom and stature, and in favour with God and man."* He felt fatigue and needed sleep, as Matthew 8:24 records, *"And, behold, there arose a great tempest in the sea, insomuch that the ship was covered with the waves: but he was asleep."* He experienced hunger and had to eat, as seen in Matthew 4:2, *"And when he had fasted forty days and forty nights, he was afterward an hungered."* Jesus even experienced the same spiritual hunger which plagues the mature believer and revealed His method for satisfying it in John 4:31 through 34:

> *In the mean while his disciples prayed him, saying, Master, eat. But he said unto them, I have meat to eat that ye know not of....My meat is to do the will of him that sent me, and to finish his work.*

But, now, from His position at the right hand of God, Christ, the Head of the Church, is omnipresent and can be everywhere at once; He is omniscient and knows what is happening everywhere at once; and He is omnipotent, all-powerful in behalf of His own everywhere at once. He can direct His Body, the Church, all over the world at the same instant. He is infinite, without any limitations whatsoever. When Jesus walked on this earth, His disciples could only communicate with Him when He was present with them and only one at a time. Now, as He sits at the right hand of the throne of God, all may reach out to Him at the same time and He will hear the prayers and the praises of every one.

Then, because of the activity of the entire Trinity in their midst, because of the energizing power of the Holy Spirit operating among them, the mature members of the Body of Christ may reach out to each other all over the world, to bear one another's burdens in prayer, provide for one another's necessities in charity, and minister to one another's needs in Body ministry. Now, all Gifts of the Spirit can operate simultaneously so that all of the needs of the Body can be met. Now, all of the members of the Body of Christ around the world can work together simultaneously to carry out the divine plan of their Head. As Christ directs the work of His Church, the members of His Body are His hands extended to the entire world, His feet bringing the Gospel message to lost and dying humanity, His voice speaking love to all. Alone, not even the Man, Jesus, could do it all, but, working together, He, as the Head, directing His Body, the Church, God's announced will can be accomplished in this world, just as Jesus declared in Matthew 28:18 through 20:

> *And Jesus came and spake unto them, saying, All power is given unto me in heaven and in earth. Go ye therefore, and teach all nations, baptizing them in the name of the Father, and of the Son, and of the Holy Ghost: Teaching them to observe all things whatsoever I have commanded you: and, lo, I am with you alway, even unto the end of the world. Amen.*

For the mature child of God, the divine strategy becomes apparent. This is the plan of the entire Trinity--Father, Son, and Holy Spirit--and it is to be carried out by those mature members of His Body, the Church, who are willing to obey His commands, teach His truth, and win His lost sheep. The Head of the Church, the Lord Jesus Christ, Himself, remains beside the throne of God, always ready to direct their efforts. And, every bit of His infinite and explosive power will be used to give them the ultimate victory in Him. This, then, is the position of the Church in this present world.

Chapter 3
SITTING DOWN IN HEAVENLY PLACES

The Old Life

Paul was writing to a body of mature believers who had already been quickened (Ephesians 2:1), the Greek, *zoopoieo*, which means, made alive and given a life which will last forever. But, that had not always been the case. When Paul considered the miserable state in which they had begun and the miraculous transformation God had made in their lives, the differences were amazing. So, Paul invited his readers to look back at the monuments of God's grace scattered through their past lives. They had begun as walking dead men (Ephesians 2:1 and 2). While their bodies and souls lived and functioned, they had been born with spirits dead in sin that could not communicate with God. If that were not bad enough, prior to salvation, they had committed trespasses and sins. Trespasses, the Greek, *paraptoma*, means to blunder or fall by the wayside and clearly presumes a fall from a position one has once occupied. It speaks of man's original state of perfection, from which he fell by sin, the Greek, *hamartia*, which literally refers to missing the mark, as in archery, and indicates man's failure to live up to the standard God has set for him, the failure of which James spoke in James 4:17, *"Therefore to him that knoweth to do good, and doeth it not, to him it is sin."* These trespasses and sins simply confirmed man's spiritual death penalty. He had been born in sin; then, he had committed sins. As a result, he was spiritually doomed, spiritually dead. In his own past and in the lives of others, the mature believer sees many who fit Paul's description perfectly, physically alive but spiritually dead. Although the evolutionist maintains that man will become better and better as he evolves from his jungle beginnings to his higher, civilized self, it's an obvious fact of history that man, without God, is a sinner who becomes worse and worse, instead.

This was the state in which the mature believers to whom Paul wrote had once walked (Ephesians 2:2), the Greek, *peripateo*, which means to walk about or walk around. In the allegorical or metaphorical sense which is used in the New Testament, however, this word signifies the way one walks in his daily activities in this world. This lifestyle may be in accord with the world's standards, but is not in accord with God's standards. Those who walk this way are on that broad road Jesus talked about in Matthew 7:13 and 14:

> *Enter ye in at the strait gate: for wide is the gate, and broad is the way, that leadeth to destruction, and many there be which go in thereat: Because strait is the gate, and narrow is the way, which leadeth unto life, and few there be that find it.*

On this road, unregenerate man will commit the sins pronounced acceptable and walk the path pronounced popular by the world. But, there's an even more sinister side to the story. While the course of this road may, on the surface, seem to be set by society, it is actually determined by Satan, himself, *"the prince of the power of the air,"* who hovers in the atmosphere above directing the downfall of unbelievers. So, sinful man finds himself, not only walking the world's path, but also walking Satan's way (Ephesians 2:2), following Satan's plan for his own destruction. It is Satan's spiritual power which energizes and directs all who choose to walk in disobedience to God (Ephesians 2:2) and operates in all who choose to walk with Satan. This was the clear message of Jesus to the Pharisees in

John 8:44, *"Ye are of your father the devil, and the lusts of your father ye will do."* Those to whom Paul wrote this letter had once walked the way of the world, the way of Satan. Their conversation, as mentioned in Ephesians 2:3, indicated more than just talk; it indicated walk, as well. It is the Greek, *anastrophe*, which refers to a way of life or a way of conducting one's life and indicates the entire pattern of one's conduct.

There's an old saying, "A man is known by the company he keeps." When one is in sin, he keeps company with others in sin; when one is controlled by Satan, he keeps company with others controlled by Satan. These *"children of disobedience,"* live their lives fulfilling the lusts and desires of their flesh (Ephesians 2:3). Lust, is the Greek, *epithumeo*, which denotes a strong, overwhelming passion which can include but is not limited to sexual desire. Desire, on the other hand, is the Greek, *thelema*, which implies an active decision of the will to satisfy a desire. Both lusts and desires originate in the mind of the sinner, as seen in Proverbs 23:7, *"For as he thinketh in his heart, so is he,"* and both are carried out by man's sinful flesh, sarx, which is used metaphorically to indicate man's sinful human nature. In Romans 6:6, Paul referred to this flesh, this sinful human nature of man, as the *"old man,"* prescribing the only cure for his behavior, *"Knowing this, that our old man is crucified with him, that the body of sin might be destroyed, that henceforth we should not serve sin."* Apart from the crucifixion of that old man, sinners are *"by nature the children of wrath"* (Ephesians 2:3), worthy only of the wrath or judgment of God. All believers were once such unregenerate people, born in sin and sinful by nature. Sin, singular, is that nature with which all are born; sins, plural, are the acts of lust and desire committed as a result. Sinners are condemned, not by the sin nature they are born with and cannot help, but by the sins which they choose, by acts of their own volition, to commit as a result. So long as they are in that state, they are children of Satan and subject to the judgment of God.

The New Life

One day, all of that changed, and that cataclysmic change was initiated by God, Himself, when man could do nothing to save his life. It happened for two reasons. The first, was God's mercy, the Greek, *eleos*, the compassion which actively reaches out to relieve misery. That mercy made God reach out to do for fallen man what he couldn't do for himself. The second reason was God's great love for those He had created. Love, here, is once again the Greek, *agape*, God's sacrificial love for man. Without doubt, the salvation plan originated in the mind of God and was motivated by His agape love. Nowhere is this seen more clearly than in what may be the single most famous verse in the entire Bible, John 3:16, *"For God so loved the world, that he gave his only begotten Son, that whosoever believeth in him should not perish, but have everlasting life."* While Jesus was obedient to the plan, it was God who conceived it, as detailed in Philippians 2:5 through 8:

> *Let this mind be in you, which was also in Christ Jesus: Who, being in the form of God, thought it not robbery to be equal with God: But made himself of no reputation, and took upon him the form of a servant, and was made in the likeness of men: And being found in fashion as a man, he humbled himself, and became obedient unto death, even the death of the cross.*

The salvation plan was born of God's great love for man and His desire to rescue man from his sinful state. While love initiated man's salvation, mercy lifted man's misery. It was God who authored it all. God first preserved the life of man until the hour of salvation. Then, God reached down and quickened, gave life to, and conferred eternal life upon that newborn babe in Christ (Ephesians 2:5). When sin had made man spiritually dead, God made him spiritually alive in the same way He quickened Christ and restored Him to life (Ephesians 2:5). The same explosive power which brought Jesus out of the grave, brings the convert out of sin; the same explosive power which resurrected Christ, gives the convert rebirth; the same explosive power which energizes Jesus for all eternity, sustains the convert's new life each day and on into eternity. Paul further explained this quickening power of God and the new life of the believer in Colossians 2:12 and 13,

> *Buried with him in baptism, wherein also ye are risen with him through the faith of the operation of God, who hath raised him from the dead. And you, being dead in your sins and the uncircumcision of your flesh, hath he quickened together with him, having forgiven you all trespasses.*

All of this was accomplished by God's grace, and God's grace, alone (Ephesians 2:5). Man could never deserve it, no matter what good deeds he may have done; he could never earn it, no matter how hard he worked; he could never repay it, no matter what he gave. Salvation, eternal life, was granted by the grace, the unmerited, undeserved favor of a loving God toward a sinful people, as recorded in Titus 2:11, *"For the grace of God that bringeth salvation hath appeared to all men."* Each mature believer can look back and see his personal monument, standing like a boulder in his memory to that wonderful day when God, in His love and mercy, reached down His heavenly hand of grace and brought him salvation. That was the day the mature believer was set on that new and narrow road; that was the day his quest for maturity started; that was the day his eternal life in Christ began.

The New Position

If God had done nothing more than save sinful man, He would have done more than manever had any right to expect, more than man could ever hope to merit. But, God did notstop at salvation; God did even more, as Paul detailed in Ephesians 2:6, *"And hath raised us up together, and made us to sit together in heavenly places in Christ Jesus."* First, God raised up together, the Greek, *sunegeiro*, which literally means to wake up together and indicates that, just as Jesus awakened from physical death to eternal life in God, so the believer is awakened from spiritual death to eternal life at the moment he is saved. Then, Godreserved for the mature believer a seat in the heavenly places with His Son, the same position of rest Christ occupies in Ephesians 1:20 and 21. Sit together, as used of believers andChrist in Ephesians 2:6, is the Greek, *sugkathizo*, which means to sit down together with another. Believers could never achieve this alone; this position of rest can only be found in company with Christ. There, the mature believer need not worry or fear. When sitting down together in Christ, he need only rest in his Lord.

Perhaps, though, the most amazing words in this passage are these: *"in heavenly places."* This is the Greek, *ouranos*, which refers to the heavens and all that they contain. Scripture indicates that there are three heavens or three divisions of the heavens. Which is meant in any passage must be determined by a careful study of the context. First, there is the atmosphere, the envelope of gas which surrounds the earth. Then, there is the universe, the galaxies, planets, the sun, moon, stars, etc., of which the earth is only a small part. These two divisions of the heavens are easily delineated in Matthew 24:29 through 31. Last, there is the abode of God, the place where God now resides and to which the believer hopes to go, the place from which Jesus came to be the Saviour of the world. This Heaven is clearly seen in John 6:33. To determine which is meant in this particular passage, one must consider that the very same Greek word is used in Ephesians 1:3, 1:20, and 2:6, where it is translated, *"heavenly places,"* and in Ephesians 3:10 and 6:12, where it is translated, *"high places."* In three of those scriptures--Ephesians 1:20 (and 21), 3:10, and 6:12--the reference is clearly to the abode of Satan and his demons, the principalities and powers, etc. Then, in Ephesians 2:2, Satan is pictured as *"the prince of the power of the air."* It seems obvious, then, that the *"heavenly places"* of Ephesians 2:6 is the spiritual realm, the area of the air or atmosphere occupied by Satan and his demons and from which they carry out their diabolical plans to destroy man. This is Satan's backyard, the playground of his demons. Yet, the mature believer in the company of his Lord has nothing to fear. He may assume a position of rest in the face of the adversary, secure in his authority in Christ.

All of this is accomplished for a reason, so that the mature believer might stand as a trophy of the grace of God for all the ages of eternity (Ephesians 2:7). One look at the misery out of which the believer came, one look at the transformation God performed, one look at the exalted and secure position in which he now sits would convince anyone of *"the exceeding riches of his grace in his kindness toward us"* (Ephesians 2:7). All of the riches of this grace are imparted to a sinful soul at the moment of salvation. When God had every right to judge and destroy, He loved and regenerated; when man deserved only rejection and ruin, God recreated and restored him. All of this happened *"through Christ"* (Ephesians 2:7). Jesus was the living Word, the Logos, of God, as John 1:1 explains, *"In the beginning was the Word, and the Word was with God, and the Word was God."*

To better understand God's love and mercy and grace, and all that they accomplished in the believer's life, consider this true story: One day, the world-famous evangelist, Billy Graham, was walking around the grounds of his mountain-top retreat in North Carolina. As he walked, he accidently stepped on an ant hill. When he stooped down to survey the scene, he saw that many ants lay dead, while others scurried about in their best efforts to repair the damage all around them. Rev. Graham felt nothing but compassion for the ants. He longed to be able to communicate to them that he was sorry for their sad state, to come down to their level and help them in some way. But, at long last, he concluded that there was only one way to communicate with an ant--that was to become an ant. When God looked down from Heaven, He saw man in a miserable state, born in sin and dead in his trespasses. There was only one way God could communicate with him and lift him out of that misery--by becoming Man. So, in His mercy, God reached out to change man's state; in His love, He became Man so that He could redeem him; in His grace, He spoke a single Word into man's heart. He said, "JESUS," as recorded in Hebrews 1:1 and 2, *"God....Hath in these last days spoken unto us by his Son."* God, through His grace, made the first move to redeem man. But, it was Jesus who was the Personification of that grace, as John 1:17 explains, *"For the law was given by Moses, but grace and truth came by Jesus Christ."*

This is what God has wonderfully wrought in the life of the mature believer. Now, he may take his position of rest and repose with his Saviour in *"heavenly places;"* he may assume his authority over the devil and all of his demons through Christ. For all of the ages of eternity, the mature man or woman of God will stand as a living monument, a vibrant trophy, of the grace and love of God.

Chapter 4
SAVED BY GRACE

The Believer's Salvation

It's a paradoxical fact of spiritual life that a new convert is often more sensitive to all God has done for him than the mature child of God who may have much more knowledge of the spiritual principles involved. The new convert is recently saved from the ravages of sin, recently separated from his old life and given a new one. He may not fully comprehend all of the spiritual implications of it, but he does know how miserable he was before, how happy he is now, and that Jesus made the difference. The mature believer who has spent some years walking with the Lord has often lost that sense of wonder concerning the miracle of salvation Christ once worked in his life. His memory of his old life of sin may have dimmed. When he looks in the mirror, he no longer sees a rank sinner; he sees a maturing man of God with talents and abilities and a life of good works. Consequently, it is often more difficult for the more mature child of God to remember that every good thing in his life is a result of the grace of God.

Paul understood this seeming contradiction and brought his mature readers back to their beginnings as he held up the mirror to their past lives and made them look. He wanted them to see the grace of God in the face of their own sin at the moment they were saved. So, Paul penned this spiritual truth quite uncompromisingly in Ephesians 2:8 and 9, *"For by grace are ye saved through faith; and that not of yourselves: it is the gift of God: Not of works, lest any man should boast."* Once again, this grace of which Paul wrote comes from the Greek root, *charis*, the undeserved, unmerited love and favor of God. Man can never hope to deserve it, earn it, or pay for it. God offers His grace to man for no other reason than His agape love, His sacrificial love for the being He created. He expects nothing in return, because He knows that man has nothing worth giving. Clearly, then, the grace which brings man his salvation is all of God and nothing of self. This grace saved, the Greek, *sozo*. In Koine Greek, this word usually referred to rescue, particularly rescue at sea, rescue from drowning. The pens of the New Testament writers transformed this simple word into a beautiful picture of God's rescue of man in danger of drowning in sin, adding depth and richness to the believer's understanding of grace. Just as a drowning sailor can do nothing to rescue himself, so man can never hope to save himself from sin. Just as a potential rescuer is not forced to toss out a lifeline and acts only out of his own volition and kindness, so God makes the first move to extend the lifeline of salvation to lost and dying man. Just as the rescued seaman can never repay his rescuer, so man can never repay the grace of God that saves him. That salvation by grace comes *"through faith"* (Ephesians 2:8), a strong, unwavering belief and trust. But, Paul made clear that even the faith by which man accepts salvation is not original with him. It, too, is a *"gift of God."* This thought is in perfect agreement with Galatians 2:16:

> *Knowing that man is not justified by the works of the law, but by the faith of Jesus Christ, that we might be justified by the faith of Christ, and not by the works of the law: for by the works of the law shall no flesh be justified.*

In both *underlined phrases,* the word, *"of,"* is in the Greek genitive case which indicates the force that originates or generates action. Clearly, the Greek text shows that the faith by which man accepts salvation is generated by Jesus Christ as a free gift of God (Ephesians 2:8). This faith, however, must never be deemed of little worth because it is free; rather, this faith is so precious it is priceless. It must be given freely by God to man, for there is nothing on earth of sufficient value to purchase it. Once generated into a life, this faith believes all of God's promises and appropriates all of God's inheritance because it is the active, working, mountain-moving faith of Jesus Christ, Himself.

After Paul explained what salvation by grace through faith is, he detailed what it isn't. First, it isn't of man (Ephesians 2:8), since unregenerate man is worthy only of God's judgment; it's not of man's ability, since there is no good thing in him (Romans 7:18); it's not even of man's thought, since he can't even see his need of salvation apart from the revelation of God to him through the conviction of His Holy Spirit (John 16:8 through 11). Second, it is not of works (Ephesians 2:9), the Greek, *ergon*, which means the business or activity of everyday life. It can also refer to the "busy work" Satan uses to distract the sinner so he'll constantly busy himself with activities of no real value. These works can't save man, no matter how good they seem, no matter how heroic they are, no matter how worthwhile they appear to the world, and no matter how much earthly praise they bring to the man performing them. Man's business can't save him, no matter how successful he may be and no matter how much of this world's wealth he may have accumulated. Paul struck at the very heart of the popular myth that if man is just "a good person," if he pays his bills, cares for his family, gives to charity, and doesn't kick his dog, he will somehow be saved. Nothing could be further from the truth, as Isaiah 64:6 makes clear, *"All our righteousnesses are as filthy rags."* Man's righteousnesses, his good deeds, are no more than dirty rags, his do-it-yourself covering for his sin. It wouldn't work for Adam and Woman and it won't work now, for the simple reason that salvation cannot be put on by man; it must be put in by God. God planned it that way so that man, who is so given to pride, wouldn't be able to boast about this. The credit for the plan of salvation must be God's and God's, alone.

The born-again believer, then, is not the workmanship, the handiwork or creation, of his own hands by his designs, his abilities, or his thoughts. If he were, he could brag, "Look what I made of my life." Instead, he is the workmanship, the handiwork and creation, of God through His Son, Jesus Christ (Ephesians 2:10). Jeremiah got a glimpse of man as God's workmanship, comparing it to the relationship between the clay and the potter who molds it, and recorded God's words in Jeremiah 18:6, *"Behold, as the clay is in the potter's hand, so are ye in mine hand."* At the moment of salvation, the Potter, God, takes the passive clay, man, and transforms him into a good and useful vessel. The clay, the vessel, is unable to do anything to enhance itself or change its state. In this process, man is created *"unto good works, which God hath before ordained that we should walk in them"* (Ephesians 2:10). Good works, is the same Greek word, *ergon*, but there are important differences. These good works are of God's design, not man's; they are God-ordained, not self-edifying; they come after salvation, not instead of it; and they flow from a continuing walk with God, not from the mind of man. The term, "before ordained," is also interesting. It's the Greek, *pronoia*, which indicates forethought in making provision. While God does not predestine or pre-program man to robotically perform good works, He does make provision for man to do so. This leads to the inescapable conclusion that God gives man good works to perform for his benefit, not God's. God is quite capable of accomplishing His desired ends apart from the assistance of man. He simply provides work for man to do for Him because it is the heartfelt desire of the mature child of God to give service back to the Lord in return for all the Lord has done for him.

The Believer's Position Before Salvation

Paul noted that the Gentiles to whom he wrote had not been circumcised at birth (Ephesians 2:11). This caused the Jews, who referred to themselves as *"the Circumcision,"* to call Gentiles *"the Uncircumcision."* To the Jews, Gentiles were, because of their uncircumcision, *"without God"* (Ephesians 2:12). But, circumcision was an outward sign of an inner covenant, as God explained to Abraham in Genesis 17:11, *"And ye shall circumcise the flesh of your foreskin: and it shall be a token of the covenant betwixt me and you."* Apart from that covenant, it meant nothing, according to Romans 2:25, *"If thou be a breaker of the law, thy circumcision is made uncircumcision."* In Romans 2:26, Paul proved that, if the covenant existed, the circumcision was implied, *"If the uncircumcision keep the righteousness of the law, shall not his uncircumcision be counted for circumcision?"* Then, in 1 Corinthians 7:19, Paul wrote, *"Circumcision is nothing, and uncircumcision is nothing, but the keeping of the commandments of God."* What may or may not have been done in the flesh wasn't the issue; what mattered was what was done in the heart (Jeremiah 31:33). God wants people whose hearts are circumcised, as Paul explained in Romans 2:28 and 29:

> *For he is not a Jew, which is one outwardly; neither is that circumcision, which is outward in the flesh: But he is a Jew which is one inwardly; and circumcision is that of the heart, in the spirit, and not in the letter; whose praise is not of men, but of God.*

By that standard, those to whom Paul wrote were as circumcised as anyone needed to be to be accepted by God; they were circumcised in their hearts, where it really mattered. At salvation, they had appropriated the circumcision of their Saviour, as Paul revealed in Colossians 2:11, *"In whom also ye are circumcised with the circumcision made without hands, in putting off the body of sins of the flesh by the circumcision of Christ."* Before, Paul's readers had been *"aliens," or foreigners,* as far as the Jews were concerned, and *"strangers," or those who don't belong,* as far as the promises of God were concerned.

The Believer's Position After Salvation

All of that changed at the moment of salvation, for all of the covenants of the Old Testament led to the new covenant in Christ, as Hebrews 10:9 declares, *"He taketh away the first, that he may establish the second."* In addition, all of the promises of Scripture are fulfilled in Christ, as Paul proclaimed in 2 Corinthians 1:20, *"For all the promises of God in him are yea, and in him Amen, unto the glory of God by us."* When Paul's readers accepted Christ, they were received into His new covenant and given access to every one of the promises of God (Ephesians 1:13).

Prior to their salvation, that state of war mentioned in Chapter 1 existed between Paul's readers and God because of their sin. Christ became their peace treaty, ending that war forever (Ephesians 2:14). Another state of war existed, too. In the Temple at Jerusalem, there was a strong stone balustrade or partition which separated the court of the Gentiles from the holy place. Any Gentile who went beyond that wall could legally be killed. Jesus Christ forever tore down that wall of separation and ended the state of emotional war which had always existed between Jew and Gentile, between "the Circumcision" and "the Uncircumcision" (Ephesians 2:14). The old animosities were resolved since both had to approach God in the same way--through the sacrificial death of His Son on the cross. The Jew could no longer trust in his laws, his commandments, or his ordinances to save him; the Gentile could no longer trust in his gods, his sacrifices, or his rites to save him, either. Both had to reach out to God and accept His Son's final sacrifice in order to be saved. Christ had transformed the state of war which existed between God and man's sin into the love of the Father for His children, He had replaced the hostility between Jew and Gentile into the love of Christian brothers, and He had converted the sin of man into the righteousness of God. Jewish and Gentile converts became one before God, one in Christ (Ephesians 2:15 and 16). On His cross, Jesus had brought both Jew and Gentile into the new covenant of His blood seen in 1 Corinthians 11:25:

> *After the same manner also he took the cup, when he had supped, saying, This cup is the new testament in my blood: this do ye, as oft as ye drink it, in remembrance of me.*

It was for this reason that Paul, a Jew, had been sent to preach to both Jews and Gentiles alike (Ephesians 2:17). Both needed to hear the same message, both needed to receive the same Christ. As Paul explained to believers in Rome in Romans 2:11, *"There is no respect of persons with God."* All were made of equal worth, because God had paid an equal price for each, so each had an equal opportunity for salvation.

The Believer's Access in Christ

Christ did it all when the veil of the Temple was torn in two, permitting both, all, everyone, whosoever will, to have free access to the presence of His Father (Ephesians 2:18). That access is designated by the Greek, *prosagoge*, and meant to lead or bring into one's presence. It referred to the entrance into God's presence provided for the believer through Christ when He rent the veil. The writer to the Hebrews drew a similar word picture in Hebrews 10:19 and 20:

> *Having therefore, brethren, boldness to enter into the holiest by the blood of Jesus, By a new and living way, which he hath consecrated for us, through the veil, that is to say, his flesh.*

Jesus is the Door, through which man may enter into salvation and, then, into the very presence of God, as Jesus taught in John 10:7 and 9:

> *Then said Jesus unto them again, Verily, verily, I say unto you, I am the door of the sheep....I am the door: by me if any man enter in, he shall be saved, and shall go in and out and find pasture.*

Those who go through that Door are no longer *"strangers and foreigners"* (Ephesians 2:19), but *"fellowcitizens,"* the Greek, *sumpolites*, which identifies one who has all the rights and privileges of all citizens. All who are born-again receive the same citizenship in the kingdom of God and the same rights as all other saints (Ephesians 1:19). They are also members of the same household, *"the household of God"* (Ephesians 2:19), the Greek, *oikeios*, which refers to those who belong to a family because they are related by blood. Through the blood of Jesus, all believers, of whatever nationality, race, age, or status, become a part of God's family. Through this very same blood, both the born-again Jew and the born-again Gentile become related to each other, brothers and sisters in Christ, all children of the same God, all members of the same family of faith, reconciled to each other and to God through the blood of Christ. Finally, Paul unrolled the blueprint of this particular household, this house, this building of God (Ephesians 2:20 through 22). It is built on the solid foundation of the twelve apostles who delivered the Gospel and were typified by the twelve foundations of the New Jerusalem in Revelation 21:14, *"And the wall of the city had twelve foundations, and in them the names of the twelve apostles of the Lamb."* Then, Jesus Christ, Himself, became *"the chief corner stone"* (Ephesians 2:20), the Greek, *akro-goniaios*, which indicates something placed at the extreme corner. In ancient construction, the cornerstone fused two walls together as one. In the same way, Christ became the living Stone which fused together the Old Testament with the New, the believing Jew and the believing Gentile into one Body, His Church. With this firm foundation, with the fusion provided by the Cornerstone, the Church of Jesus Christ became a building *"fitly framed together"* (Ephesians 2:21), the Greek, *sun-armologeo*, which refers to something bound or joined closely together.

In the ancient world, the pyramids of Egypt were an engineering and construction marvel. They still are. Each stone of each pyramid was so precisely cut, so carefully fitted into the stones around it that, to this day, not even a slip of paper may be placed between them. The building, the Church, Paul described is also so carefully and expertly joined together that it is impossible to find a space between them. Such a carefully constructed Church *"groweth unto an holy temple in the Lord"* (Ephesians 2:21). Both the growth of the maturing child of God and the growth of the Church, should produce a body of mature believers who work together to win the lost. In such a building, each individual believer will leave spiritual childhood behind to grow into spiritual adulthood. Each will come to maturity. Then, the Church, as the Body of Christ, will grow in numbers, in spiritual knowledge, and in spiritual strength. It, too, will come to maturity. Together, through the work of the Holy Spirit, all will grow and mature to become a fit and appropriate holy temple, a sanctified and set-apart, permanent dwelling place of God (Ephesians 2:22).

In Ephesus, one of the primary attractions was the temple of Diana. It was world-famous and noted for its symmetry and perfection. Paul may have been referring to it as he encouraged his readers to provide just as precise, just as perfect a temple for the true God, a temple fit for the abode of the Holy Spirit. Peter also caught this vision of this beautiful building, this glorious Church. In 1 Peter 2:4 through 9, he wrote:

> *To whom coming, as unto a living stone, disallowed indeed of men, but chosen of God, and precious, <u>Ye also, as lively stones, are built up a spiritual house</u>, an holy priesthood, to offer up spiritual sacrifices, acceptable to God by Jesus Christ. Wherefore also it is contained in the scripture, Behold, I lay in Sion <u>a chief corner stone</u>, elect, precious: and he that believeth on him shall not be confounded. Unto you therefore which believe he is precious: but unto them which be disobedient, <u>the stone which the builders disallowed is made the head of the corner</u>. And a stone of stumbling, and a rock of offence, even to them which stumble at the word, being disobedient: whereunto also they were appointed. But <u>ye are a chosen generation, a royal priesthood, an holy nation, a peculiar people; that ye should shew forth the praises of him who hath called you out of darkness into his marvellous light</u>.*

This, then is the precious privilege of the mature child of God in company with other mature children of God. Together, they may be a part of His building, His Church, held together by Him, growing in Him, praising Him.

Chapter 5
THE TOP OF THE TAPESTRY

The Top of the Tapestry Revealed

The Master's Loom
Author Unknown

Man's life is laid in the loom of time, to a pattern he does not see,
While the weavers work and the shuttles fly, till the dawn of eternity.
Some shuttles are filled with silver threads, and some with threads of gold,
While often but the darker hues, are all that they may hold.
But the weaver watches with skillful eye, each shuttle fly to and fro,
And sees the pattern so deftly wrought, as the loom moves sure and slow.
God surely planned the pattern: each thread, the dark and fair,
Is chosen by His master skill, and placed in the web with care.
He only knows its beauty, and guides the shuttles which hold
The threads so unattractive, as well as the threads of gold.
Not till each loom is silent, and the shuttles cease to fly,
Shall God reveal the pattern, and explain the reason why--
The dark threads were as needful, in the weaver's skillful hand,
As the threads of gold and silver, for that pattern which He planned.

In each life, there are circumstances that are hard to understand. Even the mature believer sometimes asks, "Why did this happen to me?" All he sees in his life are the tangled ends of the threads on the bottom of the tapestry. Sometimes, though, God will give a glimpse of the top of the tapestry, at the beautiful pattern those threads are forming.

Paul probably wondered why he was sitting in a Roman jail awaiting trial before Nero. No doubt, he also wondered why he'd had to endure so many hardships. Then, God gave Paul a glimpse of the top of the tapestry, a revelation of the plan God was carrying out in and through his life. It was a beautiful plan, one which would result in the salvation of many souls and even reach out to touch the lives of mature believers today. If Paul had not been imprisoned at least twice, he may have had neither the need nor the time to compose many of the letters which are of such value and comfort to believers of all ages.

In the third chapter of Ephesians, Paul shared part of his revelation of the top of God's tapestry. In Ephesians 3:1, he wrote *"<u>For this cause</u> I, Paul, the prisoner of Jesus Christ for you Gentiles."* That cause was the original position of the Gentiles he had detailed in Ephesians 2:11 and 12. Yet, God had a plan which would change that position forever and Paul wrote about it in Ephesians 2:13 through 19. To make it happen, God first had to let His servants know that the Jews were not the only ones to whom salvation was available; God had to show them that His plan included the Gentiles, too. Then, they could go forth to preach the peace of God to all (Ephesians 2:17). This portion of the Gospel which was to be preached to the Gentiles was the *"dispensation of the grace of God,"* of which Paul wrote in Ephesians 3:2. Paul told just how God revealed this to him in

Ephesians 3:3 and 4, *"How that by revelation he made known unto me the mystery....Whereby, when ye read, ye may understand my knowledge in the mystery of Christ."* This revelation is the Greek, *apokalupsis*, an unveiling, uncovering, or disclosure of facts and truths. God was revealing, unveiling, uncovering, disclosing His plan for the Gentiles which had, until that time, been a mystery, the Greek, *musterion*, the hidden secrets made known only to the initiated. While all born-again believers are initiated, not all will see the same part of the tapestry revealed. God will disclose what each needs to know to fulfill his part of the plan. Paul needed to know God's plans regarding the Gentiles because he, among others, was going to be used by God to preach to them. The Gentiles, too, needed to know their place in God's plan since it involved the validity of their salvation.

This particular revelation of God's grace to the Gentiles was not understood by prior generations, as Paul noted in Ephesians 3:5, *"Which in other ages was not made known unto the sons of men, as it is now revealed unto his holy apostles and prophets by the Spirit."* It was, however, foreshadowed in many ways, on many occasions. For example, when God set His people free from Egypt, He also freed others who were not children of Israel, as Exodus 12:38 records, *"And a mixed multitude went up also with them."* Then, when God gave the sacrificial Law, He made provision for those who were not Jewish but wanted to sacrifice to the God of the Jews in Leviticus 22:18:

> *And the LORD spake unto Moses saying....Whatsoever he be of the house of Israel, or of the strangers in Israel, that will offer his oblation for all his vows, and for all his freewill offerings, which they will offer unto the LORD for a burnt offering.*

Later, as the conquest of Canaan began, God ordered that the Gentile harlot, Rahab, be saved by Joshua, a type of Jesus who bore the same name. She became a member of Jewish society (Joshua 6:25). Still later, during the days of the judges, a Gentile girl called Ruth became the bride of her Jewish kinsman-redeemer, Boaz, also typical of Christ the Kinsman-Redeemer (Ruth 4:10). In addition, both of these Gentile women were included in the genealogy of Jesus Christ, the Jewish-born Son of God. In fact, they are the only two women mentioned by name in either of the genealogies of Jesus. In Matthew 1:5, we read, *"And Salmon begat Booz of Rachab; and Booz begat Obed of Ruth; and Obed begat Jesse."* Some Old Testament prophets also received an inkling of what God had in store for the Gentiles. In Isaiah 56:6 and 7, this message about the Gentiles is recorded:

> *Also the sons of the stranger, that join themselves to the LORD, to serve him, and to love the name of the LORD, to be his servants, every one that keepeth the sabbath from polluting it, and taketh hold of my covenant; Even them will I bring to my holy mountain, and make them joyful in my house of prayer: their burnt offerings and their sacrifices shall be accepted upon mine altar; for mine house shall be called an house of prayer for all people.*

Isaiah also wrote about it in Isaiah 49:6, *"I will also give thee for a light to the Gentiles, that thou mayest be my salvation unto the end of the earth."* Malachi, the last prophet to write before that long, dark, silent period between the Testaments, said this about the Gentiles of the whole world in Malachi 1:11:

> *For from the rising of the sun even unto the going down of the same my name shall be great among the Gentiles; and in every place incense shall be offered unto my name, and a pure offering: for my name shall be great among the heathen, saith the LORD of hosts.*

From these examples, it's clear to the mature believer that there is no "new truth," no "new revelation," no extra-biblical knowledge. The truth, all of it for all time and all people, is in the Word of God. It is complete; there is nothing that needs to be added to it. Still, the Holy Spirit must often uncover, reveal, and illuminate, the truths in Scripture to those for whom it is meant, as Jesus explained in John 16:13 and 14:

Howbeit when he, the Spirit of truth, is come, he will guide you into all truth: for he shall not speak of himself; but whatsoever he shall hear, that shall he speak: and he will shew you things to come. He shall glorify me: for he shall receive of mine, and shall shew it unto you.

The Holy Spirit did just that in the case of God's plan for the Gentiles. While the ancient prophets may not have fully understood the meaning and importance of the words they recorded, when God's time arrived, the Holy Spirit made the message clear to God's New Testament apostles. Peter saw it in a vision of a huge sheet lowered from Heaven that contained all sorts of animals which God commanded him to eat (Acts 10:9 through 13). When Peter refused, citing the Jewish kosher laws (Acts 10:14), God responded, *"What God hath cleansed, that call not thou common"* (Acts 10:15). After this happened three times, Peter got the message and was willing to preach the Gospel of Christ in the home of a Roman centurion called Cornelius, as recorded in Acts 10:22:

And he said unto them, Ye know how that it is an unlawful thing for a man that is a Jew to keep company, or come unto one of another nation; but God hath shewed me that I should not call any man common or unclean.

Later, Peter was called to account before the other apostles for preaching in the home of a Gentile. After he had explained his vision and the command of the Lord to him, the apostles responded with this affirmation of his action in Acts 11:18:

When they heard these things, they held their peace, and glorified God, saying, Then hath God also to the Gentiles granted repentance unto life.

Paul had received a similar revelation just after his conversion. He recounted the Lord's message to him as he testified before King Agrippa in Acts 26:16 through 18:

I have appeared unto thee for this purpose, to make thee a minister and a witness both of these things which thou hast seen, and of those things in the which I will appear unto thee; Delivering thee from the people, and from the Gentiles, unto whom now I send thee, To open their eyes, and to turn them from darkness to light, and from the power of Satan unto God, that they may receive forgiveness of sins, and inheritance among them which are sanctified by faith that is in me.

Of this revelation of the mystery of God concerning the Gentiles, Paul wrote in Ephesians 3:6, *"That the Gentiles should be fellowheirs, and of the same body, and partakers of his promise in Christ by the gospel."* These three phrases are closely related. *"Fellowheirs,"* is the Greek, *sugkleronoma*, and literally means joint-heirs. In Jewish tradition, the eldest son received a double portion of the father's inheritance, while all others received a single portion. Jesus was the eldest Son; all others who came into the family of God were assured, not a smaller portion, but an equal share of the inheritance the Father had provided. *"Of the same body,"* is the Greek, *sunsoma*, which literally means a joint-body. Gentiles who accept Christ do not become a part of the body of Jews, nor do Jews who accept Christ become a part of the body of Gentiles. Once they are born-again, both Jew and Gentile become part of a new Body, the Body of Christ, His Church. *"Partakers,"* is the Greek, *summetocha*, joint-sharers. The born-again Jew does not possess a greater share in

Christ or His promises simply because He and they were all born Jewish. Neither does the born-again Gentile, representative of all nations, possess a greater share of Christ or of His promises because He came to provide salvation to those of all nations. Rather, both Jews and Gentiles are given an equal share in Christ and in His promises because all are of equal worth and equal value in His sight and He paid an equal price, His life, for each.

It was the revelation of this mystery, the disclosure of the equality of Jew and Gentile and the uncovering of God's plan of salvation for both, that was the foundation of Paul's ministry (Ephesians 3:7 through 9). Here, we see that the revelations of God's mysteries are not given indiscriminately, nor are they given to amaze or amuse; they are given to those who need them for a purpose. It must also be noted that Paul's revelation preceded his ministry. First, he was shown that the salvation plan was to be made available to the Gentiles, then he was called to take the message of salvation, the good news of *"the unsearchable riches of Christ,"* to them (Ephesians 3:7 and 8). Because he had previously persecuted Christians, Paul considered himself *"less than the least of all saints," but he* was one of those chosen by the Lord, Himself, for this momentous ministry. The mature believer learns that Paul's experiential ministry was based on the revelation God had given him; God's revelation had not been based on Paul's past experiences or ministry. Ministry and experience must be based on God's truth as revealed in Scripture; truth cannot be based upon one's perceptions, as colored by one's experiences, either in or out of ministry.

Once God's revelation is clear, the mature believer may go forward to share it, just as Paul did (Ephesians 3:9). Then, all may see the truth of God, as revealed to His minister; all may enter into *"the fellowship of the mystery,"* a common understanding of the truth disclosed by God; all may perceive what has heretofore been *"hid."* Of course, to be a true revelation of God, it must have previously been foreshadowed, prophesied, or predicted in Scripture, just as Paul's had been. These principles can guide the mature child of God as he evaluates any revelation he feels he received from God. The first question he must ask himself is this: "Is it Scriptural?" If it isn't, it must be rejected; if it is, it must be accepted and appropriated as a basis for one's service to God. These principles can also assist the mature believer as he considers a possible call into the ministry of Jesus Christ. He must then ask himself, "Is this ministry based on a personal revelation of and by the Lord?" If it is not, it, too, must be rejected; if it is, it must be embraced and acted upon.

The Example of the Church Revealed

In addition to the love of God for both Jews and Gentiles (John 3:16), there was a definite, spiritual, and equally mysterious reason why God had included both in His salvation plan. Paul shared that revelation with his readers in Ephesians 3:10 through 12:

> *To the intent that now unto <u>the principalities and powers in heavenly places might be known by the church the manifold wisdom of God</u>. According to the eternal purpose which he purposed in Christ Jesus our Lord: In whom we have boldness and access with confidence by the faith of him.*

Here, the Church is to be an example to *"the principalities and powers,"* the same Greek words translated "heavenly places" or "high places" elsewhere in Ephesians, all referring to Satan, his demons, and the positions they occupy in the atmosphere. The example provided by the Church is that of the *"manifold,"* varied and diverse, *"wisdom of God,"* which was *"purposed in Christ Jesus our Lord."* While all of this may seem quite cryptic, it's really rather simple. The Church of believers, both Jews and Greeks, illustrate to Satan and his demons, who defied God and His plan, the fulfillment of God's perfect plan as executed by Christ in the lives of those who willingly obey Him. To understand this idea, it is necessary to examine the wise plan God carried out through His Son.

1. **Submission to Christ.** While rebellion is the very nature of Satan and his demons, the Church gives them an example of the divine principle of submission to Christ, her Lord and Saviour. The Jews were known as *"stiffnecked"* people (Deuteronomy 31:27 and Acts 7:51) while the Gentiles were pagans. It is unlikely that either would come to a Messiah who was, on one hand, Jewish and, on the other, rejected by the Jewish leaders. Only God, in His wisdom, could bring both Jew and Gentile together in submission to His Son. Only God, in His wisdom, could place the example they provided before Satan and his demons.

2. **Unity in Christ.** Satan and his demons constantly create disharmony. The Church of Christ, however, stands as an example of unity and accord, with God through His Son and with each other in the Body of Christ. The Jews had always considered all Gentiles to be unclean idolaters and would not even enter a Gentile home, while Gentiles thought Jews were strange people who had only one God and who refused to accept all of the benefits of Roman rule. Only God, in His wisdom, could bring two peoples from such diverse backgrounds together in unity through His Son. Only God, in His wisdom, could bring the Jew and the Gentile into one accord in the Body of Christ. Only God, in His wisdom, could place such a perfect example of unity before the Devil and his demons.

3. **Communion with God.** It is the avowed goal of Satan and his demons to bring a breach between God and the people He created, destroying the perfect communion He wants to have with His own. The born-again, mature children of God, His Church, illustrate the kind of communion God desires to have with His people, the kind of communion in the Holy of Holies which Paul described in Ephesians 3:12, *"In whom <u>we have boldness and access with confidence</u> by the faith of him."* Previously, Jews had so little communion with God that they didn't even recognize His Son, their Messiah, when He came. The Gentiles had no communion with God at all, preferring to commune with their idols, instead. Only God, in His wisdom, could bring both Jew and Gentile into true communion with Himself. Only God, in His wisdom, could have brought those Jews and Gentiles into communion with each other, the very communion of which John wrote in 1 John 1:7, *"But if we walk in the light, as he is in the light, <u>we have fellowship one with another</u>, and the blood of Jesus Christ his Son cleanseth us from all sin."* Only God, in His wisdom, could have established a Church which would stand as an example of that communion before the entire world and before Satan and his demons.

Clearly, the Church of Jesus Christ is meant to be a constant reminder to the devil and his demons of their sin and all that their rebellion against God cost them. The Church is also their illustration of the believers' success in Christ and all that they gain through Him. While Satan and his demons stand as an example of eternal failure, the Church stands as the symbol of eternal victory; while Satan and his demons failed miserably, the mature believers in His Church can conquer in Christ, as Paul declared in Romans 8:37, *"Nay in all these things <u>we are more than conquerors through him that loved us</u>."*

The Cost of Revelation Revealed

Such revelation in the mysteries of God had not come cheaply. Paul had already paid a high price and, within five years, he would pay with his life. Paul had suffered much persecution during his ministry which he described in 2 Corinthians 11:24 through 27:

> *Of the Jews five times received I forty stripes save one. Thrice was I beaten with rods, once was I stoned, thrice I suffered shipwreck, a night and a day I have*

been in the deep: In journeyings often, in perils of waters, in perils of robbers, in perils by mine own countrymen, in perils by heathen, in perils in the city, in perils in the wilderness, in perils in the sea, in perils among false brethren; In weariness and painfulness, in watchings often, in hunger and thirst, in fastings often, in cold and nakedness.

Paul had also experienced more than his share of physical suffering. In fact, he disclosed, in 2 Corinthians 12:7 through 10, that one particular physical problem remained with him because of the many revelations he had received in the mysteries of God:

And lest I should be exalted above measure through the abundance of the revelations, there was given to me a thorn in the flesh, the messenger of Satan to buffet me, lest I should be exalted above measure. For this thing I besought the Lord thrice, that it might depart from me. And he said unto me, My grace is sufficient for thee: for my strength is made perfect in weakness. Most gladly therefore will I rather glory in my infirmities, that the power of Christ may rest upon me. Therefore I take pleasure in infirmities, in reproaches, in necessities, in persecutions, in distresses for Christ's sake: for when I am weak, then am I strong.

The mature believer must understand that revelation in the deepest mysteries of God is going to cost something. Often, that price is very high. This must not be a cause for fainting (Ephesians 3:13) or quitting or failing to seek revelation from God. It is, rather, to be a cause for glorying, the Greek, *kauchaomai*, meaning to speak out loud or to boast. Paul's boast was not in the infirmities themselves. Notice, he did not even detail the exact nature of the infirmity. Instead, his boast was in the revelations God had given him for which he was willing to pay the price of bearing the infirmity. Specifically, Paul exulted in God's mysterious plan to bring both Jew and Gentile together into one Body of believers in Christ. No price was too high to have a part in carrying out that glorious plan.

The Gentiles to whom Paul wrote who had been included into God's provision of salvation along with the Jews, could also glory in and boast of that precious plan (Ephesians 3:13). Both Jew and Gentile could boast of God's great love for them. Both Jew and Gentile could boast that no pain, no persecution, no physical suffering had been too great a price to pay to win them, either for God's Son or for God's apostle.

The salvation of his readers was so precious to Paul that he willingly surrendered to God and to whatever He asked in order to reach them, as he avowed in Ephesians 3:14, *"For this cause I bow my knees unto the Father of our Lord Jesus Christ." "Bow the knees,"* was and is a universal idiom for one's total submission. The mystery of God, as revealed in His plan of salvation for both Jews and Gentiles, was of such overriding importance to Paul, that he dedicated his entire life to God to carry it out. Soon, he would surrender his life to that cause. The mature believer who desires the depth of revelation and the height of ministry Paul enjoyed, must count the cost (Luke 14:28 through 33) and be willing to pay the same price Paul paid. Paul counted the cost and declared his decision in Philippians 3:7 and 8, *"But what things were gain to me, those I counted loss for Christ. Yea doubtless, and I count all things but loss for the excellency of the knowledge of Christ Jesus my Lord."*

The Mystery of Love Revealed

Bowing one's knees is also the universal sign of prayer and Paul prayed for those to whom he wrote, praying to the Father of this spiritual family which included both Jews and Gentiles (Ephesians 3:15). In his prayer, Paul asked that they be granted certain blessings, but notice that Paul did not request material things for his readers, the tangible assets which so dominate the prayers of the immature in Christ. Instead, Paul asked for things of eternal value; Paul requested the benefits which God bestows on the inner man, things that cannot be purchased with man's riches but are only obtained *"according to the riches of his glory"* (Ephesians 3:16). These are the riches by which all of the believer's needs are met in Philippians 4:19, *"But my God shall supply all your need according to his riches in glory by Christ Jesus."* The believer is indeed blessed that he is not dependent on his own spiritual wealth to meet his spiritual needs; instead, he relies only on the inexhaustible spiritual riches of his God, through which all of his spiritual needs are met. Based on these riches, Paul prayed for these spiritual benefits for those to whom he wrote:

1. ***"To be strengthened with might by his Spirit in the inner man"*** (Ephesians 3:16). Strengthened, is the Greek, *krateo*, to have power, mastery, rule, or possession. The inner man, is the Greek, *esoteros*, which originally referred to the Holy of Holies, a type of the spirit of man. These terms speak of coming to a state of maturity in which God's Spirit is able to master, rule, and gain power in the inner man, one's reborn spirit. It also speaks of spiritual warfare in which the mature child of God exercises the power of God's Spirit within him to gain the victory over the enemy of his soul. This strength is received only through the work and ministry of the Holy Spirit within the spirit of the mature believer.
2. ***"That Christ may dwell in your hearts by faith"*** (Ephesians 3:17). As the Spirit of God strengthens the spirit of the mature believer, Christ takes up permanent residence in his heart, his soul. This is accomplished by faith since Christ can only truly rule and reign in the soul of man if he has, by an act of his will and a decision of his mind, chosen to believe steadfastly in Christ and to accept His saving grace.
3. ***"Rooted and grounded in love"*** (Ephesians 3:17). Rooted, is the Greek, *rhizo*, which indicates a tree which is being nourished by deep tap roots which go all the way to the source of water. Grounded, is the Greek, *themelioo*, a building term which refers to the firm foundation of the mature believer's spiritual life in God. These deep, nourishing tap roots seek the life-giving love of the Source, Christ; this firm foundation is built upon that love. It is from this position, that the mature child of God may go on--
4. ***"To know the love of Christ, which passeth knowledge"*** (Ephesians 3:18 and 19). Here is a paradox. Paul wants the mature believer to know the unknowable. Both *"know"* and *"knowledge"* are from the Greek, *ginosko*, and refer to the continuing process of accumulating knowledge. The picture drawn is similar to that of a blind man trying to discern the dimensions of an elephant. At one moment, it seems long and slender, as he examines the trunk or the tail; at another, it seems large and fat, as he touches the body; but, at still another moment, it seems round and flat, as he feels the ears. All perspectives are correct, but none is complete. The mature believer must also use all of his spiritual senses in a continuing lifelong search to comprehend anything at all of the love of Christ. Of course, he must understand that the only way to understand a subject which is beyond human understanding, is through divine revelation. First, divine revelation discloses the boundaries of the love of Christ, and the first fact uncovered about those boundaries is that there are no boundaries. The love of Christ is limitless. It's infinite. But, the human mind cannot comprehend infinity, so we're back to the beginning, trying to know the unknowable. Divine revelation also discloses that God not only has love, but He actually is love, as 1 John 4:16 assures, *"And we have known and believed the love that God hath to us. God is love; and he that dwelleth in love dwelleth in God, and God in him."* In addition, divine revelation shows that Jesus was the very Personification of His Father and, therefore, the

very Personification of His Father's love for man in everything He did on earth, as John 1:14 and 18 declares:

> *And the Word was made flesh, and dwelt among us, (and we beheld his glory, the glory as of the only begotten of the Father,) full of grace and truth....No man hath seen God at any time; the only begotten Son, which is in the bosom of the Father, he hath declared him.*

Paul prayed that his readers would receive all of these divine revelations concerning the mystery of the love of Christ for them. Then, Paul prayed that his readers would be filled to overflowing with all spiritual benefits from their Lord (Ephesians 3:19).

The Mystery of the Revealer Revealed

Paul ended his prayer for the mature believers to whom he wrote with these words, as recorded in Ephesians 3:20 and 21:

> *Now unto him that is able to do exceeding abundantly above all that we ask or think, according to the power that worketh in us, Unto him be glory in the church by Christ Jesus throughout all ages, world without end. Amen.*

It is only God who can give the mature believer a glimpse of the top of the tapestry. It is only God who can give him abundant revelation, beyond his ability to ask or even imagine, just as He revealed His mysterious plan to provide salvation for both Jews and Greeks before Peter or Paul even thought to ask about the Gentiles. This kind of divine revelation comes only by the power of the Revealer which is at work in the mature believer. That power, is the Greek, *dunamis*, the dynamite power of the King giving divine revelation to His mature children. As the mature believer comes to recognize the power and authority of God behind the divine revelations he receives, as he comes to comprehend the eternal significance of the mysteries which are disclosed to him, as he comes to know the unknowable, he, like Paul, will want to praise, worship, and glorify God, together with all of the saints, the Church, the Body of Christ, for all of the ages of eternity.

Think of it! The God of this universe takes time out of His rather busy schedule to move upon the mind of a mature believer to reveal one of His many mysteries. The God of this universe gives His mature child a glimpse of one small corner of the top of His divine tapestry.

Chapter 6
ONE BODY, MANY GIFTS

One Letter, Two Messages

In the first three chapters of Ephesians, Paul reiterated the divine truths upon which Christianity is based. He gave his readers a glorious glimpse of the top of God's tapestry, a wonderful view of the Lord's overall plan of salvation, just as God conceived it. But, as chapter four opened, Paul's emphasis changed; he began to apply the Gospel to the real lives of real people. Principles to be understood became pathways to be walked. Paul began to brief believers on the proper way to walk in this present, sinful world. The two segments of Ephesians are, however, inextricably tied by Paul's use of the word, *"therefore,"* in Ephesians 4:1, linking what went before with what comes after. Based on his knowledge of God's grace to him and His provision of salvation for all, the mature Christian will choose to walk in a way which honors God's grace and reaches out to others with the Gospel message.

One Walk

Paul identified himself as *"the prisoner of the Lord,"* since he was literally bound in a Roman prison when he wrote this letter. But, he was also bound by his love of Christ and his fellow believers. This was the bond that made Paul a prisoner of the Lord and caused him to write from his prison cell. In Ephesians 4:1, Paul asked his readers to *"walk worthy of the vocation wherewith ye are called."* That vocation is the Christian's career of coming to maturity, coming into the image of Christ, and taking the Gospel to a lost and dying world. In this brief epistle, the word, walk, appears eight times. Each time, it is used figuratively of all of the activities of one's life. It is not enough to live for Christ in church; the mature believer must live for him every day in every area of his life. If Paul could live the Christian life in jail; his readers could certainly walk for Christ free in the world. Each seasoned saint must live that life and walk that walk, too. Just as the Olympic walker uses a seemingly odd stride, the walk of the mature Christian includes certain discernable traits:

1. **Lowliness** (Ephesians 4:2). This word had originally meant low self-esteem. The New Testament writers enhanced it to mean humility and modesty, the attitude whereby one esteems himself small in comparison to his Lord.
2. **Meekness** (Ephesians 4:2). No matter what the provocation, the saint must remain gentle and even tempered. While lowliness is an attitude of heart, meekness is the outward behavior which results.
3. **Longsuffering** (Ephesians 4:2). One with this attitude of long and patient endurance before becoming angry doesn't speedily retaliate, regardless of the provocation. This longsuffering is associated with mercy, especially the mercy of God.
4. **Forbearing** (Ephesians 4:2). This patience in dealing with others, isn't always easy. Paul indicated that it can only be accomplished in love, the agape love of God working in and through the believer and governing his behavior toward others.
5. **Unity** (Ephesians 4:3). This peaceful oneness enables believers, as a group, to accomplish things for their Lord. The mature soldiers of Christ engaged in spiritual warfare

must carefully guard this bond of unity and peace and keep it intact or a breach will be created through which Satan can strike (Ecclesiastes 10:8).

Imagine a church full of such mature believers who exhibit all these characteristics! Imagine their unity! Imagine what they would be able to accomplish in Christ!

One Body

This unity will produce a Body of Christ whose members are one with each other and one with their Lord, as Paul wrote in Ephesians 4:4 through 6:

There is one body, and one Spirit, even as ye are called in one hope of your calling; One Lord, one faith, one baptism, One God and Father of all, who is above all, and through all, and in you all.

In any church, there are many people and just as many opinions. Believers often permit these differing views to divide them and build walls of misunderstanding between them. While all may be one in Christ, all are not the same. Each is different with different gifts to use and different tasks to perform. This places added responsibility on each individual since there is no other believer exactly like him, no other believer who can perform his role in exactly the same way. So, Paul called his readers to unity, to a oneness which transcends individual opinions and brings believers together with each other and with Christ. He pointed out that there are more things which unite Christians than things which divide them. Paul indicated that this ideal unity is the work of all three Members of the Trinity. As They are one in each other, so the body of believers must be one in Them.

Paul wrote of the believers' unity in the Spirit (Ephesians 4:4). It is the Holy Spirit, the same Spirit indwelling each individual believer, which brings all together into one Body, with Christ as the Head, the Brain, and believers as the Body which carries out the commands of the Brain. The Body of mature believers must work in unity with Christ or it will be handicapped and cannot long survive. It is also the Spirit of God who calls all to walk the same path leading to the same destination. While opinions vary, denominations disagree, and doctrines differ, still, all believers live with the same hope--to make Heaven their home. All are washed in the blood of the same Lamb, all worship the same Lord, and all are the servants of the same Master. He is truly their unifying Lord (Ephesians 4:4).

Since the faith of believers is generated by Him and flows from Him (Galatians 2:16), all share that same faith. While there may be many believers, there can be only one faith, the faith that originates in Jesus. While there may be many denominations, there can be only one Body, the Body unified by that faith of Christ.

There is also only one baptism. Water baptism is the common entry into Christian faith. In the early Church, once one accepted Jesus Christ as Saviour, he was baptized in water to signify the death of his old life and resurrection to his new life in Christ (Romans 6:3 and 4). Jesus had given believers His own personal example of water baptism (Matthew 3:13 through 15). Jesus also baptized those who came to Him (John 3:22) and ordered His disciples to baptize all who would come to Him in the future (Matthew 28:19), an order which His followers clearly obeyed (Acts 2:38; 8:36 through 38; 9:18; 10:47 and 48). Whether prince or pauper, whether king or commoner, all were to come into the Body by the same route; all are to receive Christ and be baptized in water, just as He had been.

Then, in Ephesians 4:6, Paul wrote of the believers' unity in God, the Father, the progenitor, protector, and nourisher of His own. He originated the plan of salvation for all (John 3:16), gives life to all, nourishes all, and protects all. He is their Father and each is His beloved child. God is above all (Ephesians 4:6), too, superior to all others and the

Sovereign God of all. Each member of the Body must submit to Him, just as Jesus was always in submission to His Father while here on earth (John 5:19; 6:38). This realization eliminates many areas of disunity and disharmony among believers which might result from the natural human quest for supremacy. God is also through all (Ephesians 4:6), the Originator of all things, the universe, the heavens and the earth and all that is in them, even man, himself. This truth shows the mature believer his own total dependence on his heavenly Father. God is also in all (Ephesians 4:6), within each believer and among the group or Body of believers. When members focus on the human nature of others, the differences bring disharmony. Mature believers, however, look for the God-nature within every member, resulting in perfect unity since the same God-nature should be shining forth from each one. Because the Trinity is in perfect unity, there can be perfect unity within the Body of Christ as members allow the Trinity to live and work in them.

Many Gifts

All members of this unified Body of Christ are gifted with the grace of God in Ephesians 4:7, *"But unto every one of us is given grace according to the measure of the gift of Christ."* Paul's writings prove that God gives His grace, His unmerited, undeserved, and unearned favor to man even before he is saved. This grace is extended to man at the moment of salvation to make the transaction (Ephesians 2:8). Yet, the grace of God doesn't stop there; God's grace continues to be poured out on the born-again believer for the rest of his life. It is God's grace which sustains him, provides for him, and guides him safely to Heaven's shores. This grace is given according to the Lord's own measure (Ephesians 4:7). While that may give the impression that the grace of God is limited, one must look at the measure the Lord uses. It's described by Jesus in Luke 6:38,

> *Give, and it shall be given unto you; good measure, pressed down, and shaken together, and running over, shall men give into your bosom. For with the same measure that ye mete withal it shall be measured to you again.*

The Lord makes certain the measure is filled to overflowing, assuring the mature child of God that he will be given all the grace he needs in any situation. This grace is measured by the gift of Christ whose identity is revealed in Luke 11:13, *"If ye then, being evil, know how to give good gifts unto your children: how much more shall your heavenly Father give the Holy Spirit to them that ask him?"* The Holy Spirit, the Gift of Christ, is at work in the life of the believer, comforting him, enlightening him, giving the grace of God to him in a measure which is all he can contain and more.

Paul had some even more interesting information to share with his readers. He began in Ephesians 3:8 through 11:

> *Wherefore he saith, When he ascended up on high, he led captivity captive, and gave gifts unto men. (Now that he ascended, what is it but that he also descended first into the lower parts of the earth? He that descended is the same also that ascended up far above all heavens, that he might fill all things.) And he gave some, apostles; and some, prophets; and some, evangelists; and some, pastors and teachers.*

The portion of this passage which appears in parentheses concerns the time when the gifts described in the remainder of the passage were dispensed among men. To understand Paul's message, it is first necessary to have some understanding of the Biblical teachings regarding death, precisely what happens to mortal man at death, and exactly what happened to Jesus at the moment of His death at Calvary.

The three parts of man's being--body, soul, and spirit--which were inextricably united during life, are instantly separated at death. Scripture is clear about what happens to each. First, the spirit of man, whether saint or sinner, goes back to God, as Ecclesiastes 12:7 explains, *"Then shall the dust return to the earth as it was: and the spirit shall return unto God who gave it."* The body of man, whether saint or sinner, decays into dust, the material from which it was first created by God, as seen in the previous verse and also in Genesis 3:19, *"For dust thou art, and unto dust thou shalt return."* But, the ultimate destination of the soul is decided by man during his life. If he followed God, his soul goes to Heaven; if he didn't, his soul is consigned to Hell. There is no other alternative. This was the primary point of the story of the rich man and Lazarus, as related by Jesus in Luke 16:19 through 26:

> *There was a certain rich man, which...fared sumptuously every day: And there was a certain beggar named Lazarus, which was laid at his gate, full of sores, And desiring to be fed with the crumbs which fell from the rich man's table....And it came to pass, that the beggar died, and was carried by the angels into Abraham's bosom: the rich man also died, and was buried: and in hell he lift up his eyes, being in torments, and seeth Abraham afar off, and Lazarus in his bosom. And he cried and said, Father Abraham, have mercy on me, and send Lazarus, that he may dip the tip of his finger in water and cool my tongue; for I am tormented in this flame. But Abraham said, Son, remember that thou in thy lifetime receivedst thy good things, and likewise Lazarus evil things: but now he is comforted and thou art tormented. And beside this, between us and you there is a great gulf fixed: so that they which would pass from hence to you cannot: neither can they pass to us, that would come from thence.*

Prior to the death of Jesus, the souls of the righteous dead went to an area of Hell or the grave reserved for them where they did not experience the torments suffered by the unrighteous dead in the other part of Hell. In the story of the rich man and Lazarus, we learn that these two areas of the grave were separated by a large and impenetrable gulf.

In the parenthetical passage found within Ephesians 4:8 through 11, Paul illuminated events that occurred immediately after the death of Christ. At the moment of His death, Jesus experienced the same separation of body, soul, and spirit common to all men. His spirit returned to God who had given it, His body was placed in a borrowed grave, and His soul went to the area of Hell reserved for the righteous dead. But, God, through David, had left this promise for His anointed Messiah in Psalm 16:10, *"For thou wilt not leave my soul in hell; neither wilt thou suffer thine Holy One to see corruption."* When Jesus died and His soul went into Hell, He did not come as captive; He came as Conqueror. When He arrived, He immediately took permanent possession of the keys of death and of hell, as John explained in Revelation 1:18, *"I am he that liveth, and was dead; and, behold, I am alive for evermore. Amen; and have the keys of hell and of death."* With these keys, Christ freed from Hell the captive righteous dead of all the previous ages, took them with Him, and left to keep an appointment He had made with a dying thief, as recorded in Luke 23:43, *"And Jesus said unto him, Verily I say unto thee, To day shalt thou be with me in paradise,"* the garden of God. Since the Lord's death, the souls of all righteous dead have immediately gone to be with Him in Paradise where their souls rest from their earthly labors. Their bodies lie in the grave awaiting the bodily resurrection that will take place at the second coming of Christ when the glorified bodies of the dead in Christ will be resurrected, as Paul described in 1 Corinthians 15:51 through 55:

Behold, I shew you a mystery; We shall not all sleep, but we shall all be changed, In a moment, in the twinkling of an eye, at the last trump: for the trumpet shall sound, and the dead shall be raised incorruptible, and we shall be changed. For this corruptible must put on incorruption, and this mortal must put on immortality. So when this corruptible shall have put on incorruption, and this mortal shall have put on immortality, then shall be brought to pass the saying that is written, Death is swallowed up in victory. O death, where is thy sting? O grave, where is thy victory?

Those believers who are still alive at that time will join the resurrected saints in the air, according to Paul's description in 1 Thessalonians 4:13 through 17:

But I would not have you to be ignorant, brethren, concerning them which are asleep, that ye sorrow not, even as others which have no hope. For if we believe that Jesus died and rose again, even so them also which sleep in Jesus will God bring with him. For this we say unto you by the word of the Lord, that we which are alive and remain unto the coming of the Lord shall not prevent them which are asleep. For the Lord himself shall descend from heaven with a shout, with the voice of the archangel, and with the trump of God: and the dead in Christ shall rise first: Then we which are alive and remain shall be caught up together with them in the clouds, to meet the Lord in the air; and so shall we ever be with the Lord.

Since the day Jesus died, certain gifts have been available to the Body of Christ, the Church of the Redeemed. This becomes even more clear, once the parenthesis in this passage has been understood and, for the moment, set aside so that the remainder of the passage may be considered. Anyone taught the principles of English grammar, recalls that a phrase placed within parentheses gives additional information but is not necessary to an accurate understanding of the sentence or paragraph. If one temporarily sets aside the parenthetical phrase contained in Ephesians 4:8 through 11, it would read:

Wherefore he saith, When he ascended up on high, he led captivity captive, and gave gifts unto men....And he gave some, apostles; and some, prophets; and some, evangelists; and some, pastors and teachers.

The particular gifts to which Paul referred are the ministry positions which provide the authority structure of the Church, the Body of Christ, in His absence. Before His death, Jesus, Himself, had performed these functions. Since after His death, He would no longer be physically present, He established a new authority structure, composed of five offices, to govern the affairs of His Church. These positions, His gift to bring order to His Church and often described as the Five-Fold Ministry, are:

1. **Apostle.** The apostle is the ambassador of the Lord, sent to do the foundational work of the Church, to teach foundational truths of God through revelation, knowledge, doctrine, and prophecy, etc. The office of apostle is the highest ranking one in the Body of Christ, as indicated by Paul, an apostle, in 1 Corinthians 12:28, *"And God hath set some in the church, first apostles, secondarily prophets, thirdly teachers, after that miracles, then gifts of healings, helps, governments, diversities of tongues."* Each of the other offices is inherent in the office of the apostle and he has the ability and authority to fill each of these offices if necessary, just as Paul often did. While he described himself as an apostle of Christ (Romans 1:1, etc.), he also often acted as prophet, evangelist, pastor, and teacher. The apostle has God-given authority over all other offices in the Body.

2. **Prophet.** The prophet is the second highest officer in the Body of Christ. He is commissioned by Christ as the messenger of God to His people and is anointed by the Holy Spirit through the Gift of Prophecy. While many think of a prophet as foretelling the future, he's more concerned with forthtelling--preaching, exhorting, delivering a message in tongues or bringing the interpretation, as well as conveying messages in the language of the people present. The prophet of God is not necessarily concerned with forecasting future events--although that, too, may be a valid part of his ministry.

3. **Evangelist.** The office of the evangelist differs from that of prophet in that the message delivered by the prophet is specific and current and comes directly from the Lord while the evangelist delivers the common and constant message of salvation as revealed in all of its glory in Scripture. The modern concept of an evangelist is one who visits the church to preach to lukewarm saints, but this is not consistent with his job description. It is the task of the evangelist, not to preach to the converted, but to reach sinners with the Gospel of Jesus Christ and to lead them to salvation. For this reason, the evangelist is primarily engaged in a mobile ministry, taking the Gospel wherever the unsaved may be. He may be called an evangelist, a missionary, etc., and, in conjunction with his message, he ministers the miracles of God to authenticate his teaching and preaching, just as Jesus did.

4. **Pastor.** The pastor is the shepherd whose task is to feed and care for God's sheep. This was the ministry to which Peter was called (John 21:15 through 17). The pastor is meant to be a mid-level officer in the Church. He is in authority over the deacons, but under the authority of the apostle or prophet. The office was never meant to be the high level position of total authority it has become in many modern churches. Pastors must serve, rather than to be served, and minister to others, rather than allow others to minister to them, as Jesus directed in Mark 10:42 through 45:

> *But Jesus...saith unto them, Ye know that they which are accounted to rule over the Gentiles exercise lordship over them; and their great ones exercise authority upon them. But so shall it not be among you: but whosoever will be great among you, shall be your minister: and whosoever of you will be the chiefest, shall be servant of all. For even the Son of man came not to be ministered unto, but to minister, and to give his life a ransom for many.*

5. **Teacher.** In the original Greek, this office is linked with that of pastor and, indeed, the pastor, as a part of his shepherding function, is expected to feed the flock on the good Word of God through his teaching.

Of course, there is much overlapping in the ministry offices. All lower offices are resident in the higher offices. An apostle may also function as a prophet, an evangelist, a pastor, and/or a teacher. Also, the office of teacher is inherent in each of the other offices, or may simply be the God-given gift and ministry of one who occupies no office at all. These ministry office gifts are given by God to the Body of Christ for very definite purposes, as outlined in Ephesians 4:12 through 14:

> *For the perfecting of the saints, for the work of the ministry, for the edifying of the body of Christ: Till we all come in the unity of the faith, and of the knowledge of the Son of God, unto a perfect man, unto the measure of the stature of Christ.*

Clearly, the ministry offices were placed in the Church by the Lord to perform several tasks. First, the officers are to perfect the saints (Ephesians 4:12), helping them to come to full maturity. Therefore, one of the goals of those occupying these offices must be to prepare the saints--the set-apart, separated, and sanctified ones--to be perfect, mature men and women of God. But, the saints must never be made dependent on their ministers; rather, they must come to maturity, capable of living stable Christian lives and entering into the ministry the Lord has prepared for them, dependent on Christ, alone. Ministers must edify (Ephesians 4:12) or build up and strengthen each member of the Body until he is able to stand alone against anything, a strong fortress of God. The minister of God must seek the unity of the Body in the faith, too, (Ephesians 4:13), the oneness that enables the Body to work together to accomplish God's will. It is particularly important that the Body be unified in the faith, in its beliefs, in its doctrine, to present a united front against Satan and the temptations he brings. Therefore, ministry officers must lead all members of the Church into clear truth, based solely on Scripture, so that doctrinal disharmony is avoided and the unity of the Body in the faith is preserved. The minister must also bring all into the full knowledge of Christ. Since this begins with a personal relationship with Jesus, God's ministers should lead each member of the Body into this relationship. To nurture them and increase their knowledge, requires the systematic teaching and preaching of Scripture. It was the prophet, Isaiah, who instructed ministers in the proper method for imparting knowledge to the mature saints of God. In Isaiah 28:9 and 10, he wrote:

> *Whom shall he teach knowledge? and whom shall he make to understand doctrine? them that are weaned from the milk, and drawn from the breasts. For precept must be upon precept, precept upon precept; line upon line, line upon line; here a little, and there a little.*

Paul left a standard for evaluating the maturity of members--Jesus, Himself, as Paul wrote in Romans 8:29, *"For whom he did foreknow, he also did predestinate to be conformed to the image of his Son, that he might be the firstborn among many brethren."* Each saint is measured against His spiritual stature and evaluated according to the fullness of His spiritual perfection (Ephesians 4:13). As the believer comes into the image and reflection of Christ, he comes to full spiritual maturity and attains complete spiritual perfection. The ultimate goal of all ministers, whatever office they occupy, should be to put themselves out of business! They should work to bring each believer to such a degree of maturity and excellence that each can stand alone. When the Lord returns to claim His own, the Church will have achieved her perfection, the saints will have come to maturity, and the work of all ministry officers will be completed for all time. The proper functioning of these five offices will have specific results within the Church, as listed in Ephesians 4:14 and 15:

> *That we henceforth be no more children, tossed to and fro, and carried about with every wind of doctrine, by the sleight of men, and the cunning craftiness, whereby they lie in wait to deceive; But speaking the truth in love, may grow up into him in all things, which is the head, even Christ.*

Again, the primary goal of ministry is the maturity of believers. Using the words, *"tossed to and fro, and carried about with every wind of doctrine"* (Ephesians 4:14), Paul painted the picture of a ship without anchor or rudder on a stormy sea. This, too, aptly describes the immature child of God, at the mercy of the cruel sea of confusion, in the grip of the destructive winds of deception. While all newborn babes in Christ may be spiritual children who are dependent on others, the true minister of the Lord won't perpetuate their babyhood. Through teaching and preaching, counseling and exhorting, he will do all he can to bring young saints to maturity in their Lord. As mature believers, they will be anchored in Christ, sheltered by the Rock that no storm can shake. The Word of God will be their rudder, safely guiding them through the hurricanes of heresy on every side.

These deceptions and heresies have two sources. The first is *"the sleight of men"* (Ephesians 4:14), a term which originally meant manipulating dice and came to mean entrapment by deceit or trickery, like a dishonest gambling game where the naive are cheated out of their cash. The immature in the Body of Christ are easy prey for the deceptions of false teachers who are, all too often, like the dishonest gambler, only in it for the money. If the ministry officers are doing their work well, the members in their care will be able to rightly divide the Word of truth and avoid these false teachers and their heretical doctrines. The second source is identified as, *"cunning craftiness"* (Ephesians 4:14). This is the same Greek word translated, *"wiles,"* in Ephesians 6:11, referring to the work of Satan. He will stop at nothing to deceive the believer. Unfortunately, the immature child of God is all too easily fooled by his wiles. If the God-appointed ministers are executing their offices faithfully, they will teach believers to recognize Satan's many devices and avoid the pitfalls he seeks to place before them. Both the false teacher and the Devil are seen lying *"in wait to deceive"* (Ephesians 4:14), or ambush from hiding. Their goal is to attack in a weakened or unguarded area where the immature child of God is particularly vulnerable. If, however, the ministry officers are performing their appointed tasks, they will, by their words and the personal example of their lives, show the young Christian how to walk the straight and narrow road safely, avoiding every ambush of the enemies of his soul.

One ambush often used successfully by Satan is the temptation to criticize others in the Body of Christ. The hostility produced can destroy, not only the life of the immature believer who falls prey to the temptation, but also the reputation of the one against whom he brings reproach. To avoid this snare, Paul advised, *"speaking the truth in love"* (Ephesians 4:15). To do it, one must express what is true, untainted by his personal prejudices, and he must do it in the agape love of God, the sacrificial love of God for man. This phrase has often been used as license to verbally abuse a brother or sister in the Lord. Anything may be said, no matter how hurtful, so long as it is true. It seems obvious that Paul, who was writing about unity and maturity, had no such thing in mind. The truth of which he wrote was undoubtedly the glorious truth of the Gospel, ministered by God's appointed officers in His agape love. As that truth goes forth in power, the Holy Spirit may be trusted to reveal and deal with whatever faults and foibles others may harbor. Rather than criticizing their failures or gossiping about their faults, the mature child of God will minister the true message of the Gospel in love to all in the Body of Christ. It is through this truth, this love, this ministry of the Holy Spirit that each member may come to maturity with every other member to form a well-functioning Body which exhibits the image and likeness of Christ and perfectly performs the will of its Head, Christ (Ephesians 4:15 and 16). This will produce a Body which fits the description given by Paul in Ephesians 4:16:

> *From whom the whole body fitly joined together and compacted by that which every joint supplieth, according to the effectual working in the measure of every part, maketh increase of the body unto the edifying of itself in love.*

The words so carefully chosen by Paul draw a perfect picture. For example, fitly joined together indicates pieces that are formed to fit with other pieces to join so closely together that nothing can come between them. Paul saw a Body composed of individual mature believers who fit together in such perfect unity, that they seem to move as one at the direction of their Lord. Compacted means knit together and the idea is one of unity, of coming together as though knitted from a single skein of yarn. This compacting occurs when every joint, every member, supplies everything possible to every other member of the Body (Ephesians 4:16), producing a Body which is strong and secure. Here is the agape love of God in action, as each member places the needs of all other members ahead of his own. Then, the Body will work together effectively. *"Effectual working,"* is the Greek, *energeia*, and one need not be a Greek scholar to know that this word means, energy at work. Of course, the energizing Force of the Body of Christ, its very heartbeat, is the Holy Spirit. As His Fruit transform the life of each believer, as His Gifts are exercised in full measure to meet the needs of every other believer, the entire Body will be blessed and come to full maturity in Christ. The proof of that maturity may be found in the final phrase of Ephesians 4:16, *"increase of the body unto the edifying of itself in love."* Such a perfect Body of Christ would be able to edify itself, to build and strengthen itself. And, all that is done would be motivated by the agape love of God, as each sacrifices himself for all others. Such a Body, each member energized by and operating in the sacrificial love of God, will continue to grow in geometric progression and will continue to strengthen.

One Standard

The standard of measurement given by Paul may be used to evaluate any church as a part of the Body of Christ. Are the ministry officers fulfilling their assigned functions? Does the Body operate in unity? Is the Body achieving the expected results in spiritual growth and maturity under the leadership of the ministry officers? Are all involved developing day by day into the image and likeness of Christ? A tree is, after all, known by its fruit (Matthew 12:33). So is a church. So is each believer. Paul explained his concept of Body ministry in even greater detail in 1 Corinthians 12:12 through 27:

> *For as the body is one, and hath many members, and all the members of that one body, being many, are one body: so also is Christ. For by one Spirit are we baptized into one body, whether we be Jews or Gentiles, whether we be bond or free; and have been all made to drink into one Spirit. For the body is not one member, but many. If the foot shall say, Because I am not the hand, I am not of the body; is it therefore not of the body? And if the ear shall say, Because I am not the eye, I am not of the body; is it therefore not of the body? If the whole body were an eye, where were the hearing? If the whole were hearing, where were the smelling? But now hath God set the members every one of them in the body, as it hath pleased him. And if they were all one member, where were the body? But now are they many members, yet but one body. And the eye cannot say unto the hand, I have no need of thee: nor again the head to the feet, I have no need of you. Nay, much more those members of the body, which seem to be more feeble, are necessary: And those members of the body, which we think to be less honourable, upon these we bestow more abundant honour; and our uncomely parts have more abundant comeliness. For our comely parts have no need: but God hath tempered the body together, having given more abundant honour to that part which lacked: That there should be no schism in the body; but that the members should have the same care one for another. And whether one member suffer, all members suffer with it; or one member be honoured, all the members rejoice with it. Now ye are the body of Christ, and members in particular.*

This Body, as described by Paul, is the virgin Bride, untainted by spot or wrinkle, for whom Christ will soon return. Being a functioning part of that Body, fully prepared for the Lord's coming, means coming to maturity in Christ.

Chapter 7
NOTHING TO GO BACK TO

The Old Life

The born-again Christian is not the only one who walks through the activities of this life; there is also a road which sinners walk, as Jesus described in Matthew 7:13 and 14:

> *Enter ye in at the strait gate: for wide is the gate, and broad is the way, that leadeth to destruction, and many there be which go in thereat: Because strait is the gate, and narrow is the way, which leadeth unto life, and few there be that find it.*

There are only two roads. Each day, each mortal must decide which of them he will take. The broad road looks good, is easy to find, and offers the companionship of many fellow-travelers, but it's the main thoroughfare of Satan's kingdom and always leads to destruction (Proverbs 14:12; 16:25). The narrow road may not look nearly as inviting, is hard to find and even harder to walk, and is often a lonely path, but it's the main street of God's kingdom and leads directly to gates of pearl and streets of gold. There's no middle road, no compromise. One travels God's highway of holiness (Isaiah 35:8) which leads to life everlasting (Revelation 22:2), or he is automatically on Satan's road (Matthew 12:30) and is on his way to spiritual death. In Ephesians 4:17, Paul advised his readers to avoid the road of sin walked by the Gentiles, typical of sinners of all nationalities. Then, in Ephesians 4:17 through 19, Paul listed some of the characteristics of the sinner's life, the old life of those to whom he wrote, the life of all who walk the wide path:

1. **Vanity of mind.** In their foolishness, sinners think they and their lifestyles are just fine, thank you. But, in Ephesians 4:1 and 2, Paul had advised his readers to, *"Walk...with all lowliness."* Then, in Romans 12:3, Paul explained this Christian humility this way:

> *For I say through the grace given unto me, to every man that is among you, not to think of himself more highly than he ought to think; but to think soberly, according as God hath dealt to every man the measure of faith.*

The believer is to evaluate himself soberly and honestly, measuring himself against the example of Jesus Christ and against the objective standard of Scripture. When viewed according to those criteria, true and heartfelt humility is bound to be the result.

2. **Understanding darkened.** These words describe a mind that the light of the truth of God has not penetrated, a mind that doesn't know the difference between right and wrong, moral and immoral. In addition, like the immature, the sinner whose understanding is darkened is unable to think ahead to the logical consequences of his wrong actions.

3. **Alienated from the life of God through ignorance because of blindness.** Here, we see one doesn't know because he doesn't want to know. He isn't born-again and he's estranged from God's family because he has chosen to refuse to permit the beautiful light of the Gospel to penetrate his soul. In 2 Corinthians 4:4, Paul described such sinners, *"In whom the god of this world hath blinded the minds of them which believe not, lest the light of the glorious gospel of Christ...should shine unto them."* They are also seen in John 3:19 and 20, *"Men loved darkness rather than light, because their deeds were evil. For every one that doeth evil hateth the light, neither cometh to the light, lest his deeds should be reproved."* But, the mature believer continually seeks the light of God. He wants all of the knowledge of

God he can find and is rewarded with greater and greater understanding of spiritual matters. He's no longer blind, he's a member of the family of God, and has everlasting life in Christ. John described him in John 3:21, *"But he that doeth truth cometh to the light, that his deeds may be made manifest, that they are wrought in God."*

4. **Past feeling.** Some sinners no longer sense the pain they are inflicting on themselves or others as a result of their activities. They are hardened, callous, insensible to the destruction they are causing. Paul told Timothy about them in 2 Timothy 4:2, *"Speaking lies in hypocrisy; having their conscience seared with a hot iron."* As the believer comes to maturity, he is increasingly aware of the terrible penalty of sin, both in this world and in the one to come, and perceives the awful consequences of sin in the lives of those around him. He becomes more and more sensitive to others and their need of salvation.

5. **Given over to lasciviousness.** While this may not be a word which comes up often in general conversation, it happens all the time. It describes anything one does to excess, but is used particularly of immoral sexual activity. Having chosen to walk Satan's road and reject the light of Jesus Christ, sinners have given themselves over, in effect, granted Satan a power of attorney he uses to lead them into all forms of sinful excesses and unrestrained behavior to which they give themselves completely. But, the mature saint practices self-control, self-restraint, and, when necessary, self-denial. He heeds the advice of Paul recorded in Philippians 4:5, *"Let your moderation be known unto all men."*

6. **Work all uncleanness with greediness.** These words paint the picture of a sinner caught in the trap of materialism, the so-called "workaholic" who willingly surrenders all of his ethical and moral standards in the pursuit of riches. We also see the image of the hedonist who "works" at finding more and more pleasure and is willing to engage in more and more sin to find it. He, like the materialist, finds that he is never satisfied with the "high" he reaches and is driven to greater excesses in his search for excitement.

If one didn't know Paul wrote this passage in the first century about first century sins, one might think it was written about life in our own times. Truly, there is no new thing under the sun (Ecclesiastes 1:9), and the Bible is proven to be timely truth to all generations. Having met Christ, the mature child of God realizes that there is nothing worth returning to, nothing worth jeopardizing one's relationship with God, nothing worth relinquishing one's home in Heaven. There is, indeed, nothing to go back to.

Putting Off the Old Life

The lifestyle previously described is not that of the mature child of God (Ephesians 4:20). He is now engaged in a lifelong process of making changes in his life. To do it (Ephesians 4:21), he must first hear. But, it's not enough just to hear; he must also obey what he hears from the Lord. Then, he must be taught. God wants His people to know "The truth, the whole truth, and nothing but the truth," so He systematically teaches them new facts about Himself, new perspectives, new principles, new precepts. Finally, he must learn that truth. As much as the Lord is determined that His children know the whole truth about Him, His mature children must be determined to learn it. It is the responsibility of the divine Teacher to teach; it is the responsibility of His mature saints to learn. Of course, hearing, being taught, and learning are all voluntary actions. The believer is never compelled, constrained, or coerced. He must voluntarily give himself to the process of hearing, being taught, and learning. Among other lessons, the maturing child of God needs to learn the things he must put off and those he must put on, as Paul explained in Ephesians 4:22 through 24:

That ye put off concerning the former conversation the old man, which is corrupt according to the deceitful lusts: And be renewed in the spirit of your mind; And that ye put on the new man, which after God is created in righteousness and true holiness.

The word picture is that of taking off clothes, piece by piece, to put on other clothes, piece by piece. As the believer walks down God's highway of holiness, as he learns more about his Lord and about His standard of perfection, he will remove aspects of the old life and the old lusts, just as though they were soiled garments fit only for discard. As he does, he also puts on the garments of God's righteousness and holiness, the white robes of the saint. In this continuing process, the maturing child of God is transformed from an old man into a new man, as in Romans 6:6, "*Knowing this, that our old man is crucified with him, that the body of sin might be destroyed, that henceforth we should not serve sin.*" One can almost visualize the straight and narrow road, lined with rows of crosses upon which travelers may place aspects of the old nature as though they were tossing old garments onto a rack. Paul gave more information about this process in Colossians 3:5 through 9:

Mortify therefore your members which are upon the earth; fornication, uncleanness, inordinate affection, evil concupiscence, and covetousness, which is idolatry: For which things' sake the wrath of God cometh on the children of disobedience: In the which ye also walked some time, when ye lived in them. But now ye also put off all these: anger, wrath, malice, blasphemy, filthy communication out of your mouth. Lie not one to another, seeing that ye have put off the old man with his deeds.

In 1 Corinthians 6:9 and 10, Paul added to the list of the old man's clothes of sin which must be put off:

Know ye not that the unrighteous shall not inherit the kingdom of God? Be not deceived: neither fornicators, nor idolaters, nor adulterers, nor effeminate, nor abusers of themselves with mankind, Nor thieves, nor covetous, nor drunkards, nor revilers, nor extortioners, shall inherit the kingdom of God.

And, in Galatians 5:19 through 21, Paul added even more to his complete description of the garments of unrighteousness which must be removed and replaced:

Now the works of the flesh are manifest, which are these; Adultery, fornication, uncleanness, lasciviousness, Idolatry, witchcraft, hatred, variance, emulations, wrath, strife, seditions, heresies, Envyings, murders, drunkenness, revellings, and such like: of the which I tell you before, as I have also told you in time past, that they which do such things shall not inherit the kingdom of God.

This process takes time and commitment. It doesn't happen instantly. In fact, it will probably take a lifetime to complete. It's also voluntary. But, the mature believer will want to remove all unrighteousness, all that is displeasing to his Lord; he'll want to put on holiness, instead. Jesus simply makes the new robes available to every one of His saints.

Putting On the New Life

As the transformation proceeds, the believer will find that his mind is also undergoing a transformation. Old ideas are rejected as new ideas replace them. The maturing Christian finds the Lord is replacing his old will with a new one. Then, in exchange for that old, sinful nature, the child of God becomes new (Ephesians 4:24). As the growing believer walks God's road, the corrupt is removed and replaced by that which is new, different, and better. The concept is that of a systematic and progressive change of garments until the wearer is clothed from head to toe in an entirely new suit. In Colossians 3:10 through 14, Paul listed some of the new garments one will want to put on:

And have put on the new man, which is renewed in knowledge after the image of him that created him: Where there is neither Greek nor Jew, circumcision nor uncircumcision, Barbarian, Scythian, bond nor free: but Christ is all, and in all. Put on therefore, as the elect of God, holy and beloved, bowels of mercies, kindness, humbleness of mind, meekness, longsuffering; Forbearing one another, and forgiving one another, if any man have a quarrel against any: even as Christ forgave you, so also do ye. And above all these things put on charity, which is the bond of perfectness.

A similar list of the latest Designer fashions for the mature saint appears in Ephesians 4:25 through 32:

Wherefore putting away lying, speak every man truth with his neighbour: for we are members one of another. Be ye angry, and sin not: let not the sun go down upon your wrath: Neither give place to the devil. Let him that stole steal no more: but rather let him labour, working with his hands the thing which is good, that he may have to give to him that needeth. Let no corrupt communication proceed out of your mouth, but that which is good to the use of edifying, that it may minister grace unto the hearers. And grieve not the Holy Spirit of God, whereby ye are sealed unto the day of redemption. Let all bitterness, and wrath, and anger, and clamour, and evil speaking, be put away from you, with all malice: And be ye kind one to another, tenderhearted, forgiving one another, even as God for Christ's sake hath forgiven you.

A closer examination of this passage reveals a great deal about the fashion statement Paul advised for the really "in" child of God:

1. **Put off lying and put on truth.** Notice that this garment of truth is to be seen by neighbors and other members of the Body of Christ (Ephesians 4:25). For the mature believer, the standard of behavior is to be the same, whether in the world or in the church.

2. **Put off sin and put on the righteous anger which does not yield to Satan.** Paul was stirring his readers to righteous anger against the temptations of Satan and against their own tendency to yield to them (Ephesians 4:27). But, Paul cautioned that this anger is not to be permitted to continue past sunset (Ephesians 4:26), so one does not become overly self-critical. Putting on this garment of righteous anger against Satan and all of his temptations will enable the mature believer to put off every garment of sin.

3. **Put off stealing and put on honest labor.** This grimy garment of compulsive stealing must be laid aside and replaced by honest manual labor (Ephesians 4:28). Paul, himself, wore well the garment of honest labor and set the example before maturing saints in his young churches. Rather than deplete their meager resources, Paul often supported himself and those who traveled with him by his trade as a tentmaker (Acts 18:3; 20:34; 1 Corinthians 4:12; 1 Thessalonians 2:9; and 2 Thessalonians 3:8).

4. **Put off corrupt communication and put on edifying speech.** The mature child of God must take off the filthy garment of profane or obscene speech so often worn by the world, and exchange it for speech that edifies, builds up, and strengthens (Ephesians 4:29). This verse has often been taken to an extreme to include general conversation and innocent jokes. This isn't what Paul had in mind, nor does he indicate that every word spoken must be about spiritual matters. One's brothers and sisters in Christ also need the gifts of friendship, sharing, and humor to lighten the burdens of their lives. They edify, too.

5. **Put off grieving the Holy Spirit and put on His seal.** There are many ways one might grieve the Holy Spirit. One might lie to Him (Acts 5:3), tempt Him (Acts 5:9), resist Him (Acts 7:51), do Him despite (Hebrews 10:29), quench Him (1 Thessalonians 5:19), and blaspheme Him (Matthew 12:31 and 32 and Mark 3:28 and 29). The mature child of God will want to put off all such garments and put on His precious seal (Ephesians 4:30), so that he is uniquely marked as being owned and operated by Jesus Christ, protected from the trespasser, and safeguarded until he is delivered to Heaven.

6. **Putting off negative emotions and putting on positive ones.** In Ephesians 4:31, Paul left a long list of negative emotions which have no place in the life of the mature saint, and which must, one by one, be put off like tattered rags. Then, in Ephesians 4:32, he listed the positive emotions which are to be put on in their place. These positive character traits are the Christlike clothing of every mature believer. Putting on new clothes, like taking off the old ones, does not happen in an instant; it's a lifelong process. And, it is always voluntary. The mature believer, however, will be anxious to remove the old garments of sin and grateful to receive his new robes of righteousness.

The final phrase of Ephesians 4:32 is an important one. There, Paul wrote, *"even as God for Christ's sake hath forgiven you,"* presenting God as the perfect Example to the mature believer. God had every right to wear the garments in Ephesians 4:31 as the robes of the angry Judge of sinful man, but, in honor of the sacrifice of His Son, He chose instead to wear the garments listed in Ephesians 4:32 as man's kind and loving Forgiver.

To be in style on the straight and narrow road, then, these are the fashions for the travelers on God's highway of holiness, and the Lord makes them available to each pilgrim on the path. All he must do is remove his old, soiled clothing of sin so that he can put on the new garments of righteousness his God has for him. In describing this change, Paul penned the words in 1 Corinthians 5:17, *"Therefore if any man be in Christ, he is a new creature: old things are passed away; behold, all things are become new."*

The mature child of God will realize that there is nothing in the old life worth returning to, nothing in his old wardrobe fit to wear to the Marriage Supper of the Lamb. He is living a new life, walking a new road which will end at the palace of the King, and he'll arrive just in time for the wedding. To prepare, as he walks that path, he is continually taking off his old garments of sin and shame, dropping them along the side of the road, and putting on the new garments of righteousness and holiness Christ offers. Then, he will arrive at his destination wearing the proper wedding garments so that he can instantly be ushered into the Bridegroom's presence. Jesus made clear the vital importance of this change of garments in Matthew 22:1, 2, and 8 through 14:

> *And Jesus answered and spake unto them again by parables, and said, The kingdom of heaven is like unto a certain king, which made a marriage for his son....Then saith he to his servants, The wedding is ready, but they which were bidden were not worthy. Go ye therefore into the highways, and as many as ye shall find, bid to the marriage. So those servants went out into the highways, and gathered together all as many as they found, both bad and good: and the wedding was furnished with guests. And when the king came in to see the guests, he saw there a man which had not on a wedding garment: And he saith unto him, Friend, how camest thou in hither not having a wedding garment? And he was speechless. Then said the king to the servants, Bind him hand and foot, and take him away, and cast him into outer darkness; there shall be weeping and gnashing of teeth. For many are called but few are chosen.*

Chapter 8
WALKING IN LOVE

The Way to Walk

To the newborn babes in Christ in Corinth, Paul, in 1 Corinthians 11:1, gave this instruction, *"Be ye followers of me, even as I also am of Christ."* When one first comes to Christ, he must learn to recognize the voice, the will, and the move of God. This takes time, time for prayer, for Bible study, for growth. During that time, the young Christian tends to follow the godly example of an older and more mature Christian. Paul recognized this and encouraged the young Christians of Corinth to follow him as their example, only so long as he faithfully followed Christ. But, Paul had a different message for the mature believers to whom he wrote Ephesians. In Ephesians 5:1, he wrote, *"Be ye therefore followers of God, as dear children."* In the life of every maturing believer, the time must come when he has heard God's voice, understood God's will for his life, and come to recognize the move of God in himself, the Church, and the world. At that point, the mature child of God must take his eyes off of men--the pastor, the deacon, the Sunday School teacher--and follow God, alone. In both passages, followers, is the Greek, *mimetes*, and means to mimic or imitate. The mature child of God must no longer imitate men, but imitate God, His nature and His attributes, just as any child might imitate the characteristics of his beloved father to the best of his childlike ability. Of the mature Christian, it should be able to be said, "Like Father, like son (or daughter)."

The fifth chapter of Ephesians begins with a *"therefore."* It's a general rule of thumb that, whenever there is a therefore, one should find out what the therefore is there for. (The grammar may not be the best, but it gets the message across.) In any event, Paul had been writing about the believer's walk on the straight and narrow road, a walk where the maturing child of God is continually taking off the old man of sin and putting on the new man of holiness. To help his readers accomplish the change, Paul placed a mirror before them--Jehovah God, Himself. In essence, Paul was saying this: As you walk along the narrow road, putting off the unclean garments and putting on your robes of righteousness, your ultimate goal is to look, not like any man, but just like God.

In Ephesians 5:1, dear, means one loved with the sacrificial, agape love of God. This agape love motivates the walk of the believer, sustains him along the way, enables him to make the necessary changes in his spiritual attire, and guides him safely to his goal. In a definite play on words, Paul went on to say that, because of that sacrificial agape love God showers on the mature saint, he must walk in the same sacrificial agape love of God toward others (Ephesians 5:2). In this way, he imitates his heavenly Father; he also imitates Christ and conforms to the example He set when He made the ultimate sacrifice of agape love for all (Hebrews 9:28 and 10:12). To do it, the mature saint must love Christ and others with agape love, give himself for them, make the personal sacrifices necessary to do God's will, and offer his life as a sweetsmelling savor, like incense, before the throne of God.

To better understand the maturity needed to reach the standard of love the Lord requires, it's necessary to eavesdrop on a conversation between Peter and Jesus which contrasted the agape love of God with the phileos love, or friendship, of the natural man. That conversation is found in John 21:15 through 17:

Jesus saith to Simon Peter, Simon, son of Jonas, lovest (agape) *thou me more than these? He saith unto him, Yea, Lord; thou knowest that I love* (phileos) *thee. He saith unto him, Feed my lambs. He saith to him the second time, Simon, son of Jonas, lovest* (agape) *thou me? He saith unto him, Yea, Lord; thou knowest that I love* (phileos) *thee. He saith unto him, Feed my sheep. He saith unto him the third time, Simon, son of Jonas, lovest* (phileos) *thou me? Peter was grieved because he said unto him the third time, Lovest* (phileos) *thou me? And he said unto him, Lord, thou knowest all things; thou knowest that I love (phileos) thee. Jesus saith unto him, Feed my sheep.*

Twice, Jesus asked Peter for agape love, the sacrificial love of God, but Peter was unable to give it. The best he could offer at his level of maturity was phileos, friendship. Jesus understood. When He asked the third time, Jesus accepted friendship as the best Peter could give. This saddened Peter, but he knew he couldn't lie or try to embellish his feelings before Jesus, who knew all things. So, it was out of friendship that Peter first began to work for his Lord and to pastor His sheep. But, by the time Peter wrote his first letter to the Christians of Asia Minor, some thirty years later, he had matured much in Christ. He had learned a deeper, higher kind of love, the sacrificial agape love for which Jesus had asked him so long before. In 1 Peter 1:8, the same Peter wrote these words, *"Whom having not seen, ye love* (agape)*; in whom, though now ye see him not, yet believing, ye rejoice with joy unspeakable and full of glory."*

The Way Not to Walk

This was the same standard of love in which Paul was calling his readers to walk, as though carefully stepping through a minefield. To do it, to imitate the love of God and His Son and to extend that love to others, there were certain attitudes and activities, old habits and sins, which had to be forsaken forever. They're listed in Ephesians 5:3 through 5:

But fornication, and all uncleanness, or covetousness, let it not be once named among you, as becometh saints; Neither filthiness, nor foolish talking, nor jesting, which are not convenient: but rather giving of thanks. For this ye know, that no whoremonger, nor unclean person, nor covetous man, who is an idolater, hath any inheritance in the kingdom of Christ and of God.

Here, Paul listed six detours along the straight and narrow road, detours which could lead the believer away from the path of Christ and into the path of sin:

1. **Fornication.** This is an all-inclusive term which refers to any intercourse outside of the legal, married kind which is blessed by God. It includes pre-marital sex, extra-marital sex or adultery, homosexuality, prostitution, incest, bestiality, masturbation, etc. The mature child of God will heed Paul's advice to Timothy in 1 Timothy 2:22 which links fornication and lust with immaturity, *"Flee also youthful lusts."*
2. **Uncleanness.** This means any sin which would render one ceremonially unclean and unable to participate in the rituals of the Temple. It, too, is an all-inclusive term indicating any sort of impure living. Once cleansed, the mature child of God will not return to an immoral way of life, fearing the penalty described in Hebrews 6:4 through 6:

For it is impossible for those who were once enlightened, and have tasted of the heavenly gift, and were made partakers of the Holy Ghost, And have tasted the good word of God, and the powers of the world to come, If they shall fall away, to renew them again unto repentance; seeing they crucify to themselves the Son of God afresh, and put him to an open shame.

3. **Covetousness.** This is blatant materialism. In Ephesians 3:5, covetousness is linked with idolatry because, in the lives of those who have given themselves over to covetousness and materialism, money and the things it can buy have become their idols. The very fact that Paul included this sin with those against which he warned his readers is proof that even mature believers can fall into this trap. In recent years, the Church has been inundated with many ministries, especially the high-visibility media ministries, that are materialistic in both their appeal for and use of funds. For even the most mature saints in the kingdom, then, covetousness and materialism are mines in the minefield through which they must walk, snares of the enemy to be avoided at all cost. If it were not so, Paul would not have issued this warning to Timothy, his mature son in the Gospel, as recorded in 1 Timothy 6:10, *"For the love of money is the root of all evil: which while some coveted after, they have erred from the faith, and pierced themselves through with many sorrows."*

4. **Filthiness.** This is obscenity or anything which violates Christian purity. Imagine the ugly blot that would come upon one's Christian testimony if he uses obscenities!

5. **Foolish talking.** This term refers, not just to idle conversation, but to talk about sin. The mature believer must severely limit his discussion of sin and of sinful activities since such talk may soon be followed by sinful action. As King Solomon, the wisest mortal who ever lived, said in Proverbs 23:7, *"As a man thinketh in his heart, so is he."*

6. **Jesting.** This referred, not to innocent humor, but to indecent and obscene jokes and to the "double entendres" of a sexual nature which are so popular in today's society. The mature believer must avoid repeating or even listening to this sort of so-called "humor." It's not innocent. It's a mine which could destroy the walk of the child of God since walking the walk of the mature Christian involves talking the talk which is approved by God. Again, as in Ephesians 4:29, it's clear that Paul wasn't referring to idle conversation or innocent humor. Conversation, sharing, and appropriate humor are valid forms of social contact and fellowship which are beneficial to mature members of the Body of Christ. Those who are truly mature in the kingdom of God know the difference.

All these forms of sin and speech are not even to be named or spoken of by the mature believer (Ephesians 5:3) since that could lead to greater involvement. Instead, Paul counseled his readers to give thanks (Ephesians 5:4), both by sharing testimonies with others and offering praise to the Lord privately. Rather than discussing the detours Paul listed, the mature child of God must walk carefully around them, avoiding each mine in the minefield. He will, instead, share with his brothers and sisters in Christ his testimony of what God has done for him and offer praise for all that has been accomplished in his life. This is the kind of talk which edifies, builds up, and strengthens each member of the Body.

Those who do take the detours along the way face an appalling penalty. They risk losing their inheritance in the kingdom of God (Ephesians 5:5), all of the benefits, both here and hereafter, which are bequeathed to the believer by the grace of God. Clearly, those who have matured in their walk with the Lord, who have confidently taken possession of their inheritance in Christ, could lose it all. There is nothing at the end of any of those detours worth such great loss to God's children. In addition, they risk incurring the wrath of God, His hot anger and righteous indignation which He pours out upon those who, though once children, have since chosen to walk in disobedience and rebellion (Ephesians 5:6). For such, God's judgment will be severe indeed.

The mature child of God must be on guard as he walks God's highway of holiness. He must beware of those who try to lead him astray with vain and empty words (Ephesians 5:6), preachers and teachers whose doctrines sound good but, when carefully examined in the light of Scripture, are found to be devoid of divine truth. Those who are not following the only acceptable roadmap through the minefield, the Bible, and are not in daily personal contact with the Leader, God, Himself, are vulnerable to such deceptions. Paul advised his readers not to be *"partakers"* (Ephesians 5:7), not to associate with the kind of people he described, for an equal share in their deception brings with it an equal share of guilt before God and an equal portion of His wrath.

Contrasting the Walks

Previously, those to whom Paul wrote had walked in darkness (Ephesians 5:8), without the light of the truth of God, and lived lives of alienation from the Lord (Ephesians 4:18). Instead, they were to *"walk as children of light" (Ephesians 5:8)*. The contrast between the darkness and light is as startling as walking from a darkened room into the sunshine. Note the differences. Darkness, the old walk, the old life of sin, is unfruitful (Ephesians 5:11), because it carries no seed, no good Word of God, no life of Christ. It's also reproved (Ephesians 5:11) or shamed, since even mentioning dark deeds done in secret brings shame to both speaker and listeners (Ephesians 5:12). This is an allusion to the sexual and sacrificial rites of heathen religions and cults which were so secret that their participants were often threatened with death for disclosure and so shameful that the child of God shouldn't even mention them. Life in the light is the exact opposite. It's fruitful, carrying the seed of the life of Christ in the form of the Fruit of His Holy Spirit (Galatians 5:22 and 23), which grow in an atmosphere of *"goodness and righteousness and truth"* (Ephesians 5:9). It's acceptable to the Lord since, although God never tempts His children to sin (James 1:13), He often tests them to see if their responses will be satisfactory and to help them recognize areas of their lives where more growth and maturity are needed. It's also a life that can be made manifest or open before God and the world because there is nothing shameful in it. The mature child of God must never enter into any activity he wouldn't want shouted from the housetops, because that could just happen (Luke 12:3).

To conclude his contrast of the life of darkness and the life of light, Paul paraphrased Isaiah 60:1 and 2 in Ephesians 5:14, *"Wherefore he saith, Awake thou that sleepest, and arise from the dead, and Christ shall give thee light."* He called on his readers to awake from the sleep of spiritual death. This requires action on the part of the sleeper; he must stir himself and move from darkness to light, from death to life. Paul promised that the Lord would give all who responded to the Gospel the sunshine of a new day in Him. The mature in the Body of Christ have answered that call and opened their eyes to the glorious light of the Gospel. They have left the old life of sin and death behind and are walking on God's highway of holiness which will lead to Heaven. Their lives are producing a full crop of the Fruit of the Spirit and they are living lives which have been tested, tried, and proven acceptable in the sight of the Lord. They are doing nothing of which they should be ashamed, nothing they need to keep secret, nothing that must be hidden. They are no longer dead in their trespasses and sins, but are eternally alive in Christ Jesus.

Walking the Walk

Paul ended with specific travel directions for those on the Lord's straight and narrow road of life (Ephesians 5:15 through 21). Again, Paul contrasted opposites, the walk of the believer on the highway of holiness with the walk of the sinner on the road to death and Hell. The walk of the mature child of God will be characterized by these strides:

1. **Walk circumspectly.** This word refers to a walk which requires great care and diligence, a walk which is accurate, exact, strict, precise, and perfect, as through a minefield. The mature child of God must carefully, accurately, exactly, strictly, precisely, and perfectly follow his roadmap, the Bible, to make it to the other side. He must walk with care to avoid the minefield of the enemy's snares which are strewn along the way. He must walk wisely, through correct teaching. This pace will bring him safely to his destination. This stride is contrasted with the walk of fools who have rejected the wisdom of God in His Word. They have refused God's roadmap, rejected His way, and renounced His truth. They will be forever lost, forever separated from God, forever unwelcome in His Heaven.

2. **Redeeming the time.** Since the time is short and the days are evil, the mature saint must take every opportunity to check his roadmap, make progress along the road, and work for his Lord. He knows that these words, penned by an unknown poet, are only too true:

> "Only one life, 'twill soon be past;
> Only what's done for Christ will last."

3. **Understanding the will of the Lord.** The mature believer will use his roadmap and carefully search the Scriptures to learn the entire will of God. Then, he will reflect on it, ponder it, and take it to his heart so he'll be able to perform it throughout his life and walk. This effort is contrasted with the lives of those who are unwise. They expend no energy in Bible study, in learning God's will, or in gaining an understanding of it. Consequently, it is quite impossible for them to walk according to its principles.

4. **Filled with the Spirit.** While there may be many who are Spirit-<u>baptized</u>, there are few who are truly Spirit-<u>filled</u> at all times, but it must be the constant goal of the mature saint to be filled to the point of overflowing with the Holy Spirit. Then, he will have enough of the life of Christ to sustain himself and to spill over and share with others. The Spirit-filled life is contrasted with the alcohol-filled life of intoxication, summed up in the word, excess, referring to the kind of drinking that causes the drinker to be lost in immorality of every kind. Paul's allusion was to the "Feasts of Bacchus," Roman rituals dedicated to Bacchus, the Roman god of orgies. These feasts began with heavy drinking and intoxication and ended with sexual excesses of all sorts. The mature child of God wisely refrains from alcohol, knowing that Satan would use intoxication as a mine along the road, a snare designed to lower his moral standards and lead him into a detour of excessive sinful behavior.

5. **Singing.** Paul advised his readers to speak to themselves in song and mentioned three specific types of songs (Ephesians 5:19). Psalms were songs of praise, particularly those from the Book of Psalms, which were accompanied by musical instruments. Hymns are more "modern" songs continually being composed and sung by believers. Spiritual songs referred to the kind of singing in the Spirit Paul wrote about 1 Corinthians 14:15, *"<u>I will sing with the spirit, and I will sing with the understanding also</u>."* Paul indicated two uses of music. First, believers may sing together as a part of their worship. But, a believer may also sing to himself wherever he might be. Either use of song is edifying to the believer as an individual, as well as to the Body as a whole. In all of these ways, using each of these types of songs, the mature child of God makes music to his Lord in his heart and also encourages himself and others in the Lord. This is a more acceptable use of man's tongue than that to which it is sometimes put. In fact, this kind of singing may just possibly be the perfect way to combat the sins of the tongue, that unruly member which is so difficult to control and whose iniquities are described in James 3:5 and 6:

> *Even so the tongue is a little member, and boasteth great things. Behold, how great a matter a little fire kindleth! And the tongue is a fire, a world of iniquity: so is the tongue among our members, that it defileth the whole body, and setteth on fire the course of nature; and it is set on fire of hell.*

6. **Thankful.** The mature saint has so much for which to be thankful. He could spend the rest of his life pouring out his praise to his Lord and, still, it wouldn't be enough. So, Paul counseled his readers to express their thanks continually, *"for all things."* The mature child of God praises Him in everything that touches his life, both good and ill, convinced of the truth of Romans 8:28, *"And we know that all things work together for good to them that love God, to them who are the called according to his purpose."* The mature believer's thanks should be expressed to God, the Father, the Object of his worship, the Originator of the plan which saved him, and the Source of his life. It should also be offered in the name of the Lord Jesus Christ, since it is in His name that the believer has access to the Father.

7. **Submissive.** This is a military term which refers to setting soldiers in order by rank under their commander. Paul was not advising that every member be submitted to every other member of the Body of Christ. That would provide for no structure and no clear lines of authority, resulting in spiritual anarchy. The plan Paul had in mind was similar to the formation of an army. Each member of the Body must know, accept, and fulfill his place in the chain of command of the Lord's army. Each soldier must submit to the officer in authority over him and officers must assume responsibility for the guidance of the soldiers in their care. The highest ranking officers, those in the five-fold ministry positions previously described, must submit to the lateral advice-and-consent authority of others of equal rank. Then, every member of the Body of Christ, every soldier in the army of God, will walk in proper order, and they will do so out of fear or respect for their ultimate Commander, the One to whom all must be subject and to whom all will answer, the Lord Jesus Christ, Himself.

The mature child of God recognizes the total sovereignty of his Lord and the precarious nature of his own narrow walk before Him. He willingly takes his place in the army of God, having sufficient knowledge and experience in spiritual matters to fear rebelling, either against God or against His ordained authority structure. This mature believer has graduated from imitating man to imitating Christ and to truly trying to follow His example. As Jesus was submissive to God in all things, so the mature Christian must submit himself, both to God and to the God-ordained authorities He has placed over him. This is the way the mature child of God must walk all the days of his life. This is the walk which will safely bring him all the way to his heavenly home.

Chapter 9
MARRIAGE IN THE LORD

On the Highway of Life

The believer is not alone on life's journey; he encounters many others on the way. He may meet some he considers "good drivers." They are usually those with whom he agrees, doctrinally and personally. There may be others with whom he does not agree and considers rather "careless drivers." There will also be those with whom he finds no agreement and considers "bad drivers." On the road of life, the saint will encounter those who are not Christians, at all. Some are so-called "good" people who pay their bills, care for their families, and are charitable toward others, people he might consider "responsible drivers." He'll also meet some who are basically good, but have one besetting sin. For example, they may have a serious problem with alcohol and be "drunk drivers." Then, there are those lost in the depths of sin who careen through life causing accident and injury to themselves and others, the "reckless drivers" of this world. The Christian will have to relate to those he encounters on the road of life, in one way or another. He will establish close connection with some of the "good drivers." He may have more cautious associations with the "careless drivers." There may even be "reckless drivers" with whom he maintains no relationship at all, in the interest of "defensive driving" and "accident avoidance." Through Paul, God gave His children some specific guidelines to govern their "road" relationships. Chapters nine through eleven of this book will examine God's specific rules for these associations:

1.	**Wife.**	4.	**Fathers** (and mothers).
2.	**Husband.**	5.	**Servants** (or employees).
3.	**Children.**	6.	**Masters** (or employers).

The basic principle governing all human relationships is found in Ephesians 5:21, *"Submitting yourselves one to another in the fear of God."* Once again, submit is that quasi-military term referring to an army set in order under a commander and Paul did not mean that every person must submit to every other person or we'd have spiritual anarchy. The saint must know, accept, and fulfill his place in God's authority structure--in the home, in the Church, and in the world. He must willingly submit to those in authority over him and faithfully take responsibility for those under his authority. Those of equal rank in the chain of command should submit to the lateral advice and consent of others of parallel status. All should assume their proper positions in the army of the Lord, under the authority of the Commander-in-Chief, Jehovah God, so that the Body of Christ can be His example to the world and the devil. By appropriately applying these principles to his life and his relationships, the mature child of God is able to mirror or typify spiritual relationships before the world. For instance, by following God's rules for the relationship of husband and wife, the believer exemplifies the mystical relationship between Christ and His Church. Utilizing these precepts in the parent-child relationship signifies the bond between God, the loving Father, and His children. Then, by also incorporating these principles in the employer-employee association, the believer symbolizes his position as the servant of Christ.

A Wife in the Lord

Paul passed along these important commands for the Christian wife in Ephesians 5:22 through 24:

> *Wives, submit yourselves unto your own husbands, as unto the Lord. For the husband is the head of the wife, even as Christ is the head of the church: and he is the saviour of the body. Therefore as the church is subject unto Christ, so let the wives be to their own husbands in every thing.*

Notice that Paul's comments were specifically addressed to wives, not to husbands who might use these words as a so-called "heavenly baseball bat" to beat their wives into submission. Husbands are never given Scriptural authorization to force submission from their wives, either physically or emotionally. In fact, the words, *"submit yourselves,"* indicate the voluntary decision of the wife. Her submission is not forced or coerced, but offered freely in obedience to God, to the authority structure He has set, and to the husband He has placed over her in His chain of command. Contrary to modern feminists, the Christian wife takes full responsibility for her attitude and voluntarily submits to her husband, not because he's smarter or better or even of greater value, but because God commands it. She knows that God is not the Author of confusion but has a definite authority structure in His kingdom. She knows there are differences between men and women, husbands and wives, that transcend the obvious physical ones. While God sees no difference in the worth or value of husbands and wives (Galatians 3:28) or in the awful price Christ paid for each, God has decreed that there are different ranks in His army, in the functions they perform, and in their job descriptions. The mature Christian wife accepts her assigned rank and function in humility, even if she may be more intelligent or more capable--even if she happens to be right on any given issue. She understands that, even if society's roles and standards change, God's roles and standards have not been revised and never will be.

In Titus 2:5, Paul wrote to Christian wives, *"Be discreet, chaste, keepers at home, good, obedient to their own husbands, that the word of God be not blasphemed."* How do these commands translate into action? As her husband's most trusted confidant and advisor, the Christian wife will offer him her honest opinions, realizing he won't always see things as she does and she won't always get her own way. So, the mature believing wife will look to her husband to make the final decision and will willingly submit to and support it. Of course, the first question posed is always, "What if he's wrong?" In that event, the submissive wife prays and trusts God to reveal his mistake to him. She never tries to manipulate her husband; manipulation is a subtle form of rebellion and she must never resort to rebellion, since this more serious wrong would be dealt with by God before He would deal with the husband's supposed error in judgment. The second question usually asked is this: "What if the husband is not a Christian? In that event, the submission of his Christian wife is even more important as revealed in 1 Peter 3:1 and 2:

> *Likewise, ye wives, be in subjection to your own husbands; that, if any obey not the word, they also may without the word be won by the conversation of the wives; While they behold your chaste conversation coupled with fear.*

As Peter made clear, the believing wife's attitude of willing submission is far more likely to result in the salvation of the unbelieving husband than her rebellion might be. On the spiritual level, the submissive wife finds her lines of communication with her Lord open, unhindered, and always available to her. On the natural level, she is able to introduce her husband to the Saviour who has made her a better and more loving wife. On the other hand, her rebellion in the name of religion would only succeed in driving her husband further away from the Lord she serves, the Lord he might reasonably conclude is responsible for her behavior.

A minister once counseled the Christian wife of an unsaved man. In the course of the session, she revealed that she attended every church service, even when he asked her to stay at home to spend time with him; she resisted having a sexual relationship with him because she did not wish to be joined to a sinner; and, to put the icing on the cake, she prayed for him and sprinkled him with holy water as he sat reading his evening newspaper. After all of this faithful effort, she simply could not understand why he drank, preferred the company of his bar buddies to her own, and refused to get saved. Why, indeed?

Notice that, in both Ephesians 5:22 and 1 Peter 3:1, *the Christian wife is to submit to her "own"* husband. This same word is found in Colossians 3:18, where Paul wrote, "*Wives, submit yourselves unto your own husbands.*" The husband of the Christian wife, whether or not he is a born-again believer, is specifically named as the only one in authority over her on this human plane. There is no ambiguity about her superior officer. So, the mature believing wife won't circumvent the authority of her husband, even if, especially if, he is not yet a Christian. She won't place herself under the authority of others--be they Christian friends, the elders of her church, her pastor, respected leaders, writers, teachers, speakers, etc., or anyone and everyone that agrees with her point of view. While all of these sources may provide her with information, counsel, and advice, she is still directed by God to submit to her own husband. She may share the information, counsel, and advice she has received. Even better, she can invite him to seek information, counsel, and advice with her. She must, however, always recognize that it is his right, duty, and obligation to make the final decision and always evidence her resolve to submit to it.

The mature Christian wife will also submit to her husband, just as though she were submitting to the Lord (Ephesians 5:22) because, in a real way, she is. It was God who established the authority structure of the family and placed her husband over her. By submitting to him, she is submitting to God's Word, God's will, God's plan, and, ultimately, to God, Himself. Scripture records two reasons for this command. First, it's for the wife's own spiritual protection. Her refusal to submit to her husband will inevitably expose her to spiritual harm through deception, as seen in 1 Timothy 2:11 through 14, "*And Adam was not deceived, but the woman being deceived was in the transgression.*" Second, the mature Christian wife submits to her husband to illustrate the mystical principle of Christ and His Church (Ephesians 5:23 and 24). Paul compared the husband to the head which thinks, reasons, makes decisions, and directs bodily action, the same comparison he drew concerning Christ as Head of the Body, in Ephesians 1:22 and 23. As such, it is the husband's God-given responsibility to consider all options in the light of God's Word, God's will, and the welfare of his family, to reason and make decisions based on those considerations, and to direct family activity to fulfill the decision he has made. Then, he is responsible before God for the effects his decisions have on his family. This is the same position Christ, as the Head of the Church, occupies (Ephesians 5:22).

The phrase, *"he is the saviour of the body,"* is most revealing. Note the lower case "s" in, saviour, indicating the husband, rather than Christ. Then, body, refers to the physical body, not to the soul which is saved by Christ, alone. Together, these words indicate the husband's role in saving or preserving the physical well-being of the wife. For example, it is his duty to provide to the best of his ability for her physical necessities, such things as food, shelter, and clothing. It is his responsibility to meet her emotional needs, such as love, security, and companionship so that she will never be tempted or deceived into seeking them elsewhere, as Paul instructed in 1 Corinthians 7:3 through 5:

> *Let the husband render unto the wife due benevolence: and likewise also the wife unto the husband. The wife hath not power of her own body, but the husband: and likewise also the husband hath not power of his own body, but the wife. Defraud ye not one the other, except it be with consent for a time, that ye may give yourselves to fasting and prayer; and come together again, that Satan tempt you not for your incontinency.*

The husband should also protect his wife from physical threat and bodily harm with his physically stronger body. This may be as simple as doing the heavy lifting and carrying for her or a complex as repelling an advance or attack by another. The husband must also protect his wife from unwise decisions which could cause her spiritual harm. This, he is to do in the same way that Adam, who was not deceived by Satan (1 Timothy 2:14), might have protected Woman, who was deceived, if he had only told her to fix something else for lunch. In short, the husband is his wife's buffer, protector, and preserver against both the world and the attacks of the enemy. In these ways, he truly saves her from harm.

It has been said, "Uneasy lies the head that wears the crown." While submission may be hard for the wife, especially at the start and especially as she swims against the tide of feminism, she must never forget that her husband actually has the more difficult role and bears greater accountability before God, for higher rank always carries more responsibility. He must think through and consider all options. He must fast, pray, and often agonize to find the mind and will of God in each matter. He must make decisions that could have far-reaching, even cataclysmic, effects on the lives of the people he loves most. Yet, most of the time, he would be the first to admit that he really isn't sure what to do. Then, he must endure the dissension within his family inevitably generated by difficult decisions. Finally, he must bear the ultimate responsibility before God for every decision made, every action taken, and every effect that results. Even those husbands who abdicate their responsibility, opting for a cold beer and a seat in front of the televised football game, are still accountable to God for the welfare of their families. Once the mature Christian wife recognizes this, she realizes that her submission is the least she can do to support him.

Ephesians 5:24, begins with another pesky *"therefore,"* and whenever there is a therefore, one must find out what the therefore is there for. Here, for all of the reasons previously given, the command that the Christian wife be submitted to her own husband is reiterated. As a general rule, whenever anything is repeated in Scripture, it is done for emphasis. This is, in effect, a call for the mature army of the Lord to come to attention and pay attention! Paul then emphasized the reason for the precept: The mature Christian wife is to be submitted to her husband as a natural illustration of a spiritual principle; her attitude and behavior symbolize the attitude and behavior of the Church before Christ.

This submission applies *"in every thing"* (Ephesians 5:24). This always raises the question, "Is the Christian wife to submit unto sin?" The answer must be a resounding, "No!" It is clear that the wife is to submit to her husband as the Church submits to Christ; the husband is the authority over the wife, as Christ is the Head of the Church. Since Christ would never ask His Church to sin or to violate God's Word in any way, the God-given authority of the husband over his wife does not mean that he may ask his wife to submit to sin or to violate the clear commands of Scripture. Neither may he resort physical abuse, since Christ would never abuse His Church. A wife suffering such abuse must, for her own safety, temporarily remove herself from the situation and seek help.

A Husband in the Lord

The Lord's commands to the Christian husband in Ephesians 5:25 through 29, were just as specific:

> *Husbands, love your wives, even as Christ also loved the church, and gave himself for it; That he might sanctify and cleanse it with the washing of water by the word, That he might present it to himself a glorious church, not having spot, or wrinkle, or any such thing; but that it should be holy and without blemish. So ought men to love their wives as their own bodies. He that loveth his wife loveth himself. For no man ever yet hated his own flesh; but nourisheth and cherisheth it, even as the Lord the church.*

Paul repeated this order to husbands in Colossians 3:19, "*Husbands, love your wives, and be not bitter against them.*" God's order to the mature Christian husband is to love. Instead of using the Lord's directions to his wife to demand, force, or coerce her submission, he must love her until he wins her complete trust. In that atmosphere of love and security, the submission of the Christian wife (that she wants to give in compliance to God's commands to her) will just naturally flow. The husband must also recognize that, just as the refusal of his wife to submit to him will cause her profound spiritual problems, his failure to love her will bring him a terrible penalty, as 1 Peter 3:7 explains:

> *Likewise, ye husbands, dwell with them according to knowledge, giving honour unto the wife, as unto the weaker vessel, and as being heirs together of the grace of life; that your prayers be not hindered.*

Weaker, here, means, more fragile, like fine crystal which is cared for gently. Gentle, caring love, then, must be the motivating force in the relationship of the Christian husband to his more delicate wife. Note, the word used of love in Ephesians 5:25, 28, and 33 is not the Greek, *philandros*, the natural love of a husband and wife for each other, the standard of love the wife is taught in Titus 2:14, "That they may teach the young women to be sober, to love their husbands." The Lord calls the husband to an even higher standard of love, to agape love, to the unselfish, self-sacrificing love of God for man. It is this love that gives asking nothing in return, that seeks the good of the other instead of self, that makes the first move toward reconciliation, even when in the right. It is this love which caused God to send His Son to the cross of Calvary, this love He ministers to all mankind. This higher standard of love can only be achieved as the husband allows the agape love of God to flow through him to his wife.

This is the kind of love that Christ showed for His Church. This love caused Him to make the first move to reconcile her to Himself, even though she had sinned and He hadn't, and to give Himself as a sacrifice for her redemption. Not only did He make a sacrifice for her; He became the Sacrifice for her. This love caused Him to seek her sanctification, setting her apart from sin and for God's use, to seek her cleansing to remove all of her impediments and make her faultless, to seek her continual washing through the effectual working of His Word, so that she might someday be free of all spots or stains, all wrinkles or flaws, and all blemishes or blame, fit to be presented before the throne of God in Heaven and introduced as His beautiful Bride. All of this continuing work that Christ does for His Church is accomplished, not for His good, for He is already perfect, but for hers. It is His expression of His agape love for Her. Because this is the Lord's personal standard for the love He has for His Church, it is also His standard for the love the husband must have for his wife. In no other way can the husband illustrate Christ's love for the Church. To meet this high standard, the husband must love his wife just as much and in the same way that he loves himself. This principle is especially valid in Christian marriage since, in the sight of God, marriage makes two persons one, as God revealed to Adam at his marriage to his newly-created mate in Genesis 2:21 through 24:

> *And the LORD God caused a deep sleep to fall upon Adam, and he slept: and he took one of his ribs, and closed up the flesh instead thereof; And the rib, which the LORD God had taken from man, made he a woman, and brought her unto the man. And Adam said, <u>This is now bone of my bones, and flesh of my flesh</u>: she shall be called Woman, because she was taken out of Man. Therefore shall a man leave his father and his mother, and shall cleave unto his wife: and <u>they twain shall be one flesh</u>.*

It should be noted that Adam made this inspired declaration about leaving father and mother to marry, even though he had no earthly father or mother to leave. He knew the wisdom of separation from in-laws, even before in-laws existed. The mature believer must recognize this wisdom, too. The covenant of marriage, as Adam described it, simply reunites the man and the woman, the husband and wife, as one in the Lord. For added emphasis, Paul reiterated this divine truth for his readers in Ephesians 5:30 and 31:

> *For we are members of his body, of his flesh, and of his bones. For this cause shall a man leave his father and mother, and shall be joined unto his wife, and <u>they two shall be one flesh</u>.*

Based on that high standard of love and that principle of oneness, the mature Christian husband is commanded to apply the Golden Rule (Luke 6:31) to his relationship with his wife; he is to treat her as he treats himself, as he would like to be treated by others. Such care will involve agape love, sacrificial love. The husband loves himself (we all do) and makes any sacrifice to do what is best for himself. If he didn't, he might be thought lacking in self-esteem, possibly even self-destructive or suicidal. He must love his wife, that reunited part of his own flesh, in the same way and make any sacrifice necessary to do what is best for her, as well. Since he never hates himself, he never has any right to hate her. He must provide her with nourishment, from the Greek, *ektropho*, which, interestingly enough, means, to nurse, feed, or <u>to bring to maturity</u>. As the husband provides for and nourishes himself, both physically and emotionally, as he comes to spiritual maturity himself, so he should provide for, nourish, and seek the spiritual maturity of his wife. He must also cherish, from the Greek, *thalpo*, which means, to warm. Just as the husband provides a warm, comfortable climate for himself, so he should provide warmth for her, both physically and emotionally. This climate includes the warmth of his embrace and the tenderness of his love. In all these ways, the mature Christian husband loves his wife as Christ loved His Church, accepts her and treats her with the deference and devotion due that reunited part of himself, and fulfills the standard of agape love to which God has called him and in which his Saviour stands as his example.

God's standard of love for the Christian husband is almost as impossible as His standard for the submission of the Christian wife. But, it's the only standard that will produce a perfect (mature) Christian marriage between a mature husband and wife, a fit representation to the whole world of the relationship between Christ and His Church.

The Mystery of Marriage Explained

Once, when a church bulletin announced that the subject of the pastor's next sermon would be, "The Mystery of Marriage Explained," one oft-married, female parishioner was heard to exclaim, "Oh, I must be here for that. Marriage has always been a complete mystery to me!" Paul explained this mystery, simply, profoundly, in Ephesians 5:32 and 33:

> *This is a great mystery: but I speak concerning Christ and the church. Nevertheless let everyone of you in particular so love his wife even as himself: and the wife see that she reverence her husband.*

Of course, a mystery is a secret revealed only to the initiated. Beyond the human contract of marriage, then, there is a mystery, a symbolism, which is opened and explained only to those who are initiated into the Body, mature men and women of God. That symbolism was always there, from the very first marriage in the Garden of Eden where God served as both the Father of the bride and the officiating Clergy, down through the ages to today, even though most marriages are between persons who have no idea of the mystical meaning of the contract into which they enter. But, because the mature Christian has been initiated into the Body of Christ, the Lord has chosen to share with him the precious symbolism of Christian marriage. As we've seen, a really successful, working Christian marriage is an allegory of the relationship between Christ and His Church. The Lord decided to signify this association using a covenant-relationship man could easily understand--marriage. Man cannot accept or reject the Lord's choice of an allegory; he can only do his best to comprehend the mystery it reveals.

Divorce and the Christian

Using the marriage relationship as an allegory of Christ and His Church, just as Paul taught it to his readers, it becomes crystal clear that divorce can never be an acceptable option for the mature Christian. The entire body of Scripture proves that Christ loves His Church eternally, enough to have given His own life for her, enough to make the first move to reconcile her unto Himself. He would never divorce her. This, too, was the message of Christ, as recorded in Matthew 19:3 through 8:

> *The Pharisees also came unto him, tempting him, and saying unto him, Is it lawful for a man to put away his wife for every cause? And he answered and said unto them, Have ye not read, that he which made them from the beginning made them male and female, And said, For this cause shall a man leave father and mother, and shall cleave to his wife: and they twain shall be one flesh? Wherefore they are no more twain, but one flesh. What therefore God hath joined together, let not man put asunder. They say unto him, Why did Moses then command to give a writing of divorcement, and to put her away? he saith unto them, Moses because of the hardness of your hearts suffered you to put away your wives: but from the beginning it was not so.*

Clearly, from the beginning, it was the plan of God that one man and one woman become one flesh for one lifetime. He had, under the Law, provided the bill of divorce in the case of adultery, but only because the hearts of His people were so hard that they were unwilling to forgive a mate guilty of marital adultery, as God had so often forgiven their spiritual adultery. It is still the will of God that one man and one woman remain one for one lifetime. Even if one should commit adultery, the most damaging sin against marriage, it is still His will that there be forgiveness and reconciliation. Only then, can Christian marriage, the covenant between two mature members of the Body of Christ, truly symbolize to the whole world the mystical union between Christ and His Church.

Chapter 10
A FATHER IN CHRIST

God's Commands to Children

In ancient civilizations, the position of children was, at best, precarious. Under Roman law, as we've seen, the father had absolute power, the patria potestas, over his child for as long as he lived. Unwanted, sickly, or deformed children could be and often were thrown away or killed at birth. Baal worshippers frequently resorted to child sacrifice during times of natural disaster, famine, or military threat. Some cultures routinely sacrificed the firstborn to insure future fertility. Even the Jews sometimes sold children into slavery to pay the debts of the family. This practice, and the right of redemption by which the slave could be bought back by his family, were extensively regulated in the Mosaic Law (Leviticus 25:39 through 55).

Through Paul, however, God set a new and higher standard governing the Christian parent-child relationship. The guiding principle was this: The Christian parent must value the life and well-being of his child to show the world the value that God, the Father, places on the lives and spiritual well-being of His children; by the same token, the Christian child must honor and obey his parents to illustrate the honor and obedience owed to God by His children. To order parent-child relationships, God gave clear commands through Paul. The first of those commands was issued to the children themselves in Ephesians 6:1 through 3:

> *Children, obey your parents in the Lord: for this is right. Honour thy father and mother; which is the first commandment with promise; That it may be well with thee, and thou mayest live long on the earth.*

Obey, is the Greek, *hupakouo*, which means, to hear and pay attention to, hence, to obey. The word implies the same willing submission the Christian wife gives her husband. Nowhere, however, does the definition imply agreement. Just as the Christian wife doesn't always agree with her husband, the Christian child won't always agree with his parents. Just as the Christian wife may respectfully express her opinions to her husband, the Christian child has this same right. But, once the parent makes the decision, the Christian child, like the Christian wife, must submit to it. The child is never given permission to rebel.

The phrase, *"in the Lord,"* (Ephesians 6:1) has been used to argue that Christian children need only obey Christian parents. Instead, parents are over children in the Lord and in His authority structure for the family, whether or not they are Christians. So, Christian children must obey their parents, even if they are not yet born-again, knowing that the unbelieving parent is more likely to be won to the Lord who inspires his Christian child to be obedient. In Colossians 3:20, Paul phrased his commands to children even more clearly, *"Children, obey your parents in all things: for this is well pleasing unto the Lord."* In the natural, the parent offers his child unconditional love, provision, protection, and guidance. The Christian parent gives his child even more. He is able to love his child with the agape love of the Lord, provide for his child both temporally and spiritually, protect his child from natural and spiritual enemies, and guide his child into a personal relationship with Christ, just as he guides him into a happy and successful future.

Honor, the Greek, *timao*, meaning, to value or hold worthy and to give added weight or value to opinions, is the second duty of the Christian child (Ephesians 6:2). While obedience refers to external behavior, honor refers to an internal attitude of heart. A child may outwardly appear to obey his parents while, in his heart, he's seething in discontent and rebellion. The child who truly honors his parents, however, honors them from deep within.

Parents have valuable insights gained from their added years of experience. The Christian child wisely learns from their history so he won't have to repeat it, knowing their experience could save him unnecessary unhappiness. The believing child must also realize that his parents are motivated by love for him. Their advice should be given in an attitude of concern and their children should receive it as evidence of that concern. Parents are, of course, human. It's possible for parents to be wrong, even good parents, well-meaning parents, Christian parents. Both parents and children should recognize this fact, accept it, and go to God for final resolution of their conflicts.

Note that children must honor and obey both father and mother. It is the child's natural tendency to honor one parent above another, depending on the situation, the issue, and the child's age and gender. But, God demands the same honor and obedience toward both parents. Notice, too, that there is no time limit on this command. Even the adult child must honor and respect his parents, even if he does not necessarily agree with them. That disagreement may be expressed respectfully, in love. Then, both the parents and their adult child must realize that his first obligation of obedience is to God and his second responsibility is the well-being of his own nuclear family, his spouse and children.

There are two reasons for these commands to children. First, there was the legal approach, *"for this is right"* (Ephesians 6:1), the Greek, *dikaios*, fulfilling one's obligations before the Lord. Obedience, submission, and honor are pronounced right before God, the only way the Christian child can fulfill his duties to God. Second, there was the appeal to pragmatism since, in Exodus 20:12, this was the first commandment in the Mosaic Law containing a promise for those who kept it, *"Honour thy father and thy mother: that thy days may be long upon the land which the LORD thy God giveth thee."*

God's Benefits for Obedient Children

God promises at least two benefits to the child who honors and obeys his parents (Ephesians 6:3). First, things will go *"well"* for him. In the natural realm, things will go well because he has a good relationship with his parents and is spared much needless sorrow as he listens to their advice and learns from their experience. He will learn valuable lessons about living under authority which will help him in school, in the military, in his future career, under the law, and in society. He will also learn, by his parents' example, the proper use of authority, so that he'll be able to function more effectively on the job, in the military, and as a parent to his own children. Spiritually, the experience and example of his parents can spare him much frustration and give him valuable guidance toward a closer personal relationship with his Lord. The child will also learn to live within God's authority structure, to submit to the authority of others as a babe in Christ, and, after coming to maturity, to assume authority over others as a father (or mother) in the Lord.

Second, Paul echoed the promise of the Law, that the obedient child would *"live long upon the earth"* (Ephesians 6:3). In the natural, the knowledge and experience of parents guide him into a healthy lifestyle of good nutrition, moderate exercise, proper rest and health care, psychological and emotional health, and the avoidance of unhealthy habits such as smoking, drinking, and drug abuse. His parents also guide him to a lifestyle of safe living, safe driving, safe recreation, and the avoidance of predictable hazards. No wonder, this obedient child will live a longer, happier life. These benefits also extend into the spiritual realm, as his parents lead him into a healthy relationship with God. They provide spiritual nourishment as they feed him on the Word of God, teach him the spiritual exercise of his faith, help him find spiritual rest by trusting the Lord in all things, guide him into the spiritual good health of praise, prayer, and Scripture reading, and teach him to avoid unhealthy spiritual habits such as failure to attend church, read God's Word, be thankful to Him, and pray. The believing parents of the obedient child will also guide him into a safe and secure spiritual lifestyle as they teach him to live safely under God's established authority so he is hedged in against Satan and protected from his attack. From them, he learns the proper conduct of his spiritual life, as they teach him the secret of being in the world while not being of the world (John 17:15). His parents show him spiritually safe forms of recreation that will not bring him under the bondages of the enemy, and they help him walk safely through the devil's minefield of temptations without falling victim to them.

Childhood is a vitally important time; it's also a very short time in one's life. God has provided the child with two parents to love him, support him, provide for him, and assist him in making the difficult transition from infancy to maturity. The Christian child would do well to heed the advice of Paul, to obey and honor his parents, to learn all that he can from their lives, their experiences, their knowledge, and their example. In so doing, he will fulfill his obligation to his Lord, reap the blessing of God on his life, and show the world a living allegory of the relationship between God and His spiritual children, a walking example of the standard of behavior the Lord requires of each of His own.

God's Commands to Fathers

To provide equity for children in a world which required none, God, through Paul, also gave specific commands to fathers in Ephesians 6:4, "*And, ye fathers, provoke not your children to wrath: but bring them up in the nurture and admonition of the Lord.*" Paul sent a similar command to the Christian parents of Colosse in Colossians 3:21, "*Fathers, provoke not your children to anger, lest they be discouraged.*" Notice that the commands are addressed only to fathers. The father, not the mother, is charged by God with responsibility for the upbringing of children. He must set the moral and spiritual standard, initiate guidance of the family, and establish discipline in the home. The mother is also accountable before God for the rearing of her children, as implicit in Paul's previous commands to wives (Ephesians 5:22 through 24). As the father's companion, she may offer advice and insight concerning the moral and spiritual standards that are set; as his helpmeet, she must assist her husband in providing guidance for the family; and, as his submitted wife, she must follow the discipline her husband has established. But, God makes it abundantly clear that the ultimate responsibility for the spiritual welfare of children rests upon their father who will answer to the Lord for his use or misuse of that authority. All too often in modern society, the father abdicates this God-given position of authority. He may be too busy with his career or too involved in his own interests to assume responsibility for the spiritual welfare of his children. Indeed, he may be entirely absent from the home and unavailable to them. In these cases, the mother often steps in to fill the vacuum and usurps the authority of the father, only adding to the problem. But, while the father may opt to abdicate his God-given authority over his children, he can never abdicate his God-imposed responsibility; he will surely and ultimately answer before God for their spiritual welfare.

Paul specifically advised Christian fathers not to provoke their children to wrath, the Greek, *parargizo*, indicating an irritation or provocation beyond measure or endurance. Some fathers are prone to excessive discipline, while mothers tend to the other extreme of over-indulgence. To guard against the irritation and provocation this disparity might cause, the standards set for home and family, the guidance given, and the discipline imposed must all be ministered consistently, by <u>both</u> parents, in an atmosphere of love, compassion, and understanding, never in a capricious, cruel, or abusive manner. Even right standards and discipline, dispensed in a wrong attitude or uncontrolled temper, will only provoke the children and engender anger, bitterness, resentment, and rebellion in them. Paul offered two guiding principles to govern the discipline of children. First, they are to be reared in *"the nurture...of the Lord"* (Ephesians 6:4). Nurture, is the Greek, *paideia*, which refers to the training that includes education, discipline, rewards, and punishments. God set clear guidelines for the education of children in the Law of Moses in Deuteronomy 6:6 and 7:

> *And these words, which I command thee this day, shall be in thine heart: and <u>though shalt teach them diligently unto thy children, and shalt talk of them when thou sittest in thine house, and when thou walkest by the way, and when thou liest down, and when thou risest up</u>.*

Though the words may be few, the principles expressed are specific and all-inclusive. An entire educational plan is found here. First, the curriculum is defined. Children are not taught man's so-called wisdom, but, rather, all of the commandments of God, including the Ten Commandments and the statutes governing social, moral, and ethical conduct. Then, the teaching methods which God deemed suitable and successful are listed:

1. **Teach diligently.** Diligently, is the Hebrew, *shanan*, which means, to sharpen, and indicates sharpening by repetition. In other words, children are to have their skills and knowledge sharpened by their parents' constant repetition of principles.

2. **Teach when sitting in the house.** There's a never-ending amount of work to be done in any home, leaving little time for sitting in the house, except perhaps at mealtimes, after work and school, and on the Sabbath when no work at all is to be done. So, God ordained that mealtime conversation, evening family times, and Sunday observances include repetitions of His precepts. These need not be formal lessons; in fact, a more informal approach will probably bring better results; these might simply be family discussions of the events of the day and the applicable spiritual principles. On Sunday and special religious holidays, simple explanations of these observances and the spiritual principles involved may be given. In modern times, the family also sits in the house when watching television. At that time, God's standards are taught through the choice of acceptable programs and the rejection of unacceptable ones.

3. **Teach when walking.** A family might walk together through the grocery store, in a shopping mall, or on a family outing. Again, God ordained that these occasions be used as opportunities to teach the young. For example, when shopping, the conversation might naturally turn to God's provision for the family. On vacation or on an outing, God's creation might be discussed as His handiwork in nature is viewed and appreciated.

4. **Teach when lying down.** One might lie down at bedtime, during an illness, or at the birth of a child. These, too, are times of training in the Christian family. At bedtime, a comforting discussion of God's providential care for His children and simple prayers for His divine protection through the night are good teaching tools. During an illness, there can be discussion of God, the Healer, prayers for recovery, and expressions of trust in Him to do the work. When a new baby arrives, parents might share with older children the simple facts of human reproduction and the creative miracle of God evident in each new life.

5. **Teach when rising up.** These lessons come in the morning, when arising for the day, or after recovery from an illness, and these are also appropriate occasions to teach. The

children will learn as they see their parents begin each new day with God, with prayers of thanksgiving for His protection through the night, and with His Word to guide them into the new day. They will learn as their parents testify to the healing of an illness or injury, whether that healing came by natural means of the body's own restorative powers or through a miracle, and they will realize that God is the Author of both.

In short, God ordained that mature Christian parents view every occasion throughout every day as an opportunity to teach their children. To do it, there must be continuing discussion of every facet of religious, family, social, and business life and constant reiteration of God's commands concerning religious, social, moral, and ethical conduct. Children should be encouraged to participate in those discussions, to ask questions and to seek answers, so they will come to maturity having been nurtured in the Lord.

Of course, in any family, there must be discipline, correction, and punishment. The Christian family is no exception. This form of nurturing must have only one goal--to mold the character of the child. To do it, family discipline must be based on firmly established and clearly understood rules set by the father and consistently enforced by both parents. Rewards and praise for good behavior that conforms to the established standards reinforce them. But, there will be times when the child does not conform his behavior to the rules, and correction or punishment must be used. This discipline should be designed to modify behavior, not to retaliate against the child or to provoke his anger, resentment, or rebellion. It should always be both fair and fitting to the offense. The issue of corporal punishment, spanking, must be left to parents to decide. It can be noted that the Bible does advise spanking for certain offenses (Proverbs 10:13 and 23:13 and 14). If and when it is used, it, too, must be done to punish and correct behavior, never to injure or abuse. To prevent excesses, the Christian parent should never administer corporal punishment out of anger or frustration, but only when well in control of his own temper and emotions.

This nurturing in the Christian home has only one motivation--love. According to Ephesians 5:2, the agape love of God, should be the driving force in all relationships. The love of Christian parents for their children must be unconditional and based on relationship, not behavior. Proper nurturing in the Christian home will have several results, all desirable. First, children will come to maturity learning to fulfill their obligations to their Lord, their parents, and others. Second, they will be taught to be good parents to their own children. There are no courses or educational requirements for prospective parents. Instead, most people learn parenting from their parents and tend to parent their own children the same way. For the sake of their grandchildren, then, Christian parents will want to follow God's instructions to the letter. Finally, such nurturing will illustrate to children the Fatherhood of God and help them respond to Him appropriately. In general, children who have a loving relationship with their earthly fathers tend to have a right concept of their heavenly Father and a loving relationship with Him. On the other hand, children who have flawed relationships with their earthly fathers, for whatever reasons, often have great difficulty developing right concepts of God, receiving His love, and accepting His discipline.

Bringing children up in the *"admonition of the Lord"* (Ephesians 6:4) was Paul's second governing principle of discipline. Admonition, is the Greek, *nouthesia*, which refers to issuing a warning. It is the duty of the Christian father to caution his children against wrong behavior and warn them of the inevitable natural and spiritual consequences of it. In the natural realm, for example, if the child violates the law, consequences may include a fine, a criminal record, even time in prison. Should he abuse his body, he risks permanent damage to his health, in the form of heart or respiratory problems if he smokes, liver and brain damage if he drinks, and addiction, brain damage, or chromosome damage if he uses drugs. Illicit sexual activity may bring an unwanted pregnancy, venereal disease, even death. The child must also be warned about the terrible spiritual consequences of sin. God has established certain laws in the universe which, if broken, bring dire results. For instance, in Galatians 6:7 and 8, Paul wrote of the law of sowing and reaping:

> *Be not deceived; God is not mocked: for whatsoever a man soweth, that shall he also reap. For he that soweth to his flesh shall of the flesh reap corruption: but he that soweth to the Spirit shall of the Spirit reap life everlasting.*

In Matthew 6:14 and 15, Jesus taught the law of forgiveness, *"If ye forgive men their trespasses, your heavenly Father will also forgive you: But if ye forgive not men their trespasses, neither will your Father forgive your trespasses."* The law of putting God first in one's life was taught by Jesus in Matthew 6:33, *"But seek ye first the kingdom of God, and his righteousness; and all these things shall be added unto you."* Paul taught the law of ultimate good which ever operates in the life of the believer in Romans 8:28, *"And we know that all things work together for good to them that love God, to them who are the called according to his purpose."* The important law of spiritual consequences is recorded in Ecclesiastes 10:8, *"He that diggeth a pit shall fall into it; and whoso breaketh an hedge, a serpent shall bite him."* Finally, the writer of the Book of Hebrews taught the law of death and of judgment in Hebrews 9:27, *"And as it is appointed unto men once to die, but after this the judgment."*

Admonition will have worthwhile results in the life of the child. First, he will be forewarned and taught to fear sin and the judgment that results. As an adult, he may not always choose God's way, but he will clearly understand the consequences he faces if he doesn't. Also, Christian parents will faithfully discharge their obligation before God by fulfilling their responsibility as watchmen over the souls of their children, according to Ezekiel 3:17 through 21:

> *Son of man, I have made thee a watchmen unto the house of Israel: therefore hear the word at my mouth, and give them warning from me. When I say unto the wicked, Thou shalt surely die; and thou givest him not warning, nor speakest to warn the wicked from his wicked way, to save his life; the same wicked man shall die in his iniquity; but his blood will I require at thine hand. Yet, if thou warn the wicked, and he turn not from his wickedness, nor from his wicked way, he shall die in his iniquity; but thou has delivered thy soul. Again, When a righteous man doth turn from his righteousness, and commit iniquity, and I lay a stumblingblock before him, he shall die: because thou hast not given him warning, he shall die in his sin, and his righteousness which he hath done shall not be remembered; but his blood will I require at thine hand. Nevertheless if thou warn the righteous man, that the righteous sin not, and he doth not sin, he shall surely live, because he is warned; also thou hast delivered thy soul.*

Finally, by bringing up their children in the admonition of the Lord, by warning them against sin, Christian parents succeed in meeting God's condition and have a right to claim His promise in Proverbs 22:6, *"Train up a child in the way he should go: and when he is old, he will not depart from it."* The Christian parent can know no greater joy than this: that his child has come to maturity and is walking with the Lord.

Chapter 11
UNDER AUTHORITY AND IN AUTHORITY

God's Commands to Servants/Employees

Rome ruled the world Paul knew. Her citizens were so enraptured with their own dominance, they felt it beneath their dignity to do mundane things like work. They had slaves to do that. In fact, there may have been sixty million--that's 60,000,000--slaves throughout the empire. Consequently, Paul had a vast audience for his next commands. Some slaves had kind masters with whom they established strong bonds of mutual respect, friendship, and even love. But, most suffered under cruel and despotic masters who considered them of no more value than a good tool or a cow, and who possessed the power of life and death over them and their families. Many slaves in the Roman Empire had become Christians. They were free in spirit, but, in body, they were bound by their slavery. Having liberty in Christ, they wondered whether they should seek freedom in the flesh. If they remained in natural slavery, they thought they might risk spiritual slavery, too. Paul's words were meant to resolve these questions with the news that servitude was not necessarily inconsistent with Christianity. While America no longer has slaves, she is home to millions of workers, the people who really keep the country humming. Some have good jobs, safe working conditions, fair salaries, and excellent benefits. But, far too many, in the words of the American existentialist and philosopher, Henry David Thoreau, "lead lives of quiet desperation." Paul's words are addressed to all of them, as well. Paul's next commands, in Ephesians 6:5 through 8, were appropriately directed to all of these people:

> *Servants, be obedient to them that are your masters according to the flesh, with fear and trembling, in singleness of your heart, as unto Christ; Not with eyeservice, as menpleasers; but as the servants of Christ, doing the will of God from the heart; With good will doing service, as to the Lord, and not to men: Knowing that whatsoever good thing any man doeth, the same shall he receive of the Lord, whether he be bond or free.*

There were, in the ancient world, several classes of servants--the apprentice who briefly joined himself to a skilled craftsman to learn the trade, the servant who committed himself to several years of servitude to retire a debt, and the bondslave who was sold into lifetime slavery. Servant, here, is the Greek, *doulos*, which referred to the lowest scale of servitude, the bondslave. But, in the allegorical sense used by many New Testament writers, this Koine Greek word expressed the highest form of devotion to the Lord, the devotion of one who is bound by chains of love alone. Paul called on servants of every kind to offer willing submission to their masters, just as a soldier submitted to his commanding officer, just as though they were obeying the Lord, Himself (Ephesians 6:6). Indeed, these Christian workers were obeying the Lord. While Jesus was their Master in the spirit, their owners were their masters in the flesh; to obey Him, it was necessary that they obey them. Paul never gave his readers permission to rebel; instead, he commanded them to live the Christian life in whatever position they found themselves (Philippians 4:11 through 13).

To understand this principle, one must have a mature understanding of the sovereignty of God and His control over everything that touches one's life. If He is truly Lord, then He had ordained the status of slaves, just as He had ordained the status of masters. So, accepting one's state is, in effect, accepting God's sovereign control over one's life. In the modern world, God, as Sovereign, has decreed that some are employees while others are employers. Acceptance of this causes the mature Christian employee to work for his employer, just as though he were laboring for God, realizing that the Lord placed him in his position, gave him his job, gives him the health and strength to do that job, and enables him to care for himself and his family with his wages (Deuteronomy 8:18). This concept is spelled out even more clearly in Colossians 3:22 through 24:

> *Servants, obey in all things your masters according to the flesh; not with eyeservice, as menpleasers; but in singleness of heart, fearing God: And whatsoever ye do, do it heartily, as to the Lord, and not unto men; Knowing that of the Lord ye shall receive the reward of the inheritance: for ye serve the Lord Christ.*

Here, Paul added the words, *"in all things,"* to the standard of obedience required of Christian servants and employees. Like the submitted wife to whom Paul wrote in Ephesians 5:24, this does not mean that the servant or employee must obey unto sin. This is clear in the addition of the qualifying words, *"as to the Lord,"* which appear in both Ephesians 6:5 and Colossians 3:23. Since Christ would never ask His servants to sin, the employer never has the right to require his employee to sin. If that kind of request is made, such as the typical, "Tell him I'm not in," the Christian employee has every right to respectfully, but firmly, refuse. Most employers will accept this refusal, realizing that if his employee will not lie for him, he will not to lie to him or about him.

There are certain attitudes of obedience expected of the saved servants/employees to whom Paul wrote and certain attitudes that are not tolerated in these Christian workers:

1. **In fear.** The Christian worker must respect the position of even the most cantankerous boss, even if the individual in that position seems unworthy of his respect.
2. **Trembling.** Trembling, is the Greek, *tromos*, which describes the anxiety of one who wants to do his utmost to fulfil his duty. It's been said that, "the Christian is so heavenly minded that he is no earthly good." It should never be the case that the Christian worker is so caught up in his religion that he's a less productive employee on his job. If anything, since he is ultimately working for his Lord, he should work even more conscientiously to do the best job he can for his employer.
3. **In singleness of heart.** The Christian worker should be the most honest, most trustworthy, most diligent employee. He must never be tempted to extend his coffee break or supply his children with pencils and paper clips at the expense of his company.
4. **As unto Christ.** All of these attributes were to characterize the attitude of the mature Christian servant (employee), just as though they were his attitudes toward his service to God. This outlook can bring an entirely new perspective and motivation to a job which might otherwise be dull, boring, repetitive, unchallenging, and unfulfilling, etc.
5. **Not with eyeservice.** This refers to service done diligently when the master is looking, but neglected when he isn't. Yet, maturity means doing what's right even when no one is looking. Christian workers must never forget that, even when no one else is watching, the eyes of their Saviour are always on them.
6. **Not as menpleasers.** This indicates servants or employees who endeavor to please men instead of God. The motivation of the Christian worker must always be to please God since, by so doing, he will naturally please the human being for whom he works.

7. **As servants of Christ.** Here, the Greek, *doulos*, has the added significance of the love bond between Christ and His servants. Because of that love bond, the servants of the Lord fulfill their duty to Him by fulfilling their duties to their earthly masters.

8. **Doing the will of God from the heart.** It is in the heart or soul, the seat of the mind, the emotions, and the will of man, that the commands of God are weighed and the decision made to obey them. Realizing that it is God's command to work diligently for one's master or employer, the Christian servant/employee must make the decision in his soul to obey. The obedience of the Christian servant or employee must never be given grudgingly; it must be offered in the same attitude he brings to his service to his Lord.

9. **With good will, doing service as to the Lord and not men.** In both Ephesians 6:8 and Colossians 3:24, God, through Paul, promised a reward to all Christian servants and employees who perform their duties according to His commands and in the attitude of obedience He ordered. While the earthly benefits of slaves might have been very different from those their masters enjoyed, while the material possessions of employers might be much greater than those their employees can afford, there will be no difference in the spiritual reward each will receive from God in return for diligently fulfilling the obligations of their particular positions (Ephesians 6:8). Each faithful servant of God, whether a slave or a master in this world, will, in the world to come, be granted his full spiritual inheritance for his service in the position where God placed him (Colossians 3:24). Having come to maturity, having executed his responsibilities fully and faithfully, each can claim his complete spiritual inheritance as a son in Christ; each will receive all that the Lord has bequeathed to him, both in this world and in the next. This is the clear and unmistakable promise of Jesus Christ, Himself, in Matthew 10:42 and 16:27:

> *And whosoever shall give to drink unto one of these little ones a cup of cold water only in the name of a disciple, verily I say unto you, he shall in no wise lose his reward....For the Son of Man shall come in the glory of his Father with his angels; and then he shall reward every man according to his works.*

God's Commands to Masters/Employers

There were also many born-again slave owners in the Roman Empire. While they may have had unlimited power under Roman law, under God's law of love, there were strict commands to govern their conduct toward their servants. In Ephesians 6:9, we read, *"And, ye masters, do the same things unto them, forbearing threatening: knowing that your Master also is in heaven; neither is there respect of persons with him."* Paul ordered Christian masters/employers to exhibit the same attitudes toward their servants/employees which those servants/employees had just been commanded to exhibit toward them (Ephesians 6:9). This command included the same obedience and submission, since, as believers, both must ultimately be submitted to Christ; it included the same posture of fear and trembling, the same singleness of heart, since, as mature men of God, they knew that only then could they fulfil their obligations to God. It also included the same diligent service to Christ since, as laborers for Him, they were ultimately working under His eye alone.

There was, however, one additional command directed only to masters/employers. By this command, masters were not only forbidden to use the generally accepted cruelty against their slaves, they were forbidden even to threaten such actions. This command also extends to the mature Christian employer, who is likewise not permitted to threaten his employees with such things as a salary cut, a demotions, an unearned negative job rating, or an unjustified bad recommendation, etc. This is the clear message of Paul's similar command to masters/employers in Colossians 4:1, *"Masters, give unto your servants that which is just and equal; knowing that ye also have a Master in heaven."*

Paul gave only one reason for the commands in Ephesians 6:9 and those in Colossians 4:1. The believing masters of Paul's day, as well as the born-again employers of our modern world are ever under the watchful eye and the ultimate authority of their heavenly Master. Just as the slave/employee is under the authority of his master/employer, that master/employer is under God in His authority structure. No one, not the slave, not the master, not even the president of the United States, acts with impunity; everyone answers to someone and everyone answers to God. The mature child of God recognizes this principle and governs his actions toward others accordingly.

The mature believer recognizes one additional fact: God is no Respecter of persons; He doesn't play favorites. He recognizes no status or station; He sees only His commands and one's actions in response. This is the clear message of Romans 2:11, *"For there is no respect of persons with God."* This fact is reiterated and elaborated upon in Colossians 3:25, *"But he that doeth wrong shall receive for the wrong which he hath done: and there is no respect of persons."* If that were not enough, Peter made the point even more forcefully. In 1 Peter 1:17, *"And if ye call on the Father, who without respect of persons judgeth according to every man's work, pass the time of your sojourning here in fear."*

A Case of Employer/Employee Relations

At about the same time Paul composed Ephesians and Colossians, he had to resolve a difficult case of master/slave, employer/employee relations. It was the case of Philemon and Onesimus, which is described in Paul's letter to Philemon.

Philemon, whose name meant loving and affectionate, was a rich and influential man who lived in Colosse. He was also a born-again Christian who had probably found the Lord through Paul's ministry (Philemon 19). In Philemon, verses 5 through 7, Paul described Philemon's character as loving (probably a play on words based on the meaning of his name), faithful, of good communication, full of good things in Christ, and a source of joy to Paul. But, Philemon was also a wealthy slave owner and one of his slaves, Onesimus, had come to Paul. While his name meant, profitable, he had not been at all profitable to his master, another play on words that Paul simply couldn't resist (Philemon 11). In fact, Onesimus had rebelled against his master and run away. There is the clear implication, in Philemon 18, that he may have even robbed his master to support his venture.

Under Roman law, a runaway slave, if recovered, could hope for little mercy. The least penalty he might expect was to be branded across his forehead with the letter "F" to forever identify him as a fugitive. In most cases, however, he would simply be put to death, as an example to other slaves with similar plans. The particular death penalty prescribed for slaves was crucifixion, arguably the most terrible death penalty ever devised by man.

But, Onesimus had become a Christian under Paul's ministry during his time on the run. He may even have met Paul when both were in prison (Philemon 10). In any event, Onesimus now knew and understood his obligations under God, the same obligations Paul had detailed in Ephesians and Colossians. He was ready to return to his master (Philemon 12) and be truly profitable to him (Philemon 11). Or, he was willing to remain with the imprisoned apostle to aid him in the ministry (Philemon 13). In an effort to intercede for Onesimus, to spare him the terrible penalties of his previous rebellion, Paul wrote to his old friend, Philemon. Then, he sent the runaway slave back to his master to deliver that letter. One can only imagine the feelings of Onesimus as he approached his master's home.

The letter Onesimus carried survives as a classic illustration of mature Christian master/slave, employer/employee relations. Paul would not permit Onesimus to remain with him without the consent of his master (Philemon 14), even though he could face the death penalty if he returned. Paul recognized Philemon's right, as the master/employer in God's authority structure, to make the final decision. Paul also expressed his confidence in Philemon's obedience to the One who was his Master in that authority structure (Philemon 21). In verses 14 through 19, to mediate a settlement of the dispute, Paul detailed two possible options to Philemon: he could willingly permit Onesimus to return to Paul as his assistant (Philemon 14), or he could accept Onesimus back, as a servant, but also as a brother in the Lord, recognizing that both ultimately labored for the same Master (Philemon 15 through 17). Notice that exacting the legal penalty prescribed under Roman law was not an option, in keeping with his commands against cruelty in Ephesians 6:9 and Colossians 4:1. While Paul countenanced no extreme punishments or brutal threats against Onesimus, he did recognize Philemon's right to just restitution for the costs incurred because of the rebellion of Onesimus. In order to effect the reconciliation, Paul even offered to repay whatever loss Philemon may have suffered (Philemon 18 and 19). Here, Paul stood as a type of Christ, who paid the price to free the rebellious of this earth from the penalty of their sin, the same Christ who will repay and reward the faithful and good in His kingdom, both masters and slaves, employers and employees. Paul expressed his confidence that Philemon would not only do what Paul had asked of him, in perfect accord with God's commands regarding the relationship of masters and slaves, employers and employees, he trusted that Philemon would do even more (Philemon 21). Here, Paul provided this general principle which the mature Christian, whether employer or employee would do well to follow: Don't just do what is required; do more than is asked; go the extra mile. Do all as unto the Lord who is the Master of all.

Paul's request was not rejected. Onesimus must have been received with open arms, restored to his home and his master, and added to the church in Colosse. Just a short time later, when Paul composed his letter to the Colossians, he made mention of Onesimus and his brand new status as a child of God and member of His Body. In Colossians 4:9, Paul wrote, *"With Onesimus, a faithful and beloved brother, who is one of you. They shall make known unto you all things which are done here."* In fact, tradition maintains that Onesimus went on to become the Bishop of the church at Berea, the church Luke commended for their faithful adherence to Scripture in Acts 17:10 and 11.

Thus, Paul concluded his instructions to the mature in the Body of Christ concerning their inter-personal relationships. It is a standard which requires great personal growth to achieve. It is a standard which will bring the Body and each of its members closer to greater perfection and maturity in Christ.

Chapter 12
THE ARSENAL OF GOD'S ARMY

A Strong Soldier of Christ

We're at war! Yes, there's a war going on against Satan and all of his demons, a spiritual war waged against every born-again believer and, to fight it, every mature saint is automatically conscripted into the army of the living Lord. Make no mistake about it. This conflict requires committed, mature men and women of God, the soldiers of the King who are commanded to go forth in spiritual warfare and to return in spiritual victory.

To better wage this warfare, it's necessary to understand it. When one is born again, he is redeemed from bondage to Satan, just as the children of Israel were freed from bondage in Egypt. But, the devil doesn't simply admit defeat and give up. Instead, he, like Pharaoh, devises a persistent campaign to recover what he's lost, a campaign in which he employs every diabolical strategy at his command and involves all of his demonic forces. That campaign has as its single goal the recapture of the freed captive, the born-again saint of God. It will include attacks on the body of the believer, with illnesses and diseases (although not every illness and disease is satanic in its source), and attacks on the soul of the believer, with temptations and torments, attitudes and appetites. That campaign will continue without truce or treaty until that saint safely reaches Heaven's shores. The Christian has no choice about engaging in this battle. The moment he was saved, Satan launched the attack against him and he must either confront the powers of hell in the victory of the Lord, or go down to defeat before his foe. This confrontation is called spiritual warfare and every mature man or woman of God is called upon to wage it.

Paul recognized the reality of this incessant struggle against Satan, so he warned his readers about it and trained them for the fight they faced. That basic training in spiritual warfare began in Ephesians 6:10, *"Finally, my brethren, be strong in the Lord, and in the power of his might."* Strong, is the Greek, *endunamoo*, an imperative verb indicating that, to survive Satan's onslaught, it is absolutely imperative that the saint have strength. But, this verb is also passive, proving that it is utterly impossible for the spiritual warrior to gain this strength by his own effort; he can only be the passive recipient of the strength given to him by his Lord. The saint has no strength of his own, no power in himself to fight the good fight of spiritual warfare; his strength in the battle before him is the strength of his Commander-in-Chief, strength his Lord operates through him. That's why, when referring to his own spiritual battle, Paul wrote these words in 2 Corinthians 12:7 through 10:

> *And lest I should be exalted above measure through the abundance of the revelations, there was given to me a thorn in the flesh, the messenger of Satan to buffet me....For this thing I besought the Lord thrice, that it might depart from me. And he said unto me, My grace is sufficient for thee: for my strength is made perfect in weakness. Most gladly therefore will I rather glory in my infirmities, that the power of Christ may rest upon me. Therefore I take pleasure in infirmities, in reproaches, in necessities, in persecutions, in distresses for Christ's sake: for when I am weak, then am I strong.*

The *"power of his might"* in Ephesians 6:10 is, however, quite a different matter. Power is the Greek, *kratos*, which refers to power and dominion. It's from a root which means, perfect and complete, referring to the perfect and complete power of the Lord. He need not receive power from any other source; His power doesn't grow when exercised or diminish when at rest. His power is always forceful, always claims its rightful dominion, and is always at its perfect and complete zenith. Might, is the Greek, *ischus*, which refers to power that's naturally resident. This is the inherent power of the almighty Lord, power which always was, which is, and which always will be, power which is forever resident within Him and which He brings into action and operates through His mature saints.

Wearing the Whole Armor

To follow Paul's instruction to be strong, it's necessary for the warrior of the Lord to obey his next instruction in Ephesians 6:11, *"Put on the whole armour of God, that ye may be able to stand against the wiles of the devil."* Paul was a master of the subtle, rhythmic play on words for which the Koine Greek language was famous. Hard on the heels of, strong, the Greek, *endunamoo*, he told his readers to *"put on,"* the Greek, *enduno*, which means, to be clothed in or to hide in. There are two facts about donning the armor that the spiritual soldier must keep in mind. First, the whole armor must be put on. It's not enough to wear part or most of the armor of the Lord; to be fully protected, one must wear every piece of armor his Commander provides. Second, putting on the armor isn't something the Lord does for His fighters. They aren't passive recipients of His armor in the same way they are passive recipients of His strength. God both prepares and presents this armor, but the warrior of the Lord must clothe himself, hide himself, in all the armor the Lord has given him. The mature soldier of Christ must take the initiative in his own defense.

This spiritual armor is absolutely necessary if the warrior of the Lord has any hope of being able to stand against Satan. Once again, the verb, stand, is in the passive form and means, to be made to stand. The message is clear. While the soldier of the Lord must take responsibility for putting on the armor, once that armor is in place, it is the Lord, Himself, who gives that soldier the ability to stand firm against every attack of Satan.

The devil's wiles are indicated by the Greek, *methodia*, the methodical schemes and strategies of Satan, his carefully conceived and conducted battle plan to attack the saint. The strong soldier of Christ must understand that these satanic strategies will never be fair, as seen in Ephesians 6:12, *"we wrestle not against flesh and blood."* Wrestle, is from a Greek root that literally meant, to vibrate or shake. It indicated the kind of hand-to-hand combat that concludes when one combatant is able to shake the other to his foundations, topple him from his standing position, and bring him down for the count. It isn't a fair match since the opponent isn't even made of flesh and blood. He is a spiritual being and is far more formidable than any mortal foe. Were the adversary mortal, he would be visible, comparable in strength and power, and vulnerable to human strategy, physical force, and natural weapons. Since he isn't mortal, he is invisible to the human eye, possesses superhuman strength, and cannot be conquered by any wile or weapon of man's devising. He can only be seen through spiritual discernment, a Gift of the Holy Spirit (1 Corinthians 12:10), can only be contested in the imparted strength of the Lord, Himself, and can only be defeated by the spiritual weapons in the Lord's arsenal. The wrestling match, then, has been unfair from the very outset. From the beginning, the warrior of the Lord has been forced to fight with the inhuman and the inhumane who are identified in Ephesians 6:12:

> *For we wrestle not against flesh and blood, but against principalities, against powers, against the rulers of the darkness of this world, against spiritual wickedness in high places.*

Here, we learn the names of the four ranks in the satanic horde which are arrayed against the army of the living God:

1. **Principalities**. Principalities, is the Greek, *arche*, which indicates one who is the first or the leader, the magistrate or ruler in first place. Since this is the same word translated, archangel, in Jude 9, referring to Michael, the warrior archangel of God, this ranking may apply only to Satan, himself, or to Satan and a few of the highest demons in his kingdom.
2. **Powers.** This is the Greek, *exousia*, which literally means, delegated authority. While these are clearly chief rulers and high in the authority structure of Satan, they derive their delegated authority from and execute the will of Satan; they have no power of their own. At the same time, however, these beings are in authority over others who must obey them. In modern terminology, these are Satan's "middle-level bureaucrats."
3. **Rulers of the darkness of this world.** This rank is the Greek, *kosmokrator*, which means, world ruler. These are demons assigned to rule specific areas of the world. The angel, Gabriel, met one of them in Daniel 10:13, *"But the prince of the kingdom of Persia withstood me one and twenty days: but, lo, Michael, one of the chief princes, came to help me."* It is through the efforts of these ruling demons that Satan is able to accomplish all that God predicted of him in Isaiah 14:16, *"They that see thee shall narrowly look upon thee, and consider thee, saying, Is this the man that made the earth to tremble, that did shake kingdoms."*
4. **Spiritual wickedness in high places.** This lowest rank in Satan's kingdom is the Greek, *porneria*, the root from which the word, pornography, comes. It refers to depravity and wickedness of every sort. The high places in which these depraved and wicked ones reside are indicated by the compound Greek word, *ep-ouranios*, which means, in or above heaven, in the heavenly regions. It may be used of Heaven, the abode of God and His angels, of the lower heavens, the universe, or of the heaven of the clouds, earth's atmosphere. Context determines which is correct. Since Paul referred to Satan as *"the prince of the power of the air"* in Ephesians 2:2, it's logical to conclude that the high places of Ephesians 6:12 are in the atmosphere above. These lower-ranking demons, hovering just above the heads of mankind, seek to work their wiles on man, to trouble him, and to trick him into the same depravity and wickedness they, themselves, practice. But, this same word, ep-ouranios, appears several times in Ephesians. In Ephesians 1:3, it identifies the place where the mature believer is blessed with *"all spiritual blessings,"* the place where God brags about His own in the presence of Satan, just as He bragged about Job. In Ephesians 2:6, it identifies the position of rest and authority occupied by the mature saint, where he can sit back, relax, and exercise his spiritual authority against the enemy. Finally, in Ephesians 3:10, it pinpoints the location from which Satan is forced to observe the Church in action, forced to view the Body of Christ executing the will of God, forced to witness the believers' victories in the Lord. Clearly, then, even though the mature child of God is engaged in an unfair fight with inhuman and inhumane spiritual opponents, through Christ and the armor and weapons He offers, the warrior of the Lord can occupy a position of complete victory, even in Satan's own backyard. This battle can be won.

"Wherefore," because the believer faces such formidable foes, Paul reiterated his previous commands in Ephesians 6:13, *"Take unto you the whole armour of God, that ye may be able to withstand in the evil day, and having done all, to stand."* But, here, instead of the passive, stand, Paul used the active, withstand, the Greek, *anthistemi*, which means, to stand against, to oppose, or to resist. This word indicates a soldier taking his place of opposition and resistance in the battle lines in a face-to-face, toe-to-toe, nose-to-nose stance against the enemy. Having put on all his armor, having taken his position against the enemy, the

soldier of the Lord has done all; he has done his part. As he stands his ground, toe-to-toe with Satan, God will do His part in defending him and bringing him out victorious.

The Whole Armor of God

In Ephesians 6:14 through 17, Paul described each piece of the armor God has designed for each of His willing warriors:

> *Stand therefore, having your loins girt about with truth, and having on the breastplate of righteousness; And your feet shod with the preparation of the gospel of peace; Above all, taking the shield of faith, wherewith ye shall be able to quench all the fiery darts of the wicked. And take the helmet of salvation....*

Note that this arsenal of armor and weaponry contains nothing to protect the warrior's back. At no time is the mature soldier of the King to turn his back to the enemy of his soul. Such a posture would leave him vulnerable to ambush or portend his retreat. Either would result in his immediate defeat. It should also be noted that all of the weapons on this list are defensive, weapons to be used as the mature soldier of the Lord stands against the attack of Satan. Those defensive weapons of spiritual warfare are:

1. **Truth.** The truth of God, the revelation of Him in His Word, protects the warrior's loins. In type, the loins, the part between the ribs and the hips, represent the reproductive area and the area of strength needed for standing securely upon one's feet. It is to be girt, or wrapped around completely, as with a girdle or a belt. The allusion is to the belt used by the ancient warrior to hold his sword securely within his grasp and to cinch up his flowing robes, giving him unencumbered freedom of movement. It is this circle of the truth of God which the soldier of the Lord uses, both to protect his firm stance from a fall and to protect the ability to reproduce the life of Christ in him and in others he may win to his Lord. When attacked, the mature soldier of God cannot stand secure apart from the truth of the victory of Christ; he cannot reproduce the life of Christ apart from the truth of the work of the Holy Spirit in the life of each believer; and he cannot win others to the Saviour apart from the truth of His death and resurrection to redeem fallen man.
2. **The breastplate of righteousness.** The breastplate is the Greek, *thorax*, and covered the thorax or chest of the soldier. This is the part of the soldier's body that contains his most vital organs, including his heart. This particular breastplate is one of righteousness, indicating the nature of one who has been justified by God and who, therefore, stands before His court as though he had never sinned. It is the judicial act of justification, accomplished by God at salvation, that makes His soldier's heart right before Him. It is that soldier's determination to stand in continued righteousness, right behavior, that continually protects his heart from yielding to the temptations to sin Satan will scheme to bring across his path. To successfully stand against Satan, the heart of the mature warrior of God--his soul with all of its emotions and affections--must remain ever right before Him.
3. **The preparation of the Gospel.** This protects the fighter's feet. Preparation, is the Greek, *hetoimasia*, which conveys the idea, not of shoes, but of the firm foundation beneath one's shoes. The mature soldier of the King stands on the Gospel, the firm foundation which gives him peace with God and the peace of God (Romans 5:1 and Philippians 4:7), the foundation upon which his feet securely stand as he faces his eternal foe, and the foundation or platform from which he witnesses to others and tells them the good news of the Gospel of Jesus Christ. It is this Gospel which promises him the power to safely tread on Satan in all his forms, in Luke 10:19, *"Behold, I give unto you power to tread on serpents and scorpions, and over all the power of the enemy: and nothing shall by any means hurt you."*

4. **The shield of faith.** In the ancient world of war and warriors, there were two types of shields. The first, designated by the Greek, *aspis*, was a small, round shield which could cover only a small part of the soldier's body at a time. The second, identified by the Greek, *thureos*, originally described the great stone used to cover the entrance of a cave but later came to be used of the large, rectangular shield which covered a warrior's entire body and behind which he could safely hide. It was this second type of shield of which Paul wrote. It is only the mature soldier's firm faith in his God that could entirely shield him.

An offensive weapon often used in the warfare of Paul's day was the fiery dart, an arrow whose tip was dipped in pitch or some other kind of flammable material. The tip of the arrow was lit, the arrow was fired, and the burning pitch at its point would stick to and continue to burn whatever the arrow struck. On other occasions, the arrow might be dipped in some sort of poisonous or infectious substance which would cause a painful skin inflammation or even kill its unfortunate victim. According to Paul, however, an unwavering belief in the promises and principles of God is the shield which will completely protect the mature Christian warrior against any such fiery darts of Satan. This faith will quench or extinguish the fire or infection, safely putting out Satan's fearful flame.

5. **The helmet of salvation.** Helmet, is the Greek, *pericephalaia*, which literally meant, around the skull. The helmet encompassed the soldiers head and, metaphorically, protected the mind. It is the mature saint's full knowledge of his own salvation that protects his mind from doubts, fears, and temptations, as well as wrong thoughts, feelings, and attitudes. In 1 Thessalonians 5:8, Paul wrote, *"But let us, who are of the day, be sober, putting on the breastplate of faith and love; and <u>for an helmet, the hope of salvation</u>."* While the mature believer engaged in spiritual warfare must have the complete assurance of his own, historic salvation experience to shield his mind from the attack of the enemy; he must also have the <u>hope</u> that his salvation will sustain him in time of future attack, along with the <u>hope</u> of his ultimate salvation at the day of his death or the day of the Lord's return.

In addition to the defensive weapons, the soldier of the Lord also has some offensive weapons. Paul listed them in Ephesians 6:17 and 18:

> *And <u>the sword of the Spirit</u>, which is the word of God: Praying always with all <u>prayer and supplication</u> in the Spirit, and <u>watching</u> thereunto with all <u>perseverance</u> and supplication for all saints.*

The offensive weapons of the mature spiritual soldier are used in the counter-attack against the onslaught of Satan, to reclaim the spiritual territory where he sits as the trespasser and the usurper. This offensive aspect of spiritual warfare is the fulfillment of the type presented in the Book of Joshua. There, God's children had been given title deed to the land of Canaan, but it was inhabited by heathen Canaanite tribesmen who had to be attacked offensively and driven from their strongholds. In the same way, the redeemed believer is given God's title deed to every aspect of his life, to bring every one of them into conformity to Christ (Romans 12:2). Some facets of his life, however, must be reclaimed from the influence of Satan. The offensive weapons to do it are these:

1. **The sword of the Spirit.** There are two kinds of swords in the New Testament. The first, the Greek, *romphaia*, was a Thracian sabre so large and unwieldy, it had to be carried on the soldier's right shoulder and swung with both hands, limiting his ability to use his shield simultaneously. The second, the Greek, *machaira*, referred to a knife worn with a sword and used for cutting or butchering. It was this second sword Paul wrote about in Ephesians 6:17, a small sword which could easily be held in one hand and used while the protective shield remained in place. This particular sword was the sword of the Holy Spirit,

the Word of God, itself. This sword and the surgical precision with which it is used by the Holy Spirit in the life of the believer are described in Hebrews 4:12:

For the word of God is quick, and powerful, and sharper than any two-edged sword, piercing even to the dividing asunder of soul and spirit, and of the joints and marrow, and is a discerner of the thoughts and intents of the heart.

The Holy Spirit wields this double-edged sword of Scripture in the believer's life to remove any impurity and to cut Satan out of any territory he may occupy. This removal of all that is malignant with sin and satanic influence is accomplished with complete surgical precision so that healthy spiritual tissue remains untouched and protected.

Jesus effectively used this sword of Scripture against Satan's temptations in Matthew 4:1 through 11. There, Satan brought three temptations against the Lord, symbolizing the three kinds of temptations in 1 John 2:16, *"For all that is in the world, the lust of the flesh, and the lust of the eyes, and the pride of life, is not of the Father, but is of the world."* First, Satan tempted the hungry Saviour to turn stones into bread (Matthew 4:2 and 3), an appeal to the lust of the flesh. But, Jesus, wielded the sword of Scripture (Matthew 4:4), saying, *"Man shall not live by bread alone,"* a quote from Deuteronomy 8:3. Next, Satan misquoted Psalm 91:11 and 12 to entice the Lord to leap from the pinnacle of the Temple to prove God would protect Him (Matthew 4:5 and 6), an appeal to the pride of life. Note that Satan can quote Scripture, often better than most Christians, and he'll misquote it, too. This shouldn't deceive the mature believer, just as it didn't deceive the Lord. He responded (Matthew 4:7) with, *"Thou shalt not tempt the Lord thy God,"* a quote from Deuteronomy 6:16. Finally, Satan showed Him all the kingdoms of the world and demanded the Lord worship him to obtain them (Matthew 4:8 and 9), an appeal to the lust of the eye. While Jesus did not dispute Satan's present possession of those kingdoms, He knew they would all one day be His (Revelation 11:15). To defeat Satan, He spoke these words, *"Thou shalt worship the Lord thy God, and Him only shalt thou serve,"* a quote of Deuteronomy 6:13.

Here, the mature soldier of Christ finds a perfect example of the effective use of the Spirit's sword to defeat the devil. But, to follow this example, the soldier of the Lord must remember two things. First, to quote Scripture against Satan with the ease evidenced by Jesus, one must read, study, and memorize it, just as He had. Second, one can't reject the Old Testament as not applicable to today's problems and temptations or as done away with by grace since it was the Old Testament Jesus used as His spiritual sword, and it was this same Old Testament with which Jesus successfully defeated His foe.

2. **Prayer and supplication.** Another effective weapon in the arsenal is prayer, and, according to Paul, it is to be offered at all times and in every way. Here, supplication indicates continual pleading until the prayer is answered. In Ephesians 6:18, prayer and supplication are inextricably linked by Paul and he also wrote that this kind of prayer and supplication should be offered *"in the Spirit."* In Romans 8:26 and 27, Paul revealed that this kind of prayer in the Spirit is an especially effective weapon against the infirmities Satan so often uses to attack the soldier of the Lord. He also explained that prayer in the Spirit is a successful weapon in the battle to remain in the perfect will of God:

Likewise the Spirit also helpeth our infirmities: for we know not what we should pray for as we ought: but the Spirit itself maketh intercession for us with groanings which cannot be uttered. And he that searcheth the hearts knoweth what is the mind of the Spirit, because he maketh intercession for the saints according to the will of God.

Paul, himself, made prayer in the Spirit, as well as prayer with the understanding or in one's own language, a part of his personal arsenal in 1 Corinthians 14:14 and 15:

> *For if I pray in an unknown tongue, my spirit prayeth, but my understanding is unfruitful....I will pray with the Spirit, and I will pray with the understanding also.*

Prayer with understanding, prayer in his own Hebrew tongue, was a weapon employed by David as he prayed for God's deliverance from the attack of the enemy. In Psalm 6:4, he wrote, *"Return, O LORD, deliver my soul: oh save me for thy mercies' sake."* As a result, in Psalm 34:4, David could write of his victory in the Lord over fear, a common attack of Satan against the believer, through prayer, *"I sought the LORD, and he heard me, and delivered me from all my fears."* The prayer and supplication of the mature spiritual warrior can also be used to intercede for other believers on the battlefield who are braving the attack of the adversary. Paul ordered intercession, here in Ephesians 6:18, with the words, *"for all saints,"* and in 1 Timothy 2:1, where he wrote, *"I exhort therefore, that, first of all, supplications, prayers, intercessions, and giving of thanks, be made for all men."* Jesus interceded for His disciples in John 17:15, *"I pray not that thou shouldest take them out of the world, but that thou shouldest keep them from evil."* Still, He intercedes for His own, as Hebrews 7:25 guarantees, *"Wherefore he is able also to save them to the uttermost that come unto God by him, seeing he ever liveth to make intercession for them."* It was with a request for the prayers and supplications of those to whom he wrote that Paul concluded this letter (Ephesians 6:19 and 20), knowing that he, too, needed this weapon, wielded by the Church, the entire Body of believers, to sustain him in the spiritual battle he was facing.

3. **Watching.** Watching, is the Greek, *agrupneo*, which means, to be so watchful that one is unable to sleep. Just as the mature soldier of the Lord must stand at his duty station to confront the attacking enemy, he must also stand spiritual guard duty. Only then, will he be forewarned of the adversary's advance so he can meet it with prayer and supplication. While on spiritual guard duty, the mature warrior of the King must never sleep, realizing that one lapse could cost him everything. He knows that it was as they slept, oblivious to threat, that Samson was shorn of his strength by Delilah (Judges 16:19), that Sisera's head was nailed to the floor of Jael's tent (Judges 4:21), and that Jonah failed to see the storm which would eventually overwhelm him and nearly take his life (Jonah 1:4 and 5).

4. **Perseverance.** When attacking the mature child of God, Satan should find himself faced with an immovable object, a soldier of Christ who is determined to be strong, to stand firm, and to endure all of the devil's temptations in patience and perseverance.

The Word of God, that sword of the Spirit wielded by the mature spiritual warrior, also reveals many other spiritual weapons in God's arsenal:

5. **Singing.** Singing encourages the singer and discourages his attacker. It may be done in the Spirit or in the language of the singer, as Paul noted in 1 Corinthians 14:15, *"I will sing with the spirit, and I will sing with the understanding also."* In Exodus 15:1, Moses sang with the understanding to praise God for victory over his adversary, *"I will sing unto the LORD, for he hath triumphed gloriously: the horse and his rider hath he thrown into the sea."* David also used this spiritual weapon to encourage himself in the Lord. All of his psalms are examples of this form of weaponry. He encouraged others to use it, too, in Psalm 98:1, *"O sing unto the LORD a new song; for he hath done marvellous things: his right hand and his holy arm hath gotten him the victory."* Paul, himself, used the weapon of singing to amazing effect in Acts 16:25 and 26:

> *And at midnight Paul and Silas prayed, and sang praises unto God: and the prisoners heard them. And suddenly there was a great earthquake, so that the*

foundations of the prison were shaken: and immediately all the doors were opened, and everyone's bands were loosed.

6. **Worship.** Worship is honoring God for who He is and coming into relationship with Him. This weapon of spiritual warfare, along with prayer and faith, was used successfully by the mother of a girl who was under spiritual attack in Matthew 15:22 and 28:

And, behold, a woman of Canaan came out of the same coasts, and cried unto him, saying, Have mercy on me, O Lord, thou son of David; my daughter is grievously vexed with a devil....Then Jesus answered and said unto her, O woman, great is thy faith: be it unto thee even as thou wilt. And her daughter was made whole from that very hour.

It was in an attitude of worship that the man known as Legion approached Jesus and was set free of the spiritual enemies that had attacked his mind in Mark 5:6 and 15:

But when he saw Jesus afar off, he ran and worshipped....And they come to Jesus, and see him that was possessed with the devil, and had the legion, sitting, and clothed, and in his right mind: and they were afraid.

This same worship will precede the great spiritual victory predicted in Revelation 14:6 through 8:

And I saw another angel fly in the midst of heaven, having the everlasting gospel to preach unto them that dwell on the earth, and to every nation, and kindred, and tongue, and people, Saying with a loud voice, Fear God, and give glory to him; for the hour of his judgment is come: and worship him that made heaven, and earth, and the sea, and the fountains of waters. And there followed another angel, saying, Babylon is fallen, is fallen, that great city, because she made all nations drink of the wine of the wrath of her fornication.

7. **Praise.** Praise is thanking God for what He's done. God's warriors must praise Him for past spiritual victories, as the psalmist advised in Psalm 107:8, "*Oh that men would praise the LORD for his goodness, and for his wonderful works to the children of men.*" In Psalm 34:1 through 4, David revealed that it was praise, coupled with prayer and supplication, that brought him victory over fear:

I will bless the LORD at all times: his praise shall continually be in my mouth. My soul shall make her boast in the LORD: the humble shall hear thereof, and be glad. O magnify the LORD with me, and let us exalt his name together. I sought the LORD, and he heard me, and delivered me from all my fears.

In Hebrews 13:15, the writer directed mature soldiers of the King to praise, even when they don't feel like it, especially when they don't feel like it, as a sweet sacrifice to the Lord, "*By him therefore let us offer the sacrifice of praise to God continually, that is, the fruit of our lips giving thanks to his name.*" In Isaiah 61:3, we discover that God placed praise in His arsenal to be an especially effective spiritual weapon against the satanic attack of depression, "*To appoint unto them that mourn in Zion, to give unto them beauty for ashes, the oil of joy for mourning, the garment of praise for the spirit of heaviness.*" David, a notable warrior as well as a psalmist, understood why praise is such an effective spiritual weapon. It was the one weapon which brought God directly into the battle, as he explained in Psalm 22:3, "*But thou art holy, O thou that inhabitest the praises of Israel.*"

8. **Submit and resist.** In the army of God, the mature soldier must take his place under his Commander, conform to His will, and submit to His authority. It would do no good to resist Satan, if he did not first submit to God. Then, the spiritual warrior can resist Satan and all of nıs spiritual attacks. Resistance is an active opposition flowing from

a systematic battle plan. That resistance, that battle plan will bring the victory promised in James 4:7, "*Submit yourselves therefore to God. Resist the devil, and he will flee from you.*"

9. **Bind and loose.** In Matthew 16:19, the mature spiritual soldier is granted the authority to use another of the weapons of spiritual warfare, binding and loosing:

> *And I will give unto thee the keys of the kingdom of heaven: and whatsoever thou shalt bind on earth shall be bound in heaven: and whatsoever thou shalt loose on earth shall be loosed in heaven.*

Jesus promised that, if the soldier of the Lord will bind Satan in faith (Mat. 12:29), God will, in response to that faith, bind him in the heavenly realm where he and his demons reside (Ephesians 6:12). This weapon, in tandem with others, will, indeed, work just as promised, just as revealed in Psalm 149:5 through 9:

> *Let the saints be joyful in glory: let them sing upon their beds. Let the high praises of God be in their mouth, and a two-edged sword in their hand; To execute vengeance upon the heathen, and punishments upon the people; To bind their kings with chains, and their nobles with fetters of iron; To execute upon them the judgment written: this honour have all his saints.*

Jesus also promised that, if, in faith, the mature soldier of the Lord will loose himself or another from the bondages in which Satan has held him bound, God will, in response to that faith, nullify those bondages in the heavenlies, making them inactive and ineffective. This loosing was accomplished by Jesus in behalf of a woman who had been under Satan's attack of infirmity for many years, as recorded in Luke 13:11 through 13:

> *And, behold, there was a woman which had a spirit of infirmity eighteen years, and was bowed together, and could in no wise lift up herself. And when Jesus saw her, he called her to him, and said unto her, Woman, thou art loosed from thine infirmity. And he laid his hands on her: and immediately she was made straight and glorified God.*

10. **The Blood of Jesus.** The blood of Jesus isn't a magic charm. When applied in faith, however, it is an effective spiritual weapon, as Revelation 12:10 and 11 reveals:

> *And I heard a loud voice saying in heaven, Now is come salvation, and strength, and the kingdom of our God, and the power of his Christ: for the accuser of our brethren is cast down, which accused them before our God day and night. And they overcame him by the blood of the Lamb, and by the word of their testimony; and they loved not their lives unto the death.*

11. **Testimony.** The mature warrior of the King can testify before Satan of all that God has done for him in the past. The devil will despise those testimonies, while they will inspire the child of God in future battles. Moses testified as he spoke before his people for the very last time in Deuteronomy 1:30, "*The LORD your God which goeth before you, he shall fight for you, according to all that he did for you in Egypt before your eyes.*"

12. **The Name of Jesus.** Just as the blood of Jesus is not to be used as some sort of a magic charm, neither is the name of Jesus to be used as though it were a magic word. Seven who tried it were nearly destroyed, as Acts 19:13 through 16 records. The mature soldier of Christ may, however, wield this weapon when operating under the direct authority of his Commander. In spiritual warfare, the name of Jesus may be used in two ways. First, it may be spoken to rebuke Satan, as the archangel, Michael used it in Jude 9, as follows:

> *Yet Michael the archangel, when contending with the devil he disputed about the body of Moses, durst not bring against him a railing accusation, but said, The Lord rebuke thee.*

Jesus promised that His mature warriors, those engaged in spiritual warfare, could use His name to cast out demons. This is guaranteed in Mark 16:17:

And these signs shall follow them that believe; In my name shall they cast out devils; they shall speak with new tongues.

13. **The hedge of thorns.** When the wife of the prophet, Hosea, insisted on pursuing her previous career of prostitution, Hosea, in faith, built a hedge of thorns around her so that she would not be able to find her lovers, as revealed in Hosea 1:6 and 7:

Behold, I will hedge up thy way with thorns, and make a wall, that she shall not find her paths. And she shall follow after her lovers, but shall not overtake them; and she shall seek them, but shall not find them: then shall she say, I will go and return to my first husband; for then was it better with me than now.

In his prayer and supplication, the spiritual warrior of the Lord can ask God to put a hedge around the sinner, just as Hosea did, to prevent him from pursuing his sin and to prevent Satan from pursuing his pattern of temptation in the sinner's life. In faith, the mature believer can also ask God to erect the same kind of hedge around himself, a hedge of thorns which will effectively keep the enemy out. Even Satan recognized the efficacy of such a hedge in Job 1:9 and 10:

Then Satan answered the LORD, and said, Doth Job fear God for nought? Hast not thou made an hedge about him, and about his house, and about all that he hath on ever side? thou hast blessed the work of his hands, and his substance is increase in the land.

So long as this spiritual hedge of thorns remains intact, there is safety. If, however, through disobedience, the soldier creates a break in his hedge of protection, Satan will be free to attack, as Ecclesiastes 10:8 warns, "*He that diggeth a pit shall fall into it; and whoso breaketh an hedge, a serpent shall bite him.*"

The Warrior's Weapons

For the mature soldier of Christ, then, these are the weapons of his arsenal, the weapons he uses to defeat the attack of the adversary. But, he must prove each piece for himself, in his own life, in his own experience, in his own position on the battlefield. Otherwise, like David in 1 Samuel 17:38 and 39, he will find that, in the day of battle, this armor does not fit and these weapons are unfamiliar to him:

And Saul armed David with his armour, and he put an helmet of brass upon his head; also he armed him with a coat of mail. And David girded his sword upon his armour, and he assayed to go; for he had not proved it. And David said unto Saul, I cannot go with these; for I have not proved them. And David put them off him.

While David was able to win his battle and defeat his foe with other weapons he had previously proven, there are no other weapons for the soldier of the King. The warrior of the Lord has access to the entire arsenal and he must train himself to use every weapon given him in the Word of God. These weapons have been proven effective in God's Word, they are instantly available, and they are designed to deal with any type of attack the adversary may mount. Therefore, when an attack comes, the soldier of the King need only choose an appropriate weapon, stand his ground, and confidently fight back against his foe. He is assured of victory. Satan, on the other hand, has not one single weapon that can defeat a mature soldier of the Lord, as Isaiah 54:17 guarantees:

No weapon that is formed against thee shall prosper; and every tongue that shall rise against thee in judgment thou shalt condemn. This is the heritage of the servants of the LORD, and their righteousness is of me, saith the LORD.

This song, composed during the Crusades to encourage Christian warriors on their way to battle, is the theme of the army of the Lord for it captures the essence of their warfare:

Onward, Christian Soldiers

Onward, Christian soldiers, marching as to war,
With the cross of Jesus going on before!
Christ, the royal Master, leads against the foe--
Forward into battle see His banner go!

At the sign of triumph, Satan's host doth flee;
On, then, Christian soldiers, on to victory!
Hell's foundations quiver at the shout of praise;
Brothers, lift your voices, loud your anthems raise!

Like a mighty army moves the Church of God;
Brothers, we are treading where the saints have trod.
We are not divided--all one Body we--
One in hope and doctrine, one in charity.

Onward, then, ye people, join our happy throng;
Blend with ours your voices in the triumph song.
Glory, laud, and honor unto Christ the King:
This through countless ages men and angels sing.

Onward, Christian soldiers, marching as to war,
With the cross of Jesus going on before.

The End of the Journey

Together, we have come to the end of the journey. We have traveled from bondage in sin to completion in Christ. We have come from the position of hopeless and helpless slaves to the status of adult and experienced soldiers of the Lord Jesus Christ, ready, willing and able to engage the enemy of our souls in spiritual warfare, competent and capable of achieving the victory in Him. We have come to full maturity in the Lord.

Thank you for making the trip with us. If you need additional copies of this book or if we can be of assistance to you or your group, please don't hesitate to contact us.

WORD OF ZION
7907 Rolling View Avenue
Baltimore, Maryland 21236
(410) 661-5890

BIBLIOGRAPHY

Alexander, Pat, *The Lion Encyclopedia of the Bible*, Lion Publishing Corporation, 1978.

Barr, George, *Who's Who in the Bible*, Jonathan David Publishers, Inc., 1975.

Barclay, William, *The Letters to the Galatians and Ephesians*, The Westminster Press, 1958.

Benton, William, *The Encyclopedia Britannica*, Encyclopedia Britannica, Inc., 1959.

Blaikie, William Garden, *The Book of Joshua*, Klock and Klock Christian Publishers, 1978.

Blaiklock, E. M., *The Zondervan Pictorial Bible Atlas*, Zondervan Publishing House, 1977.

Bohle, Bruce, *The Home Book of American Quotations*, Dodd, Mead and Company, 1967.

Boone, R. Jerome (Editor), *The New Chronological Bible*, World Bible Publishers, 1980.

Briscoe, Jill, *Here Am I--Send Aaron*!, Victor Books, Scripture Press Publications, 1981.

Buksbazen, Victor, *The Gospel in the Feasts of Israel*, Christian Literature Crusade, 1978.

Bullinger, Ethelbert W., *A Critical Lexicon and Concordance to the English and Greek New Testament*, Samuel Bagster and Sons, Ltd., 1969.

Chafer, Lewis Sperry, *Chafer Systematic Theology*, Dallas Seminary Press, 1983.

Coleman, William L., *Today's Handbook of Bible Times and Customs*, Bethany House Publishers, 1984.

Comay, Joan and Ronald Brownrigg, *Who's Who in the Bible*, Bonanza Books, Crown Publishers Inc., 1980.

Conybeare, W. J., and J. S. Howson, *The Life and Epistles of St. Paul*, William B. Eerdmans Publishing Company, 1974.

Dake, Finis Jennings, *Dake's Annotated Reference Bible*, Dake Bible Sales, Inc., 1986.

Edersheim, Alfred, *Old Testament Bible History*, William B. Eerdmans Publishing Company, 1986.

Elwell, Walter A., *Evangelical Dictionary of Theology*, Baker Book House, 1986.

Esses, Michael, *Jesus in Exodus*, Logos International, 1977.

Foxe, John, *Foxe's Book of Martyrs*, Zondervan Publishing House, 1965.

Friberg, Barbara, and Timothy Friberg, *Analytical Greek New Testament*, Baker Book House, 1989.

Gutzke, Manford George, *Plain Talk on Exodus*, Zondervan Publishing House, 1974.

Habershon, Ada R., *Hidden Pictures in the Old Testament*, Kregel Publications, 1982.

________________, *The Study of the Types,* Kregel Publications, 1974.

Harris, R. Laird, Gleason L. Archer, Jr., and Bruce K. Waltke, *Theological Wordbook of the Old Testament*, Moody Press, 1980.

Henry, Matthew, *Matthew Henry's Commentary on the Whole Bible*, Mac Donald Publishing Company.

Heslop, William G., *Extras From Exodus*, Kregel Publications, 1975.

Jamieson, Robert, A. R. Fausset, and David Brown, *A Commentary Critical, Experimental and Practical on the Old and New Testaments*, William B. Eerdmans Publishing Company, 1945.

Josephus, Flavius, *The Complete Works of Josephus*, Kregel Publications, 1972.

Law, Henry, *The Gospel in Exodus*, The Banner of Truth Trust, 1967.

Lockyer, Herbert, *All the Divine Names and Titles in the Bible*, Zondervan Publishing House, 1975.

_______________, *All the Men of the Bible*, Zondervan Publishing House, 1958.

_______________, *All the Women of the Bible*, Zondervan Publishing House, 1958.

Machen, J. Greshem, *New Testament Greek for Beginners*, The Macmillan Company, 1951.

Mackintosh, C. H., *Notes on the Pentateuch: Genesis to Deuteronomy*, Loizeaux Brothers, 1977.

Marshall, Alfred, and J. B. Phillips, *The Interlinear Greek-English New Testament*, Samuel Bagster and Sons, Limited, 1972.

Mather, Samuel, *Figures or Types of the Old Testament*, Johnson Reprint Corporation, 1969.

Mead, Frank S., *Who's Who in the Bible*, Galahad Books, Harper and Row, Publishers, Inc., 1980.

Meyer, F. B., Ephesians, *Key Words of Inner Life*, Christian Literature Crusade, 1975.

Nee, Watchman, *Sit, Walk, Stand*, Christian Literature Crusade, 1973.

Orr, James, *The International Standard Bible Encyclopedia*, William B. Eerdmans Publishing Company, 1983.

Packer, James I., Merrill C. Tenney, and William White, Jr., *The Bible Almanac*, Thomas Nelson Publishers, 1980.

Pfeiffer, Charles F., and Howard F. Vos, *The Wycliffe Historical Geography of Bible Lands*, Moody Press, 1968.

Phillips, John, *Exploring the World of the Jew*, Moody Press, 1988.

Pick, Aaron, *Old Testament Words for English Readers*, Kregel Publications, 1977.

Pink, Arthur W., *Gleanings in Exodus*, Moody Press, 1976.

______________, *Gleanings in Joshua*, Moody Press, 1975.

______________, *Gleanings From Paul*, Moody Press, 1978.

______________, *Spiritual Growth--Growth in Grace, or Christian Progress*, Baker Book House, 1971.

Redpath, Alan, *Victorious Christian Living, Studies in the Book of Joshua*, Fleming H. Revell Company, 1955.

Ritchie, John, *Feasts of Jehovah*, Kregel Publications, 1982.

____________, *From Egypt to Canaan*, Kregel Publications, 1982.

____________, *Tabernacle in the Wilderness*, Kregel Publications, 1982.

Scofield, C. I., *The Scofield Reference Bible*, Oxford University Press, 1909.

Scroggie, W. Graham, *Joshua in the Light of the New Testament*, Kregel Publications, 1981.

Simpson, A. B., *The Land of Promise*, Christian Publications, Inc., 1969.

_____________, *Walking in the Spirit*, Christian Publications, Inc., 1969.

Smith, William, *Dr. William Smith's Dictionary of the Bible*, Baker Book House, 1981.

Spence, H. D. M., and Joseph S. Exell, *The Pulpit Commentary*, William B. Eerdmans Publishing Company, 1980.

Strong, Augustus H., *Systematic Theology*, Judson Press, 1985.

Strong, James, *The New Strong's Exhaustive Concordance of the Bible*, Thomas Nelson Publishers, 1984.

Tenney, Merrill C., *The Zondervan Pictorial Bible Dictionary*, Zondervan Publishing House, 1969.

Thayer, Henry Joseph, *The New Thayer's Greek-English Lexicon of the New Testament*, Hendrickson Publishers, Inc., 1981.

Vine, W. E., *A Comprehensive Dictionary of the Original Greek Words With Their Precise Meanings for English Readers*, Mac Donald Publishing Company.

__________, Merrill F. Unger, and William White, Jr., *Vine's Expository Dictionary of Bible Words*, Thomas Nelson Publishers, 1985.

Walton, John H., *Chronological and Background Charts of the Old Testament*, Academie Books, Zondervan Publishing House, 1978.

Wight, Fred H., *Manners and Customs of Bible Lands*, Moody Press, 1953.